LINCOLN CHRISTIAN COLLEGE AND S

W9-BVJ-078

.... Global
Human Smuggling

Global
Human Smuggling

Comparative Perspectives

EDITED BY

David Kyle and *Rey Koslowski*

THE JOHNS HOPKINS UNIVERSITY PRESS
Baltimore & London

© 2001 The Johns Hopkins University Press
All rights reserved. Published 2001
Printed in the United States of America on acid-free paper
9 8 7 6 5 4 3 2

The Johns Hopkins University Press
2715 North Charles Street
Baltimore, Maryland 21218-4363
www.press.jhu.edu

Library of Congress Cataloging-in-Publication Data

Global human smuggling : comparative perspectives / edited by
David Kyle and Rey Koslowski.
    p.   cm.
Includes bibliographical references and index.
    ISBN 0-8018-6589-1 (cloth : alk. paper) — ISBN 0-8018-6590-5
(pbk. : alk. paper)
    1. Emigration and immigration.   2. Illegal aliens.   3. Smuggling.
4. Transnational crime.   5. Organized crime.   I. Kyle, David.
II. Koslowski, Rey.   III. Title.
    JV6201 .G56 2001
    364.1'35—dc21

00-011294

A catalog record for this book is available from the British Library.

■■■■■■■■■ Contents

8 3725

117929

PART II. Case Studies: Mexico, Russia, and China

PART III. The Politics of Human Smuggling

Acknowledgments

This project has its roots in our late night discussions of a paper David Kyle presented while we were fellows of a Summer Institute for Young Scholars sponsored by the German American Academic Council (GAAC) and the Social Science Research Council (SSRC), held in New York City in 1996 and in Berlin in 1997. We are very grateful to the GAAC and the SSRC and to the Institute co-conveners, Rainer Munz and Aristide Zolberg, for bringing us together. We also benefited enormously from the provocative and informative discussions we had with the other GAAC Summer Institute fellows and invited speakers. We hope this volume demonstrates the need for ongoing cross-disciplinary discussion and cooperation on the multifaceted topic of international migration and, more specifically, irregular clandestine migration.

This volume is based on a set of papers presented at two meetings that we planned together. The first workshop was held at Rutgers University–Newark, under the auspices of the Center for Global Change and Governance, on May 15, 1998. The second meeting was held at the University of California, Davis, on October 10, 1998, and was sponsored by the University of California's Comparative Immigration and Integration Program, the University of California's Institute on Global Conflict and Cooperation, and the Institute for Governmental Affairs. We are grateful to Phil Martin for co-organizing our meeting at UC Davis. Special thanks go to Richard Langhorne, director of the Rutgers Center for Global Change and Governance, for providing financial support for both meetings. We also thank the Center for Global Change and Governance for cosponsoring a June 2000 meeting in Washington, D.C., which enabled several contributors to this volume to present their findings and arguments to poli-cymakers and other academic researchers from the United States and from several other countries; we also thank the co-organizers of the Transatlantic Workshop on Human Smuggling, at which they were presented, Freder-ick Heckmann of the European Forum for Migration Studies, and Susan Martin of the Institute for the Study of International Migration at George-town University.

David Kyle is very appreciative of a year-long research fellowship and participation in multidisciplinary meetings on the topic of international migration sponsored by the University of California at Davis Humanities Institute. Rey Koslowski also thanks the Center of International Studies at Princeton University for supporting his research and writing as well as his organizational efforts to place the issues raised in the volume before the policy community. Most of all, we wish to extend our heartfelt grati-tude to the contributors of this volume for their professional efforts; they made this volume not only possible but a pleasure on which to work. Un-doubtedly, we will hear more from them on this important emerging topic.

■■■■■■■■■ Introduction

David Kyle and Rey Koslowski

If 1993 is the year human smuggling crashed into our living rooms with the *Golden Venture* fiasco (the name of an ill-fated ship carrying undocumented Chinese from Fujian Province), the year 1998 could be viewed as the year that human smuggling became an official "global problem." In that year there were major busts of human smuggling rings, denouncements of undocumented migrant exploitation by national and world leaders, several international conferences, and a popular Hollywood movie (*Lethal Weapon 4*) depicting "evil snakeheads" and their human cargo from China. For example, U.S. attorney general Janet Reno created the Worker Exploitation Taskforce primarily because of a specific case involving sixteen individuals who had orchestrated an elaborate scheme to enslave young female Mexican nationals and force them into prostitution. The women, some as young as fourteen, were smuggled into Texas, transported to Florida and South Carolina, and, instead of being given legitimate work as promised, forced to become prostitutes to pay back their smuggling debt. "We must get these modern day slavery cases off the front pages of the newspapers and into the history books," said Janet Reno (Justice Department press release, April 23, 1998). As a global phenomenon, human trafficking in slaves from such places as Ukraine, Myanmar (Burma), Laos, Nepal, and the Philippines, mostly for a commercial sex industry, is so profitable that criminal business people invest in involuntary brothels much as they would in a mining operation; in step with arms-length capitalism, Kevin Bales asserts that some investors in Asia may not even realize they are profiting from human misery in the form of slaves held in brothels (1999). Yet these cases of trafficking in humans as commodities signal a wider phenomenon of the increasing smuggling of *migrants* seeking the living standards of developed countries as well as those escaping political persecution and disasters in a world with ever more restrictive asylum policies.

While many human smuggling operations around the world are more analogous to travel agencies than to the infamous slave traders of the last century—some even offering legitimate guarantees of successful entry and work—there is, however, a diverse range of smugglers with differing levels of organization, ability, and trustworthiness; some prove to be just as deadly as the brothels of sex slaves supplied by the human traffickers. Since 1998, nearly every week has brought stories of the deaths of clandestine migrants somewhere in the world, deaths resulting from horrendous acts of violence or simple miscalculations on the part of smugglers or the migrants themselves as they attempt to evade the authorities. The most recent incident to capture world attention involved fifty-eight migrants from Fujian, China, on June 19, 2000; trapped inside a sealed tomato truck in Dover, England, they had already suffocated to death by the time a police officer had it pried opened. Given the inherent physical dangers of crossing hundreds, and often thousands, of miles while attempting not to be detected, guided by people with few scruples through the most dangerous areas of the world, it is likely that by the time this book appears in print hundreds more will have died attempting to leave one hell and, tragically, finding another. On August 4, just a few weeks after the Dover tragedy, a collection of forty-six migrants from Somalia, India, Nepal, and Afghanistan were rescued just minutes from death in a locked truck outside Budapest as they lay gasping for breath; the driver did not have the key to open it (Reuters newswire, "Hungary Police Save 46 Immigrants from Suffocation," August 4, 2000).

These two incidents illustrate not only the complex human rights issues involved in contemporary smuggling—given that some would be considered more properly asylum seekers and, hence, the smugglers are providing an escape route—but also the global nature of the human smuggling of migrants and the trafficking of people tricked into contemporary forms of slavery. Few countries of the world remain untouched by smuggling crimes, migrant tragedies and victimization, the related corruption of public officials, and the political ramifications of all of these. In fact, it is the long-term political consequences and enforcement strategies that may have a wider effect on all of us. For example, on August 25, 2000, the president-elect of Mexico, Vicente Fox, outlined his vision of a completely open border with the United States; as part of the reason, he cited the hundreds of deaths resulting from migrants running the gauntlet of a virtually militarized border with an ostensibly friendly neighbor. In another example, a top New York immigration attorney, Robert Porges, was indicted on forty-four federal charges of helping up to seven thousand Chinese gain visas through fraudulent asylum claims, allegedly making over $13 million from the scheme ("Of Lawyers and Snakes: a Smuggling Ring Cracks," *U.S. News and World Report,* October 2, 2000, p. 44). This case illustrates not only the potential for corruption of well-placed individuals and, hence, immigration policies, but also the application of broad new enforcement power. Similar to some drug laws, a new law (Civil Asset Forfeiture Reform Act of 2000) will allow the INS to seek forfeiture of all the law firm's assets.

It is very difficult to estimate the extent of human smuggling and migrant trafficking worldwide owing to their clandestine nature. Nevertheless, there has been an increase in reported cases, which researchers, particularly those associated with the International Organization for Migration (IOM), have been gathering (see figure 1 for an example of IOM's view of the phenomenon); regional estimates from around the world paint a picture of a recent increase in migrant smuggling (Salt and Stein, 1997). In 1999, the U.S. Border Patrol apprehended more than 120,000 people attempting to cross the U.S.-Mexican border and estimate that this is only a small fraction of the number of people who actually get across (see http://www.ins.usdoj.gov/graphics/aboutins/statistics/msraug99/SWBORD.HTM). A recent large-scale sociological study indicated that three-quarters of clandestine migrants from Mexico pay "coyotes" to help them on their first trip across the border and two-thirds did so on subsequent trips (Singer and Massey, 1998: 577). In addition to the well-publicized cases of Mexicans smuggled into the United States, in the summer of 1999, hundreds of Chinese were smuggled in rusty old ships to Canada's Pacific coast, and close to two thousand people from China and the Middle East were apprehended on Australian shores in the fall of that year. One of the most publicized, if not the largest, flows into the European Union (EU) was the approximately three thousand people, mostly Kurds from northern Iraq and southwestern Turkey, who paid smugglers $2,000 to $8,000 for passage to Italy by boat between July 1997 and January 1998 (IOM, 1998). Recently, increasing numbers of cases have been noted in Germany (MNS, 1998), the United Kingdom, and France (IOM, 1996) as well as in transit countries like Poland (PAP, 1998) and Hungary (MTI, 1998). Jonas Widgren of the International Centre for Migration Policy Development has estimated that some four hundred thousand people are smuggled per year ("Europe's Smuggled Masses," 1999). As far as a worldwide total, it has been estimated that as many as 4 million people are smuggled across borders on an annual basis (IOM, 1997). The U.S. Immigration and Naturalization Service (INS) estimates that transnational human smuggling, hardly a global issue in the 1980s, is now a multibillion-dollar trade worldwide, rivaling the drug trade. The IOM estimated total global revenues in 1997 of up to $7 billion (IOM, 1997), up from a 1994 UN estimate of $3.5 billion (IOM, 1996).

Though these numbers (mostly estimates) surrounding the phenomenon of human smuggling tell only part of the story, they are nearly all we do have. And because they are supplied mostly by enforcement agencies, they tend to reflect a subset of smugglers—those who have been caught. Information gained from failed smuggling operations does provide an indication of the diversity and growth of such activities, and occasionally a glimpse into the smuggling operation itself, but it also suggests several unanswered questions: What are the broader historical, political, and sociological foundations of migrant smuggling? Is there a systematic difference between failed smuggling operations and successful ones? Is the trafficking in women to be sold into slavery an outgrowth of migrant smuggling as a service, or should it be considered separately? How much of this phenomenon is inadvertently or even purposively created by states to meet other economic and security goals?

This volume explores the historical context, social organization, and political ramifications of human smuggling across national borders as a global phenomenon. It fills a gap in the current literature by presenting diverse empirical research, conducted in several different regions, that is either explicitly or implicitly comparative. More than a subcategory of international immigration, the trade in humans and migrants is a topic that intersects contemporary anxieties concerning the global political

Fig. 1. Contemporary Human Smuggling Flows around the World
Source: IOM, 1998.

economy, ethnic and gender stratification, multiculturalism, population growth, political corruption, transnational crime, the Internet, human rights abuses, and the (in)ability of states and global agencies to control any of these effectively. Using social scientific research, this volume examines the regional and organizational diversity of migrant smuggling in several of the primary sending regions. We believe that it is the combination of grounded regional and policy research and a global comparative vision that will be most fruitful to the development of theories of migrant smuggling in a wide range of contexts.

A definition of human smuggling, including its social organization and political and economic significance, is still very much a work in progress. In part, this is because while this activity is not new, its global scope, diversity, and complexity are new: professional human smugglers have plied their trade with the educated Indian middle class and impoverished Cubans; North Africans have been smuggled into Spain; Albanians and Kosovar refugees have been ferried to Italy; Chinese have been flown into the European Union via Moscow; and tens of thousands of Russian and Eastern European women have been trafficked throughout Western Europe to work as prostitutes—some unwittingly (IOM, 1996; 1998; GSN, 1997). Consequently, both governments and activists socially construct "the problem" in different ways depending on what or for whom they are advocating action. For example, sending countries have a different set of concerns than receiving countries. Because the activity also intersects with other well-known and novel social problems such as unemployment, illegal migration, prostitution, and cybercrime, preexisting advocacy groups and state agencies tend to follow a predictable pattern of either promoting or discounting certain aspects of human smuggling as a global social problem. As the contributors of this volume point out, simply defining the phenomenon of human or migrant smuggling, which is sometimes contrasted with human trafficking as a more coercive form, is one of the main stumbling points for greater governmental and nongovernmental organization (NGO) cooperation; for example, to what degree do we build into the definition of human smuggling or trafficking the intentions and knowledge of the person smuggled as opposed to the smuggler? What about cases of coercion to smuggle a third party or join a criminal enterprise, or cases of self-smuggling? Should all cases of trafficking for prostitution be treated as coercive and exploitative regardless of the specific conditions and treatment of the women, or should we conceptualize a separate category for those in which violence, or the implicit threat of violence, was used?

Public perception thus far has been guided by state enforcement agencies and news reports covering the daily busts of a human smuggling operation somewhere in the world. State immigration reforms in the 1990s have been largely focused on curtailing "illegal alien" flows and the pursuit of those who facilitate them globally. These initiatives include stepped-up border control, intensified internal policing and investigations, new laws against human smuggling and migrant trafficking, antiforgery actions and training to prevent document fraud, more prosecutions of smugglers, and increased penalties for those convicted. States have also enlisted employers as well as airlines and shipping companies in the battle by imposing fines on employers who knowingly hire illegal aliens and carrier sanctions on those who do not prevent migrants from illegal entry.

Nearly overnight, the U.S. Immigration and Naturalization Service has seen its budget balloon from $1.5 billion in FY1993 to $4.2 billion in FY1999 (Andreas, this volume, Chap. 4). Beginning in 1993, INS operations such as "Hold-the-Line," "Gatekeeper," and "Safeguard" increased the number of border guards in the most heavily crossed areas of the U.S.-Mexican border. Barricades have also been put into place along the border, and the U.S. military supports the burgeoning INS Border Patrol. Legislation passed in 1996 to combat illegal migration increased penalties for those who enter the United States illegally and made human smuggling a federal crime. It also enhanced undercover investigative authority, which includes wiretaps, expanded application of asset forfeiture laws, and enabling the INS to set up undercover businesses for sting operations to catch smugglers and counterfeiters in the act. Finally, it increased the number of assistant U.S. attorneys to handle the anticipated growth in caseloads.

In 1997, the INS devised a national antismuggling strategy, which engages all enforcement departments across the INS in coordinated operations intended to disrupt smuggling organizations (Nardi, 1999). The biggest bust came in November 1998 with "Operation Seek and Keep," which broke up an organization that had smuggled as many as three hundred (mostly) Indian nationals per month for three years (INS, 1998). Soon thereafter, the INS announced arrests of members of an organization that smuggled Chinese nationals into the United States through the Mohawk Indian reservation, which straddles the U.S.-Canadian border. In order to strengthen interior enforcement, the Congress recently authorized funds for two hundred new INS positions to form "Quick Response Teams" for deployment in transportation corridors used by smugglers and areas with increasing cases of illegal immigration (INS, 1999).

U.S. legislators have responded in particular to the growth in trafficking in women and children. Several have introduced bills to combat trafficking through prevention, prosecution, and enforcement against traffickers and protection and assistance to victims of trafficking. In the fall of 1999, Representative Chris Smith introduced the "Trafficking Victims Protection Act," which focuses exclusively on trafficking for forced prostitution and sexual exploitation and proposes increased punishment for traffickers. Representative Sam Gejdenson introduced the "Comprehensive Anti-Trafficking in Persons Act," which is similar to the Smith bill but includes trafficking in forced labor of all kinds and thereby also covers the trafficking of men. On October 28, 2000, President Clinton signed congressionally passed compromise legislation into law.[1]

There is little evidence that tighter border controls have been successful in stopping the smuggling of people across borders or in reducing the
debt bondage and forced prostitution that some of those who are smuggled endure once they get into a target country. Even immigration officials
recognize the limitations of this parochial approach: according to an INS
spokesperson, "even with all the manpower available at our disposal, the
US remains totally vulnerable to smuggling operations unless they are
stopped *at their point of origin*" (quoted in *Far Eastern Economic Review*, April 8, 1993). The antitrafficking legislation attempts to address
this problem by proposing economic sanctions on those sending and transit countries that tolerate traffickers and do not cooperate with U.S. efforts to apprehend them.

Although the United States receives the largest numbers of smuggled
people and therefore has perhaps the greatest incentives to do something
about it, other major target states have taken similar border control tightening and internal enforcement initiatives. Largely in response to the
growth of smuggling in 1997 and 1998, Germany reorganized its border
police to combat smugglers better, equipped police with night vision
scopes, and lined its border with motion and infrared detectors (Cole,
1998). Germany has additionally supported border control and antismuggling efforts in Poland and the Czech Republic, across whose borders smuggled migrants primarily enter but which will perhaps someday
become members of the EU/Schengenland—thereby transforming their
eastern borders effectively into those of Germany.

In response to the wave of boat people from China and the Middle East
washing up on Canadian and Australian shores, policymakers in these target states have adopted, or are considering, new antismuggling measures.
The Australian government instituted a new visa policy that limits refugee
visas to three years, bars refugees from bringing their families, and denies
refugee status to boat people who passed a "safe" country without lodging an asylum application. In addition, the government expanded the authority of the Coast Guard to intercept suspect ships on the high seas, and
it opened new detention facilities for the growing numbers of boat people (Stensholt, 1999). Canada's immigration minister, Elinor Caplan, said
that Canada may have to revise its rules for the detention of smuggled asylum seekers, called for putting penalties for human smuggling on par with
drug smuggling, and said that she would consider "more aggressive steps

to seize the vehicles, vessels, aircraft and other property used in the course of such operations" (quoted in Mickleburgh, 1999).

An additional factor fanning the flames of the illegal alien issue is human rights concerns because some human smuggling networks· use trickery, physical coercion, and emotional degradation either to exploit migrants economically or to force them into slavery. Typically, contemporary slaves come from the world's politically weakest groups: the impoverished, the handicapped, ethnic minorities, women, and children. However, contrary to the conventions of enforcement agencies and news reporting, which tend to identify "the bad guys" and their victims, much migrant smuggling or trafficking operates in an ambiguous area that is neither purely voluntary nor involuntary from the perspective of the migrant. Many contemporary slaves know that they will be smuggled illegally across borders to work, and they sometimes know the nature of the work—what they often do not know is the terms of the "contract." Similarly, many "voluntary" migrants who choose a clandestine route to work abroad feel compelled to leave their home communities because of economic crises, political conflict, ethnic persecution, and fear of rape at home in the case of many ethnic minority women. The treatment of contemporary migrant trafficking and human slavery among news reporters and activists is reminiscent of the earlier "white slavery" scare, with a similar evolution into a debate regarding the pros and cons of legalizing prostitution as one of the primary activities in which slaves are engaged (Scully, this volume, Chap. 3; Stange, 1998). The trafficking of women and children has become a global moral panic.

Critics contend that immigration has spun out of control and that the unintended economic, social, and political costs will be high, though no one can say with any certitude what those are or will be. What is missing from this parochial political argument, however, is the global economic and sociological context in which some U.S. "natives" compete not so much with those who come here from "Third World" countries but with the vast majority *who stay behind* and work in free-trade zones and export manufacturing enclaves set up by transnational corporations and compliant states. The transformation of the U.S. economy from an industrial base to a postindustrial service and information base, buffeted itself by global capital flows, has been painful but not unsuccessful—thus far anyway. *Globalization* is the term used both to explain and to normalize the ideology of neoliberal free-trade policies. Immigration levels increased precisely during this period of significant restructuring of the U.S. economy and the global economy more generally. As many have observed, we can explain the strong negative reaction to current immigration patterns among some Americans and Europeans as due, in part, to a scapegoating of immigrants during the transformation to postindustrialism and to what many now call the globalization of national economies. While immigrants may be blamed for facilitating the destruction of the old corporate-labor contract under industrial capitalism, they are rarely credited for helping to build the new economy in the United States, whose population rate of increase is at below replacement level. It is perhaps due, in part, to this ambiguity regarding the *economic* impact of immigrants that nearly every "immigration reform" in the past two decades has been accompanied by so many loopholes, back doors, and side doors that they have typically facilitated even greater levels of immigration (Hollifield, 1992; Cornelius, Martin, and Hollifield, 1994; Joppke, 1998).

Of course, there is much more to the contemporary immigration story than invidious comparisons of immigrants using cold economic logic, a point that comes into clearer view when we examine the politically sensitive issue of "illegal aliens" or "undocumented migrants," estimated to be around 5 million currently living in the United States (INS: http://www. ins.usdoj.gov/stats/illegalalien/index.html), which is by definition the outcome of all human smuggling operations. Some view the tripling of the immigrant population since 1970 and the fact that one in ten Americans is "foreign-born" (Escobar, 1999) as a threat to the "social order" and "political culture" of the United States (e.g., Beck, 1996; Camarota, 1998). Although high-pitched public rhetoric has been marginalized recently, owing to the fear of an immigrant minority backlash, a significant segment of the U.S. population believes that foreigners who are here illegally may carry the corrupting seeds of a more generalized lawlessness. The fear is not that they are different culturally per se, but rather different in a particularly political way that threatens state stability and constitutional democracy and undercuts labor unionization and fair wage competition. Of course, state officials and representatives, regardless of the economic logic of immigration, are especially sensitive to questions of social order and territorial integrity when so many seem to be able to cross their borders so easily at will.

Although news reports from around the world document the growing export of people for profit and some criminologists and policymakers have begun to investigate the linkage of transnational migration and crime from the perspective of the impact on states (Den Boer and Walker, 1993; ISPAC, 1996; Kerry, 1997; Smith, 1997; Wang, 1996; Winer, 1997), international migration specialists have largely ignored this phenomenon, with some notable exceptions (Salt and Stein, 1997; Ghosh, 1998). Given the strategic political and intellectual location of illicit labor mobility across international borders, it is somewhat surprising that relatively few social researchers, apart from criminologists of transnational crime, have focused on this topic. Even during the 1990s, when research on "transnational migration" (and, more generally, "transnationalism") became a social science growth industry, the topic of human smuggling or migrant trafficking was largely left to states, nonprofit organizations, and journalists to define and explain the phenomenon within their own agendas.

While large and well-established transnational criminal organizations expand their human smuggling operations in some sending regions, in other regions out-migration is facilitated by a range of local "migration merchants" (Kyle, 2000; Kyle and Liang, forthcoming), which may or may not be linked indirectly to professional criminal organizations; they are part of the general global commodification of the migration process whereby a range of actors profit, either legally or illegally, from activities that facilitate the "export" of migrants as a business (Salt and Stein, 1997). In some regions, local migration merchants recruit or lend money to would-be migrants before they are introduced to more sophisticated transnational smugglers.

In general, the role of entrepreneurial organizations as actors in undocumented migration flows has been relegated to either a secondary consideration or one activity of some "criminal gangs" (Kwong, 1997; McDonald, 1995; Chin, 1996). In contrast, ethnic-based firms established after arrival in the United States have received much more attention in the migration literature (Light and Bonacich, 1988). Similarly, the growing literature on "transnationalism" has considered the role of mutual-aid "voluntary organizations" in sustaining "transnational communities" but not the role of professional smuggling organizations (Basch, Schiller, and Blanc, 1994). Some researchers may understandably wish to avoid areas of research that may link migrants with crime for fear of further stigmatizing immigrant minorities, or they perceive such research to be too risky. This volume demonstrates that social science researchers do have a role in helping to understand a complex area of transnational social life precisely because their research and analyses are different from that of a state enforcement agency. Much of the nonacademic discussion and debate surrounding human smuggling and trafficking proceed from either estimated aggregate data using deductive logic (e.g., recent increases in smuggling *must* be due to large criminal enterprises) or emotional testimonies of women who were trafficked for sex. Although these are valid and important types of information, what is missing is a sustained historical and empirical examination of different smuggling activities using more inductive and comparative reasoning by observers not so directly tied to advocating a priori a specific state policy or political/philosophical position.

The claim that academic researchers are unbiased in their analyses of this area of social life would be naïve—in fact, it is our acute awareness of the ability of bias to color our findings, even when we have corroborating evidence, that leads to some of the seemingly cumbersome approaches and traditions of social scientists. However, there are two features of the claims of the contributors of this volume that make them different from those of state officials or journalists, who have largely shaped public opinion on this topic thus far. First, there is a great deal of diversity within "the academic community" because of our range of disciplinary and methodological approaches. It is the multiplicity of findings and theories and our ongoing debates that contribute to social research; no one researcher claims to have all the answers, but collectively we may begin to understand the different facets of a social activity as complex as contemporary human smuggling. Most important, we have the freedom from organizational policy directives and news posting deadlines to explore more diverse social, political, and historical dimensions; our intellectual goals may evolve in directions very different from, even tangential to, the immediate topic at hand as state officials would formulate it. Many of the contributors to this volume broaden their analytical frame beyond state constructions of human smuggling, thus allowing them to focus on the role of a range of state policies and actors who have both facilitated and hindered human smugglers.

This volume is divided into three parts, though, like human smuggling itself, any simple categorization of these chapters would be impossible. Part

I primarily explores historical and conceptual approaches to human smuggling, providing an overview and context for understanding some of the related topics, debates, and policy conundrums. A theme running through these otherwise disparate chapters is how politics, not just economics and criminality, creates professional human smuggling (as opposed to self-smuggling) of the scale we are witnessing today.

In the first chapter, David Kyle and John Dale compare two cases of human smuggling that would normally be viewed as the opposite ends of this phenomenon in terms of coercion and exploitation. By comparing human smuggling out of Ecuador, a country of clandestine labor migration driven mostly by migrant demand, and Burma (Myanmar), a country that has been the site of some of the most horrific forms of trafficking in girls for brothels in Thailand and elsewhere, they explore some of the basic assumptions regarding why and how such activities have arisen in the 1980s and 1990s. Although there are obvious differences between these two cases of what they refer to as "migrant exporting schemes" and "slave importing operations," there are also similarities in the high degree of tacit and active complicity required by a range of people in the sending and destination regions. Similarly, in neither case does "transnational organized crime" of the sort described by many in the news media and among enforcement agencies play a significant role; smugglers and traffickers in both regions are deeply integrated into the social fabric of indigenous settings, though not uniformly so, and are facilitated by a loose network of recruiters, middlemen, actual smugglers, local and foreign financiers, and government officials and police on the take. Though these cases have some unique features that make them unrepresentative of other cases, that is precisely their value: they help keep us attuned to the possibilities disallowed by our assumptions of why and how human smuggling operates, especially as formulated in official rhetoric and media portrayals. They also demonstrate the need to examine the broader historical-sociological forces at play in cases of human smuggling from specific subnational regions, especially those built on a foundation of either failed or abusive/extractive state regimes. These local maladies are augmented by a globalized media and production chain that nevertheless excludes the ability of labor to move freely and by government corruption as both a cause and a consequence of human smuggling.

Khalid Koser examines asylum seekers as another major source of contemporary human smuggling often falling between that uncomfortable dichotomy of "freedom fighter" and "evil smuggler"; he suggests that we should not put too fine a point on the distinction between human smuggling as a migration issue and human trafficking as a human rights issue. Asylum seekers straddle this distinction in that they are often escaping human rights violations by seeking out smugglers—much as the Underground Railroad smuggled people out of slavery during the 1800s—but then also encounter additional human rights violations along the way. For example, using data from interviews with Iranian asylum seekers in the Netherlands, Koser found that many did not control some of the most basic features of their passage, including how and where they would be smuggled. He explores the historical path to this situation as a series of unintended consequences; reducing legal avenues of migrant workers in Western Europe drove immigrants to seek asylum as the only legal path of entry; this, in turn, led to a set of restrictive control policies for would-be claimants in an attempt to filter out bogus applications; as this cycle deepens, the extreme difficulty of the asylum process has driven both labor migrants and now asylum seekers into the hands of professional smugglers as the only ones able to offer them hope of a life beyond the persecuted and discriminated communities in which they live.

In Chapter 3, Eileen Scully examines the transnational trafficking of women for prostitution from 1850 to the end of the Cold War. Scully reminds us that the issue of trafficking in women and children, which currently gets the most popular press and political attention of those being smuggled across borders, is not a new one; it was accompanied then, just as now, by a wide range of efforts of nongovernmental organizations, states, and new multilateral organizations such as the League of Nations and United Nations to control it. The underlying causes of previous forms of trafficking in women (largely a misnomer at the time) flowed directly from large mobile populations of men as indentured laborers and as the new urban workforce, especially the large movement of Asian labor following the abolition of slavery. It is intriguing that two dimensions to trafficking more than a century ago could just as easily describe the topic today: political and economic turmoil in Russia and China fueled significant flows of labor, including prostitutes; and the debates surrounding the definitions and root causes of trafficking and policy recommendations sharply divide into the two camps of those seeking sex work regulation and those who strongly feel that a prohibition of prostitution will curtail the demand. Ultimately, however, it was the misnamed and racist framework of the "white slave trade" that fell victim to a lack of credibility and hence sustained outrage when it was shown that most of the women in question were neither "white" nor slaves but rather a coethnic community of women attached to overseas laborers. Most appropriate to current actions, projects, and laws being currently developed, Scully cautions us to consider the unintended consequences of antitrafficking measures such as the Mann Act, most of which served further to assert male control over women.

In a different context, though echoing the previous three chapters, Peter Andreas, in Chapter 4, presents a fascinating story of the development of a state-smuggler symbiosis and the unintended downhill cycles in which state control actions drive would-be migrants into the arms of smugglers, which in turn is used to justify even greater levels of "border buildup." He begins by reminding us that, ironically, it was Mexico trying to keep out illegal American immigrants that in part led to the U.S.-Mexican War. The larger point is that ever since that war, the United States has either facilitated Mexican labor immigration or turned a blind eye to what has mostly been a low-cost informal affair of crossing the Rio Grande. In the 1990s, the United States sought to deter illegal aliens from crossing through brute force and high technology—not capture them once across—largely maintaining an ineffective and understaffed program of workforce compliance. The central paradox along this particular border when viewed globally is that it was precisely during the 1990s that tariffs decreased and commercial interpenetration increased between the two neighboring countries. Andreas asserts that instead of migrants and their guides being deterred from making the crossing, their operations have gotten more complex, diverse—and expensive. Thus, the nature of smuggling itself has been transformed from an informal affair to a big business attracting large criminal organizations. By tracing the reciprocal interaction between state policies and clandestine transnational actors, Andreas suggests the multiple ways in which states make smuggling and smuggling (re-)makes states.

The chapters in Part II explore, through regional case studies, the social organization of human smuggling from three of the most important source countries: Mexico, Russia, and China. In the first chapter of this section, David Spener explores the patterns and social organization of migrant smuggling along the Mexico-Texas border as they have evolved in the 1990s, precisely the period since the U.S. Immigration and Naturalization Service put into place significant physical and personnel resources along the border. Spener develops a typology of evolving migrant smuggling strategies, which are analyzed from several theoretical vantage points: informal economy, global commodity chains, and migrant autonomy/resistance. Unlike Andreas, however, his research suggests that although some larger criminal syndicates have indeed sought profits from human smuggling operations, there is evidence that multiple types of smugglers thrive following the logic of niche markets, but also because of their different sociological foundations. Emerging from his finely grained analysis is a salient fact calling into question the entire framing of a "border crossing": it is not so much a border but a border region, complete with its own binational economy and sociocultural life. Thus, instead of viewing smugglers as preying upon the migrant stream, like foxes hunting sheep, Spener describes them as part of wider "transborder networks of trust."

In the next chapter, James O. Finckenauer examines the criminal activities of Russians and others from the former Soviet Union involved in migrant trafficking. He situates "alien smuggling" in the broader context of Russian transnational organized crime in general. This context includes the structures and the scope of criminal activities of the former Soviet criminal organizations engaging in transnational crime. Finckenauer contrasts what we know to be organized crime with what is, for him, better labeled "crime that is organized." Though he emphasizes the lack of hard evidence in this area, he suggests that human smuggling (at least in the case of the Russians) may better represent the latter than the former, a distinction that has implications for transnational law enforcement policies given that large, ongoing criminal organizations are easier to infiltrate and disrupt. Finckenauer suggests that falsely portraying most trafficking from Russia as controlled by the Mafia as organized crime is counterproductive on two counts: first, we lose the possibility of a credible threat among those actually involved; it also diverts attention away from the areas of research we need most, especially a better understanding of the consumers of such human commodities and those multiple people who reap the large profits from this trade.

The following three chapters focus on human smuggling from China, specifically from the province of Fujian. Though the numbers of smuggled Chinese are relatively small from the vantage point of the receiving states, their smuggling methods, using incredibly complex and flexible operations—and the high profits they generate—have earned irregular migration from this region special global interest. In Chapter 7, Zai Liang and Wenzhen Ye review the historical and demographic trends of international migration from China; there has been a significant increase in immigrants (many of them undocumented) from China's Fujian Province to the New York metropolitan area. Their chapter argues that absolute poverty is not the cause of this new immigration; rather, it is rooted in a unique configuration of historical and contemporary factors. First, since Fujian is on the coast of China, many Fujianese are familiar with life at sea and thus are well prepared for the sometimes dangerous journeys usually to the United States. Second, because of China's transition to a market-oriented economy and remittances from overseas immigrants, the relative income disparities in Fujian have increased over time. This increase has given rise to a sense of relative deprivation among the Fujianese, a primary motivation for seeking fortune abroad. Finally, the existence of a sophisticated human smuggling network throughout the world that uses modern technology facilitates the process of immigrating to New York.

Ko-Lin Chin, in Chapter 8, describes the social organization of Chinese human smuggling. Based upon data collected from a survey of three hundred undocumented Chinese in New York and interviews with key informants in the United States and China, he examines the individual and group characteristics of human smugglers, patterns of smuggling operation, and the relationships between alien smuggling, gangs, and organized crime groups. Echoing Finckenauer's findings on human smuggling out of Russia, Chin suggests that most human smugglers are not gang or tong members, although some gang and tong members are involved in the human trade. Moreover, a human trafficking organization can best be described as a small, loosely knit group. Members of the group come from all walks; they are predominantly ethnic Chinese who are not career criminals.

In contrast, in Chapter 9, Peter Kwong disagrees with Chin's assessment in part by arguing that Chinese organized crime has developed human smuggling into a truly global business, shepherding one hundred thousand people per year to a range of destinations including Japan, Canada, Australia, the United States, France, Holland, and other parts of Europe. Kwong's primary focus, however, is on the relationship between illegal migration flows from China and the labor markets in which they are inserted. For Kwong, human smuggling can be sustained only on the premise that illegals, once they have arrived in a host country, can secure employment to pay off their debts. Thus, Kwong argues that we cannot look at human smuggling apart from the historical changes in labor conditions within both the illegal and legal labor markets.

If Part I explored how politics makes human smuggling and Part II described the social organization of human smuggling from three of the most important origin countries, Part III examines primarily how human smuggling makes politics, including its intended and unintended consequences. The politics of human smuggling are fraught with multiple, often conflicting, local and national political and social agendas, especially among those crusading to stop the trafficking of those who are economically exploited and abused, since questions of morality, cultural norms, and universal human rights naturally enter into the debate.

Picking up where Eileen Scully left off in Chapter 3, in Chapter 10 Nora Demleitner analyzes the current multiple constructions of migrants, coercion, and prostitution in the contemporary period. She argues that the legal construction of victimized migrant women often works at crosspurposes to the goal of curtailing forced prostitution through international trafficking. Noting the aggressive enforcement of migration laws but a lack of policies and laws regarding smuggling and brothel ownership, she argues that the issue of forced prostitution needs to be viewed as a problem caused in part by the current immigration law, reinforced by gender inequalities, and tolerated because of the precarious legal position of the victims. Thus, the current treatment of migrant women who prostitute themselves as both illegal and immoral serves to stigmatize them as double outcasts. She suggests that we also need to learn more about the nature of the global demand for sex services as a global business and, hence, what might be done about the fundamental structure of a world of deep inequalities and restrictive migration policies. The urgent question implicit in Demleitner's chapter is whether states can overcome their focus on migration control and inherently sexist constitutions in order to protect the human rights of those tricked, trafficked, and traded regardless of the degree of their prior knowledge of what lay ahead for them on the other side of the border.

Similar to Demleitner's approach but in a very different political context, H. Richard Friman describes how smuggled immigrants are socially constructed as threats to the social order in Japan. Though often referred to as a newcomer to immigration, Japan has, in fact, a long history of public assertions that crime is linked to immigrants or foreigners. In the past, these arguments surfaced during periods of severe dislocation such as the aftermath of the 1923 Tokyo earthquake and the American occupation. A crime-by-foreigner discourse has resurfaced in Japan in the context of increased immigration and high-profile incidents of transnational human smuggling—but in the absence of the severe dislocations of the past. Friman explores the historical political sources of this resurgent discourse and why it resonates in such a distorted manner. For example, while it is acknowledged that the *yakuza* (Japanese organized crime) have recently turned to human smuggling, the reason most often concerns economic pressure rather than their long history of labor brokering among the still necessary day laborers and other unskilled labor, much of it illegal. In the end, Friman argues that undocumented immigrants—especially Chinese—play an important scapegoat role, one that obscures the continuing need for inexpensive Chinese labor and the unintended effects of antigang legislation resulting in the diversification of *yakuza* operations into human smuggling.

Mark J. Miller examines the sanctioning of the unauthorized employment of "aliens," comparing the United States and several European states. By doing so, he elucidates important dimensions of the politics of international migration and crime. Echoing a similar conclusion by Demleitner, he concludes that we have arrived at a policy paradox: by countenancing illegal employment of aliens but not illegal migration itself, states create the conditions for greater levels of immigrant worker exploitation. Such a paradox is no longer academic, as Miller notes that "support for parties and governments, especially in Europe, can crumble or mushroom over immigration issues." All in all, Miller describes an immigration policy environment wholly inadequate to the task of stemming both illegal immigration and, especially, the insidiousness of employers hiring workers who do not hold legal visas.

In the final chapter, Rey Koslowski examines the challenges posed by human smuggling to states as well as the dilemmas of international co-operation among states to combat human smuggling. He does so by plac-ing the issue of state control in the context of the processes of economic globalization as well as the politics of linking migration and crime in the policy-making process. States have embarked on multilateral cooperation to combat human smuggling and trafficking by increasing border con-trols, passing antismuggling and antitrafficking laws, and stepping up en-forcement of these laws. If human smuggling is mostly "crime that is or-ganized" by informal transnational social networks rather than just another activity of traditional organized crime groups, as cases studies by Finckenaur, Chin, Kyle and Dale, and Spener indicate, then, Koslowski argues, international efforts to target human smugglers may be much more difficult in practice than anticipated. Moreover, as tighter border controls have the unintended side effects of pushing migrants and refugees into the arms of smugglers, multilateral antismuggling initiatives confront additional challenges, often of their own making. In the end, Koslowski argues, along with Kwong and Miller, that as long as destination states fail to enforce policies that cut demand for smuggled labor, significant re-duction of human smuggling is unlikely, and multilateral agreements, which may represent impressive feats of international cooperation, will most likely prove to have much less of an impact than policy makers had hoped.

THE TOPIC OF HUMAN SMUGGLING has evolved from sensational interest in the early 1990s to maturity as a recognized global problem at the pres-ent moment, when large amounts of public and private funds are about to be expended in an effort to deter it in different regions of the world. The collective picture this volume paints, however, is a phenomenon re-sistant to half-hearted state control efforts lacking sufficient political will to develop programs that would thwart not only the associated criminal-ity but also the complex motivations of those smuggled, the nature and organization of the demand for their labor, and states' own historical ac-tions that have inadvertently created and maintained it. Of course, the dilemma is that we cannot simply do nothing as more and more die en route or are funneled into contemporary forms of slavery. Fortunately, a wide range of state and nongovernmental-organization programs are be-ing implemented to address some of the most immediate issues of human rights violations and to aid those most victimized by the promise of a false dream. Similarly, much of the initial governmental and academic analysis on human smuggling and trafficking has been concerned with narrowly descriptive questions, which, unfortunately, often results in highly speculative numbers in an attempt to procure more funding and lend it an air of scientific objectivity. This is to be expected, but we need to keep in mind that there is still much we do not understand about this phenomenon and its potential to transform civil societies and state agencies of control.

This volume presents a mix of descriptive empirical evidence and conceptual analysis often providing a much needed historical and comparative context in which to gain a broader perspective. A central theme that emerged naturally from this first set of academic studies on human smuggling is how state officials and smugglers are locked in an embrace without straightforward solutions, primarily because the causes, social organization, and proposed solutions are much more historically and politically complex than they may at first seem. It is precisely the global nature of human smuggling that requires us to consider the wider social and economic context in which it is flourishing, rather than simply demonizing the smugglers, some of whom provide safe passage out of some very dismal situations and others who prey on the weakest of humanity. Viewing human smuggling as a global phenomenon, we can begin to develop a partial list, reinforced by the chapters that follow, of some of the broad issues worthy of further research and analysis:

1. Capital and commodities are increasingly global—labor is not. This is a fundamental tension in the world today, whereby the policies and discourse of free trade abruptly end at the point of labor mobility.

2. Related to the process and ideology of so-called globalization, the demand for cheap or free labor that the smugglers provide resonates with other labor trends of temporary and disposable workers; short-term profitability can be used to justify nearly any action and can even be framed perversely in moral terms as alleviating unemployment among some of the poorer regions of the world.

3. The current state system based on territorial sovereignty but characterized by uneven state capacity is wholly inadequate to the task at hand. This fact is exacerbated by high levels of corruption in some

sending, transit, and receiving states as well as the restrictive asylum policies implemented by several destination countries during the post–Cold War period.

4. As millions of dollars are beginning to be directed at the root causes of human smuggling and trafficking, a logical approach would be to develop economic and social aid programs in traditional sending regions. However, much of the migration research in general, and the works of the contributors to this volume, indicate that it is not what a person does not have that motivates him or her to leave; it is what that person's neighbor has that compels him or her not to be left behind—that is, *relative* deprivation. Within their national context, regions with high levels of migrant exporting tend to be some of the most dynamic. In contrast, those being tricked into slavery are more likely to come from more impoverished regions. The challenge in these latter cases is to encourage economic development and political empowerment without reinforcing the power of entrenched local elites.

5. Because we are dealing with a multifaceted social and political phenomenon, the unintended consequences of particular measures in stopping human smuggling are nearly always counterproductive without an integrated approach. For example, a militarized border without effective employer sanctions is ineffective and dangerous to the migrants and sends a message opposite to the one intended. Proposed technological measures of control of "illegal aliens" and labor settings may have consequences for all of us; because people are not intrinsically and obviously illicit in the same way as, say, a kilo of heroin, new methods of categorizing, tagging, and monitoring the world's populations, especially using digital and satellite technologies, will be a tempting, if chilling, solution to overcome the challenge of managing an increasingly highly mobile world.

In sum, continuing to locate the problem exogenously within a transnational crime framework outside the past actions and current conditions of the countries of origin and destination would seem to ensure that, at least in the short run, many more will be tempted into the hands of human smugglers; they will continue to be perceived, correctly or incorrectly, as the only credible hope of attaining the political freedoms and economic opportunities we enjoy in the world's most developed countries.

The difficult lesson is that extreme caution is needed before government and nongovernment agencies rush to solve the problem without understanding what "the problem" is beyond the immediate facts of a particular case and without sufficient political will to tackle both its supply and demand dimensions. Unfortunately, as this volume suggests, the phenomenon of human smuggling is exacerbated by multiple sets of interlocking problems such as widening social inequality, state corruption, and ethnic and gender discriminations. Further, all of these are compounded by the contradictions of a contemporary world connected economically and technologically but in no fundamental way integrated politically or culturally. In this sense, human smuggling—in all its guises—is not so much a disease but a symptom of the enormous contemporary disparities in the legitimate mobility of the world's peoples during, ironically, the historical apex of mutual global awareness and interconnectedness.

NOTE

1. See H.R. 3154, H.R. 3244, and S. 1842, available at the Library of Congress Web site:http://thomas.loc.gov

REFERENCES

Altink, S. 1995. *Stolen Lives: Trading Women into Sex and Slavery.* London: Scarlet Press.

Bales, Kevin. 1999. *Disposable People: New Slavery in the Global Economy.* Berkeley: University of California Press.

Basch, Linda, Nina G. Schiller, and Cristina Szanton Blanc. 1994. *Nations Unbound: Transnational Projects, Post-colonial Predicaments, and Deterritorialized Nation-States.* Langhorne, Pa.: Gordon and Breach.

Beck, Roy. 1996. *The Case against Immigration: The Moral, Economic, Social, and Environmental Reasons for Reducing U.S. Immigration Back to Traditional Levels.* New York: W. W. Norton & Co.

Camarota, Steven A. 1998. "Immigrants in the United States—1998: A Snapshot of America's Foreign-Born Population." Center for Immigration Studies Backgrounder Series, January.

Chin, Ko-lin. 1996. *Chinatown Gangs: Extortion, Enterprise, and Ethnicity.* New York: Oxford University Press.

Cole, Deborah. 1998. "Germany Fights Wave of Immigrant Smuggling." Reuters, November 9, 1998.

Cornelius, Wayne A., Philip L. Martin, and James F. Hollifield. 1994. *Controlling Immigration: A Global Perspective.* Stanford: Stanford University Press.

Den Boer, Monica, and Neil Walker. 1993. "European Policing after 1992." *Journal of Common Market Studies* 31 (1): 3–28.

Escobar, Gabriel. 1999. "Immigrants' Ranks Tripled in 29 Years." *Washington Post,* January 9, 1999, A01.

"Europe's Smuggled Masses." 1999. *Economist.* February 20.

Ghosh, Bimal. 1998. *Huddled Masses and Uncertain Shores: Insights into Irregular Migration.* Dordrecht: Kluwer Law International.

Global Survival Network (GSN). 1997. *Crime and Servitude: An Exposé of the Traffic in Women for Prostitution from the Newly Independent States.* Washington, D.C.: Global Survival Network.

Hollifield, James F. 1992. *Immigrants, Markets, and States: The Political Economy of Postwar Europe.* Cambridge: Harvard University Press.

INS. 1998. "INS Arrest Two Fugitives in Largest Alien Smuggling Case." News release, Immigration and Naturalization Service, December 4, 1998.

INS. 1999. "INS Enhances Interior Enforcement Strategy: Plans Deployment of New FY 1999 Resources." News release, Immigration and Naturalization Service, March 30, 1999.

International Organization for Migration (IOM). 1996. "Organized Crime Moves into Migrant Trafficking." *Trafficking in Migrants, Quarterly Bulletin,* no.11 (June).

IOM. 1997. "Trafficking in Migrants: IOM Policy and Activities." http://www.iom.ch/IOM/Trafficking/IOM_Policy.html

IOM. 1998. *Trafficking in Migrants, Quarterly Bulletin,* no. 17 (January).

ISPAC. 1996. International Scientific and Professional Advisory Council of the United Nations Crime Prevention and Criminal Justice Program (ISPAC) International Conference on Migration and Crime: Global and Regional Problems and Responses, Courmayeur Mont Blanc, Italy, October 1996.

Jenkins, Philip. 1998. *Moral Panic: Changing Concepts of the Child Molester in Modern America.* New Haven: Yale University Press.

Joppke, Christian. 1998. "Why Liberal States Accept Unwanted Migration." *World Politics* 50 (2): 266–93.

Kerry, John. 1997. *The New War: The Web of Crime That Threatens America's Security.* New York: Simon and Schuster.

Kwong, Peter. 1996. *The New Chinatown.* Rev. ed. New York: Hill and Wang.
———. 1997. *Forbidden Workers: Illegal Chinese Immigrants and American Labor.* New York: New Press.

Kyle, David. 2000. *Transnational Peasants: Migrations, Networks, and Ethnicity in Andean Ecuador*. Baltimore: Johns Hopkins University Press.

Kyle, David, and Zai Liang. "Migrant Merchants: Organized Migrant Trafficking from China and Ecuador." Ms. in authors' possession.

Light, Ivan, and Edna Bonacich. 1988. *Immigrant Entrepreneurs: Koreans in Los Angeles, 1965–1982*. Berkeley: University of California Press.

McDonald, William F. 1995. "The Globalization of Criminology: The New Frontier Is the Frontier." *Transnational Organized Crime* 1 (1): 1–22.

Mickleburgh, Rod. 1999. "Whistle-blower Migrants Offered Landed Status, Aim Is to Catch Snakeheads Who Smuggled Chinese into Canada and to Protect Victims, Caplan Says." *Globe and Mail,* November 27.

MNS. 1998. "More Human Smuggling across the Eastern Border." *Migration News Sheet,* no.186/98-09 (September), 5.

MTI. 1998. "Conference on Border Control." MTI Hungarian News Agency, April 22, 1998.

Nardi, Louis F. 1999. Statement before the Subcommittee on Immigration and Claims, Committee of the Judiciary, U.S. House of Representatives, March 18.

PAP. 1998. "Interior Minister Reports Crime Rise in 1997." Polish Press Agency, February 18.

Salt, John, and Jeremy Stein. 1997. "Migration as a Business: The Case of Trafficking." *International Migration* 35 (4): 467–94.

Singer, Audrey, and Douglas Massey. 1998. "The Social Process of Undocumented Border Crossing among Mexican Migrants." *International Migration Review* 32 (3): 561–92.

Smith, Paul, ed. 1997. *Human Smuggling: Chinese Migrant Trafficking and the Challenge to America's Immigration Tradition*. Washington, D.C.: Center for Strategic and International Studies.

Stange, Margit. 1998. *Personal Property : Wives, White Slaves, and the Market in Women*. Baltimore: Johns Hopkins University Press.

Stensholt, John. 1999. "Boat People: 'No Bypassing' Rule." *Financial Review,* November 22.

Wang, Zheng. 1996. "Ocean-Going Smuggling of Illegal Chinese Immigrants: Operation, Causation, and Policy Implications." *Transnational Organized Crime* 2 (1): 49–65.

Winer, Jonathan M. 1997. "Alien Smuggling: Elements of the Problem and the U.S. Response." *Transnational Organized Crime* 3 (1): 3–13.

PART I

Historical and

Conceptual Approaches

1 ▪▪▪▪▪▪▪ Smuggling the State Back In: Agents of Human Smuggling Reconsidered

David Kyle and John Dale

Given the immediate policy and enforcement concerns of state agencies, it is unlikely that state representatives and others concerned with developing policies to combat human smuggling will reflect on either states' own role in creating and sustaining human smuggling or the nuances of its historical and sociological foundations. When a causal story is offered by state agencies or media, it usually takes the form of either of two conceptual extremes, one global and the other highly individualistic: first, globalization has created the conditions for greater transnational crime of all sorts, of which trafficking in humans is the most recent illicit global activity; or second, some very ruthless and greedy professional criminals (organized crime) are exploiting the weak and mostly innocent migrants who are either duped or coerced into a clandestine journey. Although there is an important element of truth to these statements regarding some smuggling operations, unfortunately they cover up more than they reveal, simplify more than they illuminate. We take issue with these two general axioms in this chapter through an examination of two very different cases of human smuggling: migrants contracting migration merchants in Ecuador to facilitate a journey to the United States, and young girls and women trafficked from northern Burma to Thailand and held in slavery.

These two cases demonstrate the antithesis of the two axioms stated above; first, specific historical actions by politicians and other state actors in both sending and receiving states are largely responsible for the recent increase in global human smuggling, and, second, we need to recognize the extreme diversity of smuggling operations and activities, both among and within sending regions, and how they are integrated into wider regional social structures.

If reporting on human smuggling is rife with the two aforementioned axioms, there is also a well-recognized paradox that academic researchers have been quick to point out: state aggressiveness in combating human smuggling, in the form of tighter border controls and asylum policies, has prompted more people to seek smugglers and others to enter the migrant smuggling business, including ongoing transnational criminal enterprises attracted by the high profits and low risks of this activity. Of course, the rapid increase of United States' border enforcement activities in the mid-1990s (see Andreas, this volume, Chap. 4) drives up the costs of illegal migration and increases the profits of human smuggling, thereby attracting the attention of criminal enterprises already engaged in other types of transnational smuggling, such as the drug trade. For would-be migrants, what used to be a relatively low-cost, informal affair of crossing the Rio Grande now requires greater risks and resources and is less likely to be attempted without some type of professional smuggler (though see Spener, this volume, Chap. 5, for a discussion of market diversity). Of course, for those coming from more distant countries this has been the case for some time (Kyle, 2000).

What is telling about the positive correlation between the United States' enforcement actions along the border and the recent increase in the scope and profitability of professional smuggling is that U.S. government representatives, especially from the Immigration and Naturalization Service (INS), not only agree with this assessment but hint that this was the plan all along. However, unlike Andreas's detailed account (this volume, Chap. 4) of the unintended consequences of U.S. domestic politics leading to the militarization of the U.S.-Mexican border, which suggests a less than rational policy-making process, the specter of foreign terrorist threats is now consistently mentioned as a significant part of the border deterrence strategies of the 1990s. For example, a recent U.S. General Accounting Office report begins with these two sentences: "Alien smuggling is a significant and growing problem. Although it is likely that most smuggled aliens are brought into the United States to pursue employment opportunities, some are smuggled as part of a criminal or terrorist enterprise that can pose a serious threat to U.S. national security" (May 1, 2000:1). Hence, according to this interpretation, it wasn't the *Golden Venture* smuggling ship that ran aground in 1993 as much as the World Trade Center bombing a few months earlier that prompted U.S. government officials to reevaluate border security and strategy. In this scenario, it was desirable for the United States' security interests to diminish the chaos of small-scale mom-and-pop smuggling operations along the border in favor of larger, full-time criminal enterprises. Professional law enforcement techniques rely heavily on infiltration and disruption of stable and quite large criminal organizations rather than small-scale opportunists; in a nutshell, an ongoing professional criminal syndicate presents a much larger and weaker target than two cousins and an uncle moonlighting as migrant smugglers. Thus, by raising the physical and financial costs of a clandestine crossing it was more likely that smaller operations would be driven out of business and migrants would be funneled through (monitored) criminal syndicates.

Interestingly, both of these alternative theories of the United States constructing institutional human smuggling along its border call into question the two axioms of human smuggling reportage, that unfettered globalization is the root cause and that those being smuggled are uniformly the victims of evil smugglers. In the first instance, the concept of technological globalization is much too nebulous and macrosociological to capture the specific actions and political and economic conditions in some regions that have led to increased human smuggling of the type we see today. In the U.S. case, given state complicity in driving would-be migrants into more onerous smuggling operations run by professional criminals who routinely use violent coercion, apportioning all the blame to the smuggler conveniently avoids the moral and political complexity that is a near universal trait of actual smuggling activities. When such complexities do emerge from actual human smuggling situations, such as the prominent case of Cuban boy Elián Gonzalez, depending on one's political agenda the story can be shoe-horned to fit within a preexisting morality story. In the Gonzalez case, it is striking that many who would otherwise be on the side of illegal migration control viewed the mother of Elián, who died in a smuggling operation, not as a victim but as someone who willingly risked her life in order to reach the United States and offer her son a better life. Thus, while the Mexican smuggler helping other Mexicans—many of whom come from indigenous minorities or rural backwaters persecuted by Mexican authorities—find a better economic and political environment in the United States is described as exploitative and cruel when a smuggling operation ends in a death, his Cuban counterparts risking choppy seas in little more than rafts are almost never so described. Once again, the many paradoxes one encounters in the uneven and unbalanced control of people across state borders need to be viewed within the larger political context of conflicting strategic policy goals, of which controlling undocumented labor is only one consideration.

Migrant Exporting Schemes versus Slave Importing Operations

If the case of the U.S.-Mexican border buildup demonstrates how state policies engender professional human smuggling, it is insufficient to explain its more complex sociological and political foundations found in various regions around the world. However, it demonstrates an important point: a narrow focus on the criminal smuggler overlooks a range of people implicated and benefiting from the politics and business of human smuggling. In order to bring some conceptual clarity to the complex social phenomenon of human smuggling, we distinguish between two ideal-types: *migrant exporting schemes* and *slave importing operations*, which are exemplified in the cases of Ecuador and Burma, discussed below. One or the other usually predominates in a sending region, though sometimes both together. These conceptual categories draw attention to the entire range of activities at both ends and not simply under what immediate conditions a person is smuggled across a border. The idea is to understand two different kinds of smuggling activities that are profitable, but under different circumstances and with distinct kinds of transnational social organizations.

The primary goal of a migrant exporting scheme is to provide a limited or "package" migration service out of a sending region (see Salt and Stein, 1997). Most of the organizational activity takes place on the sending side, and the contract is terminated once the migrant has arrived at the destination. In some cases, however, financial loans for the smuggling fees become an important source of income after arrival, but the terms of interest and payment and the division of labor vary greatly; the smuggler is not necessarily the loan shark. It is quite common for family members already abroad to lend the smuggling fee for a reduced rate. Such migrant exporting schemes are often characterized by highly irregular, often short-lived criminality, much of it opportunistic. Since many are part-timers, it is not simply a matter of breaking up a stable ring or criminal organization, though there is some evidence that larger criminal syndicates have moved into the migrant exporting business. It may or may not involve high levels of state corruption. Sending states typically find little political will to disrupt such migrant export projects owing to both a lack of criminal law for most related activities and the large sums of migrant remittances. Within such schemes, migrants are often driven to professional smugglers by blocked social mobility, preexisting corruption, and uneven development—not absolute poverty. Racism and sexism are common reasons for perceived ceilings in mobility, though many would be considered middle class within their home communities.

Migrant exporting is more like money laundering than drug smuggling. The type of flow is not intrinsically illicit—unlike heroin. The principal investors do not have to accompany the commodity physically across the border. The layering process of identity laundering is built into all transactions along the way; once the migrant is integrated by crossing the border, the activity is complete—in contrast, getting heroin across the border is only the beginning because the criminal organization still needs to distribute and sell it in order to reap the bulk of the profits. And this is exactly the crucial distinction between a migrant exporting scheme and a slave importing operation.

In a slave importing operation, the goal is to import weak labor, typically minority women, though not always so, for *ongoing* enterprises by relatively stable criminal organizations or even semilegitimate businesses in the destination country. Needless to say, a slave—held in bondage for economic profit—is extremely profitable (Bales, 1999). Unlike a migrant exporting scheme, a slave importing operation nearly always involves corruption of state officials in all countries involved. In most cases, victims of such operations are duped into believing that it is a migrant exporting scheme in which they are about to embark. Slave traders can pretend to be migration exporters precisely because the latter do exist. As with many cons, it is the victim's own complicity in a relatively minor crime (illegal border crossing) that leads to the final snare of the confidence scheme. Tragically, in this case, the migrant (now an illegal alien) is stripped of all legal rights and personal dignity and made to pay off a rolling debt through coerced labor, typically prostitution. Migrants may be held for weeks, months, or years in such conditions, paying off the new debt incurred each time they exchange hands. Given the nature of this enterprise, unlike a migrant exporting scheme, often the victims come from much more dire economic and social situations; it is a combination of their desperateness, political weakness, and lack of strong social networks that leads them to believe the false promises. Most such operations are sophisticated enough to have the initial contact person be a seemingly wealthy woman from the same ethnic group as the victim. The recruiter's claims are buttressed by the ubiquitous images of idealized lifestyles of the most developed countries now beamed by satellite around the world through the global media industry.

There is a legal, political, moral, and sociological difference between the two types of smuggling activities we have outlined here. Slaves are slaves; it does not matter what unfortunate decisions were made to place them in the hands of slaveholders. By focusing on the nature of the economic enterprise spanning multiple countries, and not the degree to which a migrant agreed to be smuggled (few are actually kidnapped), we gain a better understanding of what is at stake for those at multiple levels of society who are benefiting from smuggling operations, whether directly or indirectly, and a deeper understanding of their different economic logics may lead to more appropriate policies that go beyond capturing the immediate perpetrators. We next turn to two examples of a migrant exporting scheme and a slave importing operation in order to move from an ideal-type to the historical complexities of actual cases.

Ecuador: Migrant Exporting Schemes

Most Ecuadorians abroad are from a single region of Ecuador, the southern province of Azuay, where the most recent development project in a long history of entrepreneurial efforts has come to include migrant exporting.[1] Located approximately 300 kilometers south of Quito over mountainous terrain, the province of Azuay includes Ecuador's third largest city, Cuenca (pop. 330,000), and shares a common social and political history with the neighboring province of Cañar.

Unlike neighboring regions, Azuay is characterized by an early integration with, and dependence on, the capitalist world economy. Azuayans exported cloth during the colonial period. The Azuayan elite relied on ideological control of its nominally independent peasantry, which included unusually large numbers of Spaniards and mestizos compared with the indigenous population. Unlike the rest of Ecuador, Azuay largely avoided the extremes of the colonial *encomienda* system of debt peonage but did not escape it altogether. Throughout the colonial period, policies restricting the peasantry to *reduciones,* or bounded communities, severely limited their social mobility.

After independence from Spain, the lack of royal authority and Azuay's general isolation meant that local elites could consolidate their political dominance and increase their ideological claims to the region's resources and surplus labor. For example, when the cloth trade in Azuay collapsed in the early 1800s owing to cheap British imports, Azuayan elites actively searched for economic solutions to the crisis that would not fundamentally alter the social status quo. The challenge for elites was straightforward: after several decades of placing little pressure on the Azuayan and Cañari peasantry following the decline of the cloth trade, they needed a peasant cottage industry that furthered the elite's role as intermediaries and could fill a market niche using preindustrial technology and inexpensive raw materials. Thus, local elites deliberately introduced to the region a productive activity—the weaving of straw hats—that would not upset but reinforce the existing Azuayan social structure.

In promoting the new industry, local officials noted the low cost of the straw and other materials needed and also that it was an occupation in which "all hands [could] be put to work, including men and women, elderly and children" (Dominguez, 1991:36). With such a concerted push by the elite and the quick popularity of the hats in sunny Azuay itself, the introduction was a huge success—to the extent that peasants and urban poor were soon weaving hats in nearly every corner of Azuay and Cañar. With the internal demand satisfied, the hats began to be exported for gold miners passing through Panama during the California gold rush of the

1850s (hence the name "Panama hat"); the value of straw hat exports from Ecuador jumped from 117,008 pesos in 1843 to 830,040 in 1855 (Palomeque, 1990).

The weaving of straw hats—planned and instituted by local elites— began a radical transformation that would soon articulate the region into a labor-intensive, industrial bureaucracy, closely linked to the world economy. Though the cottage industry of hat weaving was similar to that of cloth weaving, whereby both raw material and woven product were brokered to the peasantry by middlemen who were, directly or indirectly, employed by urban export "houses," the production and marketing processes entailed a greater division of labor on a much larger scale with (as city officials predicted) the participation of both men and women, young and old, each finding his or her production niche. The brokering system itself employs a hierarchy of *comisionistas,* who broker for the export houses, and independent *perros* (dogs), who sell to the *comisionistas* after paying the weaver slightly less for the hat than what the *comisionista* would have paid. At the height of the hat trade in the 1940s, Dominguez estimates that as many as 250,000 children and adults from the provinces of Azuay and Cañar were engaged in some activity directly related to making and marketing "Panama hats" (1991). Although the peasant weavers of Azuay enjoyed an unprecedented freedom in comparison with their counterparts living on haciendas or working in urban sweatshops, their ambiguous class position prevented any significant economic or social gains from being made through group mobilization; though thousands were and continue to be exploited at below subsistence-level piece rates, this common exploitation as a potential source of group action is outweighed by their conservative position as landowners in direct economic competition with their neighbors—a fact fully exploited by the *comisionistas* and *perros.*

A "long decade" of economic depression in Azuay began with the precipitous drop in Panama hat exports in 1947 and its continuous decline every year until the mid-1960s. Cuenca's principal importer of Panama hats, the United States, began to import cheaper "straw" hats from Asia after World War II.

The impact of the hat industry's decline on Azuay and Cañar was immediate and severe, initiating a quiet revolution of economic disarticulation and social disintegration. For many members of the urban elite not directly connected to the hat trade, any financial losses were compensated by their ability to exploit the new vulnerability of the rural and urban labor force. It was, instead, those diverse groups engaged in some activity related to the hat trade (which at its height included more than a quarter of the population) that had to seek external remedies to the immediate economic crisis they were experiencing. While the local and national elite did little to respond effectively to the Azuayan crisis of the 1950s, two groups—the white-mestizo exporters and the rural peasant weavers—began two different types of migration that together would set the stage for a mass exodus in the 1980s and 1990s. It was during the 1950s that the first Cuencanos arrived in New York City, mostly young men of wealthy white and mestizo families directly connected to urban hat export houses. They were looking for ways to capitalize financially on their longstanding connections with U.S. importers—and for adventure (Astudillo and Cordero, 1990). It was also during the late 1950s that regular jet airline service connected Cuenca to New York City via Guayaquil: it was now just as easy for a Cuencano to travel to New York City as to Quito, Ecuador's capital.

These pioneering migration networks notwithstanding, the mass regionwide phenomenon of international migration from Azuay, Cañar, and Morona Santiago (largely populated by Azuayans) that developed during the 1980s cannot be completely accounted for by a geometric increase, that is, a simple "snowball" effect of migrants helping family and neighbors to make the multiple border crossings—especially the high number of peasants migrating to New York City directly from the most rural areas. Unlike other historical international flows of documented and undocumented immigrants, there is no evidence of direct recruitment by North American employers to facilitate the considerable financial and legal obstacles of the journey. Yet, in just ten years, the modest international migrations of the 1970s turned into a mass exodus, making it one of the largest groups of undocumented immigrants in the New York City metro area.

This sharp increase in international migration, especially from rural, isolated areas, can be explained only by the reemergence of a centuries-old institution in the region—the usurious middleman, who profits from the economic and political space afforded by a complacent elite and a captive peasantry, in this case, an integrated network of *tramitadores*, or facilitators, who provide the range of legal and illegal services needed to make a clandestine trip to the United States. Instead of mediating the hat procurement for export houses as in the hat trade, *tramitadores* work, directly or indirectly, for unscrupulous travel agencies, which are themselves participants in larger formal and underground networks of migration merchants, or those who profit from some aspect of the migrant exporting business.

Although these facilitating networks are international in scope, they begin with a *tramitador*'s sales pitch to the would-be migrant in his or her home village, not unlike the role played by the *perros* in the straw hat trade. The *tramitador* offers to arrange all the national documents needed to leave Ecuador, visas for intermediary countries, all the physical travel arrangements, and, depending on the type of trip, a falsified U.S. visa or passport. To pay for all these services, which run from $6,000 to$10,000, an amount even the wealthiest of Ecuadorians would balk at, the *tramitador* arranges to have the money lent to the ingenuous peasant by a *chulquero* (smuggler/moneylender), at usurious interest rates of 10–12 percent, compounded monthly, with all land, animals, and possessions of the migrant held as collateral. In addition, numerous local banks and money exchange houses provide the needed financial infrastructure and legal cover for such operations. Local community-based networks of *tramitadores* and *chulqueros* typically are closely related by kinship, relying on social ties with a high degree of trust and loyalty, thus allowing for clandestine capitalism to operate with fewer costs (both monetary and psychological) related to maintaining the financial and legal security of the covert economic activity. For example, in one medium-sized Azuayan town with high levels of international migration, all the moneylenders are members of just five families, and each of these families is further interlocked through marital ties. It should be emphasized that moneylending as an economic institution with a set of rules and customs has been a historical feature of the region even before the rural economy was completely monetized. The vicissitudes of small-scale and subsistence farming among the peasantry, along with the periodic burden of financing an annual religious festival, have traditionally required the services of moneylenders, who are either coethnic villagers or white-mestizo outsiders and whose rates are officially controlled by the state. For example, in times of crop failure, a loan enabled households not only to buy the few necessary household goods but also, most important, to continue the production cycle, which could include temporary coastal migrations and handicraft production. In times of regional scarcity, loans from "outside" the village with one of the urban-based "patrons" often involved usurious practices made possible by the peasant's ignorance and general position of weakness vis-à-vis the patron.

With corrupt local officials and a network of professional forgers, the necessary local and national documents are bought by the *tramitador*. Often the forger's work is so good that U.S. embassy personnel in Quito cannot figure out how the documents can circumvent infrared detectors and laminate safeguards developed by the 3M company (personal communication). Next, working with legitimate travel agents, the *tramitador* makes the travel arrangements, which, broadly speaking, fall into either of two categories: (1) the direct route to New York City, using a "borrowed" passport or forged visa, which also entails a significant amount of cultural coaching on how to look and act like a *residente*; or (2) the tortuous overland route that includes a sophisticated network of Central American and Mexican contacts, "safe houses," and "coyotes" (those who actually lead the migrant across the Rio Grande). Since the Mexican government has made attaining a visa to its country more difficult, sometimes coyotes are also used to get into Mexico through a Guatemalan farm or by boat. At every step of the way, from the financing of the trip in Ecuador to the dependence on a nefarious international network spanning half a dozen countries, the migrant risks being swindled, jailed, deported, robbed, or violently abused, including rape and murder. Not surprisingly, the main task of the *tramitador* is to gain the confidence, whether founded or unfounded, of the potential "client." The price of land is so inflated owing to competition by return migrants in both urban and rural areas that only those who have a U.S. dollar income can hope to purchase a new plot, lending support to the recruiter's sales pitch.

The particular configuration of financial and human resources brought to bear by each migrant on the problem of getting him or her across a border is often as unique as the Azuayan villages and barrios. The financing of the trip usually involves a combination of personal savings, free loans by relatives, interest loans by friends, and usurious loans by *chulqueros*. Similarly, a catalog of the techniques used to get across the U.S. border or obtain a tourist visa could fill a medium-sized book. Kin- and community-based migration networks make use of the information and resources circulating within them, thereby making migration paths fairly consistent within a given social network. In this way, the path taken by a successful migrant pioneer gets repeated and revised within his or her network. Sometimes this evolutionary process may induce a pioneer, who has already made several trips and may be a *residente*, or "green-card" holder, to become an in-network *tramitador*, coyote, or *chulquero* whose services are provided for a lower fee or even freely (that is, monetarily speaking, though reciprocity of some sort is assumed). Conversely, it is also common for return migrants to lend money to regional intermediaries (of the *perro* mold), who in turn lend at higher rates to professional *chulqueros*, who in turn lend to the new migrant at the highest rate, thus forming a pyramid scheme that requires a constant influx of new migrants to keep capital circulating to the top.

To conclude this section, the impact of mass international migration is nothing short of an economic and social transformation for the province of Azuay. These individual, community, and regional transformations leading to one of the most important mass international migrations from South America are built not on the foundation of either individual decisions or the snowball effect of social networks but rather on a regionwide migrant exporting industry in which a wide range of people play a direct and indirect role, from the recruiter to the local banker. The explosive construction of new concrete homes in some rural villages near Cuenca, often filled with a new SUV in the garage and chickens in the upper floors, provides testimony to the general success of the migrant exporting schemes in this region. The sustainability and future changes in the social organization of these schemes are topics for future research.

Burma and Thailand: Slave Importing Operations

A guest staying in one of Myanmar's (Burma) finest hotels may be surprised to learn through an official tourist brochure that Myanmar has a unique natural resource that it would like to offer: its own female virgins (Kyaa Nyo, 1997; Knowles 1997). A male tourist may therefore be able to experience not only the virgin quality of a mysterious country dotted with hundreds of ancient pagodas, only recently opened to tourism, but also a night with a virgin girl from a rural village who may be as young as twelve years old. If the Myanmar government helps promote its virgins as a local resource for sale, it is not surprising that virgins are also an exportable and highly profitable commodity. The primary destination for young women trafficked out of Myanmar is Thailand, with some eventually continuing on to other destinations.

The transnational trafficking of women and girls between Myanmar and Thailand, while perhaps increasing in overall numbers, is not a new development. As Eileen Scully (this volume, Chap. 3) points out, by the 1890s "networks of varying sophistication and durability" were evident throughout Southeast Asia. Already, as is still the case today, "sexual service to foreigners had been commoditized and stigmatized, the fate of lowborn and marginal women." What's novel about the contemporary flow of women from Myanmar to Thailand's sex-work industry is that ethnic minority women from the countryside of Myanmar are in demand by foreign tourists and business travelers (particularly Chinese) in Thailand. This emerging, exoticizing taste for Burmese prostitutes is refined by one further criterion: these women (girls, really) must be virgins. At least, it is Burmese (ethnic Shan) virgins for whom foreign customers traveling in Thailand are willing to pay the most money. Moreover, the states of both Myanmar and Thailand are playing the most proactive role in constituting this demand. H. R. Friman (this volume, Chap. 1) explains how the state (Japan) plays a constitutive role in the ideological construction of the "Snakehead Threat" as "foreign" and how the state benefits from this construction both politically and economically. Myanmar and Thailand, however, profit by playing a more direct role in constructing the markets of transnational organized crime that we are describing here. Before turning to Myanmar, to understand the regional and international market for Burmese virgins, we must examine recent economic and demographic changes in Thailand.

In the minds of many Thai citizens, globalization has come to mean currency crisis and unemployment. Joining the prescriptive belt-tightening fiscal austerity discourse provided by the International Monetary Fund has been a more indigenous, nationalist discourse targeting illegal immigration. Curiously absent from the Thai state's remedial discussion of the causes of illegal immigration has been the state's own role in promoting it. In the summer of 1996, when financial analysts worldwide still perceived the Southeast Asian "tiger" economies as roaring, the Thai state issued a cabinet resolution allowing employers in forty-three provinces to register illegal Burmese, Laotians, and Cambodians already living in Thailand to work for two years. The purpose of the resolution was to ease the burden of Thailand's labor shortage. The unanticipated currency crisis, however, engendered a new official policy toward illegal immigration: repatriation of the approximately one million illegal alien workers in an attempt to ease the sharp increase of unemployment among Thai nationals. Most illegal alien workers in Thailand are from Myanmar.

About twenty thousand young girls and boys (ages ten to fifteen) are smuggled from Myanmar each year to work in Thailand's sex industry (Mirkinson, 1994:4). This represents about 10 percent of all prostitutes working in Thailand (Chaipipat, 1997). Most of these youths come from Shan state in the northeastern region of Myanmar, bordering Thailand. According to research presented in Bangkok at a 1997 regional conference on the prevention of human trafficking, the annual illegal income generated by sex workers (of all ages) in Thailand is between 450 billion and 540 billion baht (or roughly U.S. $10 billion).[2] To put these numbers in perspective, this is more money than is generated from drug trafficking. Moreover, Thailand's total state budget was only one trillion baht in 1995, prior to the recent currency crisis (Chaipipat, 1997). Complicating Thailand's repatriation policy objective, Myanmar insists that it will not accept illegal workers from its ethnic minority groups now employed in Thailand.

In 1988, a statewide prodemocracy movement emerged in Myanmar to challenge twenty-six years of political repression and economic mismanagement under the military regime that usurped control of the state in a 1962 coup. The military state's crackdown was more dramatic and bloody than that witnessed the following year in Beijing's Tiananmen Square. Western democratic states responded initially to what they identified as human rights abuses by passing economic sanctions against Myanmar. Sorely in need of foreign investment, the military-state regime began to privatize its state-managed natural resources (teak, jade, and oil), abandoning its isolationist economic policy, known as the "Burmese way to Socialism." The state also consented to the demands of the major opposition party, the National League for Democracy, led by Aung San Suu Kyi. Suu Kyi, who has since been awarded the Nobel Peace Prize for her efforts, is the daughter of the national hero Aung San, who was assassinated by the associates of Myanmar's current dictator shortly after he had successfully led the country to democratic independence from the British and Japanese in the wake of World War II. Suu Kyi demanded successfully that the military regime hold fair and democratic elections, and in a 1990 landslide victory she was elected with 82 percent of the vote. The military, however, refusing to honor the results, instead responded by placing Suu Kyi under house arrest and systematically arresting or assassinating the newly elected members of her party in each township throughout the state.

As prodemocracy activists from the urban centers of Rangoon and Mandalay fled to the rural Thai-Myanmar border regions to join forces with ethnic minority rebels who had been fighting the state for national autonomy since the initial coup, the Burmese military launched a new campaign to eradicate these rebel strongholds. For the past decade, the military has resorted to a systematic policy of burning local villages along the border, raping and torturing ethnic minority women, forcibly conscripting villagers to serve the military as porters, minesweepers, and human shields in its campaigns to exterminate oppositional groups, and coercively enslaving villagers to work on the military state's infrastructural projects. Some of these projects, like the oil pipeline being constructed through Myanmar to Thailand, are financed by transnational corporations like Unocal, based in the United States, and Total, based in France. Such military campaigns and development projects have generated a dramatic increase in Thailand's refugee camps situated along the Thai-Myanmar border.

In contrast to the economic sanctions initiated by Western democratic states (and encouraged by Suu Kyi's National League for Democracy Party), member states of the Association of Southeast Asian Nations (ASEAN), along with China and, of course, transnational corporations with high levels of investment in partnerships with the state-owned Myanmar Holdings Company Ltd., have continued trading with Myanmar under a policy of constructive engagement. Proponents of this policy argue that reviving official development assistance, promoting more investment, and even encouraging nongovernmental associations (NGOs) to provide humanitarian assistance will bring about much needed social and political change in Myanmar. They maintain that isolating the military-state regime through economic sanctions is ineffective. In 1997,

ASEAN inducted Myanmar as a new member of its economic regional trading bloc. Myanmar's ruling party celebrated its induction into ASEAN as a solution to its flagging attraction as a site of foreign investment. However, Myanmar was unable to cash in on this opportunity, owing to the simultaneous onset of what became dubbed in the international financial press as the "Southeast Asian currency crisis." Myanmar's potential trading allies, such as Indonesia and Thailand, were suddenly subjected to strict lending criteria imposed by the International Monetary Fund. Overt investment in Myanmar was no longer politically feasible. Yet Myanmar has pursued other sources of unofficial revenue in more clandestine transnational markets of Southeast Asia (and beyond), as illustrated in some of its official tourist brochures promoting another of its putative natural resources: Burmese virgins.

Both men and women from Myanmar concentrated in Thai refugee camps along the border have reported in interviews with humanitarian NGO workers that local Thai officials forced them upon threat of being repatriated to serve as recruiters for organized human smuggling groups engaged in the trafficking of young girls from Myanmar into Thailand's sex industry.[3] The local Thai officials, typically immigration border patrol officers, then receive a bounty from one of the agents of the human smuggling groups. Sometimes the process works the other way around, whereby the agents approach the Thai officials and pay them bribe money to pass without complication through the border checkpoints. These refugee recruiters lead the agents to their home villages in Myanmar. Along the way (and back), the agents pay bribes whenever necessary to Myanmar's military-state personnel. The refugees are needed for their skills in speaking Burmese as well as the local ethnic minority language of the target village in Myanmar. Perhaps most important, the refugees are used to establish the trust necessary for persuading the young girls' families to relinquish custody of their daughters (usually with some form of material compensation) to the Thai officials.

While some girls have a vague idea of the nature of the work they will be doing, they are not aware of the working conditions (particularly the debt peonage) that await them. Upon returning, the local official typically charges 5,000 baht per person brought by agents of the human smuggling operation into Thailand. Brothel owners in Thailand pay the agents, who pay the state authorities, but ultimately the brothel owner charges this same amount to the young girls' debt. As a "virgin," she will earn up to 15,000 baht from one customer. Virgins—particularly Burmese or Shan virgins—command top dollar in many areas of Thailand these days. Most of the demand seems to be coming from Chinese tourists and businessmen. A young girl's "loss of virginity" can be sold several times, until she can no longer pass as a virgin in the eyes of her potential customers. Through a surgical procedure, a girl can also be "revirginized." Thus, the loss of virginity is viewed not so much as an event but rather as a gradual process. Many of these young girls from Myanmar, even prior to entering the sex trade in Thailand, can recount stories of being raped by the Myanmar military. Virgins are highly valued not only for the reduced risk of their having HIV infection but also because in many Asian cultures deflowering a virgin is considered to bestow upon the perpetrator youthful potency and healthful benefits. Burmese and Shan girls are exoticized as special virgins, in part because of the relative isolation of Myanmar for several decades.

The money earned from the commodification of these young girls' virginity is significantly more than that earned by nonvirgins—a status the former are, of course, quickly on their way to assuming. Yet the percentage they actually receive is not even enough to cover their initial smuggling debt. Moreover, the local police regularly raid these brothels (typically consisting of several rooms above a karaoke bar or coffee shop) in order to collect bribe money from the brothel owners, whose business in Thailand is illegal. The cost of these bribes is added to the young girls' debt, along with the cost of their food, clothing, cosmetics, toiletries, occasional health checks, and "rent" (although they typically sleep in the same room, just big enough for a bed and sink, where they service their customers). A "Burmese virgin" can expect to spend an average of eighteen months working simply to pay off her debt to her original brothel owner or to any subsequent owner who purchases her (and her debt) from that original owner.

It is important to understand that it is not the girl who has paid the bribes to the police all along but rather the brothel owner. This money is not paid simply to prevent the girls from being arrested and deported; it is an informally institutionalized source of income for the police in exchange for their protecting the brothel owner. Sometimes the brothel owner or agent will ask the police to arrest certain girls working in his brothel when the owner or agent does not want to give the sex workers the money that he owes them. The new Thai policy of repatriating illegal alien workers has not diminished demand for the employment of these girls. It has, however, made it much more difficult for these girls to move into other areas of work and thus to remain in Thailand, once (or if) they have managed to buy back their freedom. Moreover, Thai immigration policy changes have not slowed trafficking but rather have made it easier for the brothel owners and police to threaten these women with repatriation.

Thailand's most recent immigration policy proposal might appear destined for failure (in terms of its putative intent to curb migrant trafficking), but a careful reading between the lines suggests that, in practice, it may serve the state's interests. Thailand's immigration police announced in February 1998 that they had come up with a new strategy to encourage legal and illegal immigrants working in the country to return to their homelands voluntarily: instead of launching crackdowns on illegal workers, immigration police were being instructed to provide travel expenses and free meals to alien workers wishing to return home (Charoenpho, 1998). They argued that this "psychological approach," which focuses only on illegal workers, would be more cost-effective than crackdowns, whereby arrested illegal workers are sent directly to detention centers for months (of free meals). Under the new strategy, authorities would be required to pay only travel expenses and free meals on the day that the workers leave for their countries. In addition, the Thai immigration police, according to the national press, cited their concern for curbing the activities of human smugglers: "To prevent other Burmese immigrants from sneaking through the country [Thailand], Police Lieutenant-General Chidchai said he has liased with non-governmental organizations, the army and concerned agencies to help keep close watch on the movement of human smuggling gangs" (Charoenpho, 1998: 2).

In a move that was meant to be interpreted as "putting their money where their mouth is," the Immigration Police, in the same report, assured Thai nationals that they had asked Police Region 7 (which is responsible for western provinces bordering Myanmar) to deploy more officials at border passes to prevent the influx of Burmese into the country. This move addresses the common rebuttal bandied in the press that the rate of illegal immigration influx (particularly owing to "internal" conflict in

Myanmar) outpaces that of repatriation. As a solution to preventing illegal Burmese immigration, however, the deployment of more officials at border passes, as we have seen, may serve only to exacerbate the problem. It is precisely such corrupt officials who have been making possible illegal migration from Myanmar through their complicity in human smuggling activities. In fairness to the government of Thailand, its historical and geographical location within one of the world's most volatile regions makes its triple challenges of political stability, economic development, and migration control especially severe. Similarly, few countries in the world are untouched by some degree of official corruption. Nonetheless, the evidence suggests that while Thailand has recently passed laws increasing the penalties for sexual relations with children, the ubiquitous sex industry organized mostly for local consumption and the enormous profits to be gained by investors in the sex trade call into question the notion that women and children trafficked into Thailand and held in bondage are simply the result of some criminal miscreants.

Agents of Human Smuggling Reconsidered

In this section, we examine actors who are common to both of our cases as well as to other cases of migrant smuggling. First, however, in comparing these two differing cases of human smuggling from Ecuador and Myanmar, what is most striking is what is largely missing: "transnational gangsters." Although many point to "transnational organized crime" as the driving social force behind the global increase in human smuggling (see, e.g., Godson and Olson, 1995), it plays only a supporting role, if at all, in these two cases. Given the nature of the human commodity being smuggled, it is predictable that some human smugglers are members of traditional crime organizations, though by some definitions even corrupt police could be segregated conceptually into the organized crime camp. There is much evidence that most smugglers of migrants around the world simply participate in what Finkenauer (this volume, Chap. 6) calls "crime that is organized" but not "organized crime." An additional element to this crime that is organized recalls earlier forms of widespread smuggling; for many around the world participating in migrant exporting and even slave importing is not perceived, as a result of longstanding sociocultural norms, as a "real crime" in the region of origin.

Some migrant smugglers are more akin to the historical "free traders" of an earlier era when important commodities, in this case labor, were highly regulated and usuriously taxed. Migrant smugglers from the region of Azuay are not members of transnational organized crime in any traditional meaning of the term. Most are helping family and neighbors get to New York City. This is a case that illustrates that mass undocumented migration can rapidly increase without organized crime. In contrast, Myanmar presents a case of state-organized crime (Chambliss, 1989), entailing the smuggling of an illicit and, to be sure, morally bankrupt commodity. There is all too often a belief that a victim must somehow have deserved her or his fate. Especially on the migrant exporting end of the business, smugglers and moneylenders advertise in newspapers and do little to cover the nature of their business. Moreover, we have seen in the case of Myanmar that even states may subtly advertise to tourists the availability of commodities, the consumption of which are officially designated illicit, such as virgin prostitution. Similarly, it is the very parents of young girls who will sometimes sell a daughter for a sum equal to one year's income.

Apart from problematizing the role of organized crime, our two cases implicate other, unusual suspects in the social organization of migrant smuggling: (a) states pursuing their official interests and corrupt state officials pursuing self-aggrandizement; (b) regional elites; and (c) employers at the destination.

Regional Elites

For many developing countries, local economic and political power is concentrated into relatively few regional elite families (Walton, 1977). This is especially striking in the case of Azuay, where such families are still referred to as "the nobles." Since the early 1960s, many elites have adopted the discourse, if not also the strategies, of successive waves of development experts from North America and Europe, especially as foreigners have brought financial and technological aid. Yet the results of the previous modernization period were mixed at best, in large part owing to the unwillingness of regional elites to give up real power and the ideologies of social stratification that legitimize privilege. Hence, we have a common local "development" situation in the 1990s in many parts of the world: great strides in isolated areas which raise expectations for a better life but which do not live up to their promise (Isbister, 1995).

Mass emigration may seem to be the ultimate measure of failure of a regional economy. However, mass transnational migration through an efficient, even rationalized, system of migration commodification and smuggling overcomes the two most important concerns for regional elites in the 1990s: migrant smuggling continues to profit from workers through remittances and curtails political upheaval associated with the broken promises of failed "development" projects.

Not only does the export of people have some of the advantages of other traditional exports, such as backward linkages (e.g., financial services) and forward linkages (e.g., construction), but it also does not have the most significant disadvantage—competition from other regions around the world; migrants represent a global export paradoxically contained within a locally controlled market. Hence, transnational undocumented migration is an unintended consequence of development through modernization—a sort of grassroots development project itself from which many regional elites continue to profit.

States and Corrupt State Officials

The commodification of migration affects sending and receiving states very differently, a fact that points to the real nature of human smuggling and undocumented migration vis-à-vis the saliency of the modern state system. State boundaries add to the value of any commodity needed across borders. Indeed, they are dependent on each other. In the case of human smuggling, sending states have generally viewed migration, whether legal or not, as a positive benefit. Remittances now rival many traditional sources of state revenue. Sending states have even reached out to include migrants abroad in domestic politics and have taken an active role in how undocumented co-nationals are treated in the United States and Europe. The Mexican ambassador Silva Herzog, speaking at the national convention of the League of United Latin American Citizens in Anaheim, California, observed, "It is particularly surprising that at a time of almost unprecedented success in the United States economy . . . the anti-immigration voices have once again taken the high ground. . . . Make no mistake about it, this is racism and xenophobia, and it has a negative impact on every person of Hispanic origin living in this country, regardless of their migratory status" (*Los Angeles Times,* June 26, 1997). Such aggressive campaigning for lessening immigration controls by a Mexican official in the United States is grounded not only in humanitarian concerns but also in the fear that the more than $4.5 billion remittances to families in Mexico every year will recede during a grave economic crisis at home.

Similarly, in Burma, the military government has cried foul because Thailand wants to repatriate Burmese nationals because of backlash against foreigners during a period of economic hardship. Illegal aliens from Myanmar working in Thailand manage to send substantial amounts of money home to their families (substantial, at least, to families living in a country where the annual per capita income is currently about U.S. $150). However, Myanmar's military tends to collect this remitted money through various forms of violence, bribery, and "taxation," which is paid either in cash, labor, or social capital.

Highly publicized in the international media have been the Myanmar military's violent campaigns and practices of coerced labor, extortion, "ethnic cleansing" (rape and murder), and crop burning against its rural ethnic minority communities living in the border regions of the state (see, e.g., http://www.soros.org/burma). We have also noted above how less publicized practices of bribery, or the payment of "tea money" to state employees, have become informally institutionalized.

However, the military also collects "taxes" from locals, which are typically imposed suddenly, as circumstances may dictate. Taxes may be imposed on particular villages for "beautification projects" (such as patching up ditches in the villages' dirt roads) purportedly designed to enhance tourism. Those who cannot pay the tax in cash pay the tax in labor, helping to patch up the roads. The state also collects taxes from local villages that do not produce the quota of rice required by the state—even when the state's military campaigns have destroyed the rice crops, making it impossible for the villagers to meet such quotas.

When a family within the village has no money to pay these taxes, the state requires that family to offer a male member of the household to serve either as a porter (without pay) in the military to fight in campaigns against rebel ethnic minority armies or in state construction projects. Few of these conscripts ever return to see their families. It is not uncommon to learn that they have been literally worked to death. If a poor family has neither the money nor a male member of the family to serve the military, it may be able to borrow the money from either a wealthier family in the village or from the state in order to hire a neighbor's son to serve in the military for it. In this sense, the state "taxes" the villagers' social capital.

In short, if the economically poor military state of Myanmar suspects that there are sources of wealth to be tapped within these villages, it can and does construct a justification for usurping that wealth. The state understands that a significant portion of that wealth is sustained through remittances from migrant members of the village working abroad. Thus it is not surprising that the proposal last year by Thailand's House Committee on Labor and Social Welfare met with protest from the state of Myanmar. In its effort to alleviate the burden of continuing to employ illegal workers from Myanmar, Thailand proposed to tax them all (including ethnic minorities) and remit the money directly to the state of Myanmar (Hutasingh, 1997). If Myanmar had accepted these conditions, then it would have meant that it had also accepted the status of its minority workers in Thailand—an acknowledgment Myanmar was unwilling to provide. After all, there was little to gain in doing so: Myanmar already receives at least as much in remittances by "taxing" local minorities who remain in Myanmar.

In regard to the receiving states, such as the United States, it would seem that the commodification of migration and the increasing use of smugglers would be uniformly negative. After all, some U.S. policymakers have even considered the elimination of birthright citizenship for "illegal aliens." Although employers benefit from falsely documented labor, such benefits cannot be collapsed into the interests of the state. In addition, the economic benefit of both documented and undocumented migration to the U.S. economy on the whole is an area of hot debate.

Unlike private employers, U.S. leaders and policymakers have a variety of pro-immigrant, anti-immigrant, and ethnic communities to contend with and placate (see Joppke, 1998; Freeman, 1994). Although immigration laws must be upheld by the state, and although anti-immigrant voices include some demographic and economic rationales that cannot simply be reduced to racism, there is also a political price for "bashing immigrants." High-profile state agencies can diminish the political fallout of migration controls through a diffusing strategy that relies on a variety of third-party actors such as airlines and privatized detention centers. In a similar manner, a more commodified migration process, also using third parties (i.e., smugglers), allows states to develop a discourse that emphasizes the criminality and evil of alien smuggling rings, which can then be contrasted with hard-working immigrants.

Employers and Slaveholders

North American employers of unskilled urban and farm labor directly benefit from an efficient underground source of labor. Were migrants dependent upon their own social networks to cross borders under conditions of heightened state monitoring, immigrant labor flow might subside. Thus, smugglers might be conceptualized as an extension of, and in some cases a replacement for, labor recruiters. In some undocumented smuggling streams, the migrant, and even the individual smuggler for that matter, becomes a sort of indentured servant working for the syndicate or a collaborator. In extreme cases, slavery has returned in the form of garment and sex workers held captive in Los Angeles and New York City. Contemporary slavery, as Bales (1999: 14) pointed out, is not about slave owning but "slave-holding," or complete control over people for economic profit. While this is a useful distinction between older and more contemporary forms of slavery, it is also one that is more disconcerting because the organization of work around the world under the globalization project has led to greater levels of labor control, practices that are increasingly legitimized as necessary for survival within a competitive global arena. Even when free to find employment on their own terms, illegal immigrants with large usurious debts make an especially docile and hardworking labor force—a point not overlooked by employers or states in receiving countries.

Thus, instead of conceptualizing contemporary slaves as "disposable people," the title of Bales' book, we might instead view them as an extreme, though not uncommon, example of the growing process by which labor is forced underground into invisibility as well as disposability. One could argue that the concept of "disposable people" per se is not particularly novel to the current globalization project but rather has been the lot of much of humanity historically. What is novel are the growing levels of work that is purposely hidden by employers and laborers from the global markets they are seeking to sell in or from the local clientele of "global cities" (Sassen, 1991). Tellingly, all the actors highlighted in this section—local elites, states, and employers—justify their less than honorable actions by invoking some form of the argument "globalization made me do it." Globalization *as an ideology* continues to blur the boundaries of what should be considered exploitative economic behavior first and foremost in the area of labor relations.

Conclusion

Existing studies of transnational human smuggling, its organization, and the actors that sustain this practice are typically shaped by a particularly ahistorical conception of "organized crime"—one that allows no conceptual space for analyzing the organizational sources of transnational human smuggling provided by, and thus implicating, regional elites, states, and employers (and, hence, consumers). Proceeding deductively from the common assumption that only large-scale transnational criminal organizations are driving increases in the levels of human smuggling fails to elucidate the central, proactive roles played by noncriminal migrants and criminal nonmigrants, including corrupt state representatives, in sustaining and transforming the practice of professional human smuggling. Other studies also suggest that even the premise of the deductive analysis of complex groups of transnational organized crime as necessary to the clandestine activities associated with human smuggling is faulty, especially in cases in which a previous legal activity has been converted to an illegal, heavily penalized one (see Reuter, 1985).

We have used a historical comparative approach in an attempt to understand the social organization, political benefits, and economic profitability of contemporary human smuggling as a diverse bundle of activities and participants. Our findings suggest that comparing processes of transnational migrant smuggling across different times and places reveals a wide range of social formations implicating a diverse configuration of actors. Yet we have conceptualized some significant differences between two fundamental types of smuggling enterprises: migrant exporting schemes and slave importing operations. Both can be just as deadly for the migrant and place him or her at great legal and physical risk, but we believe that effective policies need to distinguish among a range of smuggling operations, some which are aiding people to leave situations of political persecution and economic hopelessness and others that deliver them into precisely such circumstances. In broad terms, three themes emerge from this comparison of a migrant exporting scheme and a slave importing operation: global diversity, internal organizational complexity, and contradictory state involvement in human smuggling activities and human rights. Through empirical research, the following chapters help elucidate in diverse ways these three basic observations.

NOTES

We wish to thank Daniela Kraiem and John Walton for their editorial scrutiny of an earlier version of this chapter, which was first presented to the annual meetings of the Society for the Study of Social Problems, August 1999, Chicago.

1. The material in this section comes from Kyle (2000).

2. This data was presented by the Coalition to Fight Child Exploitation, the Thai Red Cross Society, and Mahidol University's Institute for Population and Social Research.

3. Fieldnotes and audio-taped interviews, February 1998, Thailand. These informants must remain anonymous; the information that they have provided is not the kind of information their organizations are mandated to collect. These informants have taken a great personal risk in providing this information, and we offer them special thanks.

REFERENCES

Albanese, J. 1982. "What Lockheed and la Cosa Nostra Have in Common." *Crime and Delinquency* 28:211–32.

Altink, S. 1995. *Stolen Lives: Trading Women into Sex and Slavery.* London: Scarlet Press.

Andreano, R., and J. J. Siegfried, eds. 1980. *The Economics of Crime.* New York: John Wiley.

Astudillo, Jaime, and Claudio Cordero. 1990. *Huayrapamushcas en USA: Flujos migratorios de la region centro-sur del Ecuador.* Quito: Editorial El Conejo.

Bales, Kevin. 1999. *Disposable People: New Slavery in the Global Economy.* Berkeley: University of California Press.

Basch, Linda, Nina G. Schiller, and Cristina Szanton Blanc. 1994. *Nations Unbound: Transnational Projects, Post-colonial Predicaments, and Deterritorialized Nation-States.* Langhorne, Pa.: Gordon and Breach.

Becker, Howard S. 1998. *Tricks of the Trade: How to Think about Your Research While You're Doing It*. Chicago: University of Chicago Press.

Braudel, Fernand. 1958. "Histoire et Sciences Sociales: La Longue Duree."*Annales E.S.C.* 13 (4): 725–53; reprinted in *Ecrits sur l'historire*. Paris, 1969.

Chaipipat, Kulachada. 1997. "New Law Targets Human Trafficking." *Nation* (Bangkok), November 30.

Chambliss, William J. 1989. "State-Organized Crime." *Criminology* 27 (2): 170–84.

Charoenpho, Annucha. 1998. "New Way to Repatriate Immigrants: Illegal Workers Lured through Incentives." *Bangkok Post*, February 2, p. 2, col. 1.

Chin, Ko-lin. 1996. *Chinatown Gangs: Extortion, Enterprise, and Ethnicity*. New York: Oxford University Press.

Dominguez, Miguel E. 1991. *El Sombrero de Paja Toquilla: Historia y Economia*. Cuenca, Ecuador: Banco Central del Ecuador.

Freeman, Gary. 1994. "Can Liberal States Control Unwanted Migration?" *Annals of the American Academy of Political and Social Science* 534:17–30.

Godson, Roy, and William J. Olson. 1995. "International Organized Crime." *Society* (January/February): 18–29.

Hutasingh, Onnucha. 1997. "Tough Fight against Illegal Alien Workers." *Bangkok Post*, December 15, p. 2, cols. 1–6.

Isbister, John. 1995. *Promises Not Kept: The Betrayal of Social Change in the Third World*. 3d ed. Hartford: Kumarian Press.

ISPAC. 1996. International Scientific and Professional Advisory Council of the United Nations Crime Prevention and Criminal Justice Program (ISPAC) International Conference on Migration and Crime: Global and Regional Problems and Responses, Courmayeur Mont Blanc, Italy, October 1996.

Joppke, Christian. 1998. "Why Liberal States Accept Unwanted Migration." *World Politics* 50 (2): 266–93.

Kerry, John. 1997. *The New War: The Web of Crime That Threatens America's Security*. New York: Simon and Schuster.

Knowles, Joe. 1997. "Come for the Pagodas, Stay for the Virgins." *Might* 15 (March/April): 19.

Kwong, Peter. 1996. *The New Chinatown*. Rev. ed. New York: Hill and Wang.

———. 1997. *Forbidden Workers: Illegal Chinese Immigrants and American Labor*. New York: New Press.

Kyaa Nno, Maung. 1997. "Myanmar Women." *Today* 4 (December 16–31): 82–84.

Kyle, David. 2000. *Transnational Peasants: Migrations, Networks, and Ethnicity in Andean Ecuador*. Baltimore: Johns Hopkins University Press.

Kyle, David, and John Dale. 1999. "The Social Construction of a 'New' Social Problem: Global Human Smuggling." Presented at the Society for the Study of Social Problems meetings, "Legislating the Boundaries of Inclusion: Immigration, Citizenship, and the Law," August 6, 1999, Chicago.

Light, Ivan, and Edna Bonacich. 1988. *Immigrant Entrepreneurs: Koreans in Los Angeles, 1965–1982*. Berkeley: University of California Press.

McAdam, Doug, Sidney Tarrow, and Charles Tilly. 1996. "To Map Contentious Politics." *Mobilization: An International Journal* 1 (1): 17–34.

McDonald, William F. 1995. "The Globalization of Criminology: The New Frontier Is the Frontier." *Transnational Organized Crime* 1 (1): 1–22.

McMichael, Phillip. 1997. *Development and Social Change: A Global Perspective*. Thousand Oaks, Calif.: Pine Forge Press.

Miller, Tom. 1986. *The Panama Hat Trail*. New York: Vintage Books.

Mirkinson, Judith. 1994. "Red Light, Green Light: The Global Trafficking of Women." See http://deepthought.armory.com/~leavitt/women.html. Pp.1–8.

Morley, Geoffrey. 1994. *The Smuggling War: The Government Fight against Smuggling in the Eighteenth and Nineteenth Centuries*. Gloucestershire: Alan Sutton.

Palomeque, Silvia. 1990. *Cuenca en el siglo XIX: La articulacion de una region*. Quito: Ediciones Abya-Yala.

Reuter, Peter. 1985. *The Organization of Illegal Markets: An Economic Analysis*. Research report, U.S. Department of Justice, National Institute of Justice. February.

Ruggiero, Vincenzo. 1997. "Trafficking in Human Beings: Slaves in Contemporary Europe." *International Journal of the Sociology of Law* 25:231–44.

Salt, John, and Jeremy Stein. 1997. "Migration as a Business: The Case of Trafficking." *International Migration* 35 (4): 467–94.

Sassen, Saskia. 1991. *The Global City: New York, London, and Tokyo*. Princeton: Princeton University Press.

Schwartz, Herman M. 1994. *States versus Markets: History, Geography, and the Development of the International Political Economy*. New York: St. Martin's Press.

Shapiro, S. 1984. *Wayward Capitalists*. New Haven: Yale University Press.

Smith, D., and R. Alba. 1979. "Organized Crime and American Life." *Society* 16: 32–38.

Smith, Paul, ed. 1997. *Human Smuggling: Chinese Migrant Trafficking and the Challenge to America"s Immigration Tradition.* Washington, D.C.: Center for Strategic and International Studies.

Tilly, Charles. 1985. "War Making and State Making as Organized Crime." In *Bringing the State Back In,* edited by Peter B. Evans, Dietrich Rueschemeyer, and Theda Skocpol, 169–91. Cambridge: Cambridge University Press.

United States General Accounting Report to Congressional Committees. 2000. "Alien Smuggling: Management and Operational Improvements Needed to Address Growing Problem." May 1. GAO/GGD-00-103.

United States Immigration and Naturalization Service. 1998. (September 21). "News Release." San Diego, Calif.: Office of the United States Attorney Southern District of California. See http://www.usdoj.gov/usao/cas/pr/cas80921.2html.

Walton, John. 1977. *Elites and Economic Development: Comparative Studies on the Political Economy of Latin American Cities.* Austin, Tex.: Institute of Latin American Studies.

2 ▪▪▪▪▪▪▪ The Smuggling of Asylum Seekers into Western Europe: Contradictions, Conundrums, and Dilemmas

Khalid Koser

I'm writing this introduction on June 19, 2000, the day of the tragic discovery of fifty-eight dead migrants in the back of a truck in the port town of Dover in the United Kingdom. Although clearly their motivations and intentions will now never be known, these migrants have quickly come to be described in the media as "asylum seekers." However inaccurate this description may be, the events in Dover have certainly brought to the attention of the media, public, and politicians a phenomenon that seems to have been growing over the past decade in Western Europe—the smuggling of asylum seekers.

As early as 1994, it was estimated that between 60,000 and 120,000 asylum seekers were being smuggled into Western Europe annually (Widgren, 1994), and there is a growing consensus that an increasing proportion of asylum seekers continues to be smuggled. The smuggling of asylum seekers presents a range of conceptual and policy challenges, which have been made all the more difficult to cope with given the shortage of empirical data. This chapter presents findings from one of the only research surveys conducted among smuggled asylum seekers in Western Europe (Koser, 1997b). It tries to address some of the crucial questions surrounding the smuggling of asylum seekers: Is smuggling necessarily an evil? Is it really a new phenomenon? And why are policymakers finding it so hard to come to terms with smuggling?

The study of smuggling is still in its infancy, and there is a lack of consensus about concepts, definitions, and terminology. One distinction that does seem to be emerging, both in the literature and in policy instruments, is between the concept of "trafficking" and the concept of "smuggling." The trafficking of human beings is increasingly associated with coercion, exploitation, deception, violence, and physical or psychological abuse. The majority of the literature on trafficking, for example, has focused on women and prostitution. In contrast, smuggling is being defined simply as the illicit movement of people across international boundaries. According to this distinction, trafficking is a human rights issue, whereas smuggling is a migration issue (Salt and Hogarth, 2000).

This chapter, which focuses on a case study of Iranian asylum seekers smuggled to the Netherlands, takes issue with this distinction. There is no evidence of coercion or violence or that the respondents were subsequently placed in exploitative industries in the Netherlands. Still, the smuggling exposed many of them to increased insecurity and vulnerability: in other words, smuggling can be both a migration and a human rights issue.

The chapter is structured around this expansion of the concept of smuggling. In the first part, the smuggling of asylum seekers is analyzed as a migration issue. Empirical evidence on the interaction between smugglers and asylum seekers is combined with a broader analysis of the changing policy context in Western Europe to lend credence to the common assertion that an increasing proportion of asylum seekers are being forced to employ smugglers in order to escape their home countries and reach a country of asylum. In the second part, smuggling is analyzed as a human rights issue. It shows how the asylum seekers in this survey were exposed to forms of political, economic, and social insecurity as a direct consequence of smuggling. Although the phenomenon may not be new, there are qualitative differences from earlier periods, specifically relating to the changing composition of asylum seekers, the growing organization of smuggling, and the changing purposes of smuggling.

Seeking Asylum in Western Europe:
The Changing Political Context

Analysis of the changing political context for asylum seekers in Western Europe, combined with analysis of data on asylum applications, provides some insight into the interactions between smuggling and asylum. In simple terms, asylum in Western Europe can be thought of as having moved through three phases over the past thirty years. During the 1960s and 1970s—and particularly before the "oil crisis" of 1973—there were two distinct legal migration channels into Western Europe, one for labor migrants and another for refugees. The majority of refugees at this time were accepted in Western Europe on the basis of a "quota" system (Troeller, 1991).

As economic recession and an environment of retrenchment struck Western Europe during the mid-1970s, the demand for overseas labor dried up, and most of the formal routes for labor migration—for example, through recruitment agreements with particular countries of origin—were closed over the following decade (Cornelius, Martin, and Hollifield, 1994). In retrospect, it is quite clear that one of the unintended consequences of these policies was to force economic migrants into the asylum channel—which had become the only remaining legal channel for entry into Western Europe. Such an analysis goes a long way toward explaining the data presented in figure 2, which show how asylum applications in the main asylum countries in the European Union (EU), and across the EU as a whole, grew steadily through the late 1980s, to an overall peak in 1992 of more than 672,000 applications. The convergence in the asylum channel of refugees and economic migrants has notoriously presented policymakers with great problems of clarification, and many human rights activists are concerned that at least some genuine asylum claimants have been ignored as the obsession with filtering out so-called bogus refugees has grown.

Largely in response to rising numbers and the impression that a majority of asylum seekers were "bogus," a raft of policies was adopted across Western Europe during the mid-1990s to try to place restrictions upon asylum. One set of policies was aimed at reducing the scale of asylum migration. This included the imposition of visas upon citizens from a growing list of countries, the promotion of so-called safe havens, the re-

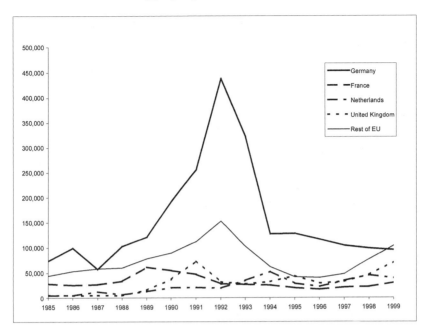

Fig. 2. Total Annual Asylum Applications in Selected EU Member States, 1985–1999
Source: Eurostat. *Note:* "Rest of EU" is an estimate.

quirement that asylum seekers submit their applications at a consulate or embassy in their country of origin ("in-country processing"), and carrier sanctions. These combined with another set of policies targeted on changing the spatial distribution of asylum applications, and specifically on diverting applications from Western Europe. Perhaps the best example is the series of Readmission Agreements signed on a bilateral basis between countries in Western and central or Eastern Europe, which have facilitated the return of asylum seekers from the former to the latter (King, 1994).

Many commentators agree that the combined effect of such policies was to reduce the number of asylum applications across Western Europe after the peak of 1992 (ECRE, 1994; Hovy, 1993; Salt, 1995). Across all the countries of the European Union, this decrease was fairly dramatic, and applications had more than halved by 1996. At the same time, the data in figure 2 indicate that across all the main EU countries of asylum except Germany, and across the EU as a whole, asylum applications began to rebound in the late 1990s. This has been particularly significant in the United Kingdom, where estimates for asylum applications in 1999 almost returned to the historical high in 1991.

One interpretation of these data is that, just as closing down the labor migration channel forced economic migrants into the asylum channel, increasing restrictions upon this asylum channel are now forcing asylum seekers into a new, illegal channel. And the indications are that this channel is increasingly monopolized by smugglers and traffickers.

Thirty-two Iranian Asylum Seekers

To illustrate these trends better, this section draws on a series of in-depth interviews conducted with thirty-two Iranian asylum seekers in the Netherlands, over a period of about a year in 1996 and 1997. Interview data were supplemented by information gathered during open-ended discussions with opinion formers and representatives from inside the asylum seeker populations. The interpretation of such qualitative data is always difficult and perhaps more so where the respondents can be considered vulnerable, as in the case of asylum seekers. It is, therefore, helpful to understand the circumstances of the respondents and to assess the validity of the data in this light.

The respondents were interviewed in two Azielzoekerscentra (AZCs, Asylum Seeker Centers) in the Netherlands. Twenty-one were women, the majority aged between twenty and thirty-five. This predominance of young and female respondents reflects quite closely the demographic composition of the Iranian populations in the two AZCs visited, although it is a reversal of the gender profile of Iranian asylum seekers in Dutch AZCs as a whole. Asylum seekers in AZCs have already passed through two earlier interview procedures in Aanmeldcentra (ACS, Initial Reception Centers), then Opvang en onderzoekscentra (OCS, Reception and Assessment Centers), and are at the stage where they are awaiting the outcome of a full assessment of their claims for asylum, or in some cases appeals against previous assessments. All the respondents had left Iran between one and two years prior to the interviews, and the length of time spent in the AZC ranged from just one week in one case to eighteen months in another.

This context imposed restrictions upon the interviewing procedure and subsequently upon data analysis. Several respondents did not speak English, which is my mother tongue. There was also a more general problem of trust, operating in two directions. The respondents were generally and understandably reluctant to discuss issues that might directly affect their claims for asylum. At the same time, given that they had already been officially interviewed a number of times by the time I interviewed them in the AZCs, several respondents appeared to be "practiced" at interviews, responding appropriately as opposed to necessarily accurately.

A number of strategies were adopted in response to such difficulties. For approximately one-quarter of the interviews, the assistance of an interpreter was necessary. In each AZC more than one interpreter was employed, as an attempt to counter the problems that can arise when a single interpreter becomes too closely associated in the eyes of a study population with a researcher. The interpreters were all drawn from within the Iranian asylum seeker populations within the AZCs; the assumption was that respondents might be even less forthcoming in the presence of two "outsiders," namely, an external interpreter and me. In most cases the gender of the interpreter matched the gender of the respondent. During the interviews, anonymity was guaranteed, this method being employed along with several other techniques to attempt to secure a degree of trust among the respondents. Despite such methodological safeguards, reservations clearly surround the validity of the data gathered. The following analysis therefore focuses on excerpts from selected interviews with only eight respondents, with whom I believe a particularly good rapport was established.

Smuggling as a Migration Issue

Twenty-nine of the thirty-two respondents admitted during our interviews that smugglers had been involved in at least parts of their journeys between Iran and the Netherlands. Smugglers were involved in three main ways: in exit strategies, in planning routes, and in entry strategies.

Exit Strategies

Nineteen of these twenty-nine respondents reported that smugglers had helped them to leave Iran, and three main exit functions were cited. First, smugglers reportedly concealed eight of the respondents, who said that they were in immediate danger of being arrested. All eight were in Tehran when they contacted smugglers, and half were taken outside Tehran to be concealed, while the other half were hidden within Tehran. One respondent had remained in hiding for about a month, waiting for his contact to make the necessary arrangements to smuggle him out of Iran.

Of eighteen respondents who were willing to provide detailed information about their journeys, six reported flying directly out of Tehran. A second function that smugglers served, for these six specifically, was to organize flight tickets and travel documents. In each case the travel documents were reported to have been forged, and the names on the tickets false, in order to try to ensure that the respondents were not intercepted at the airport. The other twelve respondents left Iran by land, most over the western border with Turkey, but three spent more than a week traveling eastward to the border with Pakistan. Only four said that they exited Iran through formal border crossings, and for these four, forged documents were also apparently provided. For the remaining eight a third exit function that smugglers had served was to move them clandestinely across the border.

The respondents generally agreed that it is easy to find smugglers in Iran. Several respondents reported having already known smugglers either personally or indirectly through other people, and others suggested that smugglers could be found on certain days in certain bazaars in most large cities in Iran, but especially in Tehran. In the cases of three respondents, their journeys had been organized by relatives already living in Western Europe—in two cases in Germany, and in one in the United Kingdom. In these cases smugglers had apparently been contacted directly in Germany and the United Kingdom, and the respondents in Iran had then been approached by their agents. It is particularly interesting to note that several of the more recent arrivals among the respondents intimated that the function of smugglers is increasingly being transformed from one of facilitation—simply responding to demand—to one of recruitment and control. Smugglers now apparently advertise their services in certain newspapers in Iran and are reported to be exercising a virtual monopoly over the supply of forged documents and over clandestine border crossings, so that in effect they can select who leaves Iran illegally.

Migration Routes

A second broad function that smugglers served was to organize the migration routes of most of the respondents. The geography of migration routes between Iran and the Netherlands fell into four broad categories (table 1). The first category covered three respondents, who reported that they had flown directly from Iran to the Netherlands. In contrast, all the remaining respondents said that they had arrived in the Netherlands via at least one other country. Three reported having flown directly from Iran to either Romania or Hungary, from where two subsequently traveled by plane and one overland to the Netherlands. A third category similarly involved a two-step route and covered five respondents who flew to the Netherlands from Turkey or Pakistan, to which neighboring countries they had initially been smuggled from Iran. The remaining seven respondents (of the eighteen who provided detailed information about their journeys) reported a three-step route, involving travel initially to either Turkey or Pakistan, then to either Romania or Hungary, and finally on to the Netherlands.

As table 1 shows, the time taken to travel between Iran and the Netherlands generally varied according to the route taken. Several respondents whose migration route involved three stages reported the total journey lasting more than a month. In one case a respondent reported having stayed in Romania for nearly three months while his contact there obtained a false passport for him. The implications particularly of long periods of time spent en route between Iran and the Netherlands are returned to in the next section, as for several respondents they became sources of both legal and economic insecurity.

The relatively restricted number of routes reported may be an indication that a limited number of routes have become well established and maintained by smugglers. It was reported that a close international network of contacts operated along these routes. Most respondents were accompanied on each stage of their journey and responsibility for them then handed on to another contact in the next destination. Interestingly, one respondent told me that a friend had been smuggled from Iran to the Netherlands about three years before she had and that that friend had come through a quite different route, via Spain. The implication may be

Table 1. Migration Routes

Number of Steps	Route	Time (in days)	Number of Respondents
1	Iran–Netherlands	1	3
2	Iran–Romania/Hungary–Netherlands	3–15	3
2	Iran–Turkey/Pakistan–Netherlands	5–20	5
3	Iran–Turkey/Pakistan–Romania/Hungary–Netherlands	10–90	7

that smugglers are responsive to the opening and closing of opportunities for negotiating entry into Western Europe.

Entry Strategies

The final principal function that smugglers served concerned entry, into transit countries as well as into destination countries. Three principal entry strategies were employed by smugglers—clandestine entry, entry with false documentation, or entry without documentation. In general these different strategies coincided with different migration routes. Clandestine entry was the main strategy for entering neighboring Turkey or Pakistan from Iran. In contrast, a majority of respondents reported using false documentation to enter Romania or Hungary. Meanwhile, the dominant strategy for entering the Netherlands was to present oneself to the immigration police without a passport.

This last strategy illustrates a wider function that smugglers were reported to have served, which was to provide information on how to remain in the Netherlands after arrival. For example, the absence of a passport hinders personal identification, the identification of a country of origin, and the identification of transit countries. Most smugglers were reported to have had very accurate information on the asylum procedure in the Netherlands. Some respondents had even been advised how to respond during interviews with immigration officials, for example, by not naming as transit countries those countries with which the Netherlands had signed a Readmission Agreement.

Perhaps the most extreme example of smugglers organizing entry strategies was in the case of eleven respondents for whom smugglers even made a decision about their final destination. Three of these respondents had simply requested that they be taken to any country in Western Europe. However, the remaining eight had intended before leaving Iran to join relatives or friends already living in countries in Western Europe—in Germany, Denmark, and the United Kingdom, but not in the Netherlands (Koser, 1997b). For all eleven respondents, smugglers had apparently stated that the Netherlands was the only country to which they could be smuggled at that time and had thus effectively made the decision about their final destinations for them.

Smuggling as a Human Rights Issue

The last section demonstrated quite clearly how, for twenty-nine of the thirty-two respondents interviewed, smuggling was a migration issue. For many of these respondents, smuggling provided what they perceived as their only options for leaving Iran, traveling to Western Europe, and entering the Netherlands. To return for a moment to the distinction described in the introduction to this chapter, there seems to be a growing consensus that smuggling is a migration issue, and the preceding empirical evidence has reinforced that consensus. However, smuggling also became a human rights issue for many of the respondents involved in this survey. Three sources of vulnerability arose for respondents as a direct consequence of smuggling—political, economic, and social insecurity.

One of the main sources of political insecurity for any asylum seeker arises from the threat of deportation. Iran is one of a number of countries where it is reported that repatriated asylum seekers often face persecution from the government arising specifically from their attempts to claim asylum in the first place (MNS, 1995). Nevertheless, during 1996 and 1997, at the time of the interviews, deportations from the Netherlands to Iran were occurring (MNS, 1996). What remains unclear is the extent to which smuggling increases the likelihood of being deported. On the one hand, the 1951 United Nations Convention on Refugees stipulates that refugees should not be penalized on the basis of their method of arrival in a country of asylum. The implication is that once asylum seekers have entered the asylum procedure, their involvement or otherwise with smugglers should have no bearing on their applications. On the other hand, it is quite clear that on certain political and media agendas, asylum seekers are increasingly becoming synonymous with illegal migrants. There is a concern among human rights activists that asylum seekers who can be shown to have been smuggled may not be allowed to enter the asylum procedure and may face the threat of deportation as illegal migrants.

For the majority of respondents, the political insecurity associated with the rejection of a claim for asylum was heightened by the fact that they arrived in the Netherlands via one or more transit countries, these migration routes having been organized by traffickers. Many were smuggled initially to Turkey, whence regular deportations of Iranian asylum seekers have been reported. At the end of 1995, 150 Iranian asylum seekers staged a sit-in at the headquarters of the United Socialist Party in Ankara demanding that deportation orders by the government of Turkey be revoked. Romania was another country through which many respondents transited. A Readmission Agreement has been negotiated by the Dutch government with Romania so that asylum seekers can be returned there. Romania, however, is one of several central or Eastern European countries considered by many authorities to be ill equipped properly to receive and protect asylum seekers (ECRE, 1995).

Traffickers were reported to have charged between $4,000 and $6,000 U.S. for their services, and meeting these costs also exposed many respondents to a form of economic vulnerability at various stages during their migration. First, even before leaving Iran, all but two of the respondents who employed smugglers were obliged to turn to friends or relatives for financial assistance. Several reported that they had been forced to risk staying in Iran despite the very immediate threat of detention in order to raise money. It is quite clear that in the absence of financial support from social networks, most respondents would not have been able to migrate.

Meeting the cost of traffickers also meant that some respondents left Iran with virtually no money, which exposed many to sources of economic vulnerability both in transit countries and in the Netherlands. As indicated in table 1, those respondents who came to the Netherlands via transit countries spent between a few days and almost three months in the latter. About half of them reported that they had been obliged to work on the black market in transit countries, in order to derive sufficient income to live. The fees paid to smugglers did not cover subsistence costs en route to the Netherlands. In contrast, other respondents had managed to borrow enough money before leaving Iran to cover the cost of living in transit countries.

Most respondents nevertheless arrived in the Netherlands without money. At the same time, most had no other source of income to supplement state allowances to meet basic expenditures, largely because of restrictions upon entry into the labor market for asylum seekers in the Netherlands during their first two years there (Groenendijk and Hampsink, 1995). Only one respondent admitted that he had worked illegally during his first year in the Netherlands, although he intimated that several other respondents had also worked illegally but were unwilling to admit as much to me. Even in those few cases in which respondents had found temporary employment after their first year in the Netherlands, in the majority of instances a substantial proportion of that income was sent back to Iran to pay debts to friends or relatives from whom money had been borrowed initially.

The role of smugglers in influencing the destinations of some of the respondents also gave rise in their case to a source of what might be described as social insecurity. As described previously, eight respondents had intended to join family or friends in other countries in Western Europe but had arrived in the Netherlands largely at the behest of smugglers. In this way they effectively became isolated from potentially supportive social networks. Interviews with several respondents who did have social networks in situ in the Netherlands confirmed that these had provided a variety of forms of assistance including emotional support, information, financial assistance, and child care. At a more qualitative level, there were quite clear indications that those without an immediate social network to which to turn for general support suffered to a far greater degree and far more frequently from depression and more regularly expressed concern about their future (Koser, 1997b). Beyond the short term, there is a considerable literature that shows how social networks can help migrants to integrate in new host countries, particularly through assisting with housing and employment (Gurak and Caces, 1992).

Contradictions, Conundrums, and Dilemmas

Before proceeding to generalize from this case study, a number of reservations need to be acknowledged. The first concerns the extent to which any asylum seeker's responses to questions about an issue as potentially sensitive at smuggling can really be trusted. As emphasized earlier in this chapter, systematic methodological safeguards were put in place to try to increase the level of trust between respondent and interviewer. Nevertheless, the preceding description of smuggling experiences focused principally on only a handful of respondents, those with whom it was felt that a specific bond had been formed. This further reduction of an already small-scale survey raises a second reservation, concerning the broader applicability of the case study. In the continuing absence of virtually any other empirical research with trafficked asylum seekers, it is impossible to assess the extent to which the experiences of the respondents in this survey were typical of asylum seekers.

Still, what is clear from this case study at least is that the smuggling of asylum seekers can be both a migration and a human rights issue. This chapter has provided empirical evidence to show the types of practical obstacles in response to which asylum seekers may be forced to turn to smugglers both to leave their countries of origin and to enter Western Europe. This evidence lends credence to the conclusions drawn from the analysis of the changing political context for asylum seekers in Western Europe and data on asylum applications over the last fifteen years. At the same time, the chapter has provided empirical evidence to show how their involvement with smugglers directly increased the insecurity of many of the respondents. And it is worth emphasizing that the nature of this research means that it necessarily provides only a limited perspective on insecurity. It covers only those asylum seekers who have in effect been "successful" in reaching Western Europe—nothing is known about the asylum seekers who cannot afford to leave Iran by paying smugglers, or those who are still stranded in transit countries, or even those who might have died en route. Neither has the research been able to consider the psychological insecurities associated with being smuggled clandestinely across borders, or traveling across Europe in the back of a truck, or trying to board a plane with false documents.

Disaggregating smuggling into a migration and human rights issue has highlighted a conceptual contradiction. On the one hand, it seems that smuggling can provide a valuable service, by enabling asylum seekers—including at least some genuine refugees—to escape persecution and reach asylum. On the other hand, it seems that at the same time smuggling can expose the already vulnerable to even greater vulnerability. Herein lies a policy conundrum: how to protect asylum seekers from the insecurity associated with smuggling without closing the door on what is one of the last possibilities for applying for asylum in Western Europe. Such conceptual contradictions and policy conundrums are perhaps surprising given that the smuggling of asylum seekers is not a new phenomenon. There is clear evidence, for example, that many thousands of Jewish refugees were smuggled both westward and eastward from Germany and Occupied Europe before and during World War II.

There is no straightforward answer to this conundrum; what is perhaps easier to explain—by breaking it down into a series of constituent policy dilemmas—is just why it is so difficult to solve. Each of these, it might be argued, arises in turn from a series of new characteristics that make the contemporary smuggling of asylum seekers qualitatively different from earlier experiences: namely, the contemporary composition of asylum seekers, the social organization of smuggling, and the emerging purpose of smuggling.

One new characteristic is the complex composition of flows of smuggled asylum seekers. Most commentators would be unlikely to disagree that Jewish asylum seekers who were smuggled from Germany and Occupied Europe before and during World War II faced vile persecution and were in clear need of protection. But most commentators, however sympathetic, would also be unlikely to disagree that at least some asylum seekers arriving in Western Europe today do not have a genuine claim on refugee status. Analysis of the changing political context for asylum seekers has shown how a range of migrant categories—from refugees to economic migrants—have now been forced to converge on a single, illegal migration channel. The policy dilemma that arises is how to balance the rights of refugees while controlling the smuggling of other migrants.

A second new characteristic arises from the changing organization of smuggling. This chapter has alluded to a variety of ways in which even the smugglers in one small case study are highly organized. Smugglers in Iran seem to have become proactive in creating a market for their services, they seem to control a close international network of agents, they seem to be very well informed about asylum procedures in Western European countries, and they have proved themselves to be responsive to opening and closing opportunities for entering these countries. The policy dilemma that arises is how to break out of the current vicious cycle, whereby smugglers consistently find new responses to new policies.

A final new characteristic arguably relates to the changing purpose of the smuggling of asylum seekers. Although helping asylum seekers to escape persecution in their countries of origin is still one important function served by smugglers, it is no longer the only function. Instead, smugglers have been shown in this case study to be involved not only in planning exit routes but also in organizing entry and even selecting destinations. The policy dilemma that arises is how to disaggregate the smuggling process, so that smuggling into Western Europe can be controlled but smuggling out of some countries can still be recognized as being necessary for those being persecuted or denied fundamental human rights.

Conclusion

As mentioned, the introduction to this chapter was written on the day of the tragedy in Dover. It is now a week later; the events in Dover have already disappeared from the media agenda. Still, they have reinforced the demand that policymakers respond to what is perceived in many circles to be a growing problem in terms of both illegal entry and obvious human rights issues connected to the treatment of asylum seekers. This chapter has tried to illustrate the complexities of the smuggling of asylum seekers and to highlight some of the inherent contradictions, conundrums, and dilemmas. The concern must be that in response to a growing public clamor, policy will be made without proper regard to these complexities and without proper regard to its consequences for the asylum seekers involved.

NOTE

This chapter is a substantial revision of an earlier chapter in Koser and Lutz (1998).

REFERENCES

Cornelius, W. A., P. L. Martin, and J. F. Hollifield. 1994. "The Ambivalent Quest for Immigration Control," in *Controlling Immigration: A Global Perspective,* edited by W. A.Cornelius, P. L. Martin, and J. F. Hollifield. Stanford: Stanford University Press.

European Council on Refugees and Exiles. 1994. *Minutes and Conference Papers from the ECRE Biannual General Meeting.* London: ECRE.

————. 1995. *Safe Third Countries: Myths and Realities.* London: ECRE.

Groenendijk, K., and R. Hampsink. 1995. *Temporary Employment of Migrants in Europe.* Nijmegen, the Netherlands: Faculteit der Rechtsgeleerdheid K.U.

Gurak, D. T., and F. Caces. 1992. "Migration Networks and the Shaping of Migration Systems," in *International Migration Systems: A Global Approach,* edited by M. M. Kritz, L. L. Lim, and H. Zlotnik, 150–76. Oxford: Clarendon Press.

Hovy, B. 1993. "Asylum Migration in Europe: Patterns, Determinants, and the Role of East-West Movements," in *The New Geography of European Migrations,* edited by R. King, 207–27. London: Belhaven.

King, M. 1994. "Policing Refugees and Asylum-Seekers in 'Greater Europe': Towards a Reconceptualisation of Control," in *Policing across National Boundaries,* edited by M. Anderson and M. den Boer, 69–84. London: Pinter.

Koser, Khalid. 1997a. "Negotiating Entry into Fortress Europe: The Migration Strategies of Asylum Seekers," in *Exclusion and Inclusion of Refugees in Contemporary Europe,* edited by P. Muus, 157–70. Utrecht: ERCOMER.

————. 1997b. "Social Networks and the Asylum Cycle: The Case of Iranian Asylum Seekers in the Netherlands." *International Migration Review* 31 (3): 591–612.

Koser, Khalid, and Helma Lutz, eds. 1998. *The New Migration in Europe: Social Constructions and Social Realities.* New York: St. Martin's.

Migration News Sheet (MNS). 1995. Various issues.

Migration News Sheet (MNS). 1996. Various issues.

Morrison, J. 2000. "The Trafficking and Smuggling of Refugees: The End Game in European Asylum Policy?" Final Draft Report for the United Nations High Commissioner for Refugees.

Salt, J. 1995. "International Migration Report." *New Community* 21 (3): 443–64.

Salt, J., and J. Hogarth. 2000. "Migrant Trafficking in Europe: A Literature Review and Bibliography." Draft Final Report for the International Organisation for Migration.

Troeller, G. G. 1991. "UNHCR Resettlement as an Instrument of International Protection: Constraints and Obstacles in the Arena of Competition for Scarce Humanitarian Resources." *International Journal of Refugee Law* 3 (3): 564–78.

Widgren, J. 1994. "Multilateral Co-operation to Combat Trafficking in Migrants and the Role of International Organisations." Discussion paper at the 11th IOM Seminar on Migration, October, Geneva.

3........Pre–Cold War Traffic in Sexual Labor and Its Foes: Some Contemporary Lessons

Eileen Scully

In early 1995, California papers announced the discovery of a "nationwide prostitution ring" based in San Diego, engaged in smuggling "hundreds of destitute women from Thailand" and selling "them into sexual slavery." Local officials were caught unawares, telling reporters that they had "never heard of a similar case in which foreigners were smuggled into this country for prostitution" (Repard, 1995: B2). A few days earlier, Seattle authorities had also uncovered the local hub "of a national prostitution operation trafficking in Asian women." A police spokesman declared: "We haven't seen this kind of thing in Seattle before" (Whitely, 1995: A1).

For historians, this Orwellian amnesia is both disheartening and provocative: the past is indeed a different country, if not yet a lost civilization. Stepping across the threshold into 2000, we do well to recall the vista that emboldened and confounded contemporaries a full century ago. The new world order of the early 1900s beheld rapid and uneven internationalization, weakening community ties, and unstable great power relationships. These factors collectively abetted a burgeoning traffic in women and children for prostitution, described by contemporaries as the white slave trade. Violence, economic turmoil, and political turbulence pushed local women from Asia and central Europe into brothels as far away as Buenos Aires and Seattle. The collapse of czarism in Russia unleashed successive waves of impoverished refugees, many of them driven into crime and prostitution. As profitability grew, organized gangs and syndicates moved to control supply, demand, and operations, spawning what one American activist described as "a system of gigantic, organized, powerful syndicates, each operating independently, but each depending on the other" (Terrell, c. 1907: 22).

To be sure, there are significant differences between what we bring into the twenty-first century and what awaited those journeying into the 1900s. Recurrence does not mean inevitability or justify indifference; a record of intractability does not make the humanitarian project less compelling. It is hoped, though, that this look at forced migratory sexual labor and its foes in the era before the Cold War will help identify such overlaps and contrasts, while also highlighting how antitraffic groups grappled with many of the same dilemmas bedeviling their counterparts today.

The pre–Cold War history of forced migratory prostitution comprised three distinct periods: (1) the 1840s to about 1895; (2) the late 1890s to World War I; (3) 1919 through World War II.

To the 1890s

The geography and animating forces of modern migratory prostitution were discernible many decades before the white slave trade scare at the turn of the century. The traffic in sexual labor, both coerced and voluntary, took hold in the 1840s and continued to grow and complexify thereafter. Demand was generated by three interlocking developments, all involving the mobilization and migration of large numbers of single males.

The first of these was the deployment of nonwhite, indentured labor to replace African slaves in plantation economies, to fuel extractive industries (such as diamond and gold mining), and to undertake monumental construction projects (such as railroads and canals). Abolition of the slave trade was uneven and sporadic, spanning the whole nineteenth century: for example, the British abolished colonial slavery in 1833 but excluded India, Burma, and Ceylon, then under the control of the East India Company. Revolutionary France abolished slavery in its colonies, reestablished it in 1802, and again abolished it in 1848 (Klein, 1994: 211–13). "Emancipation came at a time when an expanding capitalism was still hungry for labour, and free labour migration was not capable of meeting that demand" (212). This meant the large-scale recruitment of unfree labor in India, China, Japan, Vietnam, Indonesia, and the Pacific islands, "where poverty and landlessness created a pool of willing migrants" (212; Aldrich, 1990: 161).

Together, Asian indentured workers supplied the world with sugar, tea, rubber, minerals, gems, artificial waterways, and railroads. One scholar estimates that a total of 10 million to 13 million Chinese were part of this great labor migration into Southeast Asia, the Americas, the West Indies, and Africa (Tong, 1994: xv–xvii). Western colonial domination in these areas abetted the process; although officials condemned practices such as "black birding," kidnapping, and debt bondage, imperial managers and private concerns effectively combined to transfer labor within and across empires (Aldrich, 1990: 163–64). Indigenous middlemen also played a critical role, bringing labor from the rural hinterlands to transfer points and undertaking "migrant smuggling" to bypass immigration controls against Asians in Western countries, such as the United States.

Second, and concomitantly, was the mobilization and migration of non-Western males within the colonial matrix and Western-dominated world market. At one end of the spectrum, Western imperial enclaves—such as Hong Kong, Singapore, Shanghai, and New Delhi—attracted, and indeed depended upon, the emergence of wealthy, indigenous urban elites. At the opposite end, monetized economies linked to international trade impoverished rural populations, pushing proletarianized peasants into growing cities, into vast colonial armies, or into the migratory labor traffic described above. For example, Spanish rule over the Philippines transformed the city of Manila into a magnet for indigenous "vagrants, vagabonds, and displaced persons" driven from rural areas (Dery, 1991: 475). Concentrations of indigenous males, both rich and poor, most often unattached, provided a ready market for a range of services provided by migratory women, from prostitution to domestic chores.

Third on the demand side was the large-scale, long-distance movement of unattached, wealth-seeking men from Europe and North America, drawn to frontiers, mammoth construction projects, and colonial opportunities. This momentum led to large settlements of single white males, ranging from frontier boomtowns in the American West, Australia, and South Africa to the more socially elevated colonial communities of maritime Asia, such as Hong Kong and the Federated Malay States. The relative ease and affordability of travel, widespread economic depression from the mid-1870s into the 1890s, and great power deployment of personnel throughout the colonial world brought significant numbers of First World men, whose presence irrevocably altered the demographics and sexual economies of non-Western societies.

Together, these three interlocking developments generated an international traffic in sex workers, expanded regional migratory prostitution, and intensified local, indigenous prostitution. At each of these levels— international, regional, and local—women entered the trade under a variety of circumstances, ranging from astute entrepreneurial calculation to entrapment. They operated along a spectrum of autonomy, from full control over their labor conditions to the virtual enslavement of locked brothels.

At the international level, the most important dynamic was the emergence of universal racialized sexual hierarchies: race, ethnicity, and nationality combined to determine women's market value, while also determining men's access to sexual and domestic services. Where racial or colonial domination is exercised, there is a marked "tendency of [the] female body to become symbolic of . . . groups' privilege, something off limits to natives, by way of controlling indigenous groups and intra-foreign gender relations" (Callaway, 1987: 237). Multinational sex markets thus tended to be "highly stratified," with status determined by a "combination of race, ethnicity, education, sociability and sexual skill" (Murphy, 1992: 287). Numerous commentators have discerned in the eighteenth and nineteenth centuries an "exoticist movement" wherein Third World peoples became "the anthropological Other," not only "despised [and] destroyed" but also constituted as a "projection of western fantasies" (Kempadoo, 1998a:10).

The most visible manifestation of this pervasive racialization of sexual hierarchies was the push to supply transported, indentured labor with the sexual services of women of their own race or ethnicity. The cultural preferences of indentured workers dovetailed with the drive among employers and "host" societies to keep white women off limits to non-Western males (Hunt, 1986: 124). The movement of Chinese "coolie" labor to

North and South America, the growth of Chinatowns in the United States, and the proliferation of boomtown vice on the American frontier thus brought Chinese prostitutes to the region as early as the 1840s. Chinese women were brought to Latin America, Southeast Asia, South Africa, and Australia—again, to subsidize and reproduce male indentured Asian labor. Japanese women followed in the 1870s, after the Meiji Restoration overthrew Tokugawa feudalism and emigration was decriminalized. Sex workers from Japan could be found in the hundreds in America's Pacific Northwest, Australia, coastal China, and Southeast Asia.[1]

Although initially Chinese and Japanese women tended to venture out on their own initiative, the element of organized coercive procurement increased over time (Ichioka, 1977; Mihalopoulos, 1993; Hirata, 1992). For Chinese women in the American West, there was a brief period (1849–54) of individual agency, entrepreneurship, and consent, and the clientele was primarily non-Chinese (Hirata, 1992). However, by 1854, secret societies or triads had gained full control of the trade, as only they could pay the high cost of the journey, bribe local police, negotiate with Chinatown landlords, and protect the women from pervasive anti-Asian violence (Tong, 1994:10). Procurers, brokers, and secret societies constituted an identifiable network linking the Americas to South China and inland; by 1850, there were well over fifteen hundred Chinese prostitutes in San Francisco's Chinatown alone (Hirata, 1992). Continuing economic distress, political chaos, and social violence in South China ensured rising numbers of recruits not only for prostitution rackets but for the trade in male indentured labor as well. Then, as now, Asian women signed contracts providing for eventual release but were virtually entrapped through trickery and debt bondage; those at the lowest end of the spectrum were worked in sweatshops during the day and brothels at night (Tong, 1994: 73–75).

On the more privileged end of racialized sexual hierarchies, the establishment of white commercial and military garrisons in the colonial world, the opening of various frontier boomtowns, and the commercialization of urban prostitution evident across the globe led also to the migration of sex workers from Western societies. Donna Guy's study of modern Argentina notes that European prostitutes first arrived there in 1797, when a penal ship en route to Australia ended up in the Rio de la Plata after a mutiny; by the 1860s, there was a well-established, easily supplied market for central and Eastern European women, largely under the control of procurers and pimps of their own nationalities (Guy, 1991a: 14–20). Edward Bristow's (1983) authoritative investigation of the trade in Jewish women points to economic distress and the launching of anti-Semitic pogroms in Russia and Eastern Europe after 1860 as the primary "push" factor in the equation. Some went the short distance to western Russia, hoping to earn dowries or help families through difficult economic times (Engel, 1989; Bernstein, 1995). Others traveled greater distances, as suggested by complaints of Singapore newspapers in 1862 about threats to white prestige from "the unwholesome immigration" of immoral women from Eastern Europe (*Straits Times*, May 17, 1862, 1).

Women from Western Europe and North America (the United States and Canada) typically already professional sex workers, traveled to these expanding areas and colonial markets. Chinese sources assert that the earliest European prostitutes arrived with the thousands of British troops sent to fight in the first Opium War (1841–42); however, these women were most likely from Portuguese-controlled Macao in South China (Sun, 1988: 47–48; Porter, 1996). In the 1860s and 1870s, American, British, and French women did undoubtedly join this specialized international migration, following the opening of the Suez Canal (1869), the mid-nineteenth-century establishment of British coaling stations and military garrisons in Asia, and the concurrent inauguration of regular steamship service from Europe and the United States to Asia (Bristow, 1983).

In contrast to both Slavic and indigenous sex workers, American and Western European women generally enjoyed an elite status within the hierarchy of colonial prostitution. In the nineteenth century, these "Occidental" women enjoyed a good living, privileged status (as foreigners exempt from indigenous laws, for example), and substantial control over their working conditions. American women overtly engaged in prostitution in East Asia from the 1860s to about 1900 were typically white, literate, aged between twenty-seven and thirty-five, married at some time, and prostitutes before they arrived. On the run from the law, or pushed out of the U.S. market by younger compatriots and incoming Asian and European women, these older sex workers went out to the colonies to capitalize on the sellers' market within white settler communities. Successfully limiting their clientele to men of their own race, they remained a small but enduring elite in the echelons of migratory prostitution (Scully,

1998). Non-Western courtesan-class women constituted a parallel elite in the nineteenth-century colonial setting, largely off limits to all but wealthy indigenous males (Hershatter, 1989).

White commercial and military colonial establishments and the gathering of unattached males at massive extractive and construction projects not only attracted long-distance migratory prostitution but also expanded and intensified local and regional indigenous prostitution. There is continuing debate around the degree of agency, initiative, and consent involved in the activities of indigenous women in frontier and colonial settings (Butler, 1985; Berger, 1988). This debate over the past is central to ongoing discussions about the post–Cold War traffic in sex workers; Third World activists and scholars reject as cultural imperialism a First World discourse on the phenomenon that depicts non-Western women, past and present, as "ignorant, poor, uneducated, tradition bound, domestic, family-oriented, [and] victimized" (Kempadoo, 1998a:11; Doezema, 1998: 37; Murray, 1998: 59). These commentators promulgate "subaltern understandings and lived realities of sexuality and sexual-economic relations . . . where one can speak of a continuum of sexual relations from monogamy to multiple sexual partners and where sex may be considered as a valuable asset for a woman to trade with" (Kempadoo, 1998a: 12).

It is true that in various historical settings, "sexual bartering, explicit and implicit," has provided "the coin with which women, in so far as they could, converted . . . dependency into a reciprocal relations" (Stansell, 1986: 179). In early modern Southeast Asia, for example, sexual liaison with foreign males was not necessarily a bitter fate. The "temporary wife" of a foreign trader might well have been a woman of high birth, acting as the de facto partner of her husband in local business (Andaya, 1998). Luise White's (1986) well-known work on prostitution in colonial Nairobi makes clear, as well, the complexity, range of activities, and entrepreneurialism termed "prostitution" by contemporaries.

However, over time the ever widening economic inequalities between core and peripheral regions after the 1880s ensured significant wage differentials, making the services of Third World women relatively inexpensive for most First World men across the globe. As noted earlier, an initial phase of agency and initiative among migratory Chinese and Japanese sex workers was quickly overtaken by more coercive, exploitative arrangements (Tong, 1994: 161–63). In the American West, the vast majority of sex workers were impoverished women of color—Asian, African American, Native American, and Latina (Butler, 1985; Hurtado, 1999: 86–88). Western Australia's mining frontier and pearling settlements witnessed similar dynamics, as aboriginal women found themselves driven into the lowest echelons of commercial sex (Hunt, 1986: 137).

In colonial entrepôts, there was a similar long-term degradation of sex work for indigenous women; by the 1890s, sexual service to foreigners had been commoditized and stigmatized, the fate of lowborn and marginal women (Andaya, 1998). Hong Kong provides a good example of the dynamics. Three years after cession to the British, there were an estimated thirty-two brothels in the "Fragrant Harbor" ("Census of Registration Office," 1845). Procurement was facilitated by the expansion and distortion of customary practices, such as the adoption of female servants (*mui-tsai*); vested interests—both foreign and indigenous—then tended to defend such customs as essential to social functioning and properly off limits to colonial policing. In 1857, Hong Kong (a crown colony under the Colonial Office) instituted a system for registration and inspection of brothels, compulsory medical examination of inmates, punishment of prostitutes who infected clients, and detention in a Lock Hospital until cured (Miners, 1987: 191). Epidemic levels of venereal disease among British sailors and soldiers led to the implementation in 1867 of amended Contagious Diseases Ordinances. The CDO regime comprised controlled brothels divided racially by clientele, compulsory medical examination for inmates, and expansive police powers.

By 1883, Hong Kong had 1,274 registered female prostitutes; 1,000 of them were Chinese inmates in 78 brothels closed to foreigners ("native brothels"), 220 were Chinese and Japanese women in 39 brothels opened to foreigners and Chinese men ("foreign brothels"), and 54 were foreign women, including American, Australian, and Portuguese (from Macao), described as "voluntary submission women" because they registered voluntarily but lived alone or in small clusters, rather than in brothels, and were unofficially exempted from examination. The number of unregistered prostitutes and "sly" brothels was unknown but thought high (Scully, 1998).

Contemporaries themselves conceded that the ultimate goal of regulated prostitution was to provide "clean native women" for foreign military personnel ("Contagious Diseases Ordinances," 1883). The CDOs, operative from 1857 to 1889, were effectively limited to Asian women servicing foreigners. Hong Kong authorities observed: "It is the foreign houses used by soldiers, sailors and foreign riff-raff where disease and cruelty flourish, and only the most degraded women will enter them except under compulsion" (*Parliamentary Papers,* 26:46).

By the mid-1890s, networks of varying sophistication and durability were evident throughout Asia, the Middle East, the Americas, and Europe. Well-traveled routes included Poland and European Russia to London, Buenos Aires, Rio de Janeiro, North Africa, Saudi Arabia, Turkey, and Syria; France to North and South Africa, South America, the Low Countries, British India; colonial enclaves in East and Southeast Asia; Greece to the Levant; Hungary to Romania; Poland and Austria to Turkey; China and Japan to the United States, Latin America (especially Argentina and Brazil), Australia, Singapore, Malaya, India, and Hong Kong (Bristow, 1983: 35).

Contemporaries in this initial phase of modern migratory prostitution understood and discussed the problem within several coexisting paradigms: colonial management, immigration politics, social hygiene, and urban angst. Then, as now, public discourse on prostitution became entangled with issues of class, gender, race, and nationality. Across the world, from New York to Moscow, discussions of urban commercial sex served as "the symbol of what was perceived as the social and moral disintegration of society" (Hill, 1992: 17). Regulation and policing tended to pit authorities against one another, as health professionals battled law enforcers and self-appointed vigilantes took on allegedly feeble and corrupt police forces (Guy, 1991a: 35–39; Gilfoyle, 1986: 640). The critique of prostitution emerged as part of a larger assault on urbanization (Lees, 1979: 70). Prostitution became "a metaphor for upper- and middle-class fears about the lower class and the future of the . . . nation" (Guy, 1991a: 44; Gilfoyle, 1986: 645). Typically, regulation of sexual commerce embodied "elite concerns to define the effective boundaries of nationality and citizenship, as well as to discipline working-class women" (Guy, 1991a: 44).

The all-important link between nationality and sexuality in the discourse on migratory prostitution was forged in this early period. In part, this owed to the importance of nationality as a criterion in the state and colonial regulation of prostitution at home and abroad (Guy, 1991a: 14). However, it also arose from the bonding of "respectability" and nationalism in the modern era (Mosse, 1985: 9). "Woman as a national symbol was the guardian of the continuity and immutability of the nation, the embodiment of its respectability" (Mosse, 1985: 18). Although nonindigenous prostitutes had been long entrenched in places such as Shanghai and Buenos Aires by the 1880s, their presence and activities made them lightning rods in debates over nation building and citizenship (Guy, 1991a: 14–16; Scully, 1995, 1998). Prostitutes—homegrown and otherwise—became "the pretexts for defining one nation's sovereignty against another's" and "a focus and symbol in ideological discourse used in the construction, reproduction, and transformation of ethnic/national categories" (Guy, 1991b: 201–2). In colonial and less developed areas, debates about prostitution were infused with ambivalence toward modernity, "Westernization," and Euro-American dominance of the international system (Bernstein, 1995: 8; Hershatter, 1989).

Circa 1895 to World War I

The late 1890s brought the expansion and transformation of migratory, multinational prostitution. At the same time, the tactics of reform groups and the complex anxieties of contemporaries sensationalized and distorted the phenomenon, generating much debate and hyperbole about a worldwide "white slave trade."

The perceptible expansion of migratory prostitution, particularly in colonial areas, owed to several factors. There was a sizeable influx of women into China, colonial Asia, and South Africa. Some came from Manchuria, fleeing the chaos of the Russo-Japanese War; others had been driven by urban reformers from the United States and Western Europe. New market demand was stimulated by the multinational suppression of the Boxer Rebellion in North China circa 1900, the Boer War, and the Spanish-American-Philippine War. Contemporary British sources estimated that Shanghai alone had about two thousand non-Chinese prostitutes in the first years of the twentieth century, most of them Russian, Eastern European, and Japanese (Hyam, 1986: 68–69).

This post-1895 phase brought large-scale, organized prostitution, facilitated by improved and more affordable rail and water transportation lines. Itinerant women "attach[ed] themselves to the canteens and hotels," drawing upon those facilities and clienteles, giving politically powerful real estate agents, landlords, and entertainment purveyors a vested interest in the process (van Onselen, 1982: 107–9). The increase of women brought foreign prostitutes out to street-level solicitation and across racial boundaries, making them more visible and more controversial; the increased competition among women led to more elaborate advertising, moving beyond personal introductions and letters passed to hotel guests to spectacular promenades and public placards. Policing and regulatory responses exacerbated the situation, as migratory prostitutes under siege became more reliant on pimps and more vulnerable to corrupt officials (Scully, 1998).

The question of migratory prostitution engaged the era's full spectrum of activists, academics, philanthropists, officials, professionals, and social tinkerers. It was in the late 1890s that public discourse beheld domestic and migratory prostitution as an integrated, international problem to be dealt with multilaterally. In 1898–99, various antiregulationist groups formed the London National Vigilance Association (NVA), which became the nucleus of a broad coalition against the white slave trade (WST); this group asserted the existence of "a highly organized traffic" decoying English women to the Continent.

In fact, this was a rhetorical internationalization of a decades-old regional traffic in English girls to Belgium and France ("Correspondence Respecting Immoral Traffic," 1881). In the 1880s, this intra-European traffic had given limited currency to the term *white slavery* (Bristow, 1983: 35, 36; Nadelmann, 1990: 514).[2] NVA leaders toured the Continent in the 1890s, forming national committees in Germany, Holland, Denmark, Sweden, Russia, Belgium, France, Switzerland, and Austria (League of Nations, 1921: 13). By 1899, the NVA had gathered sufficient momentum for an international conference in London. It was here that the campaign against the WST burst into public discourse, as conferees learned of a European-wide network of procurers and brothels and established an international bureau to coordinate among national committees and disseminate propaganda. By 1904, they had orchestrated an international convention among European states, recognizing white slavery as a juridical concept in international law but limiting signatories to vague pledges to adjust domestic law to punish procurers who had used force or fraud to procure women (Grittner, 1990; Bristow, 1983).

The consensus among historians is that the NVA's internationalist thrust was an adaptation of the tactics and rhetoric of the battle against black slavery from decades back (Bristow, 1983: 37; Walkowitz, 1982: 89). So too was it a reasonable response to the ongoing campaign among public health officials to legalize prostitution worldwide as an anti–venereal disease measure (Nadelmann, 1990: 486, 514–15). This latter dimension was a constant source of tension between abolitionists and regulationists within the antitraffic coalition. Famed abolitionist Josephine Butler criticized the 1899 conference for admitting avowed regulationists. Likewise, Lady Henry Somerset was forced to step down in 1897 as president of the British Women's Temperance Association for remarks to the *Times* endorsing regulated brothels in colonial India.

Any hint of tolerance ran counter to the campaign by temperance and reform groups in London, whose combined force had led to the abolition of the CDOs in Hong Kong and the Straits Settlements and the inauguration of colonial cleanup campaigns in the 1890s. Colonial officials and police resisted the abolitionist push as regards indigenous women, however, arguing that it would generate geometric increases in clandestine prostitution and unmanageable infection rates. The end of the CDOs did not mean the end of tacit regulation, and imperial managers were permitted this de facto policy until the interwar era.

Domestic constituencies back home increasingly required colonial authorities "to make empire respectable," through programs of "native uplift" and a tighter supervision over colonial sojourners themselves, particularly those straddling and blurring racial and cultural boundaries (Stoler, 1989; Levine, 1986; Scully, 1998). An influx of "wage-earning white women in African and Asian colonies" further complicated colonial demarcations, "especially where their work was not within the confines of family—and official attempts to restrict the movements and often the choice of employment of such women were common" (Levine, 1998: 109; Davidson, 1984: 176–79).

In the United States, the judicial expansion of the interstate commerce clause in the 1890s brought trafficking in women under federal jurisdiction (Grittner, 1990: 48–50). American delegates did attend the 1899 London conference but opted not to bring home with them the "white slave trade" phenomenon (40). The United States acceded to the 1904 international convention, but not until 1908. Until 1909–10, migratory prostitution as an issue was manifest in the overlapping domains of nativism, municipal reform, and—to a lesser extent—concern about what the *Stars and Stripes* abetted in the new insular possessions and American communities overseas (Scully, 1995).

In 1906, the American Purity Alliance became the American National Vigilance Committee, later (1913) merging with the American Federation for Sexual Hygiene, to become the American Social Hygiene Association (Grittner, 1990: 51, 61, 14–15). This core group, renamed several times, became the primary U.S. representative at international gatherings and the vehicle of American participation in later League of Nations investigations of trafficking in persons. Notwithstanding sensationalist exposés by such pressure groups, concerns about constitutionality and federal-state divisions kept the United States from signing the 1910 international convention. However, the 1910 Mann Act served the purpose to a certain extent. Aimed at redressing constitutional barriers, the act made it a felony to transport knowingly any woman or girl across state lines or abroad for the purpose of prostitution or debauchery or for other immoral purpose (Grittner, 1990: 86–90). The unintended impact of the legislation was to enhance the power of pimps and procurers over sex workers (Beckman, 1984).

By 1910, the image of the white slave trade conjured up by London purity groups had taken full hold of the American imagination. Lurid stories of sullied white womanhood and organized syndicates linking major cities helped bring on board southerners who otherwise would have argued states' rights in the face of a broad expansion of federal police powers (Grittner, 1990: 90–97). The vision of a vast network of Jewish and French procurers kidnapping and luring white women from Europe and America to service lowly natives and "eastern rich potentates" was captivating, combining as it did racial anxieties, colonial debates, immigration politics, and public morality issues (Feldman, 1967). Similar sensationalism and bourgeois prurience was evident elsewhere, from London to Moscow to Buenos Aires (Grittner, 1990; Bernstein, 1995; Guy, 1991a, 1991b).

Although this image of kidnapped, debauched white women unified disparate groups, in the long run it was counterproductive. Those who might have been able to shut down the traffic as completely as had been the African slave trade were white, metropolitan populations easily outraged by tales of their young pure women brought to the outposts of barely veiled barbarity. However, 99 percent of traffic victims were in fact women of color—broadly defined by contemporaries to include Jews—distributed throughout the world but concentrated in colonial areas.

For Americans—as for Westerners more generally—foreign prostitutes at home were an immigration problem, not an object of sympathy; in the colonial context, they were a class to be despised but tolerated as necessary for sexual stability and military readiness. Metropolitan opinion over the white slave trade did force some changes in imperial management, but only as regards the small cadre among migratory prostitutes known as Occidentals.

Interwar Period and the League

On the eve of war, the agenda agreed upon by the broad coalition of antitraffic groups, enunciated at the 1913 Madrid conference, included (a) efforts by various national committees to push for abolition of licensed brothels universally; (b) initiatives to develop an information bank based on declarations from victims; (c) assisted repatriation and rehabilitation of victims; (d) provision of adequate protection for women emigrants en route; (e) campaign for uniform legislation allowing supervision of employment agencies offering jobs abroad; (f) a push to exclude the question of consent with regard to traffic in minors; (g) full suppression of colonial prostitution; (h) more attention to punishment of procurers and third parties (League of Nations, 1921: 15–16).

When reestablishing ranks in 1919, reformist groups perceived that World War I had "closed, in general, all frontiers, and rendered the traffic in women very difficult. . . . On the other hand, it let loose upon the world violent passions, immorality and even worse disorders" (League of Nations, 1921: 8). In the British colonies—such as Singapore and Hong Kong—European prostitutes had been deported as a wartime measure ("Prostitution in Singapore," 1933). More generally, European emigration decreased noticeably. However, regional and indigenous prostitution had multiplied in response to the continued presence of large military garrisons. Although some earlier lucrative routes were now less traveled, the postwar reopening of commerce and frontiers provided fertile ground for a dramatic increase in the volume and intensity of the traffic in women and children (League of Nations, 1921: 17).

In 1920, the newly established League of Nations took primary responsibility for combating the forced traffic in persons. The racially exclusive and misleading term *white slavery* was abandoned, having come under attack as early as the Brussels and Madrid conferences in 1912 and 1913, respectively (League of Nations, 1921: 55). An officer within the Secretariat was exclusively charged with information gathering and coordination. The assembly assigned to the Secretariat the task of issuing a questionnaire not simply to league members but to signatories of the 1904 and the 1910 conventions, asking what domestic measures had been undertaken to implement these international agreements. In addition, plans were put in motion for the 1921 international conference on the trafficking, to be held in Geneva.

Optimism and expansiveness characterized early league proclamations on the subject. Speakers declared that the "feebleness" of earlier arrangements was "to-day visible to every eye" (League of Nations, 1921: 10). Delegates envisioned a comprehensive, multilateral attack on public and private fronts, to "vanquish this powerful evil" (League of Nations, 1921: 11). However, self-reporting by signatories, annual conferences, and traveling commissions of inquiry constituted, in the main, the league's entire arsenal in this regard. As in diplomatic matters more generally, the league was organically unequipped to force compliance; territorial sovereignty and imperial governance came before collective security.

The dimensions and geography of the interwar traffic can be conveyed by looking at four groups: Occidental, Chinese, Japanese, and Russian. Although the first of these groups was the smallest, it remained the only effective point of access into the conscience and consciousness of Western metropoles. Deported during World War I, Western women returned in the 1920s though in much fewer numbers (League of Nations, 1934). The election of a Labour government in London in 1929 strengthened the hand of domestic reform groups; a planned League of Nations commission visit to Asia and the Middle East turned up the pressure on colonial prostitution (Miners, 1987; "Prostitution in Hong Kong," 1931). Hong Kong officials were warned: "All we can do is to play for time, having at the back of our minds the intention to meet the storm when it breaks," and they took the path of least resistance by targeting Western, rather than indigenous, prostitutes ("Social Hygiene," 1930). In the early 1930s, Hong Kong, Singapore, the Federated Malay States, Ceylon, Malaya, and Palestine closed brothels with European, Australian, and American women; the status quo continued in Syria, Iraq, Persia/Iran, parts of British India, Indo-China, Siam/Thailand, China, Manchuria, Korea, Japan, and Macao (IBSTP, 1934).

The treaty ports of mainland China—Shanghai in particular—were forced to undertake official, if unenergetic, antivice programs in the mid-1920s. However, the byzantine foreign legal system known as extraterritoriality hindered prosecution of either victims or traffickers ("Social Disease, Prostitution," 1935). By the 1930s, even as the number of Occidental women dwindled to double and single digits, a more racially charged version of the white slave trade panic decades earlier took hold back home. Exposés described a huge chain of men passing the women from hand to hand from origin to destinations, warning that *the prostitution of White women in Asia,* is the cheapening of our White race, in the eyes of the Coloured races, through the medium of the most sacred things it possesses" (Champly, 1930: 278).

The league inquiry commission in the mid-1930s, funded privately by the American Bureau of Social Hygiene, found "an international traffic in women and girls of the Near, Middle and Far East. . . . The bulk of this traffic was in Asiatic women from one country in Asia to another." There were an estimated 17,000 women and girls of many nationalities registered as prostitutes—an equal number of clandestine sex workers—throughout the major cities visited. Only 174 of them were Occidental. Chinese, Japanese (including Korean and Formosan), Eurasians, and Asiatic Russians (east of the Urals) were the most numerous. Smaller groups included Malay, Annamite, Siamese, Filipino, Indian, Iraqi, Persian, and Syrian (League of Nations, 1934).

The Chinese women had been, the league found, recruited from the poorest classes and shipped throughout Asia and the Middle East. There were an estimated 6,000 in British Malaya alone (League of Nations, 1934). Procurers were generally middle-aged or elderly Chinese women, themselves prostitutes, former prostitutes, brothel servants, or brothel managers; traffickers were of the same ilk but posed as maidservants or traveling vendors. Male trafficker were typically "runners" in cahoots with lodging houses, passage brokers, or shipboard employees. The demand was, as it had long been, the large overseas settlements of men. In Shanghai alone, about 100,000 prostitutes operated in the 1930s, in a setting that saw the transformation of what was "essentially a luxury market in courtesans" to one "primarily geared to supplying sexual services for the growing numbers of unattached . . . commercial and working-class men of the city" (Hershatter, 1997: 53, 203).

In the 1920s, Japan's policy was to repatriate its national migratory prostitutes in Singapore, Malaya, India, Hong Kong, and Thailand ("Prostitution in Singapore," 1933). However, in expanding to Manchukuo and thence to China proper, Japan extended its own domestic system of prostitution, staffed by Korean, Formosan, and Japanese women (League of Nations, 1934: 10–13; Lie, 1995: 110–15). Everywhere outside China and Manchuria, Japanese females could not travel without the consent of parents or husbands, and women of the "immoral classes" were barred entirely. The nodal points of regimental prostitution in China were Shanghai, Tientsin, Mukden, Vladivostok, and Harbin.

White Russian women, with few exceptions, were under the control and management of traffickers. Tens of thousands of Russians fled into Manchuria and China after the Bolshevik Revolution; many of the women among them were pawned as prostitutes to local Chinese or went into China and Southeast Asia. Their stateless status and utter destitution pushed them to capitalize on their sexuality, with varying degrees of degradation. White Russian prostitutes comprised the full range of sex labor, from brothel to hostess to mistress (League of Nations, 1934).

As for the United States, by the advent of war in Europe Immigration and Justice Department enforcers of the Mann Act had been made cautionary by constitutional challenges and fiscal constraints (INS, 1914). The U.S. draft act of 1917 included "campfollower" provisions prohibiting prostitution within a prescribed area around military and naval installations (Grittner, 1990: 63). Some Immigration agents saw the wartime hiatus in incoming European prostitutes as an opportunity to "get a better grip on and rid the country of Asiatic aliens" (INS, 1914). However, in general from 1914 until well into the interwar period, Americans came to see the white slave trade as a foreign problem, if not simply the delusion of zealots. With the establishment of the League of Nations, the United States became a passive presence in the campaign against forced migratory labor beyond American borders.

Casualties of scholarly deconstructionism, interwar foes of trafficking in prostitution are too often dismissed as paternalistic, elitist, racist, misogynist do-gooders more interested in social control than genuine structural transformation. Though representatives of the type are readily found, such a blanket dismissal is unwarranted and counterproductive to current antitrafficking efforts. Then, as now, remedial efforts were undermined by conflicting imperatives, vested interests, the absence of options for victims, and the entrepreneurial opportunism of traffickers.

The modern mind sees in every social problem the medical conundrum: extirpate the roots of a disease or address only the symptoms? In this regard, there are more similarities than differences between then and now. Sociologically minded humanitarians fought for long-term solutions and attention to cognate problems, such as the legal status of women, employment opportunities, punishment of clients and procurers, abolition of licensed prostitution, and so on. Pragmatists and enforcement agencies looked to the symptoms, through heightened scrutiny of travelers, stricter immigration restrictions, and beefed-up policing resources. The disparate worldviews are succinctly summed up in a confrontation between French and Dutch delegates at the 1921 Geneva conference. To the former's suggestion that the league limit its attention to the traffic rather than to prostitution more generally, M. DeGraff impatiently declared: "It is as though you said: we have a cholera Congress but you must not speak of bacilli" (League of Nations, 1921: 69).

Overlapping but distinguishable from this roots-versus-symptoms divide was the clash in the British colonies between universalism and racially infused, paternalistic exceptionalism. Ironically, the cultural relativism now propounded by Third World activists was in this earlier setting a defense of the status quo put forward by colonial offices and indigenous misogynists. When, for example, antitraffic groups pushed for twenty-one as a universal age of consent by way of undercutting those Asian religious and social customs most easily abused by procurers, both British and French delegates obtained a clause by which "in Eastern countries where, owing to climatic conditions and social and religious customs, the above standard of age cannot be applied, the definition of a minor for the purpose of the above provisions . . . shall be fixed by the National Legislatures of those countries" (League of Nations, 1921: 61). Anticipating the arrival of the league commission of inquiry touring Asia in the early 1930s, the Colonial Office took refuge in the argument that the league's purview was international, not internal.

Finally, remedial efforts ran up against a tension still with us today, that is, between protection and patriarchy. In combating the traffic, delegates suggested a range of measures that clearly crossed the line: special passport requirements for females; bans on women traveling alone; registration with local police when working abroad; forced repatriation and retraining of prostitutes; and the like. Various national governments in Asia and the Middle East enacted legislation, in the name of the international conventions, that banned marriages to foreigners and prohibited female emigration.

Women's groups throughout Europe effectively blocked a league proposal to repatriate women forcibly, saying: "Long experience in the past has shown them that protection sometimes comes to be a hidden form of slavery, a masked tyranny inspired by the best of intention" (League of Nations, 1921: 80). Abolitionists and women's rights groups opposed targeting victims rather than victimizers; jurists noted that as most countries still tolerated prostitution, extradition was not practical or likely; repatriated women tended to return to foreign brothels, thus making the proposition a costly one for governments or private organizations; feminist organizations warned that coercion and restrictions on suspected women would bring abuse and restriction on women in general ("Repatriation of Prostitutes," 1930). The compromise solution was compulsory repatriation of underage prostitutes (IBSTP, 1931).

Pre–World War II efforts to combat the traffic in women and children for prostitution "accomplished, in the final analysis, relatively little toward its objectives" (Nadelmann, 1990: 515). Indigenous women, particularly Eurasians, supplanted migratory sex workers, and a general decrease in trafficking came about as a result of changing "social, economic and demographic conditions" (516). As Ethan Nadelmann has shown persuasively, the WST never inspired a "global prohibition regime" of the sort that spearheaded the eradication of the African slave trade: such a regime turns upon the shift from a common perception of a given activity as legitimate under certain conditions and with respect to certain persons to redefinition of the activity as evil; the delegitimation of government involvement in the activity and the shift to official abolitionist activism; and the erection of effective criminal laws and conventions. This failure owed to a fundamental lack of consensus—still evident today—as to the meaning and morality of prostitution, the ease of concealment, the adaptability of entrepreneurs to changing policing strategies, and the durability of demand (Nadelmann, 1990: 486).

World War II and After

Wartime deployment of troops throughout the colonial world undercut international efforts to control prostitution. Reports in the early 1940s described Singapore as a clearinghouse for traffickers, serving Burma (Myanmar), Ceylon (Sri Lanka), India, Indonesia, Japan, Philippines, and Thailand (IBSTP, 1949). Estimates ranged from 8,000 to 20,000 sex workers in Thailand alone circa 1940, half of whom were concentrated in the metropolitan areas of Bangkok and Dhonburi. Urban and regional markets were supplied from the countryside: "Prostitution is reported to be a big business, operated on a syndicate basis, with supply lines running in and out of Bangkok to most towns and cities in the country" (IBSTP, 1949: 47; League of Nations, 1940/41: 74).

Postwar traffic was nearly all local and regional, with demand generated mostly by standing troops (United Nations, 1948). The new United Nations assumed supervision over international conventions and took on the reporting function earlier performed by league officials. Figures given for the period 1948–50 show this same local and regional concentration: migratory women moved short distances, for example, back and forth from Syria and Lebanon to Palestine/Israel; between Vietnam and Cambodia; Costa Rica and Panama; Somaliland and Aden; France and Poland; between and among Bulgaria, Turkey, Iran, Germany, Greece, Yugoslavia; and the United States, Canada, and Mexico (United Nations, 1952; "International Review of Criminal Policy," 1950).

The primary United Nations response to continued trafficking in sex workers was the 1949 "Convention for the Suppression of the Traffic in Persons and of the Exploitation of the Prostitution of Others." As before, nation-states bore primary responsibility for reporting their own compliance, passing remedial legislation, and dealing with both traffickers and victims (Farrior, 1997: 219–20). Nonbinding provisions and self-reporting allow countries to "gain the moral highground by loudly proclaiming that they have signed a document condemning the buying and selling of women's bodies, when in reality prostitution continues unchecked in their own countries" (Toepfer and Wells, 1994: 92).

Up through the 1970s, the determining factor in multinational prostitution markets in Asia was the large-scale, semipermanent stationing of troops and regularized movement of naval personnel through the region. Since World War II, it has been the U.S. military that has supplied the chief demand for commercial vice in East and Southeast Asia (Tadiar, 1993; Enloe, 1983; Moon, 1997). In the words of one author, "the U.S. presence in the Pacific is . . . a transnational garrison state that spans five sovereign states and the vast expanse of Micronesia" (Bello, 1992: 14). This "transnational garrison state has spawned a subeconomy and subculture that has had distorting effects on the larger economy and culture of the host societies," generating excessive demand for sexual labor and eroticized entertainment (15).

In the 1980s, observers and activists began to detect dramatic qualitative and quantitative changes in sexual trafficking. A decrease in the U.S. military presence in Asia, combined with global economic trends, led countries most dramatically affected to turn to "sex tourism" as a viable, if inhumane, income generator. This sector continued to expand into the 1990s, fueled by the "global restructuring of capitalist production and investment" (Kempadoo, 1998a: 15). Efforts to keep down labor costs and remain competitive had intensified rural displacement and urban unemployment; at the same time, the spread of consumer culture created widespread demand among Third World populations for goods, such as televisions and cars (Kempadoo, 1998a: 16; MacKenzie, 1998). An increased demand for children among customers fearful of AIDS is thus more than met by children themselves seeking disposable income or parents who "deploy the income-generating capacity of their children in order to ensure that the household survives" (Kempadoo, 1998a: 7; Quiambao, 1998).

Free-market reforms in Eastern Europe, Russia, Cuba, Vietnam, and the People's Republic of China (PRC) contributed to a resurgence of prostitution in those areas (Litherland, 1995; Pringle, 1998; Langfitt, 1998). "It's like the Klondike during the Gold Rush," one Albanian journalist said recently of war-torn Kosovo (Viviano, 1999: A1). The pre–World War II pattern of women from underdeveloped areas going into wealthier markets continues but is more than matched by movement in the other direction, or from one Third World area to another (Kempadoo, 1998a: 15; Charoenpo, 1998; *Bangkok Post,* July 22, 1998). Long-distance trafficking becomes less necessary with the emergence of areas specializing in sex tourism (Friedman, 1996). Traffickers typically have a diverse portfolio, often involved in narcotics, credit card fraud, money laundering, and so on (MacLeod, 1998).

As in the pre–Cold War era, remedial efforts tend to exacerbate the problem and worsen the conditions under which sex workers operate (Murray, 1998). Stricter immigration controls raise the cost of doing business, allowing organized crime to drive out less organized competitors; increased costs and potentially higher profits push traffickers—and immigrant smugglers more generally—to seek greater control over sex workers, through locked brothels, threats to family members back home, violence, and so on (*Salt Lake Tribune,* June 17, 1994). Continued state reliance on deportation does nothing to diminish the traffic and instead makes women less likely to report their situation and more dependent upon traffickers and pimps.

Most significant, there is even less consensus among antitrafficking groups than before World War II. The prewar divide between regulationists and abolitionists has been complicated by a schism as to whether prostitution may be a legitimate form of labor and prostitutes rational choosers (Doezema, 1998: 37). Various national prostitutes' rights groups have championed this latter interpretation and have found support among Third World academics and activists (Murray, 1998). They reject the nongovernmental organizations' (NGO) and Western media's view of "trafficking . . . as a global conspiracy which can be dismantled through international co-operation and the paternalistic rehabilitation of victims" (Murray, 1998: 62). Although redefining prostitution as work, and migratory prostitutes as workers, may open up new avenues of reform, this ever widening definitional divide portends a repetition of pre–World War II failures.

CHRONOLOGY OF THE CAMPAIGN AGAINST THE WHITE SLAVE TRADE
AND THE TRAFFIC IN PERSONS, UP TO 1980

1885   Jewish Association for the Protection of Girls and Women founded in London.

1895   Penitentiary Congress of Paris—search for international agreement and national legislation to deal with conditions known to encourage prostitution.

1899 London Congress—convened by a private group, National Vigilance Association (NVA); reveals to the world the existence of an organization covering all of Europe that had taken the place of isolated procuring, which up to then alone had been dealt with by repressive laws; reveals that underage women had been duped into debauchery abroad. Agreed on need for an international agreement and changes in national laws. Establishment of International Bureau and national committees.

1902 Paris Conference 1902—first diplomatic conference; arranged by French government. Leads to signing of an agreement March 18, 1904.

1904 International Agreement for the Suppression of the White Slave Traffic, March 18, 1904—signatories agree to establish national central authority to collect and share information; bind themselves to general administrative measures regarding vigilance at ports and depots, notification about suspected persons, taking declarations from alien prostitutes to get broad range of information, to protect and maintain victims before repatriation, and to supervise registry offices and employment agencies. Signatories: Brazil, Denmark, India, Italy, Norway, Sweden, Switzerland. In 1908 the United States signs on.

1910 Paris Conference 1910.

1910 International Convention for the Suppression of White Slave Traffic—Austria, Belgium, Bulgaria, Canada, France, Germany, United Kingdom, Hungary, Netherlands, Poland, Portugal, South Africa, Spain, Uruguay. Not ratified by: Belgium, Brazil, Denmark, Italy, Portugal, Sweden. The United States does not accede, arguing constitutional problems. Signatories agree to work for the enactment of national legislation to criminalize and punish procurement of girls and women, either minors or of full age, notwithstanding that the various acts constituting the offense may have been committed in different countries.

1910 Madrid Congress—400 delegates, produces book of relevant laws and ordinances.

1912 Brussels Congress 1912—reveals new facts about children, so "Traffic in Children" added. "White slavery" challenged as racially exclusive.

1913 London Conference 1913—31 official delegates representing 24 countries and between 400 and 500 delegates from national committees. Resolutions concerning need for international legislation prohibiting the employment in theaters, circuses, concerts, and music halls of girls under 16 years of age; with special provision for the protection of girls under age who accept employment abroad to perform in those places of amusement; establishment in each country of an official commission, composed of members of both sexes, to ascertain the extent of the traffic in women and children and its causes.

1919   International Conference at Washington 1919. Respect for women and children the topic.

1919   League of Nations covenant stipulating league oversight of conventions against traffic in women and children.

1920   Conference of 7 Latin American states agreeing to push for cooperation in tracking dangerous individuals.

1921   League of Nations International Conference on Women and Children. Albania, Austria, Belgium, Brazil, Bulgaria, Canada, Chile, China, Czecho-Slovakia, Denmark, Estonia, France, Germany, Great Britain, Greece, Hungary, India, Italy, Japan, Lithuania, Monaco, Netherlands, Norway, Panama, Poland and Danzig, Portugal, Romania, Serb-Croat-Slovene State, Siam, South Africa, Spain, Sweden, Switzerland, Uruguay.

1921   Seventh International Conference for the Protection of Girls (at Neuchatel). This conference made recommendations to the League of Nations, including defining traffic in women as an offense sui generis; criminalizing attempts and preparatory acts; establishing standard age of consent at 21 or higher; punishing internal traffic in same way as international traffic; making punishment as severe as possible.

1921   Convention for the Suppression of Traffic in Women and Children. Seeks to suppress the traffic using three approaches: prosecuting persons who traffic in children, licensing and supervising employment agencies, and protecting immigrating and emigrating women and children.

1926   Slavery Convention. Effort to borrow rights and duties from conventions against arms trafficking. Signatories commit to prevent and suppress the slave trade and bring complete abolition.

1930   Forced Labor Convention. Defined "forced labor" as "all work or service which is exacted from any person under the menace of any penalty and for which the said person has not offered himself voluntarily."

1933   International Convention for the Suppression of the Traffic in Women of Full Age—requires punishment of persons who traffic in women of full age and declares that consent is no defense to the crime of trafficking. Includes colonies and protectorates.

1936 Advisory Committee on Social Questions fuses Traffic Committee with Committee for Protection of Children.

1937 League tries to increase the scope of coverage to full age, either sex, whether or not consent exists, and whether or not person was taken abroad. War interrupts passage of this convention.

1949 UN consolidates the four prior treaties, plus a 1937 League of Nations draft Convention for the Suppression of the Traffic in Persons and of the Exploitation of the Prostitution of Others. Weak enforcement clauses; limited measures. Focuses on punishing procurers, persons exploiting prostitution, and brothel owners.

1957 Abolition of Forced Labor Convention.

1966 International Covenant on Economic, Social and Cultural Rights.

1976 International Covenant on Civil and Political Rights (ICCPR) required signatories to protect citizens against being trafficked for prostitution, by promulgating information about civil rights, imposing penalties, and providing a forum for individual claims. It also established an oversight body, the Human Rights Committee, to monitor compliance.

1979 Convention on the Elimination of All Forms of Discrimination against Women (CEDAW)—includes measures regarding suppression of traffic in women.

Source: Extrapolated from Stephanie Farrior, "The International Law on Trafficking in Women and Children for Prostitution: Making It Live Up to Its Potential," *Harvard Human Rights Journal,* 1997: 10:213; Wanda Grabinska, "Introductory Notes on the Legislative Development of the International Convention for the Suppression of the Traffic in Persons (1899–1949)," International Bureau for the Suppression of Traffic in Persons (IBSTP) Papers, 1955, box 193/6, Fawcett Library, London.

NOTES

1. By the mid-1890s, Japanese officials (under)estimated the numbers of Japanese prostitutes in Southeast Asia as follows: Hong Kong, 100; Singapore, 300; Penang, 200; Australia, 200; Tonkin, 80; Saigon, 160; British India, 200; Siam, 40. "Japanese Women Abroad," *Japan Weekly Mail,* May 30, 1896, 609.

2. The term *white slavery* was first used in the 1830s by London reformers in reference to East End Jewish pimps, as well as in discussions of the conditions of

factory labor for girls. Commentators agree that the phrase was first used by Count de Gasparin at the time of the abolition of the African slave trade and was later repeated by the French writer Victor Hugo in his observation: "In Europe we have another Traffic, not the Black Slave trade, but the White Slave Traffic, which is even worse." By the 1870s, it referred to state-regulated vice and by 1880 had come to include the image of white women kidnapped or lured to foreign brothels (Bristow, 1983: 35, 36; Nadelmann, 1990: 514).

REFERENCES

Aldrich, Robert. 1990. *The French Presence in the South Pacific.* Basingstoke, Hampshire: Macmillan.

Andaya, Barbara Watson. 1998. "From Temporary Wife to Prostitute: Sexuality and Economic Change in Early Modern Southeast Asia." *Journal of Women's History* 9 (4): 11–34.

Assavanonda, Anjira. 1998. "Child Prostitution on the Rise." *Bangkok Post,* September 24.

Beckman, Marlene. 1984. "The White Slave Traffic Act: The Historical Impact of a Federal Crime Policy on Women." *Georgetown Law Journal* 72:1111–42.

Bello, Walden. 1992. "From American Lake to a People's Pacific." In *Let the Good Times Roll: Prostitution and the U.S. Military in Asia,* edited by Saundra Pollock Sturdevant and Brenda Stoltzfus, 14–21. New York: New Press.

Berger, Mark. 1988. "Imperialism and Sexual Exploitation: A Response to Ronald Hyam's 'Empire and Sexual Opportunity.'" *Journal of Imperial and Commonwealth History* 17(1): 83–89, with Hyam's response, 90–98.

Bernstein, Laurie. 1995. *Sonia's Daughters: Prostitutes and Their Regulation in Imperial Russia.* Berkeley: University of California.

Branigin, William. 1999. "A Different Kind of Trade War." *Washington Post,* March 20, A27.

Bristow, Edward. 1983. *Prostitution and Prejudice. The Jewish Fight against White Slavery, 1870–1939.* New York: Schocken Books.

"Brothel Madam Faces Execution." 1998. *South China Morning Post.* November 22, 5.

Burrell, Ian. 1998. "Britain Calls Child Sex Trade Summit." *Independent.* August 4, 7.

Butler, Anne. 1985. *Daughters of Joy, Sisters of Misery: Prostitutes in the American West, 1865–1890.* Urbana: University of Illinois.

Callaway, Helen. 1987. *Gender, Culture, and Empire: European Women in Colonial Nigeria.* Basingstoke, Hampshire: Macmillan.

Capella, Peter. 1998. "Swiss Put Russian 'Mafia Boss' on Trial." *Guardian,* December 1, 14.

"Census of Registration Office." 1845. Colonial Office [CO] 129/12.

Champly, Henry. 1930. *The Road to Shanghai: White Slave Traffic in Asia.* London: J. Long.

Charoenpo, Anucha. 1998. "Thai Girls Lured to Sex Trade in Africa." *Bangkok Post,* August 24.

Chuang, Janie. 1998. "Redirecting the Debate over Trafficking in Women: Definitions, Paradigms, and Contexts." *Harvard Human Rights Journal* 11:65–107.

"Colombia Frees Child Sex Slaves." 1998. *Sun-Sentinel,* September 27, 12A.

"Contagious Diseases Ordinances." 1883. Colonial Office [CO]-129/207, #29 [Microfilm Collection].

"Correspondence, Dispatches, Reports, Returns, Memorials, and Other Papers Respecting the Affairs of Hong Kong, 1862–1881." 1974. *Parliamentary Papers.* China, vol. 25. Shannon: Irish University Press.

"Correspondence Respecting Immoral Traffic in English Girls in Belgium." 1881. British Foreign Office, Belgium No. 1.

"Cuba Cracks down on Vice, Crime." 1998. *Chicago Tribune,* November 2, 6.

Davidson, Raelene. 1984. "'As Good a Bloody Woman as Any Other Bloody Woman . . . ': Prostitutes in Western Australia, 1895–1939." In *Exploring Women's Past: Essays in Social History,* edited by Patricia Crawford et al., 171–206. Sydney: G. Allen & Unwin.

DeGroot, Joanna. 1989. "'Sex' and 'Trace': The Construction of Language and Image in the Nineteenth Century." In *Sexuality and Subordination: Interdisciplinary Studies of Gender in the Nineteenth Century,* edited by Susan Mendus and Jane Rendall, 89–128. London: Routledge.

Demleitner, Nora. 1994. "Forced Prostitution: Naming an International Offense." *Fordham International Law Journal* 18:163–97.

Dery, Luis. 1991. "Prostitution in Colonial Manila." *Philippine Studies* 39 (4): 475–89.

Doezema, Jo. 1998. "Forced to Choose: Beyond the Voluntary v. Forced Prostitution Dichotomy." In *Global Sex Workers: Rights, Resistance, and Redefinition,* edited by Kamala Kempadoo and Jo Doezema, 34–50. New York: Routledge.

Engel, Barbara Alpern. 1989. "St. Petersburg Prostitutes in the Late Nineteenth Century: A Personal and Social Profile." *Russian Review* 48 (1): 21–44.

Enloe, Cynthia. 1983. *Does Khaki Become You?: The Militarisation of Women's Lives.* Boston: South End Press.

Farrior, Stephanie. 1997. "The International Law on Trafficking in Women and Children for Prostitution: Making It Live Up to Its Potential." *Harvard Human Rights Journal* 10:213–55.

Feldman, Egal. 1967. "Prostitution, the Alien Woman, and the Progressive Imagination, 1910–1915." *American Quarterly* 19 (2): 192–206.

"France Bids Adieu to 40 Vice Girls." 1999. *Bangkok Post,* April 7.

Friedman, Robert. 1996. "India's Shame: Sexual Slavery and Political Corruption Are Generating an AIDs Catastrophe." *Nation,* April 8, 11–20.

Gilfoyle, Timothy. 1986. "The Moral Origins of Political Surveillance: The Preventative Society in New York City, 1867–1918." *American Quarterly* 38 (4): 637–52.

Grittner, Frederick. 1990. *White Slavery: Myth, Ideology, and American Law.* New York: Garland.

Guy, Donna. 1991a. *Sex and Danger in Buenos Aires: Prostitution, Family, and Nation in Argentina.* Lincoln: University of Nebraska Press.

———. 1991b. "'White Slavery,' Citizenship, and Nationality in Argentina." In *Nationalisms and Sexualities,* edited by Andrew Parker et al., 201–17. New York: Routledge.

Hershatter, Gail. 1989. "The Hierarchy of Shanghai Prostitution, 1870–1949." *Modern China* 15 (4): 463–98.

———. 1997. *Dangerous Pleasures: Prostitution and Modernity in Twentieth-Century Shanghai.* Berkeley: University of California.

Hill, Marilynn Wood. 1992. *Their Sister's Keepers: Prostitution in New York City, 1830–1870.* Berkeley: University of California.

Hirata, Lucie Cheng. 1992. "Free, Indentured, Enslaved: Chinese Prostitutes in Nineteenth-Century America." In *History of Women in the United States,* edited by Nancy F. Cott, 9:123–49. Munich: K.G. Saur.

Honore, Carl. 1998. "Sexual Slavery Growing in Europe." *Milwaukee Journal Sentinel,* December 20, 9.

Hunt, Susan Jane. 1986. *Spinifex and Hessian: Women's Lives in North-Western Australia, 1860–1900.* Nedlands: University of Western Australia.

Hurtado, Albert. 1999. *Intimate Frontiers: Sex, Gender, and Culture in Old California.* Albuquerque: University of New Mexico Press.

Hutchison, Elizabeth Quay. 1998. "'*El Fruto Envenenado del Arbol Capitalista*': Women Workers and the Prostitution of Labor in Urban Chile, 1896–1925." *Journal of Women's History* 9 (4): 131–52.

Hyam, Ronald. 1986. "Empire and Sexual Opportunity." *Journal of Imperial and Commonwealth History* 14 (2): 34–90.

Ichioka, Yuji. 1977. "*Ameyuki-san:* Japanese Prostitutes in Nineteenth-Century America." *AmerAsia* 4 (1): 1–21.

International Bureau for Suppression of Traffic in Persons (IBSTP). 1931. "International Bureau for Suppression of Traffic in Persons." Box 193/6, IBSTP Papers, Fawcett Library, London.

———. 1934. "Traffic in Women: Official and Non-Official Co-operative Action in Combatting the Traffic in the East." Box 193/7, IBSTP Papers, Fawcett Library, London.

———. 1949. "Post-War Europe as a Field for the Traffic in Women and Children." Box 193/6, IBSTP Papers, Fawcett Library, London.

"International Review of Criminal Policy." 1950. United Nations serial.

Kempadoo, Kamala. 1998a. "Globalizing Sex Workers' Rights." In *Global Sex Workers: Rights, Resistance, and Redefinition,* edited by Kamala Kempadoo and Jo Doezema, 1–28. New York: Routledge.

———. 1998b. "The Migrant Tightrope: Experiences from the Caribbean." In *Global Sex Workers: Rights, Resistance, and Redefinition,* edited by Kamala Kempadoo and Jo Doezema, 124–38. New York: Routledge.

Klein, Martin. 1994. "Slavery, the International Labour Market, and the Emancipation of Slaves in the Nineteenth Century." *Slavery and Abolition* 15 (2): 197–220.

Ko, Michael. 1998. "Mission Possible: Life Skills to Russian Orphans." *Seattle Times,* July 9, B1.

Lakshmanan, Indira. 1998. "Macao Isn't Going Quietly." *Boston Globe,* June 13, A1.

Lamberti, Rob. 1998. "Raids Free 'Sex Slaves' Prostitution Ring Hit in Massive Sweep." *Toronto Sun,* December 3, 4.

Langfitt, Frank. 1998. "China's Freer Market Beckons Old Customer; Prostitution's Return Met by Tax Collector." *Baltimore Sun,* November 17, 1A.

League of Nations. 1921. Records of the International Conference on Traffic in Women and Children, June 30–July 5.

———. 1934. "Commission of Enquiry into Traffic in Women and Children in the East." Summary of the Report to the Council. IV. Social 1934.IV.3.

———. 1935. "Position of Women of Russian Origin in the Far East." A.12.1935.IV 1935. Geneva from Traffic in Women and Children Committee. Social 1935.IV.3.

———.1940/41. Advisory Committee on Social Questions. Summary of Annual Reports for 1940/41 prepared by the Secretariat, Traffic in Women and Children.

Lees, Andrew. 1979. "Critics of Urban Society in Germany, 1854–1914." *Journal of the History of Ideas* 40 (1): 61–83.

Levine, Philippa. 1986. "Rereading the 1890s: Venereal Disease as 'Constitutional Crisis' in Britain and British India." *Journal of Asian Studies* 55 (3): 585–612.

———. 1998. "Battle Colors: Race, Sex, and Colonial Soldiery in World War I." *Journal of Women's History* 9 (4): 104–30.

Lie, John. 1995. "The Transformation of Sexual Work in Twentieth-Century Korea." *Gender and Society* 9 (3): 310–27.

Litherland, Susan. 1995. "Children—Human Rights." *InterPres Service*, May 16.

MacKenzie, John. 1998. "Sex Industry Booming As Asia Busts." *Scotland on Sunday,* October 18, 21.

Macklin, Simon. 1998. "Hit-List Plan to Combat Child-Sex Tourists." *South China Morning Post,* October 6, 7.

MacLeod, Ian. 1998. "'Chasing Ghosts': The Asian Mafia Explosion." *Ottawa Citizen,* October 25, A3.

McElroy, Damien. 1999. "Portuguese Flee Macao As Their Rule Comes to a Bloody End." *Sunday Telegraph,* January 10, 26.

Mihalopoulos, V. Bill. 1993. "The Making of Prostitutes: The *Karayuki-san.*" *Bulletin of Concerned Asian Scholars* 25 (1): 41–56.

Miners, Norman. 1987. *Hong Kong under Imperial Rule, 1912–1941.* Hong Kong: Oxford University Press.

Moon, Katharine H. S. 1997. *Sex among Allies: Military Prostitution in U.S.-Korea Relations.* New York: Columbia University Press.

Mosse, George. 1985. *Nationalism and Sexuality: Respectability and Abnormal Sexuality in Modern Europe.* New York: H. Fertig, 1985.

Murphy, Brian. 1998. "Inquiry Paints Greece as Prostitution Hub." *Boston Globe,* November 22, A18.

Murphy, Mary. 1992. "The Private Lives of Public Women: Prostitution in Butte, Montana, 1878–1917." In *History of Women in the United States,* edited by Nancy F. Cott, 9:286–98. Munich: K.G. Saur.

Murray, Alison. 1998. "Debt-Bondage and Trafficking: Don't Believe the Hype."

In *Global Sex Workers: Rights, Resistance, and Redefinition,* edited by Kamala Kempadoo and Jo Doezema, 51–64. New York: Routledge.

Nadelmann, Ethan. 1990. "Global Prohibition Regimes: The Evolution of Norms in International Society." *International Organization* 44 (4): 479–526.

"NPA to Attend International Meeting on Prostitution." 1998. *Daily Yomiuri,* October 21, 2.

"Paedophile Tourists Face Crackdown." 1995. *Independent,* July 2, 5.

Philps, Alan. 1998. "Welcome to 'Las Vegas of Middle East.'" *Daily Telegraph,* September 17, 26.

Porter, Jonathan. 1996. *Macau: The Imaginary City: Culture and Society, 1557 to the Present.* Boulder, Colo.: Westview.

Pringle, James. 1998. "Owner of Beijing Brothel to Be Shot." *Gazette,* November 19, A24.

"Prostitution in Hong Kong." 1931. C[olonial] O[ffice]-129/533/10.

"Prostitution in Singapore." 1933. C[olonial] O[ffice]-273/659/13.

Quiambao, Cecilia. 1998. "Trading in the Innocent—Child Prostitution." *Bangkok Post,* October 18.

Quilligan, Patrick. 1995. "International Community Acts to Combat Child Sex Exploitation." *Irish Times,* June 1, 10.

Repard, Pauline. 1995. "Ring Importing Prostitutes from Thailand Is Broken Here." *San Diego Union-Tribune,* February 25, B2.

"Repatriation of Prostitutes." 1930. League of Nations archives, United Nations, Geneva, 11b/16984/3293.

Salt Lake Tribune. 1994. June 17, no title, A15.

Sandos, James. 1980. "Prostitution and Drugs: The United States Army on the Mexican-American Border, 1916–1917." *Pacific Historical Review* 49 (4): 621–45.

Scully, Eileen. 1995. "Taking the Low Road to Sino-American Relations: 'Open Door Expansionists' and the Two China Markets." *Journal of American History* 82 (1): 62–83.

———. 1998. "Prostitution as Privilege: The 'American Girl' of Treaty Port China." *International History Review* 20 (4): 855–83.

"Sex Trade Trafficking of Children on the Rise." 1998. *Bangkok Post,* July 22.

Singapore *Straits Times.* 1862. May 17, 1.

"Social Disease, Prostitution Have Been Investigated Many Times in City, Official Says." 1935. *China Press,* July 16, 9.

"Social Hygiene." 1930. Colonial Office-129/522/3. Microfilm Collection.

Stansell, Christine. 1986. *City of Women: Sex and Class in New York, 1789–1860.* New York: Knopf.

Stoler, Ann. 1989. "Making Empire Respectable: The Politics of Race and Sexual Morality in Twentieth-Century Colonial Cultures." *American Ethnologist* 16 (4):634–60.

Sturdevant, Saundra Pollock, and Brenda Stoltzfus. 1992. *Let the Good Times Roll: Prostitution and the U.S. Military in Asia.* New York: New Press.

Sun Kuo-chun. 1988. *Chiu Shang-hai ch'ang-chi mi-shih* (A secret history of prostitution in Old Shanghai). Honan: Ho-nan Sheng Hsin Hua Shu Tien Fu Hsing.

Tabet, Paola. 1998. "I'm the Meat, I'm the Knife: Sexual Service, Migration, and Repression in Some African Societies." In *Global Sex Workers: Rights, Resistance, and Redefinition,* edited by Kamala Kempadoo and Jo Doezema. New York: Routledge.

Tadiar, Neferti Xina M. 1993. "Sexual Economies in the Asia-Pacific Community." In *What Is in a Rim?: Critical Perspectives on the Pacific Region Idea,* edited by Arif Dirlik. Boulder, Colo.: Westview.

Terrell, Rev. F. G. c. 1907. *The Shame of the Human Race: The White Slave Traffic.* Chicago, n.p.

"Thais Account for 90% of Vice Arrests in Hong Kong." 1999. *Bangkok Post,* April 23.

Thompson, Tony, and Nicole Veash. 1999. "Sex Slavery Spreads across UK." *Observer,* March 14, 7.

Toepfer, Susan J., and Bryan S. Wells. 1994. "The Worldwide Market for Sex: A Review of International and Regional Legal Prohibitions Regarding Trafficking in Women." *Michigan Journal of Gender and Law* 2:83–128.

Tomich, Dale. 1988. "The 'Second Slavery': Bonded Labor and the Transformation of the Nineteenth-Century World Economy." In *Rethinking the Nineteenth Century: Contradictions and Movements,* edited by Francisco O. Ramirez, 103–18. New York: Greenwood Press.

Tong, Benson. 1994. *Unsubmissive Women: Chinese Prostitutes in Nineteenth-Century San Francisco.* Norman: University of Oklahoma.

Turnbull, C. M. 1977. *A History of Singapore, 1819–1975.* Kuala Lumpur: Oxford University Press.

United Nations. 1948. Economic and Social Council. "Traffic in Women and Children." Summary of Annual Reports for 1946–47.

———. 1952. Economic and Social Council. "Traffic in Women and Children." Summary of Annual Reports for the Period 1948–1950. Prepared by the Secretariat.

United States. Immigration and Naturalization Service (INS). 1914. A. Warner Parker, Law Officer, to Commissioner General of Immigration, August 7, 1914, 52809–7.

van Onselen, Charles. 1982. *Studies in the Social and Economic History of the Witwatersrand, 1886–1914.* Vol 1. New York: Longman.

Viviano, Frank. 1999. "Albanians Try to Take Over Kosovars' Crime Network." *San Francisco Chronicle,* May 11, A1.

Walkowitz, Judith. 1982. "Male Vice and Feminist Virtue: Feminism and the Politics of Prostitution in Nineteenth Century Britain." *History Workshop* 13:79–93.

Wallen, David. 1995. "Britain Joins the Move against Child Sex Tours." *South China Morning Post,* July 15, 18.

Warren, James. 1993. *Ah Ku and Karayuki-san: Prostitution in Singapore, 1870–1940.* Singapore: Oxford University Press.

Watenabe, Satoko. 1998. "From Thailand to Japan: Migrant Sex Workers as Autonomous Subjects." In *Global Sex Workers: Rights, Resistance, and Redefinition,* edited by Kamala Kempadoo and Jo Doezema, 114–23. New York: Routledge.

Waters, Elizabeth. "Restructuring the 'Woman Question': Perestroika and Prostitution." *Feminist Review* 33:3–19.

"What on Earth?" 1998. *Washington Post.* September 5, A21.

White, Luise. 1986. "Prostitution, Identity, and Class Consciousness in Nairobi during World War II." *Signs* 11 (2): 255–73.

Whitely, Peyton. 1995. "Prostitution Probe: 5 Asian Women Freed." *Seattle Times,* January 31, A1.

Wijers, Marjan. 1998. "Women, Labor, and Migration: The Position of Trafficked Women and Strategies for Support." In *Global Sex Workers: Rights, Resistance, and Redefinition,* edited by Kamala Kempadoo and Jo Doezema, 60–78. New York: Routledge.

4 ▪▪▪▪▪▪▪ The Transformation of Migrant Smuggling across the U.S.-Mexican Border

Peter Andreas

Immigration control across the nearly two-thousand-mile-long United States–Mexican border has been transformed during the past decade from being a low-profile and politically marginalized activity into a high-intensity campaign attracting a great deal of policy and media attention.[1] "The border build up," as one journalist observes, "represents by far the most expensive and prolonged budgetary initiative ever undertaken to reduce illegal immigration" (Suro, 1998: 1). Strikingly, the unprecedented effort to build a police barrier along the border has come at the same time that the United States and Mexico have eagerly been constructing a barrier-free economy. Even though migrant labor is one of Mexico's most important exports and an integral component of the U.S.-Mexican economic integration process, it is noticeably missing from the North American Free Trade Agreement. While most economic barriers have been falling, barriers against the cross-border movement of labor have been rising in the form of more intensive policing. These sharply contrasting developments reinforce Jagdish Baghwati's broader observation that immigration controls are "the most compelling exception to liberalism in the operation of the world economy" (Bhagwati, 1984: 680).

In this chapter I trace how the interaction between law enforcement and clandestine labor migration across the U.S.-Mexican border has perversely generated a more organized and sophisticated migrant smuggling business and how this, in turn, has helped to propel a more expansive and intensive border-policing effort. I emphasize that while the relationship between law-evading smugglers and law-enforcing state actors has been purposefully conflictive, in practice it has in many ways been unintentionally symbiotic. In short, this is a story about how the state has helped make smuggling and how smuggling has helped to (re)make the policing apparatus of the state.[2] I first provide an overview of the emergence and evolution of migrant smuggling across the border and how this has intersected with various state practices over time. I then focus on the post-1993 period, characterized by a boom in both immigration control efforts and organized migrant smuggling activity in the U.S.-Mexican borderlands.

A Brief History of Migrant Smuggling across the U.S.-Mexican Border

If smuggling can be defined as the practice of bringing in or taking out without state authorization, then all population flows involving a clandestine border crossing are by definition a form of smuggling. What has varied across time and place is the degree, nature, methods, and organization of such smuggling. In the case of crossing the U.S.-Mexican border, this has ranged from self-smuggling (i.e., migrants illegally crossing the border without hiring the services of a professional smuggler), to local-level individual smuggling entrepreneurs (the traditional "coyotes"), to highly organized and sophisticated transnational smuggling networks (often specializing in the smuggling of non-Mexicans across the border—such as Chinese and Central Americans).

The first wave of illegal immigration involved self-smuggling from the United States to Mexico. A century and a half ago, Mexico unsuccessfully tried to curb illegal American immigration to its northern regions. To a significant extent, the Mexican War was a conflict over immigration and immigration control. After the Treaty of Guadalupe Hidalgo of 1848 and the Gadsden Purchase of 1853, these territories formally became part of the United States. Large numbers of white settlers (many of them recent European immigrants) moved west to these sparsely populated lands. But while the political boundaries that were redrawn through war remain, the migratory movement has been turned around, with millions of people of Mexican origin populating these areas.

The movement of people across the border remained largely unregulated throughout the nineteenth century. The first real U.S. initiative to restrict migration flows in the Southwest actually targeted Chinese. One side effect of the Chinese Exclusion Act in 1882 was to turn Mexico and the border into a corridor for smuggling Chinese laborers. Boats of Chinese migrants would land south of the California-Mexico border at Ensenada, Guaymas, or Mazatlan. The migrants paid five dollars for the trip to the border and then up to forty dollars to be smuggled into California (Metz, 1989: 365). The migrants also traveled deeper into the Mexican interior and were then smuggled across the border between Juárez and El Paso (Stoddard, 1976: 180). Federal law enforcement officials (called "Chinese inspectors") were deployed to the border area to curb the smuggling of Chinese (McDonald, 1997: 74).

Many Mexicans were informally recruited by U.S. employers to work in southwestern agriculture in the early twentieth century. Whereas legal entry was cumbersome, crossing the border illegally was relatively simple and largely overlooked. The Mexican Revolution, U.S. labor shortages during World War I, and the expansion of southwestern agriculture fueled a further influx of Mexican workers across the border. Restrictions on European immigration in 1921 and 1924 also had the unintended effect of turning the U.S.-Mexican border into a backdoor for illegal European immigrants. Thus, when the U.S. Border Patrol was formed in 1924, with a total force of some 450 officers, the primary immigrants targeted along the border were Europeans and Asians.

An estimated half a million Mexicans entered the United States during the 1920s (Calavita, 1994). When they were no longer needed during the depression era, hundreds of thousands were deported. And when the demand for cheap labor increased again in the 1940s (as a result of labor shortages during World War II), Mexican workers were encouraged to come back. This time the state played a more formal role in the labor recruitment process. The Bracero Program, a guest-worker arrangement in place between 1942 and 1964, was created to provide a cheap source of labor for agribusiness.

The long-term consequence of the Bracero Program was to institutionalize mass labor migration from Mexico to the United States. As one immigration scholar has observed, "by the time the Bracero Program ended, a relationship of symbiosis between Mexican immigrants and U.S. employers had become well-entrenched, facilitated and nurtured by more than 50 years of U.S. policymaking. With the end of the program, employment of Mexican labor went underground as the guest workers of one era became the illegal immigrants of the next" (Calavita, 1996: 289). After the Bracero Program was terminated in the 1960s, Mexican workers continued to be welcomed by employers. Legal sanctions did not worry employers, since the hiring of unauthorized workers was not a felony.[3]

Even as illegal immigration increased rapidly during the 1960s and 1970s, the enforcement capacity of the Immigration and Naturalization Service (INS) remained limited. Interior enforcement was largely nonexistent, while border controls were minimal. Even as the number of border apprehensions increased from approximately 71,000 in 1960 to more than 1 million in 1978, the budget of the Border Patrol remained less than the budget of many city police departments (Teitelbaum, 1980).

The limited presence and effectiveness of law enforcement meant that migrant smuggling was a fairly simple and inexpensive practice; migrants either smuggled themselves across the border or hired a local border guide. However, the sheer magnitude of the migration flow, competition between smugglers to service this flow, and the dispersion of the flow from agricultural to urban areas meant that smuggling gradually became more organized. As Peter Reuter and David Ronfeldt have noted, "After the termination of the Bracero program in 1965, smuggling of aliens into the United States was conducted by adventurous loners who had little concern for security and by small family-based operations. But the growth and competition for new business, the increased importance of operational skill and security, and the shift from agricultural areas to cities as the destination of many aliens created a need for larger, better organized operations" (1991: 14). Government reports suggest that smuggling organizations had grown substantially in size and complexity by the mid-1970s (Comptroller General of the United States, 1976).

Still, hiring a professional smuggler remained more of a convenience than a necessity. In FY 1970, only 8.4 percent of the illegal migrants caught by the Border Patrol in the southwestern region had attempted entry with the use of a smuggler. This increased to 13.5 percent in FY 1975 (ibid.:

5–6). These statistics probably understate the amount of professional smuggling, since those migrants who hired the services of a smuggler were more likely to evade detection and arrest. Penalties against smugglers remained minimal: fewer than 50 percent of the smugglers caught between 1973 and 1975 were prosecuted, most on a misdemeanor charge (18).

In one study, smugglers report that there was little demand for their services in the 1970s because migrants could easily enter the United States on their own. Smugglers were often hired for special needs, such as the smuggling of women, children, the elderly, and non-Mexican nationals (López Castro, 1998: 970). Using a smuggler to cross the border generally meant a faster and safer trip. This involved some personal risks, but attempting the crossing without a smuggler heightened the possibility of assault by bandits and abuse by the authorities.

Failing as a meaningful barrier, INS control efforts remained largely symbolic (Heyman, 1995). The Border Patrol could cover only a small portion of the borderline. While the INS insisted that "prompt apprehension and return to country of origin is a positive deterrent to illegal reentry and related violations" (INS Annual Report, 1978, cited in Kossoudji, 1992: 161), in practice migrants simply kept trying to cross until they succeeded. Repeated arrests did little more than postpone entry.

As migrants flowed north across the border for work, the Mexican government largely sat on the sidelines. Freedom of exit is guaranteed in the constitution, and the export of excess labor has long been an economic safety valve. Nevertheless, while not blocking the exit of Mexican citizens, in the late 1970s Mexico began to cooperate with the United States in targeting professional smugglers. This was partly due to the Mexican government's rising concerns over the smuggling of Central Americans to the United States through Mexican territory. During the Carter years, the INS created a special unit called the National Anti-Smuggling Program, which generated increased arrests and prosecutions of smugglers operating on the U.S. side of the border. Mexico, in turn, collaborated by arresting hundreds of smugglers on its side of the line. During the 1980s, cross-border immigration control cooperation continued to focus primarily on the smuggling of third-country nationals through Mexico, especially Central Americans. Nevertheless, smugglers and those being smuggled remained largely undeterred (Nevins, 1998: 326–28).

The most significant U.S. policy response to illegal immigration was the passage of the Immigration Reform and Control Act of 1986 (IRCA). IRCA introduced employer sanctions, authorized an expansion of the Border Patrol, and offered a general legalization program (as well as a special legalization program for agricultural workers). Some 2 million Mexicans were eventually legalized. IRCA's proponents argued that this supply of newly legalized workers would satisfy the U.S. demand for cheap imported labor, while the employer sanctions would inhibit the hiring of illegal workers. This, at least theoretically, would curb future migration.

IRCA, however, reinforced the very problem the law was promoted to rectify. As one immigration researcher notes, "IRCA stimulated interest in coming to the U.S., and the possibility of obtaining a green card via the legalization programs led to a huge increase in the demand for coyote [smuggler] services" (López Castro, 1998: 970). Those who were legalized under IRCA provided a stronger base for the arrival of new unauthorized immigrants. "By handing out more than 2 million green cards to former undocumented migrants," observes Douglas Massey, "Congress dramatically raised the odds that millions of other family members still in Mexico would themselves enter the United States as undocumented migrants" (1997: 26–27).

The employer sanctions law, meanwhile, provided no effective document verification system. The perverse impact of the law was to generate an enormous business in fake documents. Since IRCA did not require employers to check the authenticity of documents, they could simply continue to hire illegal workers at minimal risk—as long as the documents looked genuine and they made sure to fill out the proper forms. In the short term, IRCA helped to defuse some of the domestic pressure to "do something" about illegal immigration. But the law's failures would help make immigration control an even more daunting task in years to come.

The New Border Enforcement Campaign

As the public mood toward illegal immigration soured in the early 1990s, policymakers from across the political spectrum rushed to outdo one another in proposing tougher control measures. In this heated political context, President Clinton launched an aggressive new campaign to "regain control" of the southwestern border. Noticeably less attention was given to the enormous employer demand for cheap migrant labor or the fact that as much as half of the illegal immigrant population in the country had entered legally (as students or tourists, for example) and then overstayed their visas.

The heightened political status of immigration control has been reflected in the dramatic expansion of the INS. The INS budget grew from $1.5 billion in FY 1993 to $4 billion in FY 1999—making it one of the fastest—(and one of the only) growing federal agencies. The single most important growth area has been border enforcement. In FY 1998, the INS spent $877 million on border enforcement, up from about $400 million in FY 1993. More than half of the $413 million increase in INS funding from FY 1998 to FY 1999 was allocated for border control. According to the Congressional Research Service, more than $3.3 billion has been spent on the Border Patrol since 1994 (cited in Suro, 1998: 3).

As a result of its recent hiring spree, the INS now has more officers authorized to carry a gun and make arrests than any other federal law enforcement agency (*Migration News*, February 1998). Between FY 1993 and the end of FY 1998, the size of the Border Patrol along the southwestern border more than doubled—from 3,389 agents to 7,231 agents. Reflecting the intensified monitoring of the border, total line watch hours for the Border Patrol increased from 2,386,888 in FY 1993 to 4,807,669 in FY 1997 (Bean, Capps, and Haynes, 1999). In addition, as of March 1997, the INS had about 1,300 inspectors at thirty-six ports of entry on the southwestern border. The inspections' appropriations totaled $151 million for FY 1997—a 78 percent increase from FY 1994 levels.

The new border enforcement campaign has also involved a massive influx of new equipment, such as infrared night-vision scopes, low-light TV cameras, ground sensors, helicopters, and all-terrain vehicles. The increasingly high-tech nature of border enforcement has included a new electronic identification system called IDENT, which stores the fingerprints and photographs of those apprehended at the border. The military has also played a supporting role by assisting with the operation of night scopes, motion sensors, and communications equipment, as well as building and maintaining roads and fences. Along the border south of San Diego, for example, army reservists built a ten-foot-high steel wall that extends for fourteen miles. Similarly, in Nogales, army engineers constructed a fifteen-foot tall fence that is nearly five miles long.

Congress has assured that the border buildup continues by passing the

Illegal Immigration Reform and Immigration Responsibility Act of 1996. The sweeping immigration law authorized the hiring of 1,000 Border Patrol agents a year, reaching a total force of more than 10,000 by the year 2001. The 1996 law promoted other measures to secure the border, including a sharp increase in the penalties against migrant smugglers. The new sentencing guidelines in some cases call for a doubling of penalties and mandatory minimum sentencing for smuggling aliens for commercial gain.

The border control offensive has been based on a strategy designed by the INS in 1993–94 called "prevention through deterrence." By using more physical barriers, surveillance equipment, legal sanctions, and law enforcement agents, the objective has been to inhibit illegal entry rather than trying to catch entrants once they have entered the country. The infusion of law enforcement resources at the most popular entry points has been designed to disrupt traditional border-crossing methods and routes, forcing migrants to give up or attempt entry in more difficult and remote areas and at official ports of entry.

The deterrence strategy has its origins in Operation Blockade (later renamed Hold-the-Line), which was launched in El Paso on September 19, 1993. Some 450 agents were paid overtime to cover a twenty-mile stretch of the borderline. The sudden show of force led to a sharp drop in attempted illegal entries in the area. Prior to the operation, there were up to 10,000 illegal border crossings per day, and only 1 person out of 8 who made the attempt was apprehended (Ekstrand, 1995). The high-profile operation drew the applause of Washington, the media, and local residents. Importantly, the operation also attracted the attention of political leaders in California, who pushed to reproduce the El Paso "success story" along their portion of the border.

Impressed by the El Paso experience and the domestic support it generated, in 1994 the INS announced a comprehensive plan to apply the "prevention through deterrence" strategy across the entire southwestern border. The strategy would first target the busiest entry points—the El Paso and San Diego sectors, which in FY 1993 accounted for 68 percent of all southwestern border apprehensions. Thus, El Paso's Operation Hold-the-Line was matched by Operation Gatekeeper south of San Diego in October 1994, which targeted the fourteen westernmost miles of the border (traditionally the location of 25% of all border apprehensions).

The strategy would then be expanded to the Tucson sector and south Texas, where migrants were expected to move after the El Paso and San Diego sectors had been secured. As envisioned by the Border Patrol, the strategy would eventually be applied along the entire border (U.S. Border Patrol, 1994).

As predicted, the tightening of border controls in El Paso and San Diego has pushed migrants to attempt entry elsewhere along the border.[4] Thus, apprehensions in the El Paso sector have remained far below the levels prior to Operation Hold-the-Line but have skyrocketed to the west in New Mexico and Arizona. Similarly, apprehensions in the Imperial Beach sector south of San Diego (traditionally the single most important gateway for illegal entry) have declined sharply since Gatekeeper began, but arrests have jumped in the more remote areas of east San Diego County.

Even though apprehensions have now reached a twenty-four-year low near San Diego and have fallen by half in El Paso since 1993, overall apprehensions along the southwestern border are actually up. The Border Patrol made more than 1.5 million apprehensions in FY 1999—an increase of 300,000 over 1993 apprehension levels (*Austin American-Statesman,* November 28, 1999). Although apprehension statistics are notoriously difficult to interpret, it seems that the border deterrence strategy has done more to shift rather than reduce the cross-border flow of migrants.

These shifts in human traffic have provided a political and bureaucratic justification to expand the border-policing campaign geographically. Thus, Operation Safeguard was launched in Nogales, Arizona, and Operation Gatekeeper, which first concentrated on the 14 westernmost miles of the border, was extended in October 1996 to cover 66 miles. Similarly, in January 1997 Operation Hold-the-Line was extended 10 miles west into New Mexico. And in late August 1997 the INS announced Operation Rio Grande in southeast Texas, which includes setting up portable floodlights, 20-foot watchtowers, low-light video cameras, and high-powered infrared vision scopes along the Rio Grande. As part of Operation Rio Grande, the Border Patrol and the military's Joint Task Force 6 have started building 240 miles of roadway, a dozen helicopter pads, and fifty high-intensity lights in the Laredo area (Spener, this volume, Chap. 5).

Meanwhile, the heightened Border Patrol presence between the official ports of entry has created more pressure at the ports of entry. Operations such as Gatekeeper have generated attempted illegal entries through the ports of entry, and the INS has in turn responded by deploying new port inspectors. Between FY 1994 and FY 1997, the number of INS port inspectors increased from 1,117 to 1,865, representing a 67 percent rise. The added personnel have been reinforced by higher penalties for those who attempt entry through fraudulent document use (*Migration News,* February 1997).

The Boom in Migrant Smuggling

Breaking up the traditional routes and methods of clandestine entry has turned the once relatively simple illegal practice of entry without inspection into a more complex underground web of illegality. Past entry methods primarily involved either self-smuggling or limited use of a local smuggler. But with the buildup of border policing, the use of a professional smuggler has become more of a necessity. The growing reliance on smugglers, a 1997 report of the Binational Study on Migration concluded, "helps to explain why most migrants attempting unauthorized entry succeed despite significantly more U.S. Border Patrol agents and technology on the border" (Binational Study, 1997: 28).

Not surprisingly, as the demand for smuggling services and the risks of crossing the border have grown, so too has the price of being smuggled. Prices along some parts of the border have doubled and in some cases more than tripled. The smuggling fee can exceed a thousand dollars. The trip from Agua Prieta to Phoenix, for example, cost as little as two hundred dollars in 1994 but reached as high as fifteen hundred dollars in early 1999 (*Arizona Daily Star,* July 11, 1999). The exact price varies depending on location, the quality of service, and the set of services being purchased. As one Border Patrol agent explains, "It's much like a full-service travel agency, all depending on how much you're willing to spend" (*Los Angeles Times,* April 7, 1996). According to the INS, the increase in prices is an indicator that the deterrence effort is effective. Yet higher prices are not necessarily a substantial deterrent, given that smuggling fees tend to be paid for by relatives and friends in the United States rather than by the immigrants themselves (López Castro, 1998: 971). Alternatively, some immigrants may be given the option of paying off the fee by working in a job arranged or provided by the smuggler (Binational Study, 1997). Although the amount paid to be smuggled across the border is not insignificant, it can be earned back in a relatively short period of time working in the United States.

The most consequential impact of higher prices has been to enhance the wealth and power of smuggling groups. As Miguel Vallina, the assistant chief of the Border Patrol in San Diego, noted, "the more difficult the crossing, the better the business for the smugglers" (*Los Angeles Times,* February 5, 1995). INS commissioner Doris Meissner explained in January 1996 that "as we improve our enforcement, we increase the smuggling of aliens that occurs, because it is harder to cross and so therefore people turn more and more to smugglers" (*Federal News Service,* January 12, 1996). But at the same time that Meissner recognizes that the Border Patrol has created more business for smugglers, she also emphasizes that we are "moving as aggressively as we can . . . so that we can put them [the smugglers] out of business" (Meissner, 1996). The president's International Crime Control Strategy has similarly emphasized the need to target organized smuggling, calling for "aggressive efforts to protect U.S. borders by attacking and decreasing smuggling and smuggling-related crimes" (quoted in Bach, 1999).

Beefed-up policing has removed some smugglers but simply increased the market position of others. Moreover, many of those arrested are the lowest-level and most expendable members of migrant smuggling organizations—the border guides and drivers who are the "foot soldiers" of the business. Smugglers are first and foremost travel service specialists. And as long as there continues to be a strong demand for their services—which the tightening of border controls and the strong domestic employer demand for migrant labor guarantee—smuggling will most likely persist. The high profits from smuggling—inflated by law enforcement pressure—assure that there will be smugglers willing to accept the occupational hazards. As one smuggler explained, "Figure it this way. If I work in a factory five days, I make $125 a week. If I take one person across the border, I get $300" (*Los Angeles Times,* May 2 , 1992). A good guide can reportedly make $60,000 a year along the border (*San Diego Union-Tribune,* April 28, 1996).

U.S. officials have gone to great lengths to portray migrants as the victims of smugglers, and they use this both to deflect criticism and to provide a further rationale to crack down on smuggling. Assistant U.S. Attorney Michael Wheat, for example, suggested that "basically, alien smuggling is modern-day slavery. The whole idea behind slavery was moving humans to perform labor. The way the aliens are moved, the way they are treated, this is just a sophisticated form of slavery" (*Los Angeles Times,* February 5, 1995). Migrants, however, generally view smugglers as simply a "necessary evil," a clandestine business transaction that they willingly engage in to evade the expanding border enforcement net. Within Mexico, migrant smuggling is considered a shady business, but one that is seen as relatively harmless (López Castro, 1998: 970). Smugglers, after all, have a clear economic motivation to deliver their "clients" unharmed across the border, since most of the payment is generally made only upon delivery (see Spener, this volume, Chap. 5). Of course, as has been well documented in media reporting, smugglers can be abusive and reckless, and their efforts to bypass law enforcement can place migrants at great risk. But it should be remembered that smugglers are hired precisely because they generally provide a safer and faster border-crossing experience. Indeed, many smugglers depend on customer satisfaction for future business, since migrants who have had a successful experience are likely to recommend their smuggler to other friends and relatives. A smuggler's reputation can matter a great deal.

Smugglers have become more skilled as border enforcement has become more intensive. As one senior INS official noted, "alien smugglers have developed a sophisticated infrastructure to successfully counteract U.S. Border Patrol operations along the Southwest Border" (Regan, 1997). Those smuggling operations that have the greatest transportation and communication capabilities are the ones most capable of evading arrest, which leaves small-time smugglers at a competitive disadvantage. Pressured by law enforcement, some smugglers have even turned to using commercial trucks to move migrants across the border, blending in with the massive boom in cross-border trucking brought on by the liberalization of trade and transportation. Northbound truck crossings have doubled since 1993. Overwhelmed by the high volume of cross-border traffic, U.S. port inspectors can realistically search only a small percentage of the trucks crossing the border. Enhanced border policing has also prompted smugglers to become more technologically sophisticated. Peter Skerry and Stephen Rockwell note that "as the Border Patrol pours more resources into night-vision scopes, weight sensors and giant X-ray machines for seeing into trucks, smuggling rings counter with their own state-of-the-art equipment paid for by increased [smuggling] fees" (1998).

Although many of the local freelance entrepreneurs who once dominated migrant smuggling along the border are being squeezed out by the border enforcement campaign, they are being replaced by better organized and more skilled smuggling organizations. One INS intelligence report suggests that many smuggling groups that were once based in the United States have relocated to the Mexican side, helping to insulate principal leaders from the grasp of American law enforcement (cited in U.S. General Accounting Office, 1997: 42). A federal task force has estimated that up to ten to twelve family-based smuggling organizations have come to dominate the trafficking of migrants across the border (*Migration News*, June 1998). Of course, it is easy to overstate these claims for political gain. One INS agent has even gone so far as to say that the border smugglers have become "huge, inter-locked cartels." Such threat inflation makes effective media sound bites even if the empirical evidence is thin (*Arizona Daily Star*, July 11, 1999).

Further complicating the challenge of organized migrant smuggling along the border has been an unintended result of U.S. efforts to deter the maritime smuggling of Asian migrants. As officials began to target the use of boats to smuggle Asian migrants into the country in 1993, much of the smuggling has been diverted to other routes, including land routes through Mexico. The arrival of Chinese smuggling boats (such as the *Golden Venture*) in 1993 attracted a great deal of media attention, sparking a quick law enforcement crackdown. Smugglers reacted by using less visible transportation methods and routes, which in turn has created more work for law enforcement officials. As Meissner noted, "We've stopped that illegal boat traffic, but there are still a lot of people coming from Asia, mainly through Central America and Mexico" (*New York Times*, May 30, 1996). Chinese pay up to thirty thousand dollars for the trip (ibid.). It should be noted that such long-distance smuggling of non-Mexicans is only a small part of migrant smuggling across the southwestern border, but it is by far the most profitable part of the business. For example, a typical boat from China landing in the northern Mexican state of Baja in 1993 carried human cargo worth $6 million (Rotella, 1998: 75–78).

As migrant smuggling has become a more organized and sophisticated enterprise in reaction to tighter controls, this has served to justify tougher laws and tougher enforcement. For example, Operation Disruption was initiated in May 1995 to target drop houses used by migrant smugglers in the San Diego area. The operation produced 120 arrests of smugglers and the uncovering of 117 drop houses (*Migration News*, February 2, 1996). The crackdown in San Diego has displaced much of the smuggling farther east to the Imperial Valley, as well as to Arizona. The Border Patrol, in turn, has responded with a nearly tenfold increase in the number of agents assigned to combat smuggling rings in the area (*Los Angeles Times,* May 10, 1998). Other federal agencies, such as the FBI, have also deployed new agents to the border in response to the increase in organized migrant smuggling (*Los Angeles Times,* May 29, 1996).

The number of smugglers prosecuted has mushroomed. In San Diego, for example, the busiest federal court in the country for migrant smuggling cases, prosecutions increased from 33 in 1993 to 233 in 1996 (U.S. Department of Justice, 1996). Nationally, the INS presented 1,547 principal smugglers for prosecution of alien smuggling violations in FY 1998—a 19 percent increase from the previous year (Bach, 1999). Tougher sentencing guidelines have significantly increased the length of prison terms for smugglers. The INS has also been given new enforcement powers to target organized smuggling, such as federal racketeering statutes and the authority to use wiretaps. On the Mexican side of the border, smugglers can now be given a ten-year prison sentence. In 1995, 700 smugglers were given prison terms in Mexico, almost a doubling of the 1994 total (*Migration News*, June 1996). Mexico has increased prison terms from five years with bond to up to twenty years without bond (*Arizona Daily Star,* July 11, 1999).

The border crackdown, however, has so far failed to cause a shortage of smugglers. One senior official from the Border Patrol's antismuggling unit has commented that the smugglers "just get paid more for taking more risks" (interview with author, U.S. Border Patrol, San Diego Sector Headquarters, April 8, 1997). And as the risks for smuggling have risen, so too has the incentive for smugglers to use more dangerous methods to avoid law enforcement. This partly explains the increase in high-speed chases and accidents that have resulted when smugglers try to circumvent INS checkpoints along the highways leading north from the border. It also helps explain a particularly creative but cruel smuggling trend: because the law does not allow jailing illegal migrants with children, children are sometimes bought, rented, or stolen to facilitate the crossing. The children are then often left to fend for themselves on the U.S. side (*Trafficking in Migrants,* June 1996).

Border corruption has also become a more serious problem. Increased enforcement has increased the need for smugglers to bribe or buy entry documents from those doing the enforcing. And as smuggling groups have become more sophisticated and profitable—as a consequence of the higher demand and cost for their services and the heightened risks involved in providing these services—the capacity and means to corrupt have also grown. In one well-known case at the San Ysidro port of entry south of San Diego, U.S. Customs inspector Guy Henry Kmett was arrested for helping a major smuggling ring move migrants through his inspection lane. The three vans busted in Kmett's lane carried Salvadorans, Guatemalans, Dominicans, and an Egyptian. Kmett came under suspicion after the Border Patrol noticed that the vans were parked at Kmett's house the day before. Kmett had spent about $100,000 in cash during the previous year on such items as a swimming pool, computers, and televisions. Law enforcement officials estimated that the Peraltas smuggling organization, which was trying to transport migrants through Kmett's lane, earned $1 million per month for smuggling one thousand migrants per month across the border (*Los Angeles Times,* February 5, 1995).

On the Mexican side of the border, there have been numerous cases of official corruption involving migrant smuggling (Rotella, 1998). In one high-profile case, the Mexican migration service's regional head in Tijuana, his deputy, and his chief inspector were all fired and charged with assisting the smuggling of non-Mexican migrants. The Tijuana office reportedly brought in as much as $70,000 weekly from the proceeds of migrant trafficking (*San Francisco Chronicle,* July 11, 1994). It has also been reported that Tijuana police have taken bribes that amount to as much as $40,000 a month to permit the operation of safe houses where migrants stay before attempting to cross into the United States (*Los Angeles Times,* February 5, 1995).

Conclusion

The relationship between law enforcers and law-evading migrant smugglers across the U.S.-Mexican borderline has been not only conflictive but in many ways symbiotic. The business of smuggling and the business of policing smuggling have grown up together. And they continue to expand because of each other. Each law enforcement move has provoked a law evasion countermove, which in turn has been matched by more enforcement. The future remains uncertain, but there is little indication that this enforcement-evasion dynamic will end any time soon.

While the focus here has been on the U.S.-Mexican border experience, it is important to emphasize that the interdependence between policing and smuggling is equally evident across other borders in other regions where new barriers have been built to deter unwanted immigration. This is perhaps most striking along the eastern and southern edges of the European Union, where the beefing up of border policing has been matched by the emergence of more expansive and organized migrant smuggling operations (Koslowski, 2000). National police bureaucracies and transnational smuggling organizations have been leading beneficiaries of the push by western powers to tighten their immigration controls. Building this "wall around the west" (Andreas and Snyder, 2000) will no doubt continue to fuel a thriving business for both law enforcers and law evaders.

NOTES

1. For a more detailed analysis, see Andreas (2000).

2. This case is an example of what the sociologist Gary Marx calls the interdependence between rule enforcers and rule breakers. See Marx (1981).

3. In 1952, Congress passed an act that made it illegal to "harbor, transport, or conceal illegal entrants." But employment was not considered harboring. This was the result of an amendment to the provision (called the Texas proviso), which was a concession to agribusiness interests (Calavita, 1994: 60).

4. For example, apprehensions by the Border Patrol in the San Diego sector fell from 531,000 in FY 1993 to 284,000 in FY 1997, but apprehensions to the east in the El Centro sector jumped from 30,000 to 146,000 in the same period (*Migration News*, July 1998).

REFERENCES

Andreas, Peter. 2000. *Border Games: Policing the U.S.-Mexico Divide*. Ithaca, N.Y.: Cornell University Press.

Andreas, Peter, and Timothy Snyder, eds. 2000. *The Wall around the West: State*

Borders and Immigration Controls in North America and Europe. Lanham, Md.: Rowman & Littlefield.

Bach, Robert. 1999. Executive Associate Commissioner for Policy and Planning, Immigration and Naturalization Service. Testimony before the House Judiciary Committee, Immigration and Claims Subcommittee, July 1.

Bean, Frank D., Randy Capps, and Charles W. Haynes. 1999. Testimony for the hearings of the Subcommittee on Immigration and Claims, Committee on the Judiciary, U.S. House of Representatives, February 25.

Bhagwati, Jagdish N. 1984. "Incentives and Disincentives: International Migration." *Weltwirtschaftliches Archiv* 120 (4): 678–704.

Binational Study on Migration. 1997. *Migration between Mexico and the United States: Binational Study.* Mexico City and Washington, D.C.: Mexican Foreign Ministry and U.S. Commission on Immigration Reform.

Calavita, Kitty. 1994. "U.S. Immigration and Policy Responses: The Limits of Legislation." In *Controlling Immigration: A Global Perspective,* edited by Wayne A. Cornelius, Philip L. Martin, and James Hollifield, 55–82. Stanford: Stanford University Press.

———. 1996. "The New Politics of Immigration: 'Balanced Budget Conservatism' and the Symbolism of Proposition 187." *Social Problems* 43 (3): 284–305.

Comptroller General of the United States. 1976. *Smugglers, Illicit Documents, and Schemes Are Undermining U.S. Controls over Immigration: Report to the Congress by the Comptroller General of the United States.* Washington, D.C., August 30.

Ekstrand, Laurie E. 1995. U.S. General Accounting Office. Testimony before the Subcommittee on Immigration and Claims, Committee on the Judiciary, U.S. House of Representatives, March 10.

Federal News Service. 1996. News Conference with Janet Reno and Doris Meissner, Washington, D.C., January 12.

Heyman, Josiah McC. 1995. "Putting Power into the Anthropology of Bureaucracy: The Immigration and Naturalization Service at the Mexico–United States Border." *Current Anthropology* 36 (2): 261–87.

Koslowski, Rey. 2000. "The Mobility Money Can Buy: Human Smuggling and Border Control in the European Union." In *The Wall around the West,* edited by Peter Andreas and Timothy Snyder. Lanham, Md.: Rowman and Littlefield.

Kossoudji, Sherrie A. 1992. "Playing Cat and Mouse at the U.S.-Mexican Border." *Demography* 29 (2): 159–90.

López Castro, Gustavo. 1998. "Coyotes and Alien Smuggling." In *Migration between Mexico and the United States: Binational Study.* Research Reports and Background Materials, vol. 3. Mexico City and Washington, D.C.: Mexican Ministry of Foreign Affairs and U.S. Commission on Immigration Reform.

Marx, Gary T. 1981. "Ironies of Social Control: Authorities as Contributors to Deviance through Escalation, Nonenforcement, and Covert Facilitation." *Social Problems* 28 (3): 221–46.

Massey, Douglas S. 1997. "March of Folly: U.S. Immigration Policy under NAFTA." Paper presented at the Meetings of the American Sociological Association, Toronto, Canada, August 8–13.

McDonald, William F. 1997. "Illegal Immigration: Crime, Ramifications, and Control (the American Experience)." In *Crime and Law Enforcement in the Global Village,* edited by William F. McDonald, 65–86. Cincinnati: Anderson Publishing Co.

Meissner, Doris. 1996. U.S. Commissioner of the Immigration and Naturalization Service. Testimony before the Commerce, Justice, State, and Judiciary Subcommittee of the Appropriations Committee, U.S. House of Representatives, May 8.

Metz, Leon C. 1989. *Border: The U.S.-Mexico Line.* El Paso, Tex.: Mangan Books.

Nevins, Joseph. 1998. "California Dreaming: Operation Gatekeeper and the Social Geographical Construction of the 'Illegal Alien' along the U.S.-Mexico Boundary." Ph.D. diss., University of California at Los Angeles.

Regan, George. 1997. Acting Associate Commissioner of Enforcement, Immigration and Naturalization Service. Testimony before the Subcommittee on Immigration Claims, Committee on the Judiciary, U.S. House of Representatives, April 23.

Reuter, Peter, and David Ronfeldt. 1991. *Quest for Integrity: The Mexican-U.S. Drug Issue in the 1980s.* Santa Monica, Calif.: RAND.

Rotella, Sebastian. 1998. *Twilight on the Line.* New York: Norton.

Skerry, Peter, and Stephen Rockwell. 1998. "The Cost of a Tighter Border: People-Smuggling Networks." *Los Angeles Times,* May 3.

Stoddard, Ellwyn. 1976. "Illegal Mexican Labor in the Borderlands: Institutionalized Support for an Unlawful Practice." *Pacific Sociological Review* 19 (2): 175–210.

Suro, Robert. 1998. "Tightening Controls and Changing Flows: Evaluating the INS Border Enforcement Strategy." *Research Perspectives on Migration* 2 (1). Carnegie Endowment for International Peace.

Teitelbaum, Michael. 1980. "Right versus Right: Immigration and Refugee Policy—the United States." *Foreign Affairs* 59 (1): 21–59.

U.S. Border Patrol. 1994. "Border Patrol Strategic Plan 1994 and Beyond: National Strategy." U.S. Border Patrol, Washington, D.C., July.

U.S. Department of Justice. 1996. *Annual Report of the Office of the United States Attorney, Southern District of California.* Washington, D.C.: U.S. Department of Justice.

U.S. General Accounting Office. 1997. *Illegal Immigration: Southwest Border Strategy Results Inconclusive; More Evaluation Needed.* Washington, D.C.: GPO, December.

PART II

Case Studies: Mexico, Russia, and China

5 ▪▪▪▪▪▪▪ Smuggling Migrants through South Texas: Challenges Posed by Operation Rio Grande

David Spener

In this chapter, I report preliminary findings from a research project that explores how migrant smugglers known as *coyotes* or *pateros* continue to move undocumented migrants through the south Texas–northeastern Mexico border region despite concerted efforts of U.S. authorities to stop them. The purpose of the research is to bring these central players in the migration process out of the shadows, where they have traditionally lurked, and into the light, where their functional roles and modes of operation can be subjected to critical examination and reflection. Engaging in such critical analysis based upon empirical data is needed in order to avoid having our understanding of the migration process distorted in significant ways by reliance on conjecture, stereotype, and myth with regard to who smugglers are and what they do. This is especially important today as U.S. immigration authorities have come to regard smugglers as their "public enemy number one" and undocumented Mexican migrants contract their services in ever greater numbers.

The Regional Context

This section of the U.S.-Mexican border region is of special interest to the study of smuggling for several reasons. First, the process of undocumented migration along this stretch of the border has been less well documented in the research literature than it has in the Tijuana–San Diego corridor. This is ironic given that a pioneering work in the contemporary study of undocumented migration from Mexico—Julian Samora's *Los Mojados*—was researched there in the late 1960s and hundreds of thousands of migrants have passed through the region every year since its publication. Although Tijuana–San Diego has traditionally been the busiest and most dramatic crossing point for undocumented Mexicans, its geographical characteristics are very different from those obtaining elsewhere. Because of this, there are limits to generalizing findings about the phenomenon of unauthorized crossing into southern California to other portions of the border. Now that a substantial portion of the undocumented flow has been rerouted away from San Diego as a consequence of Operation Gatekeeper, it becomes all the more important to consider how the characteristics of other stretches of the border influence the process of undocumented migration, including the role played by smuggling enterprises.

In addition, the south Texas–northeastern Mexico border has its own unique characteristics that set it apart from other subregions along the border and make it an especially fruitful place for studying the business of migrant smuggling. Unlike Alta and Baja California, it is a large, difficult-to-patrol region that is relatively isolated from major population centers in Mexico or in the United States. Also unlike most of the rest of the border, this region features a particularly high level of cross-border social, cultural, and economic interdependence. More than a quarter of south Texas residents were born in Mexico and together with U.S.-born Mexican Americans make up more than 80 percent of the population of Texas border counties. Relatedly, members of many families residing on one side of the border have immediate or extended family members living on the opposite side with whom they are in regular contact. These cross-border family networks have historically formed the basis for a great deal of commercial activity in the region. Much of this activity has involved the movement of various types of contraband, including undocumented migrants. These geographical and social characteristics combine to create a more daunting context for U.S. border control efforts than elsewhere.

Research Methods

Findings reported in this chapter are based upon a review of the relevant academic and journalistic literature on the smuggling of Mexicans through the region, data published by the Immigration and Naturalization Service and the Administrative Office of the U.S. Federal Court System, and records of about two dozen smuggling cases prosecuted in San Antonio and Brownsville. In addition, I conducted field interviews in San Antonio, Laredo, McAllen, Harlingen, Brownsville, Nuevo Laredo, Reynosa, and Matamoros in July 1998, in Laredo-Nuevo Laredo in March 1999, and in Monterrey in July 1999. My informants included Border Patrol agents, assistant U.S. attorneys, U.S. public defenders, immigration attorneys, human rights activists, recruiters for smugglers, and two coyotes themselves, as well as several migrants who had been smuggled on one or more occasions. Unlike Conover (1987), I did not engage in participant observation of smuggler-led crossings of the Río Bravo or treks through the south Texas brush country. I have not yet, in this preliminary stage of my study of smuggling activities, conducted systematic interviews with Mexican migrants about their experiences crossing the border aided by smugglers. Rather, I have relied primarily upon the accounts of the other types of informants mentioned above who also have in-depth knowledge of smuggling practices.

Analytic Framework

As noted by Rodríguez (1996), the Mexican transnational migrant community is currently engaged in a veritable "battle for the border" with U.S. government forces. In this battle, Mexican weapons are primarily social—a complex web of relationships spanning the border that have been built up over the course of more than a century of labor migration to the United States. U.S. government weapons, on the other hand, are mainly paramilitary and bureaucratic. Until recently, they have not seemed particularly effective. Since 1965, the number of unauthorized Mexican migrants who have successfully penetrated the U.S. southern border has grown at an exponential rate (Massey and Singer, 1995). By the mid-1990s, more than 7 million Mexican nationals had settled in the United States, most of them having entered the United States illegally at the outset (Binational Study, 1997). As noted by scholars such as Massey et al. (1987), Rouse (1991), and Smith (1995), these Mexican nationals remained active in their communities of origin, returning frequently, assisting friends and kin who wished to join them to live and work in *el norte,* and sending important cash remittances back home (Lozano Ascencio, 1993). Nearing the century's end, Mexican migrants seemed to have nearly "disappeared" the border separating their country from the United States and in so doing called into question its functional logic (Spener and Staudt, 1998).

In 1993, the U.S. government launched a counteroffensive against Mexican migrants in an attempt to reassert control over its territory adjacent to Mexico. This "rebordering" effort has taken the form of a massive increase in the number of Border Patrol agents policing the international boundary, backed up by an unprecedented battery of technologically sophisticated surveillance and population control equipment (Andreas, this volume, Chap. 4; Spener and Staudt, 1998). It has made unauthorized entry into U.S. territory considerably more difficult for migrants, though it has not yet halted their march northward. In the face of this counteroffensive, Mexicans have had to develop new strategies for crossing the border utilizing the same social resources that have traditionally propelled them. Logically, these strategies include a renewed reliance upon a renowned figure on the border: the coyote, or smuggler of human contraband.

Coyotes have come to play a crucial role in the current battle for the border by assisting millions of Mexicans to live out their "crossover dreams" in the United States. Recent research evidence suggests that the majority of undocumented migrants from Mexico enter the United States for the first time with the assistance of a smuggler (Casillas Bermúdez, 1998; López Castro, 1998; Singer and Massey, 1998). Migrant smuggling is an informal, for-profit business whose success depends upon the same general set of transborder social networks and sociocultural capital as the migrant community itself. Mexican participation in informal economic activities both north and south of the border is well documented in the social science literature (see, for example, Escobar, 1986, and Vélez-Ibáñez, 1983). As Staudt (1998: 161) notes, when such informal activities begin to transcend and transgress the border, they have the potential to become *counterhegemonic practices* that challenge the state's "propaganda, rules, and surveillance."

This politicized view of informal activity as a challenge to the state's power to regulate the population is especially salient for analyzing the operation of the migrant smuggling business on the border because it challenges one of the nation-state's most basic prerogatives: the right to regulate foreign access to its territory. The informal economic activity of the smuggling enterprise at the border not only challenges the hegemony of a single state, however. It also poses a challenge to the hegemony of the international system of states—the *world* system—by contributing to the development, maintenance, and extension of transnational communities. These communities, as Portes (1996: 164) notes, have the potential to subvert one of that system's central premises, namely, "that labor stays put and that its reference point for wages and work conditions remain local" while capital transcends national boundaries and enjoys a global reference point for investment conditions. This premise is reflected in the policies of the Clinton administration, which simultaneously promotes "free trade" with Mexico while trumpeting the fact that it has "taken a strong stand to stiffen the protection of our borders" by "increasing border controls by 50 percent" (from President Clinton's 1996 State of the Union address, cited in Andreas, 1996: 53). Not surprisingly, part of the administration's increased border control consists of trying to put alien smuggling rings out of business by imprisoning their members following capture by the Border Patrol. Indeed, the Immigration and Naturalization Service recently announced that it would step back from raids of workplaces in the U.S. interior in order to redeploy enforcement resources to the breaking up of international smuggling enterprises, including those along the southwestern border (Alonso-Zaldívar, 1999).

As I argue further below, it may be difficult to put entire smuggling enterprises out of business through criminal prosecution because most of their members are not engaged in the transportation of migrants on U.S. territory in areas that are heavily patrolled by the immigration authorities. Moreover, smuggling enterprises do not just feed off or prey upon the migrant stream. Rather, they themselves are an integrated part of it. These enterprises are structured around tightly bound, transborder networks of trust that link Mexican immigrants in the U.S. interior to friends and kin in the Mexican border cities, the Texas border cities, and the migrant sending regions in Mexico's interior. This does not necessarily mean that migrants being smuggled and their smugglers are linked to one another in the same networks of kinship and *compadrazgo*—although some certainly are—but rather that the activities of both are structured by similar bonds resulting from the migration process itself. These bonds, in turn, constitute both the migrants' and the smugglers' principal resource in countering the hegemony of the U.S. government's border control policies.

Types of Smugglers and Smuggling Operations

The objective of the migrant smuggling enterprise along the so-called Tex-Mex border, whether a single individual or an organization, is to deliver undocumented migrants safely to their U.S. destination in return for monetary payment. Smugglers have devised a variety of strategies for achieving this objective and offer a panoply of specific services to migrants, which are summarized in table 2. The fees charged to migrants vary depending upon the specific set of services included and their quality. A number of types of smuggling operations move migrants through the south Texas–northeastern Mexico border region. Some offer a comprehensive menu of services listed in table 2, while others specialize in only one or two. A smuggling enterprise may consist of a single individual or may involve the coordination of dozens of persons from a base along the border or in a city or town in the Texas interior. Its operation may depend strictly upon supply and demand and cash transactions or may center primarily on facilitating the migration of townsfolk and kin from a particular sending community in Mexico. For purposes of simplification, it is useful to classify smuggling enterprises into four basic types.

Type I: *Pateros*

These smugglers (known on the Tamaulipas-Texas border as *pateros*) dedicate themselves exclusively to leading migrants across the Río Grande. They do not organize movement farther into the Texas interior,

Table 2. Menu of Services Provided by Smugglers to Mexican Migrants

In Mexico	In the United States
Organization of a party of migrants in sending community in Mexican interior	Purchase of airline tickets and transportation to airport in Harlingen or Laredo
Arrangement of bus or other transportation to town on U.S. border	Guided passage on foot into Texas border town to evade detection/apprehension by U.S. Border Patrol and to avoid assault and robbery
Assembly of a party of migrants in a Mexican border town	
Lodging in hotel or other private dwelling in Mexican border town while awaiting departure	Lodging in safe house in a Texas community
	Guided passage on foot through south Texas brush country to evade highway checkpoints and detection/apprehension by the U.S. Border Patrol
Sale or rental of forged or fraudulent documents	
Crossing of the Rio Bravo del Norte	Motor vehicle transport (car, van, truck, or tractor trailer) to San Antonio, Dallas, or Houston
	Rail freight car transport to San Antonio
	Lodging in safe house in San Antonio, Dallas, or Houston
	Arrangement or provision of transportation to other points in U.S. interior
	Delivery to employer in United States

although they may routinely work in concert with larger smuggling organizations that do. At the present time, their services are probably of limited utility to long-distance migrants, since the main challenge facing these migrants is not getting into south Texas but getting *through* it on their way to interior U.S. destinations. This type of smuggler can frequently be found loitering around international bridges in addition to the bus stations of Mexican border cities. Migrants who are unaware of the realities of the journey they have undertaken are often victimized by these smugglers, who take their money in advance, lead them across the river, and abandon them to their fate once on the Texas side. This fate usually includes quick apprehension by the Border Patrol and often includes assault and worse by bandits who lurk in the darkness near the river on the U.S. side. A frequent complaint is that the assailants in these cases include the smugglers themselves.

Type II: Local-Interior Coyotes

Gustavo López Castro (1998) of the Colegio de Michoacán describes these smugglers as natives of towns and cities in the traditional migrant sending states of Guanajuato, Michoacán, Zacatecas, San Luís Potosí, and Jalisco. Known to residents of the region where they live as experienced guides, local-interior coyotes, often with an assistant or two, lead small groups of five or six migrants on an occasional basis. Their knowledge of crossing routes and ways to avoid apprehension by U.S. authorities has been gained from their own experiences as migrants. These guides typically accompany the group on its entire voyage to the final destination in the United States, using their knowledge of terrain in the border region to help the group cross the river and bypass checkpoints on roadways in south Texas. These smugglers do not usually arrange for private vehicle transportation out of the border region, instead relying on buses or freight trains.

According to López Castro, the principal advantage to working with this type of smuggler is that he is known in the sending community as honest, reliable, and concerned with the safety of those traveling with him.[1] A second advantage is that costs are kept to a minimum because the smuggling operation is simple and involves few people. In addition, unlike working through a border *patero,* advance payment for services is not typically required. Instead, payment is made upon arrival in the final U.S. destination city, either by friends/family members of the migrant in that city or by relatives in the sending community. A disadvantage under the present conditions of intensified border control by U.S. authorities is that this type of smuggler, because he does not live on the border, may not be able to monitor the day-to-day deployment of Border Patrol agents and equipment along the river. Thus, the likelihood of migrants being apprehended in Texas immediately after crossing the border may be higher than if they worked through a smuggler based on the border itself. At the same time, interviews I conducted in Monterrey in July 1999 indicated that some local-interior coyotes have partners/accomplices at the border itself, who may also be involved with commercial smuggling operations (see Type IV below); these partners enable them to overcome this disadvantage.

Type III: Friends and Kin

One of the major findings of the research literature on international migration in general, and Mexican migration to the United States in particular, is that migrants rely on social networks in the receiving country to ease the way for their own migration and settlement. Not surprisingly, some Mexican migrants to the United States count on friends and family members to guide them through the obstacles facing them at the border (Singer and Massey, 1998). In addition to being accompanied on their journey by experienced kin, some migrants who have crossed the river on their own or with the assistance of a *patero* may be picked up in private vehicles by friends or family members who are legal residents of the United States (see Pérez, 1991: 48–51). Although there are no reliable data indicating how common it is for friends and kin to move undocumented Mexicans through south Texas in this manner, it seems likely that the practice is less common now than it may have been in the past. The region is much more heavily patrolled by Border Patrol agents, and it is difficult to find a highway route north that one can drive without passing through an INS checkpoint. In addition, penalties for immigration law violations have increased substantially since the passage of the Illegal Immigration Reform and Immigrant Responsibility Act of 1996 (IRIRA). On the other hand, the ready availability of high-quality false documents, including resident alien cards, Social Security cards, and driver's licenses (see Immigration and Naturalization Service, 1998a and 1998b), may make it easier for legal U.S. residents to move their undocumented friends and kin through the south Texas border region in this manner.

Type IV: Border Commercial Smugglers

This type of smuggling operation is the most prominent along the Mexico–south Texas border and probably moves more migrants through the region than any of the other types. Commercial smugglers may be large or small scale, tightly or loosely organized, high tech or low tech, and high priced or relatively cheap. The clientele served by these enterprises may come to them through established regional social networks or through recruitment of strangers at the local bus terminal. With regard to Tijuana and migrant streams emanating from central western Mexico, López Castro (1998) distinguishes between two types of smuggling operations located in Mexican border communities. One type, which he calls "local and border," is run by a person who is from a traditional migrant sending community and specializes in moving people from that region on a relatively ad hoc basis, i.e., that is, in response to occasional demand from that specific community. The other type, which he refers to as "border business coyotes," is a professional organization dedicated to providing well-executed smuggling services to all migrants who wish to cross, whether they are referred by other migrants or are recruited directly by the organization at the bus stations of Mexican border towns.

Although distinguishing between these two ideal types has some heuristic value, it may tend to oversimplify the variety of commercial enterprises that offer smuggling services in the region. Smugglers who begin by moving small groups of migrants from their own hometowns on an ad hoc basis may expand and professionalize. Other commercial smugglers may work full-time at their enterprise, recruit strangers from the bus station, but offer a quality of service that is no better than the part-timer serving hometown migrants. Some commercial smuggling enterprises are vertically integrated with a centralized command and control structure, while others consist of individuals who come together on a flexible basis to move a particular party of migrants. This flexibility can also make it difficult to regard commercial smuggling enterprises as being "based" at the border itself, since a given trip may be organized from either the Mexican or the Texas interior and participants in the enterprise may travel from their base either toward or away from the border (see Type II above). Thus, at least in the south Texas–northeastern Mexico border region, it is probably best to view "commercial smugglers" as a single category consisting of a variety of organizational arrangements that range along a continuum of size and sophistication. Because commercial smuggling operations appear to be the most important to moving undocumented Mexican migrants through the border region at this time, I focus on their operations in the remainder of this chapter.[2]

Methods of Moving Undocumented Mexicans through the South Texas Border Region

Commercial smuggling operations along this section of the border have been described in brief passages in several books, including Julian Samora's *Los Mojados* (1971), Ted Conover's *Coyotes* (1987), Ramón Perez's *Diary of an Undocumented Immigrant* (1991), and Daniel Rothenberg's *With These Hands* (1998). Findings from research I conducted in the Texas-Tamaulipas border region in July and August 1998 indicate that the methods of operation of commercial smugglers had not changed remarkably since 1969, when Samora and his colleagues were in the field. Figure 3 illustrates the stages through which the typical smuggled migrant party passes.

The journey as "human contraband" begins for most migrants when they arrive by bus in a Mexican border city such as Matamoros, Reynosa, or Nuevo Laredo; they are met at the bus station by smugglers' recruiters or go to a hotel, bar, or restaurant frequented or operated by smugglers. At this time, services offered and price charged are negotiated. Some portion of the total fee charged is paid by the migrant up front to cover the costs of the *brinco,* or immediate "hop," across the border. Typically, the deposit covers any repeat attempts needed to get through the Border Patrol forces amassed immediately along the border on the Texas side. Then a call is typically made to a friend or relative of the migrant in the final destination of the smuggling trip, typically San Antonio, Houston, or Dallas. The contact in the destination city "responds" for the migrant, agreeing to pay the balance of his or her smuggling fee when the group arrives.

Next, the migrant or group of migrants waits in a hotel or other lodging for the smugglers to form a complete crossing party and to identify the best place to cross the river into Texas. Where the best place is at any given time is determined by "scouts" stationed along the Mexican bank of the Río Bravo del Norte/Río Grande who observe the day-to-day and hour-to-hour changes in deployment of the Border Patrol across the river.

Stage 1   **Communities in the Mexican interior**
- Migrants recruited by smugglers' representatives
- Migrants contact smugglers at border
- Respondents contacted by migrants

Stage 2   **Bus terminal**
- Migrants recruited by "greeters"
- Referred/taken to hotel/residence where group is to be assembled

Stage 3   **Hotel/private residence**
- Crossing party assembled
- Initial crossing fees collected
- Respondents contacted
- Migrants await departure

Stage 4   **International bridge/riverbank**
- Scouts observe Border Patrol activities
- Some migrants recruited
- Some returned migrants received
- Some early A.M./night crossings attempted

Stage 5   **River crossing**
- Migrants taken across river by local guide (swimming, wading, inner tube, or raft)
- Migrants led to safe house or to nearby point in United States where met by guide

Stage 6   **Point of unauthorized U.S. entry**
- Migrants received by local/long-distance guide
- Guide takes migrant to safe house or on trek to auto pickup point

Stage 7   **Safe house**
- Local guides deliver migrants
- Respondents contacted
- Migrants housed and fed
- Migrants picked up by guides or driven to site where guide awaits in order to be led around Border Patrol checkpoints

Stage 8   **Auto pickup points**
- Guides deliver migrants
- Drivers pick up/escort migrants
- Guides return south or accompany migrants to drop house

Fig. 3a Activities at Each Stage of the Commercial Smuggling Process

Stage 9　　　　　　**Safe house/drop house in Texas interior city**
- Respondents contacted
- Migrants housed and fed
- Remaining fees collected
- Migrants released to respondents

Fig. 3a *(Continued)*

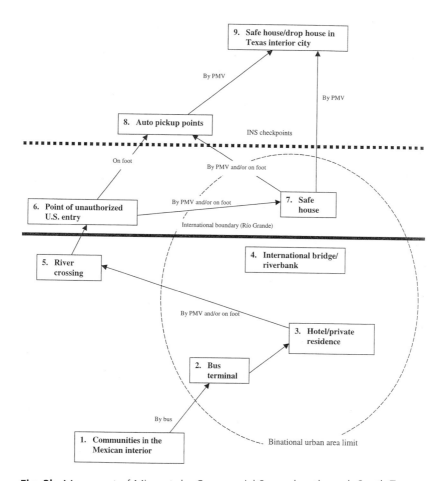

Fig. 3b. Movement of Migrants by Commercial Smugglers through South Texas, Summer 1998

Note: PMV = private motor vehicle.

When the group is completely formed and the best crossing spot is chosen, migrants are transported in cars, vans, or pickup trucks to the river, where they make a hurried crossing, usually at night. Crossing may involve wading through a shallow spot; swimming, sometimes with aid of inner tubes or inflatable rafts; or being rowed to the opposite bank in a launch. It should also be noted that Mexican police patrol the Mexican bank of the river in urban areas and frequently detain smugglers and their migrants, sometimes arresting them (migrant smuggling is against the law in Mexico). Thus, smugglers who routinely cross migrants typically must reach an accommodation with local authorities, usually in the form of cutting police in on some portion of revenues.

Upon crossing the river into Texas, the group of migrants may be guided on foot or taken by motor vehicle to a safe house operated by the smugglers. Migrants may spend several days and nights in one of these houses waiting to head farther into the Texas interior by motor vehicle or on foot.[3] Whether or not migrants are led to a safe house near the border, the next leg of the journey involves moving the migrant party out of the heavily patrolled border region. This is most typically accomplished by leading migrants on foot through the brush country around INS checkpoints on the highways headed away from the border. Once past these checkpoints, migrants are picked up in private motor vehicles and driven to a city in the Texas interior.[4] Alternatively, migrants may be hidden in car trunks or in small, commercial truck compartments and sneaked through highway checkpoints (most vehicles are not thoroughly inspected). Although the practice does not appear to be common, in the last two years some smuggling organizations have begun to move large groups (fifty or more migrants) out of the border region in tractor-trailer compartments (see, e.g., Schiller, 1999a). In addition, smugglers in the freight yards of Laredo and Brownsville continue to load migrants into locked rail cars on trains headed north, despite the fact that the Border Patrol and train companies have cracked down on the practice.

Once a group is out of the border region, its likelihood of being detained by immigration authorities is minimal.[5] Upon arrival in San Antonio, Dallas, or Houston, migrants are taken to a safe house, where their respondents are contacted. After the remaining fees are collected, migrants are released into the community. In some cases, migrants whose own employment or that of their respondents can be verified are allowed to pay their fee in installments after their release.

Changing Cost and Risk Factors Owing to Heightened Control Efforts

Since 1993, the United States has dramatically intensified its efforts to diminish illegal migration across its southern border with Mexico. These efforts include massive increases in personnel and equipment available to the Border Patrol to block unauthorized border crossing and to apprehend migrants who enter U.S. territory without official authorization. The size of the Border Patrol has grown to more than nine thousand agents, more than double the number of agents in FY 1993 (Schiller, 1999b). A series of operations—Hold-the-Line in the El Paso sector, Gatekeeper in San Diego, Safeguard in Arizona, and Rio Grande in Texas between Del Río and Brownsville—have significantly enhanced the Border Patrol's ability to deter illegal entry by migrants in urban areas abutting the international line. Elements of the operations include redeployment of agents and vehicles to the international line itself; the installation of lights, sensors, and video surveillance equipment; the construction of new walls and fences along the border; the expansion of detention facilities; and the introduction of the IDENT computerized database, which permits U.S. authorities to identify repeat illegal entrants by their fingerprints.

In addition to increasing the capacity of the Border Patrol to prevent entry by and detain unauthorized migrants, in 1994 the U.S. Department of Justice initiated a policy of more vigorously prosecuting immigration law violations. In 1996, the Illegal Immigration Reform and Immigrant Responsibility Act significantly increased penalties for alien smuggling and illegal entry into the United States. Illegal entry by itself is a misdemeanor; illegal entry following conviction of misdemeanor illegal entry is a felony and carries a jail term of up to five years in prison. This prosecution is aided by the IDENT system, which has enabled the Border Patrol to identify persons who have been repeatedly apprehended by its agents. Oftentimes, alien smugglers are prosecuted for felony illegal entry rather than for "harboring and transporting" illegal aliens, since this charge is easier to prove (see below) and can now by itself result in a substantial jail sentence. In Texas, intensified prosecution of immigration crimes has resulted in a trebling of felony alien smuggling convictions and an eightfold increase in felony illegal reentry convictions (Spener, forthcoming).

In October 1997, the Immigration and Naturalization Service (INS) produced an on-line report titled "Cracking Down on Alien Smuggling" (Immigration and Naturalization Service, 1997c). In this report, the INS outlined several effects that its new border control efforts were having on the business of alien smuggling that are relevant to the concerns of this chapter:

1. Increased border enforcement has made it harder to cross than ever before and has boosted illegal migrants' reliance on smugglers.
2. As the demand for smugglers has gone up, the price of alien smuggling has increased as well. Along the southwestern border, fees charged by smugglers have doubled in many areas, and in some cases have increased from $250 to $900.
3. As the price for alien smuggling goes up, so too does the potential for exploitation and abuse. As INS enforcement has increased, so has the ruthlessness of the smugglers.
4. While many smuggling operations along the southwestern border are still locally run, alien smuggling rings now are often connected with international criminal syndicates engaged in other illegal activities including illicit drug trafficking, prostitution, money laundering, and financial fraud.

In the remainder of this section, I examine each of these claimed effects against the evidence I have been able to gather in recent years. I wish to emphasize that my discussion is limited only to the movement of *Mexican* migrants by smuggling organizations based in the border region itself. Although migrants from Central America, Asia, Eastern Europe, and Africa are smuggled through the south Texas–northeastern Mexico border region, their numbers are quite small relative to the number of Mexicans who are smuggled. Moreover, I wish to draw some distinctions between the characteristics of the smuggling process involving Mexicans and those reported elsewhere for groups from other parts of the world. I would also like to make clear that this discussion applies only to the south

Texas–northeastern Mexico stretch of the U.S.-Mexican border, from Brownsville-Matamoros to Del Río–Ciudad Acuña, not to other sections of the border. As has been argued elsewhere (see Staudt and Spener, 1998), the U.S.-Mexican border region is a heterogeneous space within which local conditions vary substantially. In the case of border control, unauthorized migration, and the operation of smuggling enterprises, this internal heterogeneity must be taken into account in the analysis so as not to make erroneous generalizations. Finally, I wish to make clear that the situation "on the ground" in south Texas is dynamic; findings reported here are valid only through early 1999. Subsequent changes in the elements constituting Operation Rio Grande may well alter the context for migrant smuggling in Texas.

Effect 1. Increased border enforcement has made it harder to cross than ever before and has boosted illegal migrants' reliance on smugglers.

There is little room for doubt that it is considerably more difficult to enter the United States illegally away from official ports of entry in south Texas than it was before the buildup of the Border Patrol force in the region. This buildup began in the early 1990s, was intensified with the launching of Operation Rio Grande in the summer of 1997, and continued throughout 1998 as an additional 600–700 agents were added to the force patrolling the Texas-Mexico border. Formerly, it was relatively easy to cross the border in or near urbanized, heavily populated areas and "disappear" into the downtown or residential areas of Texas border cities such as Laredo or Brownsville. Now, the buildup of agents and equipment along the international line in these areas has made apprehension more likely and has forced migrants to make their crossings in more remote places. The need to make nocturnal river crossings and travel through harsh, hazardous, and unknown terrain for considerable distances once in Texas surely increases the utility of a smuggler's services, especially to inexperienced migrants.

Nonetheless, studies of Mexican migration and border-crossing practices prior to the launching of new border control initiatives and operations in 1993 and 1994 suggest that some caveats need to be placed on the finding that migrants now rely on smugglers to a considerably greater extent than they did in the past. First, we must distinguish between local and long-distance migrants. Many residents of Mexican border cities and towns "commute" illegally to work or to conduct other affairs on the U.S. side of the border (Alegría Olazábal, 1992; Herzog, 1990; Martínez, 1994). Other Mexicans reside illegally in a U.S. border town but routinely visit friends and family on the Mexican side, making their return crossings to the U.S. side away from authorized ports of entry. These local migrants make up a large proportion of persons apprehended by the Border Patrol in Texas.[6] Local migrants are generally quite familiar with places to cross, practices of the Border Patrol in the area, and the best times and strategies for making an illegal crossing. They are much less likely to employ a smuggler to make their crossing than are long-distance migrants who are less knowledgeable about local conditions.

A recently published study of the border-crossing practices of long-distance undocumented migrants suggests another distinction that may be made among this group as well. Using data collected retrospectively from male household heads from interior regions in Mexico for the years 1977 through 1994, Singer and Massey (1998) found that although migrants' reliance upon smugglers increased in tandem with the intensity of border control efforts, experienced migrants and migrants who had been apprehended previously by the Border Patrol were considerably less likely than other undocumented migrants to purchase the services of a smuggler to enter the United States illegally. Following Heyman (1995), the authors argue that undocumented migrants who have been apprehended a number of times by the Border Patrol realize that apprehension has few negative consequences for them other than a few hours of lost time. Such migrants are routinely sent back across the border into Mexico after having consented to a "voluntary departure" order, that is, without having to be detained while waiting for the completion of formal deportation proceedings. Thus, experienced migrants realize that paying a smuggler a fee to cross, even in situations in which apprehension is likely, is not necessarily worthwhile. The provisions of IRIRA that increase criminal penalties for illegally entering United States, the introduction of the IDENT system to identify repeat illegal entrants, and the Department of Justice's new commitment to vigorous prosecution of immigration law violations are all designed to change this "voluntary departure complex" by assessing misdemeanor criminal penalties for repeated apprehension by immigration authorities. Subsequent arrest for illegal entry can lead to the filing of felony charges. To the extent that the "voluntary departure complex" can be overturned through these measures, we might expect an increased demand for smugglers' services as a consequence, as well as increased risk of prosecution for felony illegal entry to smugglers themselves.

At present, however, it would appear that there are simply not sufficient resources in terms of prosecutors, magistrates, or available INS detention or federal jail space to threaten most migrants and smugglers entering Texas with probable criminal prosecution and incarceration for entering Texas illegally. In FY 1998, the Border Patrol made 563,783 apprehensions of migrants along the Texas-Mexico border (Immigration and Naturalization Service, 1999). That same year, 15,479 defendants were prosecuted for misdemeanor immigration crimes (mainly illegal entry) in the Texas border region, and another 2,586 faced prosecution for immigration felonies (Administrative Office of the U.S. Courts, 1998a, 1998b). Thus, less than 4 percent of apprehensions in Texas resulted in criminal cases being prosecuted. Clearly, the INS and federal prosecutors are exercising a great deal of discretion regarding whom to prosecute, with the vast majority facing no criminal penalties for their illegal actions. And, of course, a substantial proportion of unauthorized border crossings do not result in apprehension at all. At the same time, intensified prosecution of immigration crimes has placed a substantial strain on the federal court system as a whole (Patrick, n.d.) and on the federal courts along the Texas border in particular (Schiller and Robbins, 1999).

If we disregard the effects of previous border-crossing experience on undocumented migrants' decision-making process and presume that increased enforcement efforts have, in fact, increased the demand for smugglers' services, we are still left with the question of the magnitude of this increased demand. Here, again, Singer and Massey's (1998) findings are instructive. In their data—which cover the period *before* the implementation of most of the elements of the United States' new border control initiative—80 percent of migrants' first illegal trips and 70 percent of subsequent trips from 1977 through 1994 were made with the assistance of a smuggler. In other words, a substantial majority of illegal border crossing trips made by Mexican men from interior sending communities already depended upon a smuggler, raising the question of just how big an increase in demand for smuggling services was possible in response to tighter border enforcement.[7]

Effect 2. Increased border enforcement has led to dramatic increases in smugglers' fees.

The INS reports that increased border control efforts in recent years have led to substantial increases in the prices that undocumented migrants must pay to smugglers in order to enter the United States. Along the Arizona-Mexico border, an INS progress report notes that fees charged by smugglers has risen from $150–200 to $400–500 (Immigration and Naturalization Service, 1997a) A similar report on Operation Gatekeeper states that smuggling fees charged to migrants in southern California doubled and even tripled in some cases as a response to the operation (Immigration and Naturalization Service, 1997b). The INS reports that "elsewhere" smuggling fees have risen from $250 to $900 (Immigration and Naturalization Service, 1997c).

There are several reasons to expect the price of smuggling services to rise. First, increased patrolling of the border results in a higher probability of apprehension of migrants, including those being smuggled. This results in smugglers having to make repeated attempts to get groups through the Border Patrol's lines of defense. Second, the Border Patrol's strategy of saturating the urbanized portions of the border forces smugglers to lead migrants through more remote areas, resulting in longer trips requiring more elaborate coordination among members of the smuggling organization as well as increased capital investments. Increased efforts required by smugglers to get migrants through the border region lead them to charge more for their services. Third, smugglers are more likely than ever before to be apprehended by the Border Patrol and prosecuted with either felony illegal entry or alien smuggling, both of which carry much stiffer criminal penalties than previously. Fourth, it is now easier for prosecutors to seize vehicles and other assets used to transport aliens unlawfully, increasing the risk of financial loss to smugglers. Fifth, and finally, the increased capital investments associated with the smuggling enterprise will force smaller operators out of business and raise substantial barriers to entry to those seeking to enter the business. As a consequence, competition among smugglers is reduced, and the larger smuggling rings are free to charge higher prices for their services.

Surprisingly, my preliminary investigation did not produce evidence of a dramatic, unequivocal, across-the-board increase in smuggling fees charged to migrants since Operation Rio Grande's implementation.[8] The limited data I have been able to collect suggest that real prices charged to migrants generally fell from the late 1960s through the mid-1990s. Since the imposition of Operation Rio Grande in August 1997, the upper range of the distribution of prices charged seems to have risen considerably, to as much as $1,500, while through the mid-1990s the upper range of prices was less than $800. At the same time, even in 1999, I found fees in the range of $300-800 per person for a trip from the Tamaulipas border to San Antonio, Houston, Austin, or Dallas. The wide range in fees charged to migrants probably results from variations in the type and quality of service being provided—means of river crossing, car, van, or truck versus rail transportation out of south Texas, safe houses provided in Texas border cities, bribes paid to U.S. officials, rental of fraudulent documents, et cetera. Even if we presume that the average cost for an average trip across the border doubled from, say, $500 preoperation to $1,000 postoperation, we should bear in mind that the absolute increase was not of such a magnitude that it was likely to deter many migrants from making the trip. With the U.S. economy booming and most trips financed by loans from friends and relatives already in the country, the price difference could be earned quite quickly upon finding employment north of the border.

Why would south Texas smuggling fees be lower in the eighties and early nineties than in the late 1960s? Since Border Patrol presence in south Texas did not decline during the period, there does not appear to be a prima facie case to be made that the border was more heavily guarded in the late 1960s. Rather, we presume that the enormous increase in volume of Mexican migrants through the region tended to reduce the demand for smugglers' services in two ways. First, growth in the number of undocumented migrants relative to growth in the number of Border Patrol agents in the region may have decreased the odds of apprehension for migrants.[9] Second, the human, social, and cultural capital accumulated by Mexican transnational communities may have made it increasingly possible for migrants to negotiate the border without resorting to the services of a commercial smuggler. This accumulation of capital would facilitate the transmission of knowledge in the form of best routes to follow, ways of evading the Border Patrol and other more serious hazards (e.g., drowning, exposure, assault by thieves), the "rules of engagement" regarding apprehension, detention, and voluntary departure, and so on. It would also allow migrants already in the states to themselves assist in moving incoming friends and kin through the heavily patrolled region of south Texas with or without the use of false documents.[10]

How, though, do we explain the apparent lack of a consistently large rise in smuggling fees between the years immediately preceding Operation Rio Grande and the period since its undertaking? Field interviews I conducted in the summer of 1998 with Border Patrol agents, federal prosecutors, immigrant rights activists, and attorneys who routinely defend smugglers provide some clues as to how this outcome is possible. One important factor to take into account is that the geography of the south Texas border region is different than that of southern California in a way that makes the immediate doubling or trebling of smuggler fees in response to increased Border Patrol activity less likely. The Tijuana–San Diego corridor is a densely populated urban area in which the major challenge to undocumented migrants before Operation Gatekeeper was to move as quickly as possible through a narrow band of heavily patrolled territory and disappear into the streets of San Diego. Once in San Diego, most migrants were "home free" for all intents and purposes. Though many migrants used a coyote to accomplish this, prices charged were generally low given the short distance involved and limited arrangements that coyotes needed to make. After Gatekeeper effectively shut down this route for most migrants, costs jumped dramatically because what had been a relatively easy, inexpensive crossing suddenly became a considerably more complex and arduous undertaking requiring a much higher level of organization and effort on the part of smugglers. In south Texas, getting through the border region was already a complex and arduous undertaking before the launching of Operation Rio Grande. We may think of the fees formerly paid to coyotes in Tijuana–San Diego as equivalent to paying a Matamoros *patero* to ferry a migrant across the Río Bravo del Norte into Brownsville. Getting into Brownsville has never been the major challenge to undocumented migrants in south Texas—getting out of Brownsville and through the ranch country to Corpus Christi and Houston has always been the major hurdle. Thus, shutting down the urban corridors in northeastern Mexico–south Texas to illegal crossings by creating a Border Patrol line of defense at the river itself does not by itself affect arrangements for the major portion of the journey through south Texas. Furthermore, south Texas is a large geographical area—saturating it with

Border Patrol agents requires far greater equipment and personnel resources than shutting down a narrow band along the border itself in San
Diego.

A second factor to consider is that smuggling enterprises are not very
capital intensive. Even after the implementation of Operation Rio
Grande, the start-up requirements for a viable smuggling enterprise are
fairly minimal: someone to recruit migrants at the border or in the Mexican interior; a knowledgeable guide to lead migrants across the Rio
Grande and around INS checkpoints; a driver and a vehicle to pick migrants up and drive them out of south Texas; and somebody with a house
or apartment in the destination city to receive migrants and to collect payment from their respondents. In order to move larger groups of migrants,
an enterprise would also need access to trucks and vans as well as
dwellings to serve as safe houses in Mexican and Texas border cities. In
principle, these might require considerable up-front capital investments,
thereby limiting the scale of operations for many Mexican smuggling entrepreneurs. In practice, however, these vehicles and dwellings can be
rented or leased by smugglers in order to avoid up-front investments, reduce their businesses' fixed costs, and protect against financial losses due
to forfeiture of property in the event of arrest by U.S. authorities. For this
reason, the vehicle of choice for some smuggling enterprises is the Ryder
rental truck or van (see, e.g., Sandberg, 1999).[11] The falling price of leased
cellular and digital phone service has also brought sophisticated communications equipment well within the reach of even small-scale smuggling
operations. Thus, intensified patrolling of the border may not drastically
raise smugglers' capital costs.

By increasing the likelihood of apprehension of migrant parties and
forcing them to traverse more remote areas, Operation Rio Grande raises
the amount of time and effort smugglers must invest in moving a given
group of migrants through the region. Trips take longer and are more
likely to have to be attempted multiple times. While the increased labor
time required of smugglers surely creates some upward pressure on prices
charged to migrants, labor time is not the principal component of smuggler fees. More important to determining the cost of their services is the
risk they assume in smuggling migrants. Smugglers have developed several risk-reduction strategies in the face of Operation Rio Grande that do
not imply increased per migrant costs:

- When a migrant party is apprehended in the field, its guide frequently attempts to blend into the group. Migrants have little incentive to identify their smuggler to the Border Patrol because they will rely on him for making subsequent crossing attempts.[12] Alternatively, if apprehension appears imminent or members of a party seem unlikely to make it through the brush to be picked up on the other side of INS checkpoints, guides sometimes abandon their charges in the field, sometimes with deadly consequences (see Schiller, 1998b, 1998c).

- It is now common for smugglers to use two vehicles to guide and transport migrants on Texas highways. The smugglers drive the lead vehicle and induce one of the migrants to drive the group in a second vehicle at a safe distance behind. If the Border Patrol pulls over the second vehicle, the smugglers—who may be U.S. citizens or legal residents—continue driving up the highway.

- Smuggling rings have taken to employing legal minors to guide migrants through the brush because juveniles are not subject to the same harsh criminal penalties as adults (see Associated Press, 1999).

- Because the Border Patrol seldom refers cases involving the transportation of five or fewer persons for felony prosecution, some smugglers are induced to move smaller groups of migrants. Conversely, greater risk of prosecution leads other smugglers to increase the number of migrants moved at one time in order to raise the payload per trip. Larger group size also keeps per migrant fees down, although the physical risks to migrants can be greatly increased as a consequence.

- Smuggling organizations may bribe INS officials to gain safe passage for their parties. In other cases, Border Patrol agents themselves have gone into business as smugglers (see Crissey, 1998).

In sum, a number of strategic innovations on the part of smugglers appear to have combined to keep per migrant prices from skyrocketing as a consequence of intensified border control in the south Texas–northeastern Mexico region. With regard to all these strategies for reducing risk, it is worth bearing in mind that it is mainly the U.S.–side guides and drivers who are in most serious danger of arrest and prosecution. This raises the question of whether the costs of increased risk to incumbents in these positions are shared among all participants in the smuggling enterprise or are borne by guides and drivers alone, who are treated as expendable "mules" by the enterprise as a whole. In the latter case, increased risk might not produce much in the way of higher overall fees charged by smuggling organizations.[13]

Effect 3. As the price for alien smuggling goes up, so too does the potential for exploitation and abuse. As INS enforcement has increased, so has the ruthlessness of the smugglers.

As illustrated by the headline-grabbing case of the enslaved deaf Mexican peddlers in New York City discovered in the summer of 1997 (McDonnell and Tobar, 1997; Sexton, 1997), smugglers of Mexican migrants are certainly capable of the abuses committed by smugglers of other nationalities. Indeed, it was the 1997 conviction of a Mexican immigrant family in Kerrville, Texas, on alien smuggling *and* peonage (involuntary servitude) charges that initially provoked my interest in the smuggling enterprise in south Texas (Crouse and McCormack, 1997; Prentice, 1997). Tales of abuse of migrants at the hands of smugglers are routine and legendary in the border region. They include reports of rip-offs, rape, robbery, abandonment, extortion, kidnapping, and death in high-speed car chases or in the sealed compartments of rail cars. These reports are credible, and many such abuses are well documented. What is less clear is the extent to which they represent the actions of "typical" border commercial smuggling enterprises whose principal business is delivering live Mexican migrants to jobs and kin in the U.S. interior. A close reading of news reports in the Tamaulipas newspapers *El Mañana* and *El Bravo* suggests that many of the abuses, especially those involving defrauding migrants of their money, robbing them, or abandoning them to thieves or the Border Patrol once across the river, are committed not so much by smugglers themselves as by individuals who prey upon naïve migrants by posing as smugglers.[14]

In addition, migrants who lack previous border-crossing experience and are not enmeshed in dense transboundary migrant networks may be convinced to pay a substantial sum of money to a *patero* who does no more than take them immediately across the river, a service of limited utility since the implementation of Operation Rio Grande. In this regard, it behooves immigration scholars to remember that not all Mexican migration to the United States is driven/facilitated by established social networks. Economic crisis in Mexico in the 1990s propelled many urban Mexicans from nontraditional sending communities into the migrant stream. It is these new migrants who are particularly vulnerable to exploitation and risk of death as they cross the border.

With regard to Mexicans, at least, there are several reasons to question whether the rising price of alien smuggling (itself called into question in the preceding section) and intensified border control by themselves increase the abusiveness and ruthlessness of smugglers. On the one hand, the fees charged to Mexican migrants have not yet reached a level anywhere near the $30,000 to $40,000 reportedly charged to Chinese and other Asian groups bound for the United States (see Kwong, 1997). Although several hundred or even a thousand dollars is not a trivial sum to most Mexican migrants, it is one that can usually be paid by friends and kin. Thus, the potential for violent confrontations between smugglers and migrants and their "sponsors" over terms of payment is considerably less than for nationalities for whom the sums involved are far greater. On the other hand, the "contract" between migrants and smugglers typically stipulates that the majority of the fee for passage through south Texas to Dallas, Houston, or San Antonio will be paid only upon arrival in the destination city. This gives smugglers a strong incentive to deliver migrants safely to their sponsors, for that is the only way they can collect their full fee.[15] Moreover, unlike the "snakeheads" who sink thousands of dollars of their own funds into moving Chinese nationals around the world across multiple national boundaries by land, air, and sea, Mexican coyotes have relatively little actual cash invested in the movement of individual migrants. This is not to say that there will not be grave consequences for migrants who fail to pay their smugglers, but that the stakes are considerably lower.[16] Finally, smugglers of Mexican migrants in the region are seldom armed. This suggests that violent coercion is not usually an integral part of the smuggling enterprise and also helps explain why very few Border Patrol agents have been shot over the years while carrying out their migrant apprehension duties.

By raising these reasons for skepticism about the worsening of their behavior in response to changes in border enforcement, I do not mean to portray smugglers as victims of some sort of smear campaign organized by the INS. By all accounts, the primary motivation of commercial smugglers on the Texas-Mexico border is maximizing their own profit and minimizing risks to themselves. In pursuit of these goals, smugglers often demonstrate little concern for the comfort and safety of the migrants in their care. At the same time, we probably misunderstand the smuggling process if we reflexively portray the smuggler as the predator and migrants as his hapless prey, animalizing him into the coyote who rustles defenseless *pollos* from the coop. Migrants are not a commodity that is bought and sold by smugglers on a speculative basis. Rather, they are human beings with a will of their own who contract smugglers to provide them with a service that they strongly desire. Moreover, though not universally the case, migrants frequently are informed consumers who exercise choice in a marketplace for smuggling services that offers a panoply of different "packages" at different levels of price, quality of service, and risk. For all the stories of abuse and exploitation of migrants at the hands of smugglers, literally millions of Mexican nationals have successfully entered the United States by employing a smuggler over the past thirty years. Despite the well-known moral failings of smugglers, migrants rely upon them because the service of a smuggler makes it more likely that they will "arrive alive" in San Antonio, Houston, or Dallas. Indeed, as migrants perished by the score in the scorching south Texas heat in the summer of 1998, more than one informant I interviewed speculated that there were many among the dead who had tried to make the crossing on their own.

Effect 4. Alien smuggling rings now are often connected with international criminal syndicates engaged in other illegal activities including illicit drug trafficking, prostitution, money laundering, and financial fraud.

Paterismo and *narcotráfico* are linked in the folklore of south Texas and northeastern Mexico in the verses of numerous *corridos* dealing with both themes. Both are criminal activities that have a special prominence in the border region, and both involve the secretive movement of contraband across the international line. To the extent that individuals disposed toward illicit activities could profitably apply their cultural skills, social contacts, and intimate knowledge of the border region's geography to migrant smuggling and drug smuggling interchangeably, it is plausible that a single criminal enterprise might integrate both activities. Nevertheless, although there seems to be evidence that some criminal *individuals* in the south Texas–northeastern Mexico region participate in both types of smuggling (e.g., prosecutors going after alien smugglers with prior convictions for drug smuggling), most of my informants agreed that migrant smuggling and drug smuggling in Texas were typically separate businesses.[17] Migrant smugglers did not usually transport narcotics along with migrants, nor did drug smugglers pack migrants into their narcotics shipments.

Presumably, there are a number of practical reasons for not mixing the two types of smuggling. Drug traffickers, for instance, probably would not want to allow large numbers of untrustworthy migrants to learn their methods of bringing drugs into the United States or give them the opportunity to pilfer or commandeer their highly valuable cargo (not to mention finger them to the U.S. or Mexican authorities). On the other hand, several informants said they believed that some drug traffickers had moved into the migrant smuggling business because it could be nearly as profitable while involving far less risk, in terms of both potential jail time faced and the dangers posed by rival drug traffickers. In principle, criminal syndicates involved in drug trafficking should also find migrant trafficking attractive and be able to enter that trade effectively as well. Whether such syndicates could effectively dominate the region's migrant trade or not is another matter, since that would involve controlling the activities of the large and mobile migrant population as opposed to the supply and distribution of an inanimate commodity. If a highly trained and disciplined paramilitary force of nearly ten thousand using the latest territorial control technologies—the U.S. Border Patrol—cannot accomplish this task, it is difficult to imagine that a much smaller criminal syndicate could.

Conclusion

There can be no question that the U.S. government's intensified policing of the south Texas–northeastern Mexico border has made it more difficult for Mexican migrants to enter the country illegally. Nevertheless, it has not yet come close to halting the large-scale, unauthorized movement of Mexicans into Texas. Undoubtedly, the continued ability of smuggling enterprises to penetrate Border Patrol operations in the region—and do so at a price that is affordable to most migrants—goes a long way toward explaining the persistence of Mexican undocumented migration in the late 1990s. In this chapter I have attempted to outline how such enterprises function and illustrate why U.S. enforcement efforts thus far have neither put them out of business nor led them to raise their fees so dramatically that migrants are unable or unwilling to pay them. Attorney General Janet Reno recently announced that she would not be requesting funds in the FY 2000 budget for any additional Border Patrol agents to be brought into the region (Schiller, 1999b). It seems unlikely, therefore, that this situation will change dramatically in the immediate future.

At the same time, we should not leap to the conclusion that the "battle for the border" is over. It would be a mistake to assert that the U.S. government is *unable* to put an end to undocumented migration from Mexico and to put migrant smugglers out of business. History is replete with examples of other nations effectively sealing their borders to incursions from both within and without. Checkpoint Charlie between the two Berlins was still with us barely ten years ago, after all. The bureaucratic-military apparatus of the state was not effectively countered by the cross-border social networks of Germans for many years. Indeed, on two occasions in the previous century—during the Plan de San Diego uprising at the time of the Mexican Revolution and again during Operation Wet-back in the 1950s—U.S. authorities have effectively exercised a far more draconian control over the movement of Mexican nationals than is currently being attempted (Calavita, 1992; Dunn, 1996). Thus, we have reason to doubt the ability of the informal economic activity of smuggling enterprises to counter state hegemony under all circumstances. Instead, we can more safely say that at the beginning of the twenty-first century smugglers are immersed in a massive migrant stream emanating from Mexico. The course of this stream can be altered at the border only by imposing far more extreme paramilitary and bureaucratic control measures whose costs—economic, political, and humanitarian—the U.S. government does not yet seem willing to pay.

NOTES

The research on migrant smuggling reported here has been generously supported by the Tom and Mary Turner Junior Faculty Fellowship of Trinity University. The author thanks Randy Capps, Karl Eschbach, David Kyle, Joseph Nevins, Néstor Rodríguez, and Audrey Singer for helpful comments made on earlier drafts of this chapter. Thanks also go to Monica Shurtman and Rubén Hernández León for their assistance in making contact with key informants in the field.

1. Interviews with migrants and coyotes I conducted in Monterrey, Nuevo León, in July 1999 corroborated López Castro's observation.

2. Although smugglers are known to provide undocumented workers to employers in the United States, I do not undertake an examination of this aspect of the commercial smuggling enterprise in south Texas–northeastern Mexico. There are two reasons for this. First, it does not appear that most employers have a need to work directly with smugglers, since they may rely upon existing migrant networks to recruit new workers and arrange for their passage from Mexico. Second, my fieldwork to date has not provided me with sufficient data on such smuggler-employer collaborations to comment upon them meaningfully.

3. There are many safe houses located in the various towns and cities of the Texas border region. Periodically, one is discovered by the Border Patrol and raided, sometimes resulting in the apprehension of one hundred or more migrants. Although none of the safe houses in question offers luxury accommodations, sometimes the conditions uncovered are truly deplorable, as was the case in a house discovered in the summer of 1998 outside Eagle Pass, Texas (Schiller, 1998a).

4. Migrants entering Texas near Del Rio or Eagle Pass sometimes walk all the way from the border to Junction or Kerrville, Texas, a distance of more than one hundred miles. In Kenedy and Kleberg Counties, Texas, migrants are frequently found walking across the enormous King Ranch in an effort to avoid INS checkpoints on U.S. 77 running north from the lower Rio Grande Valley toward Victoria, Texas.

5. This is not only because very few Border Patrol agents are stationed outside the immediate border region. Within fifty miles of the border, Border Patrol agents need only have a "reasonable suspicion" to detain a vehicle. Farther into the interior the stricter standard of "probable cause" applies.

6. In 1993, Silvestre Reyes, chief of the El Paso sector of the Border Patrol, told researchers that approximately 60 percent of Mexicans apprehended by his agents on the eve of Operation Blockade were residents of neighboring Ciudad Juárez (Bean et al., 1994; Bean and Spener, forthcoming). A recent INS Progress Report on Operation Gatekeeper showed that 51, 55, and 70 percent of apprehendees in the Del Rio, McAllen, and El Paso sectors, respectively, were local "commuters" who lived in or near the Mexican border cities of Ciudad Acuña, Reynosa, Matamoros, and Ciudad Juárez ("San Diego: A Corridor for Long-Distance, Determined Crossers," October 17, 1997, downloaded on March 9, 1999, from *http://www.ins.usdoj.gov/public_affairs* /progress_reports/Gatekeeper/238.html).

7. Here it should be noted that the majority of illegal crossings in Singer and Massey's data were made in Tijuana–San Diego. Nonetheless, the authors found that migrants crossing illegally into the United States in Matamoros and Reynosa in the lower Rio Grande Valley were no less likely to use a smuggler than were migrants crossing in California. Migrants crossing in the two Laredos, Juárez, or Piedras Negras were considerably less likely to use smugglers, however, suggesting that geographical barriers to crossing (such as river depth and distance from a city center on the U.S. side) may play a large role in whether to use a smuggler.

8. My data on smuggling fees derive from published accounts in regional newspapers (the *Austin-American Statesman,* the *San Antonio Express-News* and the *Houston Chronicle* in Texas and *El Mañana* and *El Bravo* in Tamaulipas) and books (Conover, 1987; Pérez, 1991; Samora, 1971), examination of federal court records in San Antonio and Brownsville, and also from interviews with Border Patrol agents, prosecutors, public defenders, migrants, and several members of smuggling enterprises. Because the data used here are not comprehensive, conclusions regarding the evolution of smuggling fees must be regarded as tentative. I have controlled for the effects of inflation using the U.S. Consumer Price Index.

9. Results obtained by Massey and Singer (1995) suggest that odds of apprehension were falling across the U.S.-Mexican border as a whole in the 1965–90 period, owing in large measure to the rapidly growing number of attempts by Mexicans to enter U.S. territory by illegally crossing the border. The authors estimated that around 322,000 such attempts were made in 1969 (the year Samora's researchers were in the field in south Texas). By 1989, the number had skyrocketed to 2,850,000.

10. Singer and Massey's more recent research (1998), which treats undocumented border crossing as a social process, emphasizes the importance of this type of accumulated social capital in guiding the strategies that migrants pursue with respect to employing smugglers.

11. In 1998 in San Antonio, Ryder rented moving trucks with 15-foot compartments for $29.99 per day and $0.49 per mile. Thus the total costs, excluding gas, for a two-day run from Dallas to Laredo (a round trip journey of around 800 miles) would be approximately $450. A $600 fee charged to each of fifteen migrants produces gross revenues of $9,000 for such a trip.

12. Use of the IDENT database may now make it possible to charge suspected smugglers who are apprehended multiple times with misdemeanor and subsequently with felony illegal entry, but it is not yet clear how credible the threat of

this type of prosecution is. Although I have not confirmed that it is occurring, it is plausible that smuggling organizations could "rotate" guides into Mexican-side operations after they have been apprehended on multiple occasions in order to avoid prosecution.

13. Many, if not most, persons prosecuted for alien smuggling in south Texas are defended by a court-appointed attorney, usually a public defender. This suggests that such defendants are not highly valued by the smuggling rings or that smuggling rings have fewer financial resources at their disposal than is often supposed.

14. In a case reported recently in Nuevo Laredo, Tamaulipas, for example, a supposed *patero* took one hundred pesos from each of fifteen migrants and locked them in a railroad container on the Mexican side, promising that an accomplice would release them from the container once the train crossed the river. The train never crossed, and the migrants would have suffocated in the container had they not been rescued by a railroad security guard ("Rescatan a quince ilegales," 1998). In response to abuses committed by *pateros*, human rights organizations in Reynosa and Nuevo Laredo have been calling for Mexican authorities to crack down on smuggling activities on the border.

15. Indeed, in his *Diary of an Undocumented Immigrant*, Pérez (1991) notes that Mexican migrants rely upon coyotes not only for guidance but also for protection against thieves. He quotes a companion as saying, "The good thing about the coyotes is that they can't collect from a dead man, so they have to protect us against all kinds of dangers" (27).

16. Even before the launching of Operation Rio Grande, failure to pay one's smuggler could lead to violence. In 1996 a Mexican man living in Austin was murdered by one of his coyotes for failing to pay off the two-thousand-dollar smuggling fee for himself and family members (Harmon, 1999).

17. Although my review was by no means exhaustive, none of the two dozen or so 1997–98 alien smuggling indictments I read in the federal courthouses in San Antonio and Brownsville included drug charges as well.

REFERENCES

Administrative Office of the U.S. Courts. 1998a. "Criminal Cases Commenced during the Twelve Month Period Ended September 30, 1998: Table D-3." Mimeo. Washington, D.C.: Administrative Office of the U.S. Courts.

———. 1998b. "Misdemeanor Petty Offense Defendants Disposed of by U.S. Magistrate Judges by Nature of Offense during the Twelve Month Period End-ing September 30, 1998." Mimeo. Washington, D.C.: Administrative Office of the U.S. Courts.

Alegría Olazábal, Tito. 1992. *Desarrollo urbano en la frontera México-Estados Unidos*. Mexico City: Consejo Nacional para la Cultura y los Artes.

Alonso-Zaldívar, Ricardo. 1999. "INS to Cut Workplace Raids, Target Employers Immigration: Focus to Shift to Firms Suspected of Collaborating with Smugglers." *Los Angeles Times*. March 16. Electronic edition.

Andreas, Peter. 1996. "U.S.-Mexico: Open Markets, Closed Border." *Foreign Policy* 103:51–69.

———. 1998. "The Escalation of U.S. Immigrant Control in the Post-NAFTA Era." *Political Science Quarterly* 113 (4): 591–615.

Associated Press. 1999. "Immigrant Smugglers Use Youths as Guides." *San Antonio Express-News*, February 21, 2B.

Bean, Frank D., Roland Chanove, Robert G. Cushing, Rodolfo de la Garza, Gary P. Freeman, Charles W. Haynes, and David Spener. 1994. *Illegal Mexican Migration and the United States/Mexico Border: The Effects of Operation Hold the Line on El Paso/Juárez*. Washington, D.C.: U.S. Commission on Immigration Reform.

Bean, Frank D., and David Spener. Forthcoming. "Controlling International Migration through Enforcement Mechanisms: The Case of the United States." In *International Migration at Century's End: Trends and Issues,* edited by Joaquin Arango and J. Edward Taylor. Cambridge: Oxford University Press.

Binational Study on Migration. 1997. *Migration between Mexico and the United States: Binational Study*. Mexico City and Washington, D.C.: Mexican Foreign Ministry and U.S. Commission on Immigration Reform.

Calavita, Kitty. 1992. *Inside the State: The Bracero Program, Immigration, and the I.N.S.* New York : Routledge.

Casillas Bermúdez, Karla. 1998. "La frontera México-EU, la más dinámica del mundo: A los 12 años inician la aventura migratorio muchos mexicanos, revela estudio." *El Financiero*. May 9, 38.

Conover, Ted. 1987. *Coyotes: A Journey through the Secret World of America's Illegal Aliens*. New York: Vintage Books.

Crissey, Michael. 1998. "10-Year Border Patrol Vet Arrested: Officer Allegedly Found Smuggling Immigrants." *Valley Morning Star* (Harlingen, Texas), July 16, A1+.

Crouse, Jacque, and Zeke McCormack. 1997. "Family Held in Smuggling of Humans." *San Antonio Express-News,* July 22, 1A.

Dunn, Timothy J. 1996. *The Militarization of the U.S.-Mexico Border, 1978–1992: Low-Intensity Conflict Doctrine Comes Home.* Austin: Center for Mexican American Studies, University of Texas.

Escobar, Agustín. 1986. *Con el sudor de tu frente: Mercado de trabajo y clase obrera en Guadalajara.* Guadalajara: El Colegio de Jalisco.

Harmon, Dave. 1999. "Don't Ask, Don't Tell: Austin's Red Hot Economy Relies Heavily on Illegal Immigrants." *Austin-American Statesman,* December 5. Electronic edition.

Hellman, Judith Adler. 1994. *Mexican Lives.* New York: New Press.

Herzog, Lawrence A. 1990. *Where North Meets South: Cities, Space, and Politics on the U.S.-Mexico Border.* Austin: Center for Mexican American Studies, University of Texas.

Heyman, Josiah. 1995. "Putting Power in the Anthropology of Bureaucracy: The Immigration and Naturalization Service at the Mexico-United States Border." *Current Anthropology* 36:261–87.

Immigration and Naturalization Service. 1997a. "Aliens and Smugglers Find Illegal Entry More Problematic: Progress Report." Retrieved from http://www.ins.usdoj.gov/textonly/public_affairs/progress_reports/CrackDown/293.html on December 31, 1998.

———. 1997b. "Anti-Smuggling Operations." Retrieved from http://www.ins.usdoj.gov/public_affairs/ progress_reports/Gatekeeper/224.html on March 9, 1999.

———. 1997c. "Cracking Down on Alien Smuggling: Progress Report." Retrieved from http://www.ins.usdoj.gov/public_affairs/progress_reports/CrackDown/169.htm on December 31, 1998.

———. 1998a. "INS Busts Major Counterfeit Document Ring." News release. May 21, 1998. Retrieved from http://www.ins.usdoj.gov/public_affairs/news_releases/bust.htm on March 5, 1999.

———. 1998b. "INS Cracks National Counterfeit Document Operation." News release. November 13, 1998. Retrieved from http://www.ins.usdoj.gov/public_affairs/news_releases/fineprnt.htm on March 5, 1999.

———. 1999. "Southwest Border Apprehensions by Sector: Fiscal Years 1960 through January 1999." Mimeo. February 26, 1999.

Inspector General. 1998. *Review of the Immigration and Naturalization Service's Automated Biometric Identification System (IDENT): Report Number I-98–10.* Washington, D.C.: U.S. Department of Justice, Office of the Inspector General.

Kwong, Peter. 1997. *Forbidden Workers: Illegal Chinese Immigrants and American Labor.* New York: New Press.

López Castro, Gustavo. 1998. "Coyotes and Alien Smuggling." In *Migration between Mexico and the United States,* vol. 3, written and edited by the Mexico/ United States Binational Study on Migration, 965–74. Washington, D.C.: United States Commission on Immigration Reform.

Lozano Ascencio, Fernando. 1993. *Bringing It Back Home: Remittances to Mexico from Migrant Workers in the United States.* La Jolla, Calif.: Center for U.S.-Mexico Studies, UCSD.

Martínez, Oscar J. 1994. *Border People: Life and Society in the U.S.-Mexico Borderlands.* Tucson: University of Arizona Press.

Massey, Douglas S., and Audrey Singer. 1995. "New Estimates of Undocumented Mexican Migration and the Probability of Apprehension." *Demography* 32 (2): 203–13.

Massey, Douglas S., et al. 1987. *Return to Aztlán: The Social Process of International Migration from Western Mexico.* Berkeley: University of California Press.

McDonnell, Patrick J., and Hector Tobar. 1997. "Mexicans Link L.A. to N.Y. Ring: Group Peddling Trinkets Smuggled Deaf Recruits into Southland and Sent Them East, Investigators Say." *Los Angeles Times,* July 23, B3.

Patrick, Pragati. N.d. "Immigration Cases and Their Impact on Federal District Court Criminal Findings: A Fact Sheet." Mimeo. Washington, D.C.: Administrative Office of the United States Courts.

Pérez, Ramón. 1991. *Diary of an Undocumented Immigrant.* Houston, Tex.: Arte Público Press.

Portes, Alejandro. 1996. "Transnational Communities: Their Emergence and Significance in the Contemporary World-System." In *Latin America in the World Economy,* edited by Roberto Patricio Korzeniewicz and William C. Smith, 151–68. Westport, Conn.: Greenwood Press.

Prentice, Melissa. 1997. "3 in Family Plead Guilty to Peonage, Smuggling." *San Antonio Express-News.* December 3, 2B.

"Rescatan a quince ilegales." 1998. *El Mañana* (Nuevo Laredo, Tamaulipas), March 31.

Rodríguez, Néstor. 1996. "The Battle for the Border: Notes on Autonomous Migration, Transnational Communities, and the State." *Social Justice* 23 (3): 21–37.

Rothenberg, Daniel. 1998. *With These Hands: The Hidden World of Migrant Farmworkers Today.* New York: Harcourt, Brace, and Co.

Rouse, Roger. 1991. "Mexican Migration and the Social Space of Postmodernism. *Diaspora* 1 (1): 8–24.

Samora, Julian. 1971. *Los Mojados: The Wetback Story.* Notre Dame, Ind.: University of Notre Dame Press.

Sandberg, Lisa. 1999. "Deputy Uncovers Immigrants in Van." *San Antonio Express News*, February 24, "Crime and Crisis" section of electronic edition.

Schiller, Dane. 1998a. "Border Patrol Grabs 59 in Raid: Sweltering Hideout Filled with Sewage." *San Antonio Express-News.* August 7. Electronic edition.

———. 1998b. "'Coyotes' Deal in Human Cargo: Immigrants Seek Smugglers' Aid as Border Patrol Tightens Grip." *San Antonio Express-News*, August 2, 15A.

———. 1998c. "Perilous Journey: Immigrants Say Dangers Are Worth Chance for Better Life." *San Antonio Express-News*, August 2, 1A+.

———. 1999a. "121 Immigrants Discovered in Rig." *San Antonio Express-News.* April 19. Electronic edition.

———. 1999b. "Reno Says New Agents Not Answer for Border." *San Antonio Express-News*, March 10, 1A+.

Schiller, Dane, and Mario Robbins. 1999. "Border Courts Face Backlog." *San Antonio Express-News.* July 9. Electronic edition.

Sexton, Joe. 1997. "More Deaf Mexicans Are Found 'in Bondage' in North Carolina Raids." *New York Times,* July 26. Electronic edition.

Singer, Audrey, and Douglas S. Massey. 1998. "The Social Process of Undocumented Border Crossing among Mexican Migrants." *International Migration Review* 32 (3): 561.

Smith, Robert C. 1995. "Los Ausentes Siempre Presentes: The Imagining, Making, and Politics of a Transnational Community." Ph.D. diss., Columbia University.

Spener, David. Forthcoming. "The Logic and Contradictions of Intensified Border Control in Texas." In *The Wall around the West: State Borders and Immigration Control in North America and Europe,* edited by Peter Andreas and Timothy Snyder. Lanham, Md.: Rowman and Littlefield.

Spener, David, and Kathleen Staudt. 1998. "Conclusion: Rebordering." In *The U.S.-Mexico Border: Transcending Divisions, Contesting Identities,* edited by David Spener and Kathleen Staudt, 233–57. Boulder, Colo.: Lynne Rienner Publishers.

Staudt, Kathleen. 1998. *Free Trade?: Informal Economies at the U.S.-Mexico Border.* Philadelphia: Temple University Press.

Staudt, Kathleen, and David Spener. 1998. "The View from the Frontier: Theoretical Perspectives Undisciplined." In *The U.S.-Mexico Border: Transcending Divisions, Contesting Identities,* edited by David Spener and Kathleen Staudt, 3–33. Boulder, Colo.: Lynne Rienner Publishers.

Vélez-Ibáñez, Carlos. 1983. *Bonds of Mutual Trust: The Cultural Systems of Rotating Credit Associations among Urban Mexicans and Chicanos.* New Brunswick, N.J.: Rutgers University Press.

6 ▪▪▪▪▪▪▪ Russian Transnational Organized Crime and Human Trafficking

James O. Finckenauer

The criminal activities of Russians and others from the former Soviet Union are today of serious concern to many nations. Not the least of these nations are the newly independent states formed after the collapse of the USSR in 1991. In the relatively short time since that cataclysmic event, crime emanating from the former Soviet empire has swept across national borders into Eastern and Western Europe and moved east to Afghanistan, China, and Japan, south to Israel, and across the Atlantic to Canada and the United States. A looming threat of Russian organized crime and what is called a global "Russian Mafia" has become fixed in the minds of many—especially those in the media and law enforcement.

As attention to and concern about a Russian Mafia have risen, a certain mythological quality has enveloped how it is perceived (See, e.g., Rosner, 1995; Finckenauer and Waring, 1998; and Rutland and Kogan, 1998). In their article "The Russian Mafia: Between Hype and Reality," Rutland and Kogan concluded that there is a "myth of the Russian mafia" that fits with a longstanding demonic image of Russia itself (1998: 1). Hollywood and the news portray Russian criminals as more clever, devious, and ruthless than the criminals of any other nation. Why this hype? Because, they say, there are many in Russia today who have vested interests in maintaining an especially ominous image of organized crime as being mafia or mafialike. These are interests that have something to gain from the existence of a Russian Mafia—be it bigger budgets, selling newspapers, or a scapegoat to blame for policy failures. Those interests include the Russian police, the Russian president, the reformers, opposition politicians, journalists, international advisers, and even organized criminals themselves (2).

Many of these same pressures and interests—and for some of the same reasons—exist in the United States as well. Now that the original Italian Mafia threat on our shores has receded, what better replacement to galvanize political support for law enforcement and to sell newspapers, books, and movies than exotic criminals from the former "evil empire"?

Here I want to look at this Russian organized crime, or mafia, threat. And I want to do so with respect to a particular type of crime that has itself become very visible on the global scene—a type of crime that is viewed with a special kind of horror because of its insidious nature and the special vulnerability of its victims. The crime is that of human trafficking and its associated exploitation and victimization of women and children. The most flagrant type of victimization occurs when women and children are smuggled for commercial sexual purposes. The sex industry that exploits these victims encompasses everything from old-fashioned prostitution to escort services, topless dancers, massage parlors, video porn, and child pornography. It is estimated to be a multibillion dollar business (see, e.g., Robinson, 1998).

In order to look at the role of Russian organized crime in trafficking women and children for commercial sexual exploitation, we need to consider a number of broader questions, beginning with just what is organized crime and what is the current picture with respect to organized crime in Russia? Then, what is the transnational nature of this crime? Are there any indications that Russian organized crime per se is engaged in people smuggling? Finally, are there such indications with specific respect to the trafficking of women and children for the sex industry? In each instance we should ask what do we actually know and how do we know it?

Let me also clarify the use of the term *Russian* in the context of this discussion. Undoubtedly it would be more precise to refer to all peoples from what was formerly the USSR as former Soviet—more precise, but a bit cumbersome. The same is true of attempting to break down the hundreds of specific ethnic identities of all such peoples. I thus adopt the conventional use of the term *Russian* to refer to all former Soviet peoples and activities (including crimes and criminals), while recognizing that the use of this term is strictly for convenience's sake.

Although Russia, most especially Moscow, is in fact the epicenter of organized and transnational crime from that part of the world, many of those involved in that crime are not ethnic Russians. Indeed, Armenians, Belarussians, Chechens, Jews, Georgians, and Ukrainians, among others, account for a considerable share. Russian officials, journalists, and scholars with whom I have spoken have pointed out this misnomer, and some have suggested Eurasian organized crime as a more accurate descriptor. I grant their concern but will leave that discussion for another day.

Definition and Overview of Russian Organized Crime

True organized crime is much more than just crime committed by organized groups. It is also more than what might be called professional organized criminality (Amir, 1996). Beyond being simply crime that is organized, *organized crime* has a number of additional defining attributes. These attributes include the structure and continuity of criminal networks engaging in crime—structure that facilitates committing certain kinds of crimes. Then there is the sophistication of the crimes and the skill levels required to carry them out; the violence (and a reputation for violence) that is systematically used to attain and retain monopoly control of criminal ventures; the capability to mount multiple and simultaneous criminal enterprises; and a capacity to corrupt political and legal authorities.

Criminal groups or organizations can likewise be defined by their capacity to do harm—economic, physical, psychological, and societal harm (Maltz, 1990). Those criminal organizations that qualify as true organized crime groups have significant capacity for these types of harm. On the other hand, small ad hoc groups do not have the harm capacity that would make them sophisticated criminal organizations of the type to constitute organized crime. Although their individual victims are certainly harmed, such groups do not have the capacity to carry out the serious, long-term economic, physical, psychological, and societal harm that marks real organized crime. Instead, they are most typically somewhat amorphous collections of individuals, usually made up of enterprising young men who come together around a particular criminal opportunity. They exploit that opportunity and then drift apart.

This is also not to say that the individual crimes of these loosely arranged, opportunistic groups can not at times be organized—sometimes even highly organized—but rather that they are not the same as organized crime (Finckenauer and Waring, 1996). The committing of a single crime can sometimes involve considerable planning and implementation of the resulting plan by a number of individuals fulfilling very specifically defined roles and carrying out specific functions relative to that crime. Such would be an example of a crime that is organized. The sense of *organized crime,* however, goes beyond this.

It is not just the crime with which we should be concerned, nor even the organization of the crime, but also the organization of those committing the crime. In a similar vein, Russian criminologist Azalia Dolgova has pointed out the distinction between ongoing criminal organizations, with their economic and political connections, and the simple organization of a particular crime or crimes (Dolgova, 1997). The former, she says, are not created in individual cases for purposes of committing individual crimes, whereas the latter are.

"Real" organized crime groups possess criminal sophistication, structure, self-identification with the group, and reputation. They are characterized not by undertaking particular criminal activities but rather by the monopoly control of criminal enterprises—by their ability to dominate the criminal underworld. They possess the capacity to use violence, and a reputation for violence, that facilitates this monopoly control. They also have the resources and political connections to corrupt the legal and political systems at the highest levels. Indeed, there are such criminal organizations in Moscow and in Russia, as there are elsewhere in the world, but there are certainly not thousands of them as some have claimed. With respect to their criminal ventures, the issue of interest to us is whether any of the organizations that can accurately be said to be organized crime are engaged in human trafficking.

Why do these distinctions matter? What is wrong with calling something organized crime (or more particularly mafia) when it is neither? First, from a research perspective (simply trying to describe, understand, and explain the phenomenon of interest), if organized crime is so loosely or ambiguously defined as to encompass practically any crimes committed by, say, three or more persons, then it is a meaningless concept. Without a clear and focused definition of what the phenomenon is, description, explanation, and understanding are impossible. It then follows that mapping trends and measuring the impact of countermeasures will also be impossible. Even mounting countermeasures becomes problematical under circumstances of ignorance and misperception.

Martens (1998) has pointed out a further complication from the promiscuous application of the label *organized crime.* "Bad reputation," he says, is a valuable asset that permits criminals access to criminal markets that would, absent this reputation, be closed to them. Victims or potential victims who believe they are confronted by some omnipotent force called organized crime (or more especially mafia) are more fearful, more likely to succumb, and less likely to go to the police than would otherwise be true. Thus, he says, "law enforcement must not facilitate this perception, and in fact enhance the value of a bad reputation when it is undeserved" (Martens, 1998: 3). Feeding the stereotype of a Russian Mafia, according to this view, can actually increase criminals' chances of successfully victimizing others.

With respect to organized crime control policy, relatively amorphous and short-lived criminal groups (of the kind that are the norm) are not particularly vulnerable to the strategies and tactics designed to counter genuine organized crime. Use of such techniques as informants, undercover agents, and wiretapping, or (in the United States) of the RICO (Racketeer Influenced and Corrupt Organizations Act) statute, for example, assumes a degree of continuity both over time and over crimes. This continuity is not present in the simpler opportunistic crimes. The absence of hierarchical structure also makes infiltration difficult. Use of the standard organized crime fighting tools in a false belief that the enemy is the mafia will be ineffective, inefficient, and costly—not only in dollar terms but in human terms as well. At the same time, it should be recognized that true organized crime is not vulnerable to the usual techniques used against street crime because the ringleaders—the bosses—of sophisticated criminal organizations are insulated from direct association with the actual crimes and because these organizations have economic and political clout. For all these reasons, knowing who is the real enemy is important.

There have been numerous accounts of thousands of organized criminal groups operating in Russia in recent years. In 1995, for example, the Russian Ministry of Internal Affairs reported that 8,222 "organized criminal rings" had been uncovered by law enforcement agencies (Dolgova, unpublished). These rings were said to have some 32,000 members—meaning the average group had to be relatively small (approximately 4 persons). It is difficult, however, to interpret just how "8,000 organized criminal groups" should be understood in this context. This is because, as in most other countries including the United States, there is no clear definition of organized crime or organized crime group in Russian law. An offense (any offense) can be said to have been "committed by an organized group, if it has been committed by a stable group of persons who had previously united to commit one or more offenses" (Nikiforov, unpublished). Such groups can and do include, for example, several youths stealing from street stalls or committing any of a number of other crimes in concert. This rather broad definition probably accounts for the fact that nearly 40 percent of all persons convicted in Russia in 1995 were said to be members of organized criminal groups.

In Russia, the elites of the criminal organizations operate internationally as well as domestically. Their overseas operations extend into Austria, Britain, Turkey, Jordan, the Netherlands, the former Yugoslavia, Poland, Hungary, Germany, Italy, Israel, Canada, China, Japan, Afghanistan, and the United States. One of their main international criminal activities is money laundering and other banking-related schemes. In addition to these financial crimes, their major transnational activity most often includes some kind of trafficking—of stolen cars, drugs, arms, and so on.

Just as with the reported numbers of organized criminal groups, the estimates of the number of criminal organizations from the former Soviet Union engaged in these transnational activities vary enormously. For example, Dunn (1996) concluded that there are really only 6 groups in Moscow and 30 in the whole of Russia that wield the kind of power and have the extensive overseas operations that enable them to monopolize the criminal world and to infiltrate Russian business and government. On the other hand, according to a recent report on Russian Organized Crime, the FBI estimates that there are 200 to 300 such groups. The Russian Ministry of the Interior (MVD), using the same information as Dolgova, reported that there are more than 8,000. And at the upper end of the scale, at least in numbers of individual participants, the 1994 United Nations World Ministerial Conference on Organized Transnational Crime reported that there were 3 million individuals in 5,700 criminal groups operating in Russia (Center for Strategic and International Studies, 1997).

Despite their wide disagreement on the numbers involved, there is some agreement that the multiple criminal enterprises of Russian organized crime include crimes that are part of the traditional bailiwick of organized crime. These include drug smuggling, prostitution, counterfeiting, and extortion. They also include, however, many criminal ventures that are more typical of the white-collar crime variety, for example, financial swindles, illegal oil deals, and illegal exportation of raw materials. Of all these crimes, prostitution is most closely tied to the human trafficking issue.

Organized Crime and Human Trafficking

There are a number of possible ways that organized crime could be connected to human trafficking (Schmid and Savona, 1995: 28–31). For instance, organized crime figures might induce people to leave their homes, usually with false promises of employment. Promised jobs as models, dancers, tourist guides, or waitresses, for example, are one way that trafficked women are duped and then forced into prostitution. People who have decided to seek their fortune in another country might knowingly or unknowingly get involved with an organized trafficker who is part of a migrants trafficking network. Or the collection of the debt owed the traffickers might be turned over to organized crime, which then threatens the migrant and his or her family or forces them into prostitution or drug selling or other crime in order to pay off this debt.

With the possible exception of debt collection—and even that is not an open and shut case—it seems very reasonable that criminals not associated with organized crime, and indeed persons not otherwise involved in crime, could also become engaged in trafficking activities. Persons who decide to make money from human trafficking do not have to be members of organized crime to deceive women with false employment possibilities or even to organize a trafficking ring. Because the state of knowledge at present is so spotty, as we will see, there is much room for interpretation, and there are many gray areas. Such circumstances are often ripe for myth making and stereotyping. But from the relatively little that is now known, human trafficking does seem to fall more into the "crime that is organized" category than it does into true organized crime. The range of types of organizations involved is quite broad, with smugglers being everything from individual operators to members of possibly sophisticated international smuggling rings (Winer, 1997).

Two recent cases illustrate the organized (but not organized crime) nature of human trafficking. In the first case, which is the largest U.S. case of its kind, U.S. officials arrested twenty-one of thirty-one suspected smugglers named in indictments stating that they were operators of three international immigrant smuggling cartels (*Dallas Morning News,* November 21, 1998). The three ringleaders were natives of India. They were charged with transporting more than seven thousand immigrants from the Indian subcontinent to the United States for a profit of some $150 million. Their organization included transit routes through Moscow to countries in South and Central America. They had safe houses, forged documents, and transportation systems with both small boats and planes. Although INS commissioner Doris Meissner called them a "well-organized, well-financed international criminal network," there were no indications that the persons indicted were members of organized crime or that they had any connections to organized crime.

In the second case, a Thai woman was arrested in Karachi, Pakistan, for being the "matriarch of a Bangkok-based syndicate involved in the smuggling of sex workers, mainly Chinese, to North America and Europe" (Dawn News Service, Karachi, November 23, 1998). Again there is evidence that this was an organized operation. But apart from some local agents in China, the principals of the "syndicate" were the Thai woman and her Laotian partner. As with the previous case, no connections to organized crime were reported.

Salt and Stein (1997) conceptualized the organized nature of human trafficking and, using some of the limited empirical data now available, proposed a theoretical model illustrating how it works. Their model supports the idea that this is a crime that is organized. What they call the "migration business" is a "system of institutionalized networks with complex profit and loss accounts, including a set of institutions, agents and individuals, each of which stands to make a commercial gain" (468). This system is maintained by the performance of a variety of tasks: planning the smuggling operations, gathering information, financing, and certain specific technical and operational tasks (477). These tasks can be carried out by either larger or smaller trafficking organizations; but most important, they can be carried out by organizations engaged in no other forms of criminal activity. For example, Salt and Stein describe trafficking from Albania to Italy as typically involving mom-and-pop operations. These mom-and-pop trafficking rings "employ about a dozen people, including a driver in charge of getting the boat over and back, one or two crew members acting as enforcers during the voyage, and various others in charge of rounding up customers, collecting money, transporting passengers to secret departure points and acting as look-outs" (476). Describing this same sort of Albania to Italy trafficking, the International Organization for Migration said that there is usually a direct relationship between the women being trafficked and their traffickers. "Interviews suggest that traffickers are often young criminals, attracted by the possibility of earning easy money even at the cost of profiting from girls/women that were friends, school mates or neighbors in their home town or village" (1996, in *Trends in Organized Crime,* 1998: 33). The traffickers in these latter types of cases include relatives, friends, or boyfriends.

With respect to trafficking in children for child prostitution, the same sort of situation seems to prevail—namely, that a wide variety of organizational patterns are found. "The intermediary [who links demand and supply] can be an agent who buys children in rural villages and transports them to the towns or cities where they are turned over to brothel owners (who can be either individual entrepreneurs or members of criminal groups)" (ibid., 7).

Is the situation the same in Russia? There is indeed some anecdotal evidence that this same sort of mom-and-pop (or brother-and-brother) system operates. For example, the *Russian Magazine* described an interview with a man running a prostitution ring in Moscow. "I took a group of 'volunteers' to work as waitresses, strippers and dancers," he said. "I made fake papers. We had sort of a family business. My brother made visas and passports. . . . I never dragged anyone by force. They knew perfectly well what lay ahead—maybe not completely, but that was their problem. Once the plane landed, I dealt with them as I pleased" (ibid., 42).

It appears that human traffickers can range all the way from being enterprising individuals not previously or otherwise involved in crime, to individual criminals (not of the organized variety), to mixed groups of these types of individuals, to families, to local criminal groups, to networks made up of both criminals and noncriminals, to sophisticated organized groups operating nationally and internationally. True organized crime *may* play a role in some of these operations. As previously indicated, they may become debt collectors. Or, they may demand a "mob tax" to permit trafficking in their territory. What seems clear, however, is that viewing all the possible arrangements as being the same—and labeling them all as organized crime or worse, mafia—is both incorrect and unwise, from both a research and a policy perspective.

The Russian Connection to Human Trafficking and Prostitution

The specific question for us is whether what would be regarded as genuine Russian organized crime is participating in human trafficking and its derivative prostitution. We should state at the outset that the evidence of involvement by organized crime in general and Russian organized crime in particular in human trafficking is quite limited.

Let us start with the possibilities. There appear to be four possible ways in which Russian participation in trafficking might come about. For one of these types, however (trafficking in children), so little information is available that we cannot say anything about it. Trafficking in children was outlawed in Russian law only in 1995, and just four offenses were reported during that year. We will, therefore, focus on the other three.

Smuggling of Migrants from Other Countries

It is reported that on any one day there are thousands (200,000–300,000 est.) of illegal Asians (mostly Chinese), Africans, Afghans, Kurds, Somalis, and Iraqis in Moscow awaiting trans-shipment to Western Europe and the United States. Moscow is a central distribution point for these migrants (Ulrich, 1994: 7; 1997: 122). Some Russians collaborate in this smuggling with traffickers from other countries, for example, from China. It is not clear, however, just who these Russians are and with what criminal organizations they might be affiliated, if any. The Chinese in Russia often operate their Moscow pipeline themselves, whereas in other cases Russians operate as middlemen in the various transnational networks. As Salt and Stein show in their model, trafficking needs middlemen, and it would make sense to have middlemen who know the Moscow scene. Further, it would seem that the easy money and the relatively low risks entailed in human trafficking might attract local criminal elements as well as others looking for a fast buck.

Illegal immigrants need high-quality paperwork (documentation, visas, airline tickets, and so on) in order to cover their immigration. These documents are often highly sophisticated and of high quality—and the higher the quality, the greater is the cost. According to the International Organization for Migration, "the illicit trade in fraudulent documents feeds from organized migrant trafficking. Stealing, forging and altering travel documents and work and residence permits has become a major criminal activity as the ability to migrate largely depends on possessing the necessary documents" (1996: 1–2). These are all specialties of the Russians. With their long experience of circumventing Soviet bureaucracy, they are highly skilled in producing the necessary documentation. I was told by the INS that much of the problem of illegal immigrants in Moscow had to do with documentation, with "the paper." The U.S. State Department cannot keep up with the volume of requests emanating from Moscow—from all sources—for permissions to enter the United States.

A 1994 United Nations report addressed this problem of false documentation: "Blank, unissued passports are stolen from passport-issuing authorities around the world. Issued passports are stolen from tourists and travel agencies, and corrupt officials provide passports to smuggling rings" (United Nations, 1994: 3). This has been said to be a problem in Moscow.

Given the complex planning and coordination on an international scale that would be necessary to operate a large network carrying out these tasks, such trafficking operations would certainly seem to qualify as an example of a crime that is organized.

Smuggling Illegals from the Former USSR

A second type of trafficking involving Russians is of persons from the countries of the former Soviet Union who simply want to establish legal residence in Europe, Israel, or the United States. Israel has reported an increase in the use of forged documents both to acquire immigrant rights and to carry out crimes. According to Israeli authorities, the subject of documentation and the issuance of immigrant visas and other permits are said to be so lax in Moscow that they cry out to be misused. There is said to be literally an industry operating out of Moscow producing false documents certifying Jewishness.

In the United States, the INS told me in 1996 that there were increasing indications of Russian involvement in bringing illegal aliens into the United States (mostly by air and many through Seattle, Washington). As of that time, however, the numbers caught had been rather small; for example, twenty-seven illegals from the former USSR were processed by the INS in 1992–93 and thirty-six in 1995–96. There were reports that female illegals from the former USSR had been put to work as prostitutes, bar girls, and go-go dancers and in peep shows in the United States and, in one known instance of women from Estonia, as nannies. But there were no criminal cases involving such activities. The situation in Israel has been said to be similar, where women are put to work in massage parlors, for example. Males were likewise said to be exploited, often as drug couriers and even small-time extortionists. In all these cases, the persons trafficked were forced to pay back the costs incurred in bringing them into the country. Here we see examples of both people being induced to leave home under false promises and migrants being forced into crime to pay their debt.

Prostitution has historically been one of the illegal services operated as a criminal enterprise by traditional organized crime in the West. Human trafficking through and from Russia has especially been linked to prostitution, as Russian women who are illegal migrants have become a source of providers of this illegal service. Prostitution may have become one of the main criminal exports from Russia to the rest of the world. "Organized prostitution by post-Soviet criminals has become an export commodity to foreign countries mainly since 1990. It has reached epidemic proportions as post-Soviet and East European prostitution rings develop in far-flung areas of the globe. Russian, Polish and Ukrainian women, for example, have been turning up in many of the countries of Eastern Europe, Germany, Austria, the former Yugoslavia, Israel, Greece, the United States, China, Turkey, Belgium, the Netherlands, Finland, Sweden, Italy, South Africa, Thailand, Hong Kong, Korea and Cyprus" (Ulrich, 1996: 36).

Prostitution from Russia figures into the issue of human trafficking in a number of ways. For example, in 1995 Greek authorities arrested a number of Greek policemen who were masterminding foreign call-girl trafficking rings in Greece. Scores of Russian and Eastern European women were enticed to come to Greece with promises of wealth and a better life. Once they arrived, their passports were confiscated and sold to nightclub owners. The women were turned into virtual prisoners and forced to prostitute themselves. More recently, it was reported that Greece had become a "European Union foothold for prostitution rings with links throughout the former Soviet bloc" (Murphy, 1998: 22:56). All the arrests in these cases so far have been Greeks, and thus possible Russian organized crime involvement remains an unknown.

Galeotti (1995) reported that German authorities had identified 10,000 women from Eastern and central Europe and the former Soviet Union working as prostitutes there—many of them under duress. Likewise in Israel, it was estimated that as of 1995 approximately 2,500 Russian prostitutes, and a variety of other criminals, had been smuggled in. In the case of the prostitutes, some were said to have come willingly whereas others were coerced.

The number one form of visa fraud involving Russians in the United States is said to be the establishment of false companies that are then used as a basis for inviting "co-workers" into the country. According to the U.S. Immigration and Naturalization Service, in the most common practice, Russians pay "firms" to "transfer" them to the United States. In a related scheme, bogus companies established in the United States sell "business invitations" to migrants in Russia. Once in the United States, these companies may help the migrant regularize his or her status.

In each of these possible types of Russian participation in human trafficking, the smuggling of people might simply be another moneymaking venture for those entrepreneurs who are able and willing to engage in such trafficking, as well as for some professional criminal types. It could be just another example of the crimes of deception at which the Russians are so good. After all, smuggling people might be simply of a kind with smuggling consumer goods, raw materials, and vehicles, in each of which some of the same persons could be involved. If the Russian traffickers are indeed affiliated with organized crime, they might use the money they get from would-be migrants in other criminal ventures. In this way trafficking could be a sideline form of investment.

Smuggling Criminals

The third form of human trafficking involves exporting known criminals—prostitutes, hit men, and so on. In these cases the refugee status is used as a cover for criminal activity. The INS told me in 1996 that people they regarded as leaders in Russian organized crime were "piggybacking" onto legal migrants to insert criminals into the United States. Some of these criminals were reported to be assassins and others fugitives from justice in Russia who had been sent out of the country to "cool off."

Whither the Russian Mafia?

Given these possibilities, what concrete links might be established between this illegal trafficking and the Russian Mafia? Before we turn to the evidence, let us first look at some of the claims that are being made—keeping in mind that we started off by alleging that there might be a Russian Mafia–hyping phenomenon in all of this. Are there allegations that Russian organized crime and specifically the Russian Mafia are in this human trafficking business? Yes indeed there are!

Let us look at just a few examples. The first two come from the media. An article entitled "Slavic Women in Demand in Sex Slave Markets" appeared on the Web site of the Office of International Criminal Justice at the University of Illinois at Chicago. Along with poverty and social disintegration, wrote Tim Stone (1998: 1–2), the "aggressive tactics of Russian organized crime have led to Slavic sexual slaves surpassing all other nationalities." Ukrainian and Russian women are said to be earning criminal gangs "upwards of $500 to $1,000 each." "Predatory Russian organized groups lure women into slavery," and "the Russian Mafia utilizes front companies" to facilitate this enslavement. Stone tells us that Moscow-based Russian crime gangs control international slavery routes, often through cooperative ventures with the Japanese Yakuza, the Italian Mafia, and other organized crime groups. But beyond some very general citations of various authorities, the article offers no hard evidence to support any of these claims.

An earlier article that appeared in the *New York Times* for January 11, 1998, described the human trafficking somewhat less dramatically than the Stone piece but concluded similarly. "Centered in Moscow and the

Ukrainian capital, Kiev, the networks trafficking women run east to Japan and Thailand, where thousands of young Slavic women now work against their will as prostitutes, and west to the Adriatic Coast and beyond. The routes are controlled by Russian crime gangs based in Moscow" (Specter, 1998: 1). A UN official based in Vienna was cited as a source for the article. But interestingly, this official was reported as saying that despite his belief that tens of thousands of women were "certainly" sold into prostitution each year, "he was uncomfortable with statistics since nobody involved has any reason to tell the truth" (3).

Some of the most serious investigation of this issue has been done by the advocacy organization Global Survival Network. And it has made perhaps the strongest argument that it is Russian organized crime that is organizing the trafficking in women from the former Soviet Union. After a lengthy undercover investigation, the organization concluded: "Trafficking in Russia and throughout the world is organized by criminal groups. . . . Even in instances where they are not directly responsible for trafficking women overseas, Russian criminal groups provide a 'krisha' ('roof'), or security and protection, for the operations, and . . . they have incorporated the traffic of women as an increasingly profitable part of their activities inside and outside the country" (Global Survival Network, 1997: 34). But in reaching this conclusion, the Global Survival Network (GSN) seemed to lump together all the thousands of criminal groups identified by the Russian authorities into what they called "mafiya." They also concluded that "mafiya involvement in trafficking amounts to providing 'protection' to sex businesses," that is, the *krisha* concept. For many legitimate businesses in the former Soviet Union, and most particularly in Moscow, having a *krisha* is deemed necessary to their survival. A variety of individuals and groups, including criminal groups and former members of the security establishment, are in the business of providing insurance against trouble with criminals. That these businesses would perhaps include criminal enterprises in general, and human trafficking specifically, is certainly plausible. But without in any way detracting from the importance of the valuable contribution that the GSN has made in its groundbreaking research on the problem of trafficking in women for prostitution, concrete conclusions about a Russian Mafia connection seem at this point to be unwarranted and at best hypothetical.

Recalling the admonition to avoid helping criminals and criminal groups be bigger and tougher than they are, let us first deal with the label *mafia*. Unless one adopts only the most vague and all-encompassing definition of what a mafia is (the one commonly used by the media and the general public), the more than eight thousand criminal groups identified by the Russian Ministry of Internal Affairs are not a mafia or mafias. If a mafia is everything, it is nothing. Preferable, it seems to me, is the carefully delineated definition of mafia set forth by Gambetta (1993), which says that the core business of a mafia is supplying protection. Under this definition, mafias have a quasi-governmental role, and it is this that distinguishes them from simple criminals and criminal entrepreneurs and even from other forms of organized crime. Traditional mafiosi (in the Sicilian sense) are men of honor and respect. They ensure trust and credibility in transactions. As indicated, some Russian criminal groups, although it is unclear just how many, do indeed have the mafialike characteristic of being in this kind of protection business. And they may be providing protection (albeit extortionate)—as a *krisha*—to groups that are trafficking in women and children. But the only evidence for this so far is very limited and strictly anecdotal.

This lack of evidence is at the core of our problem in being able to understand and explain how much of human trafficking is controlled by organized crime. According to a series of reports by the International Organization for Migration, the organization that most closely follows developments in this area, there is a profound absence of data and information about this problem. IOM says that trafficking in women is a considerably underreported offense throughout Europe, but it nevertheless concludes that it is a "numerically small problem" (IOM, 1995: 11). In part because laws are not enforced, there have been few arrests and only a handful of prosecutions and convictions. Even in instances in which there have been arrests and convictions, trafficking in women for prostitution and prostitution in general may not be distinguished. For example, in the data of the Russian MVD for 1995, 1,756 cases of "keeping dens and promoting prostitution" were reported as organized criminal activities. Besides the fact that this seems to be a relatively small number, it does not distinguish between prostitution of the traditional domestic kind and possible cases of trafficking-related prostitution. This same lack of distinction is made between legal and illegal entry of women who may subsequently engage in prostitution.

As pointed out previously, trafficking may be carried out by individual persons as well as by organizations. Unless arrests are made and convictions ensue, the only source of information with respect to who the traffickers are is the women. But in some cases they refuse to testify because they fear legal repercussions or are personally afraid. In almost all cases, they do not know if there is a criminal organization running their trafficking. They do not know who and how many persons might be involved in such organization. "Women usually know about only part of the trafficking network, and often only come into contact with one person" (IOM, 1995: 29). In a report on trafficking and prostitution from central and Eastern Europe, the IOM concluded: "If trafficked women and their advocates are correct in their estimates, the number of known victims represents only the tip of the iceberg. Hardly any statistics are available on the extent of trafficking in women, partly because it is an illegal activity and, hence, difficult to assess, and partly because those agencies which might compile statistics do not regard the practice as important enough to warrant collecting data. Trafficking in women receives considerable media publicity, not so much because of concern for the welfare of victims, but because journalists know that stories about sex and prostitution attract attention" (1995: 33).

Salt and Stein (1997) made the point about lack of data over and over. It is "not yet clear," they said, how the migration business is organized and subdivided because statistics are not generally available (469). "It is uncertain how large a business trafficking has become, how much money it generates, and how many people it employs" (472). They, too, pointed out that the victims of trafficking—who have been almost our only sources of knowledge—often have little useful information because they know about only a minute part of the whole trafficking enterprise (478).

In my interviews with representatives of the Immigration and Naturalization Service (perhaps the U.S. agency most closely associated with the human trafficking problem), the view expressed was that there was organized smuggling involving Russians. But on the question of whether it was organized crime, the answer was "We don't know!" The INS conclusion was that the Russians were not then (1996) entrenched in trafficking activities but that their potential for becoming so was certainly great.

Conclusions

The absence of hard and reliable information leaves this subject open to speculation, to relying upon anecdotal information, and obviously to media sensationalism with respect both to the sex angle and to the Russian Mafia connection. Unfortunately, this can result in poorly informed and misdirected policies.

Ironically, in one sense it might make law enforcement easier if human trafficking were controlled by true organized crime. The targets for investigation and prosecution would at least be much clearer, and the effort could be more focused. It might also mean that law enforcement success against one area of criminal activity would spin off into other criminal ventures controlled by the same organizations. Thus, successful prosecution of a money-laundering scheme could also bring down a human trafficking scheme as well.

On the other hand, an absence of Russian organized crime control of trafficking would mean that the persons involved are in all likelihood less criminally sophisticated, not so well connected politically, and perhaps not as well organized. Mom-and-pop operators, although more numerous, are also more likely to be deterred by serious threats of being caught, prosecuted, and punished. In order for the latter to occur, of course, the threat must be credible.

Portraying human trafficking as almost exclusively linked with organized crime and mafia is also self-defeating in another way. The ultimate solution to the human trafficking problem will not come from law enforcement alone. There must be effective global migration policies that close off the opportunity for exploitation and victimization by criminal elements. But as with many of the business enterprises of organized crime, the ultimate foundation for profits from illicit goods and services is the customers for these goods and services. In this particular case those customers are the consumers and the buyers in the sex industry. It is those customers who make human trafficking profitable, and it is here that attention should be focused. Rationalizing commercial sexual exploitation as being caused by and controlled by the Russian Mafia furnishes a convenient scapegoat and allows the others who are responsible, including the supposedly respectable businessmen who avail themselves of the sexual services offered, to escape blame. Success in combating this problem will only come from a clear assessment of just what the problem is and who is involved.

This is clearly an area that requires much more attention and investigation. Such investigation must, however, avoid the sensationalism and hyperbole associated with a mythical Russian Mafia. Such simplistic explanations ignore the multilayered and complex nature of the trafficking problem. At the same time, attributing trafficking to the Russian Mafia inflates the reputations of two-bit traffickers so as to enhance their criminal success. Neither of these is a desirable outcome.

REFERENCES

Amir, Menachem. 1996. "Organized Crime in Israel." *Transnational Organized Crime* 2 (4): 21–39.

Center for Strategic and International Studies—Global Organized Crime Project. 1997. *Russian Organized Crime.* Washington, D.C.: Center for Strategic and International Studies.

Dolgova, Azalia. 1997. "Organized Crime in Russia."

Dunaeva, Victoria. 1997. "Selling Souls: Russia's Oldest Profession Takes a Grim Turn onto the International Market." *Russian Magazine* (Los Angeles) (October): 36–39. Reprinted in *Trends in Organized Crime* 3 (4) (1998): 40–43.

Dunn, Guy. 1996. "Major Mafia Gangs in Russia." *Transnational Organized Crime* 2(2–3): 63–87.

Finckenauer, James O., and Elin Waring. 1996. "Russian Émigré Crime in the United States: Organized Crime or Crime That Is Organized?" *Transnational Organized Crime*, 2/2/3 (Summer/Autumn): 139–55.

———. 1998. *Russian Mafia in America: Immigration, Culture, and Crime,* Boston: Northeastern University Press.

Galeotti, Mark. 1995. "Cross-Border Crime in the Former Soviet Union." *Boundary and Territory Briefing* (Durham, UK) 1(5).

Gambetta, Diego. 1993. *The Sicilian Mafia.* Cambridge: Harvard University Press.

Global Survival Network. 1997. "Crime and Servitude: An Expose of the Traffic in Women for Prostitution from the Newly Independent States," http://www.globalsurvival.net/femaletrade/9711russia.html, March 26.

International Organization for Migration (IOM). 1996. "Organized Crime Moves into Migrant Trafficking." *Trafficking in Migrants* (Geneva, Switzerland), no. 11 (June): 1–2.

———. 1995. "Trafficking and Prostitution: The Growing Exploitation of Migrant Women from Central and Eastern Europe" (May).

———. 1996. "Trafficking in Women to Italy for Sexual Exploitation." Migration Information Program, Budapest, Hungary (June). Reprinted in *Trends in Organized Crime* 3 (Summer 1998): 32–35.

LaGesse, David, and Ed Timms. 1998. "Immigrant-Smuggling Rings Broken Up, Authorities Say: Dallas-Based Cartels Accused of Moving 7,000 Workers in 3 Years." *Dallas Morning News*, November 21.

Maltz, Michael D. 1990. *Measuring the Effectiveness of Organized Crime Control Efforts*. Chicago: Office of International Criminal Justice.

Martens, Frederick T. 1998. "The 'Russian Mafia': Reinventing The 'Cold War' or a Social Reality." Paper presented to the Canadian Intelligence Officers' Symposium, Ottawa, Canada, September 30.

Murphy, Brian. 1998. "Prostitution Scandal Stuns Greece." Associated Press Office (Athens, Greece), November 19, 22:56.

Nikiforov, Alexander S. "What Shall We Have to Do with Organized Crime?" Unpublished.

Robinson, Laurie Nicole. 1998. "The Globalization of Female Child Prostitution." http://www.law.indiana.edu/glsj/vol5/no1/robinson.html, November 2.

Rosner, Lydia S. 1995. "The Sexy Russian Mafia." *Criminal Organizations* 10 (1): 29.

Rutland, Peter, and Natasha Kogan. 1998. "The Russian Mafia: Between Hype and Reality." http://www.ijt.cz/transitions/thrusmaf.html, November 5.

Salt, John, and Jeremy Stein. 1997. "Migration as a Business: The Case of Trafficking." *International Migration* 35 (4): 467–94.

Schmid, A. P., with E. U. Savona. 1995. *Migration and Crime: A Framework for Discussion*. Milan: International Scientific and Professional Advisory Council of the United Nations Crime Prevention and Criminal Justice Programme.

Siddiqui, Tahir. 1998. "Arrested Thai Woman Turns Out to Be Woman Trafficker." Dawn News Service, November 23.

Specter, Michael. 1998. "Traffickers' New Cargo: Naive Slavic Women." *New York Times*, January 11, A1.

Stone, Tim. "Slavic Women in Demand in Sex Slave Markets." 1998. *C & J International*, Office of International Criminal Justice, University of Illinois at Chicago, May, pp. 1–6.

Ulrich, C. J. 1994. "The Price of Freedom." Conflict Studies 275, Research Institute for the Study of Conflict and Terrorism, London (October), pp. 1–30.

___. 1996. "The New Red Terror: International Dimensions of Post-Soviet Organized Crime." *Low Intensity Conflict and Law Enforcement* 5 (1): 29–44.

———. 1997. "Transnational Organized Crime and Law Enforcement Cooperation in the Baltic States." *Transnational Organized Crime* 3 (2): 111–30.

United Nations. 1994. "Measures to Combat Alien-Smuggling." Report of the Secretary-General. August 30. Pp. 1–23.

Williams, Phil. 1998. "Overview." *Trends in Organized Crime* 3 (4): 3–9.

Winer, Jonathan M. 1997. "Alien Smuggling: Elements of the Problem and the U.S. Response." *Transnational Organized Crime* 3 (1): 50–58.

7 ▪▪▪▪▪▪▪ From Fujian to New York: Understanding the New Chinese Immigration

Zai Liang and Wenzhen Ye

One of the most dramatic episodes of illegal immigration to the United States occurred in the early morning of June 6, 1993, when a Honduran ship ran aground off the coast of Queens in New York City. The captain shouted: "The boat is owned by Honduras, jump and swim to the American shore and you will be free." Some of the 286 people on the ship jumped into the chilly Atlantic, but others waited to be picked up by the U.S. Coast Guard (Fritsch, 1993; McFadden, 1993). The ship that carried these undocumented Chinese, called the *Golden Venture* (*Jinse Maoxian Hao*), had traveled some 17,000 miles in 112 days and arrived in New York City via Africa. Most of the 286 Chinese who were aboard came from Fujian (also known as Fukien) Province on the southeastern coast of China and suffered subhuman conditions during the voyage.[1]

Although this was the most publicized incident of undocumented migration from China in the 1990s, it represents only a small chapter in a much larger operation of underground smuggling of Chinese to the United States that started in the 1980s. Chinese immigration to the United States has had a long history and can be dated at least as far back as the middle of the nineteenth century (Nee and Nee, 1972; Tsai, 1983). However, the recent wave of immigration from China has some unique characteristics that deserve analysts' attention. Compared with earlier waves, the current one involves undocumented immigrants who have been smuggled in through a dense network of connections in New York's Chinatown, Southeast Asia, and China. With the help of sophisticated modern technology, the smugglers communicate between locations, make fake documents (such as passports and visas), and find routes that are difficult for the U.S. Coast Guard and immigration officials to detect. They are also able to smuggle people by whatever means possible, such as mingling them with formal delegations using fake passports, entering the United States through Mexico, and landing directly on the U.S. coast (as occurred in Queens in June 1993).

The smuggling business is extremely lucrative given that undocumented migrants pay as much as forty-seven thousand dollars each for the trip. Therefore, any policy measure aimed at stemming the flow of these migrants is likely to encounter difficulty. Despite the tough measures announced by the Clinton administration after the *Golden Venture* fiasco, undocumented immigrants from Fujian continue to enter the country (Butterfield, 1996; Chen, 1998; Holmes, 1998; McFadden, 1998).

Although journalistic accounts are abundant ("China Arrested 256 Snake Heads," 1996; Faison, 1995; Fritsch, 1993; Kinkead, 1992; Lii, 1996a; McFadden, 1993; Noble, 1995; Schemo, 1993a, 1993b; Treaster, 1993) and two novels on human smuggling have been published in China (Cao, 1995; and Li, 1995), the scholarly literature on the illegal migration from China is just emerging (Chin, 1997, 1998; Kwong, 1997; Skelton, 1996; Smith, 1997). Some analysts contend that China's one-child policy has driven people out of Fujian to the United States as political refugees, whereas others argue that poverty in China and relaxed governmental policies are the major factors (Herbert, 1996). On the basis of interviews with illegal immigrants and smugglers, Kwong (1997) presented a compelling account of the smuggling network and the hidden world of undocumented Fujianese in the labor market, especially in New York City. He stated that the heart of the problem is "the ever-healthy demand of American business for vulnerable, unprotected labor" (Kwong, 1997: 6). In contrast, authors of chapters in Paul Smith's (1997) edited volume documented many aspects of the smuggling process: the network connections between migrants and smugglers, the potential of a large volume of illegal migration from China in the future, the relationship between China's large floating population and illegal migration from China, and the experiences of newly arrived undocumented Chinese. So far the most comprehensive study of illegal migration from China and the social organization of human smuggling is by Chin (1998) who conducted interviews with three hundred illegal migrants in New York's Chinatown.

Despite recent scholarly efforts in this area, several critical questions remain. For example, why have undocumented Chinese migrants come primarily from Fujian instead of other provinces? What are the basic characteristics of Fujian and major immigrant-sending communities that are conducive to international migration? Are immigrants mainly from the bottom of the socioeconomic hierarchy? The complex process of smuggling migrants from Fujian defies simplification and requires the examination of many factors at different levels—individual, community, national, and international.

In this chapter, we examine the causes of the recent surge in migration from Fujian to the New York metropolitan area, drawing on historical documents, secondary statistics from China, a survey conducted in Fujian, and our two field trips to Fujian in 1994 and 1998. First, we briefly review the literature on undocumented immigration to the United States and the significance of immigration from Fujian. Next, we present a profile of several major immigrant-sending communities in Fujian. Then we offer explanations for the flow of undocumented migrants from Fujian. We argue that undocumented migration from Fujian is a continuation of its long-term tradition of international migration. For centuries, Fujian sent a large number of international migrants to Nan Yang (Southeast Asia) and, to a lesser extent, to the United States. Current undocumented migration from Fujian does not stem from absolute poverty. Rather, it is based on a sense of relative deprivation caused by increasing inequality that is driven by China's transition to a market economy and remittance from overseas Fujianese. The involvement of international smuggling organizations has been instrumental in making this undocumented migration possible.

Significance of Recent Fujianese Immigration

Although there has been little research on undocumented immigration from China, there is a large body of literature on undocumented immigration to the United States, particularly from Mexico (Massey et al., 1987; Heer, 1992). The size and patterns of undocumented aliens have been carefully documented along with the impact on the U.S. economy (Massey et al., 1987; Massey and Singer, 1995; Smith and Edmonston, 1998; Warren and Passel, 1987). The focus on undocumented Mexican immigrants mainly reflects the fact that Mexicans constitute the largest volume of undocumented immigrants to the United States (Espenshade, 1995). Although the most comprehensive volume on international migration (Massey et al., 1998) claims to summarize patterns of international migration in all regions of the world, illegal migration from China in the 1990s is barely discussed.

The recent surge in undocumented migrants from other countries (such as China) provides an opportunity to study this type of migration from a country other than Mexico. We argue that because of the unique geographical position of Mexico and the unique relationship between Mexico and the United States, the findings from studies of Mexican immigrants may not necessarily be generalizable to the patterns of undocumented migration from other countries. Massey et al. (1994: 739) made a similar point: "Far too much research is centered in Mexico, which because of its unique relationship with the United States may be unrepresentative of broader patterns and trends. . . . More attention needs to be devoted to other prominent sending countries, such as the Philippines, the Dominican Republic, Jamaica, Colombia, El Salvador, Korea, and China." Our research is a step in this direction.

Furthermore, in our view, the current immigrants from Fujian differ in many aspects not only from Mexican immigrants but also from earlier Chinese immigrants. Previous waves of immigrants from China came predominantly from Guangdong, a province in southern China, and settled in Chinatowns throughout the United States (Lin, 1998; Zhou, 1992). In contrast, most of the recent undocumented Chinese immigrants have come from rural Fujian and have mainly settled in the New York metropolitan area. The *Golden Venture* fiasco is not an isolated incident, and it indicates a new trend in Chinese immigration to the United States. The exact number of Fujianese in New York is, however, difficult to estimate because many of them are undocumented and therefore are not countable in formal surveys or censuses conducted in the United States. However, Einhorn (1994) estimated that as many as 100,000 Fujianese were living in New York in 1994 and that an additional 10,000 enter each year.

One way to get a sense of the extent of immigration from Fujian is to use the Chinese census and survey data. In a recent paper, Liang (forthcoming) describes the trends of emigration from Fujian over time. According to his findings, in 1990, Fujian had already surpassed Guangdong (29,580 versus 18,688) and ranked third (after Shanghai and Beijing). By 1995, however, Fujian ranked first in the number of emigrants, sending 66,200 people (or 28% of China's emigrant population) abroad, and Guangdong ranked ninth, with only 7,200 emigrants. It should be noted that the number of emigrants identified in Chinese censuses and surveys includes both legal and illegal migrants. It is possible that family members simply do not report that another family member has migrated illegally. Therefore, the number of emigrants for Fujian as reported in Liang's paper is likely to be an underestimate of the actual number of emigrants.

The common destinations for Fujianese immigrants are Japan, Taiwan, the United States, and Australia (Kwong, 1996). Fujianese actually would rather immigrate to Japan because it is much less expensive to go there and the wages are higher than other places. But the only problem is that "the Japanese government routinely deported those arrested back to China after informing the Fujian provincial authorities" (Kwong, 1997: 61). Many Fujianese believe that immigration officials in the United States are much more lenient than those in Japan and Taiwan. Thus some who are unsuccessful in entering Japan or Taiwan try to go to the United States (Ye, 1995). Within the United States, the most frequent final destination of Fujianese immigrants is New York City, partly because smuggling organizations in Chinatown orchestrate the smuggling process and partly because of the availability of jobs in restaurants and the garment industry.

As a result of the large volume of immigrants from Fujian to the New York area, the Fujianese population and community have quickly emerged and challenged the traditional dominance of immigrants from Guangdong. Fujianese have a dense social network, speak their own dialects, and have their own lawyers who help them get green cards and resolve other legal matters. In a stroll along East Broadway in Manhattan's Chinatown, one sees many Fujianese-owned businesses, such as driving schools, dating services, service centers for naturalization, and employment agencies. All these services make the settlement process much easier for the undocumented Fujianese.

What Drives Immigration from Fujian?

Historical Roots and Legacy of Emigration

Fujian is the province closest to Taiwan across the Taiwan Strait and is near such Southeast Asian countries as Singapore, Malaysia, the Philippines, and Indonesia. It had a population of 31 million in 1993. Fujian can be characterized as "a mountain province in Southeast China"; 80 percent of its geographical area is covered by mountains (CMEC, 1993). Because Fujian is also a coastal province, its fishing industry is an important aspect of its economy and employment.

Emigration from Fujian started during the Ming dynasty in the middle of the fifteenth century and gained significant momentum during the Qing dynasty in the seventeenth century (Zhu, 1991). Some Chinese emigrated voluntarily, but millions (particularly those from Fujian and Guangdong) were imported by European colonials to work at their tropical plantations and tin mines (Alexander, 1973; Kwong, 1996).

The large exodus of the Fujianese did not start until after the Opium War, which China lost to Great Britain. As part of the war settlement, China signed the Treaty of Nanking on August 29, 1842 (Spence, 1991). Article 2 of the treaty permitted the opening of five Chinese port cities—Guangzhou, Fuzhou, Xiamen, Ningbo, and Shanghai—for residence by British subjects and their families. Two of the port cities—Fuzhou and Xiamen—are located in Fujian.

The signing of this treaty greatly facilitated the exodus of Chinese laborers (Pan, 1990). This was also a time in which the Industrial Revolution was in high gear. Having abolished the international slave trade, Britain was looking for alternative cheap labor for its colonies. The discovery of gold in California provided a stimulus for the Chinese to emigrate to the United States (Sung, 1967; Zhou, 1992).

With regard to push factors within China, one was the country's unprecedented population growth during the late Ming and mid-Qing periods. The best estimates suggest that in 1685 China had a population of 100 million. About a hundred years later, in 1790, its population was 301 million—an increase of 200 percent (Ho, 1959; Spence, 1991). The rapid growth of China's population created enormous pressure on the forces of production and plunged many people into poverty. This was especially the case in Fujian, about 80 percent of whose geographical area is covered by mountains. Meanwhile, rich merchants and landlords held large tracts of land, which deprived many peasants of their means of livelihood (Zhu, 1991). Finally, the Taiping Rebellion (1850–64), which attempted to overthrow the Qing government, also created some uncertainties for Chinese society, especially in the south.

It was under these historical conditions that a large exodus of Chinese emigrants took place. The majority of Chinese emigrants were either contract laborers or debtor (indentured) laborers, who had to work a certain number of years to pay off their transportation expenses, after which they would be free. However, whether these Chinese came as contract labor or debtor labor, many of them were actually treated as de facto slaves. This chapter in Chinese history is commonly known as "coolie trade" or "piglet" (Ye, 1995; Zhu, 1991).

From 1845 to 1874, Fujian's level of emigration from the port of Xiamen was modest. Emigration began to increase in 1875 when 16,683 left Fujian, rising to 43,613 in 1885, 105,416 in 1990, 126,008 in 1915, and then dropping to 77,781 in 1920 (Zhu, 1991). Unfortunately, statistics for migration by countries of destination are not available for these years. However, there seems to be a consensus among scholars that the majority of these emigrants left for Southeast Asia and that others went to the United States, Australia, and New Zealand.

The massive Chinese emigration has changed the demography of many Southeast Asian countries and others as well (Poston, Mao, and Yu, 1994). For instance, 80 percent of the Chinese in the Philippines, 55 percent in Indonesia, 50 percent in Burma, and 40 percent in Singapore are of Fujian origin (Zhu, 1991).

Many of the Chinese in Southeast Asian countries have been economically successful (Alexander, 1973). The overseas Chinese also play an important role in the economic development of China by sending remittances back home and by contributing money to educational institutions in China. One of the most prominent Chinese businessmen was Dr. Chen Jiageng, who emigrated from Fujian to Singapore. He founded Xiamen University in Xiamen, Fujian Province, and became a legendary figure of overseas Chinese.

It is because of these earlier emigrants from Fujian that many villages in Fujian are "overseas Chinese villages" (*qiao xiang*) with intensive networks between them and the overseas Chinese of Fujian origin. Thus it is common for Fujianese to have relatives living abroad. As has been shown, emigration is deeply rooted in Fujian's cultural heritage. However, this tradition of emigration came to a halt with the Chinese Revolution of 1949 to 1978 because its citizens were not permitted to leave China.[2]

Escaping Poverty or Relative Deprivation?

Do undocumented Fujianese migrants come to the United States because they are poor in China? Our answer is yes and no. The Fujianese are certainly poor according to the standard of living in the United States, but they are by no means poor compared with people in the rest of China. We first analyze Fujian's economic conditions in relation to the rest of China and then analyze the economic conditions of some of the major immigrant-sending regions within the province of Fujian.

Fujian's level of economic development is closely connected to its geographical position in relation to Taiwan. As the province of mainland China closest to Taiwan, Fujian had long been treated by both China and Taiwan as a military frontier province, and people on both sides of the Taiwan Strait were expecting a war to break out at any time. In fact, the exchange of canon fire between Fujian and Taiwan lasted for about three decades. The tension in the Taiwan Strait began to ease only in the 1970s when Chiang Kai-shek died and his son Chiang Ching-kou assumed power. For this reason, Fujian, which did not have a strong industrial base to begin with, received less investment from the Chinese central government.

However, ever since China initiated the transition to a market-oriented economy in 1978, Fujian has enjoyed a steady economic growth. The quality of life has also improved significantly compared with that in the other provinces. In 1979, China announced the opening of four Special Economic Zones, including Xiamen in Fujian (Crane, 1990), with the intention of attracting foreign investment and stimulating the economy. It is also because of its close proximity to Taiwan that Fujian received a large investment from Taiwan, which further boosted its local economy. In 1992, a year before the ill-fated voyage of the *Golden Venture*, Fujian received $6 billion in foreign investments, whereas other Chinese provinces received on average only half that amount. The investment capital from Taiwan is particularly noticeable: $6.96 billion from 1978 to 1999 ("Experimental Region of Collaboration," 1999). Because of the relatively flexible economic policies and preferential treatment that Fujian has received since 1978, some sociologists classify it as a laissez-faire province, along with Guangdong Province in southern China (Lyons, 1994; Nee, 1996; Parish and Michelson, 1996).

The overall economic prosperity in Fujian since 1978 is further supported by the statistics on per capita income of rural households in various Chinese provinces in 1992. It is more relevant to study per capita income for rural households because most of the undocumented Fujianese migrants are from rural areas. In 1978, when China's transition to a market-oriented economy had just started, the per capita income in rural Fujian households was only about 134 yuan, compared with 133 yuan for China as a whole. What makes Fujian distinctive is that Fujian's rural household per capita income grew at a much faster rate than that of the average province in China. For example, from 1978 to 1988, Fujian's per capita income for rural households increased by 168 percent, compared with 146 percent for rural China as a whole.[3] The difference is even more pronounced for the period 1978–92. During that time, Fujian's rural household per capita income rose by 229 percent versus 179 percent for rural households of China as a whole. As a result, the per capita income of Fujian's rural households rose to eighth place (out of thirty provinces) in 1992 (compared with twelfth in 1978). These data indicate that in contrast to other provinces in China, Fujian has enjoyed a particular advantage in the process of transition to a market-oriented economy. Therefore, at the provincial level, there is no evidence that Fujian is poor compared with the rest of China.

We further examine the economic conditions of major immigrant-sending regions in Fujian—Fuzhou (the capital of Fujian), Fuqing, Changle, Lianjiang, and Pingtan—all of which are concentrated in the eastern part of Fujian and are geographically very close to one another. Fuzhou is a large metropolis with a population of 5 million and is the center of political and economic activities in the province. Fuqing and Changle are extremely close to Fuzhou. Pingtan County is an island off the east coast and is the farthest county from Fuzhou of the immigrant-sending regions. Un-

Table 3. Characteristics of Major Immigrant-Sending Regions in Fujian Province, 1993

Region	Population (thousands)	Average Salary (yuan)	Per Capita Income (yuan)
Fuzhou city	5,507	4,803	N.A.
Fuqing city	1,101	4,853	1,640
Changle County	654	4,176	1,538
Lianjiang County	613	4,101	1,305
Pingtan County	344	4,101	1,065
Fujian Province	30,992	4,890	1,211

Source: State Statistical Bureau (1994).

like the northern provinces of China where Mandarin is the standard language, people in Fujian speak many local dialects. Thus a person who speaks the Fuzhou dialect, for example, would not be able to communicate in Xiamen, another well-known city in Fujian that is not in these five regions. However, because of the geographical proximity of these five immigrant-sending regions, they all share a common dialect: the Fuzhou dialect. This common local dialect has implications once Fujian immigrants move to the New York metropolitan area.

Table 3 reveals several characteristics of Fujian's five major immigrant-sending regions. Column 3 shows the average salary for urban workers in each region. The average yearly salaries for workers in urban Fuzhou and Fuqing are almost equivalent to the average of Fujian Province as a whole. These data indicate that Fuzhou and Fuqing are not poor by Fujian standards. Workers in the urban areas of the other three regions (Changle, Lianjiang, and Pingtan) are paid slightly lower than the average for Fujian. However, as we discussed earlier, since most undocumented Fujianese are from rural areas, it is more relevant to examine the corresponding figures for such areas.

The per capita incomes for rural households in these immigrant-sending regions are quite different. In fact, with the exception of Pingtan, rural households in these regions enjoy an advantage in per capita income, especially in Fuqing and Changle. This finding is consistent with the macrolevel portrait of development in Fujian in general. Kristof (1993), a reporter for the *New York Times*, went to Fujian after the *Golden Venture* episode and made similar observations.[4]

If absolute poverty is not the reason for migration, why are Fujianese risking their lives to come to the United States? We argue that a sense of relative deprivation is causing Fujianese peasants to make desperate attempts to migrate. The theory of relative deprivation was first suggested by Stouffer et al. (1949) in their study of army life, especially in relation to promotions during World War II. According to this theory, an individual makes judgments about his or her welfare that are based not only on his or her absolute level of material possessions (such as income) but perhaps more important on the relative level of welfare in reference to others in the community. This sense of relative deprivation has strong implications for an individual's behavior.

In the 1960s and 1970s, the concept of relative deprivation was used to study mobilization and rebellion (see, e.g., Gurr, 1969; Tilly, 1978). More recently, economist Stark and his associates have used this concept to study migration, and the concept is now a major component of the "new economics of migration" (Stark, 1991). In a study of migration from Mexico to the United States, Stark and Taylor hypothesized that "given a household's initial absolute income and its expected net income from migration, more relatively deprived households are more likely to send migrants to foreign labor markets than are less relatively deprived households" (Stark and Taylor, 1989: 4). This hypothesis is supported by data on migration from Mexico (Stark and Taylor, 1989; see also Portes and Rumbaut, 1996).

We argue that the relative deprivation approach has particular relevance for explaining undocumented migration from Fujian Province. China's transition to a market-oriented economy has dramatically increased overall income inequality because many people seized the opportunity to get rich quickly by whatever means possible (Khan and Riskin, 1998; Liu, 1995). The most commonly used measure of income inequality is the Gini index (Xie and Hannum, 1996). A Gini index of .4 or larger is considered to be exceptionally high inequality. The World Bank (1996) reported that China's Gini index was .374 in 1992. More recently, according to a study conducted by the People's University of China in Beijing, China's Gini index was .434 in 1994 (He, 1996). The large and growing value of the Gini index is consistent with the findings from social surveys in China that have suggested that a substantial proportion of respondents have complained about the rising income inequality over time

(CND, 1996). The increased inequality in China makes people at the bottom feel a sense of relative deprivation and desperate to find ways to make money and become rich. Going to the United States, through either legal or illegal channels, is an alternative way of getting rich, they think.

With regard to Fujian Province, Lyons (1998) conducted the most systematic study on trends in income disparity in Fujian. Using county-level data from Fujian Province from 1978 to 1995, Lyons analyzed changes in income distribution. He found that the county coefficient of variation (a measure of relative disparity in income) in rural households increased from .209 in 1983 to .273 in 1995. One source of increased relative income disparity is remittance. Although no direct information is available on the amount of remittance sent to Fujian each year, one can gauge the impact of remittance through other channels. As Lyons (1998) argued, part of the remittance was used to start nonagricultural enterprises that have increased rapidly since 1978.

The impact of remittance can also be detected through consumption patterns. One of the ways emigrant households spend the remittance is to build new houses or improve housing conditions. On our recent trip to Changle, one of the major immigrant-sending regions in Fujian, we saw many newly built brick houses. Using data from the 1995 China 1% Population Sample Survey, Liang and Zhang (1999) further analyzed the impact of emigration on housing conditions in Fujian. They found that, controlling for other important sociodemographic characteristics (such education, age, and occupation), families with emigrants are more likely to live in larger houses and have better housing conditions (including the type of cooking fuel used and the availability of a private bathroom and kitchen).

Local Fujianese also like to build fancy tombs for their ancestors to symbolize the good virtue of the ancestors in making the overseas venture possible. We also saw some elementary schools that were supported by money from overseas, many of which bear the names of the overseas Fujianese who donated money for them. The flow of a large amount of remittance also changes the income distribution in the communities, creating a sense of relative deprivation for those Fujian peasants who do not receive it, and provides further impetus for going abroad.

The lavish spending and consumption patterns of Fujianese who return from abroad also contribute to a sense of relative deprivation by the local Fujianese. From the founding of the People's Republic of China to 1977, having a relative abroad was not something of which to be proud. In fact, during the Cultural Revolution of 1966–76, it was a major source of trouble and cause for political persecution. Many families with relatives abroad were accused of spying for foreign countries and therefore severely punished. However, since 1978, China has changed its policy toward the overseas Chinese and has encouraged them to visit China and especially to invest in businesses. As a result, more and more of the overseas Chinese return to visit relatives (*sheng qin*) and to do business in their hometown.[5]

Most of the overseas Chinese of Fujian origin visit relatives during the Chinese New Year. They stay in luxury hotels, bring fancy gifts from abroad, give *hong bao* (red purses, money) to friends and relatives, go to karaoke clubs, and have big feasts in expensive restaurants for relatives. Ye (1995) estimated that almost 80 percent of the customers who stay in hotels in Fuzhou during the Chinese New Year are overseas Chinese of Fujian origin who are visiting relatives. Because of the large volume of overseas Fujianese who visit, some hotels depend on them for business. One manager at a hotel in the city of Fuzhou put it in this way: "To tell you the truth, without the Fujianese returning home for visits, our business could not survive."

Local Fujianese are overwhelmed by how much wealth one can accumulate abroad. What they are rarely told is how hard one has to work to make it and often under subhuman conditions; they only see how glamorous it is to work abroad. The return of the overseas Chinese has particularly motivated peasants in Fujian to migrate internationally because of the extravagant lifestyles that the visiting overseas Fujianese display.

The large volume of emigration and remittance have had a major impact on the local economy. In other provinces of China, it is customary to build the major airport in the capital city of the province. In Fujian, however, the biggest airport was built in Changle, not in the capital city of Fuzhou. In a casual stroll along a street in Changle, one sees many business banners with the word *hua qiao* (overseas Chinese) attached. To accommodate overseas Chinese, several hotels and travel agencies are named *hua qiao* hotels or *hua qiao* travel agencies.

Under such circumstances, migration is perceived as "the thing to do"—the only way that young people can advance economically (Portes,

1997). In some villages in Fujian, almost 90 percent of the young people have gone abroad (Ye, 1995). Young people who are reluctant to go abroad are considered *mei chu xi* (no great future). As more and more people emigrate to other countries, more and more Fujianese communities emerge (especially in New York), which further facilitates the process of migration for other family members from the same communities in Fujian. This is the nature of the cumulative causation of migration, which has been documented clearly in the case of Mexican migration to the United States (Massey et al., 1994).

We have so far discussed changes in income disparity in Fujian from 1983 to 1995 and examined various ways remittances have been spent and their impact on the local economy and in further stimulating more emigration. To substantiate further our argument about relative deprivation, we turn now to the question of who migrated internationally from Fujian. Table 4 compares the sociodemographic characteristics of emigrants and nonemigrants from Fujian Province. This comparison is important, because research on Chinese immigration to the United States usually focuses on the Chinese immigrants and rarely examines how immigrants compare with the people who choose to stay. As table 4 shows, men are heavily represented in the emigrant population, accounting for 74 percent of the emigrants. The mean ages of the emigrant and nonemigrant populations are similar, but they actually mask a major difference in the age distribution of the two groups. Nearly 70 percent of the emigrants versus 27 percent of the nonemigrants are in the working age of twenty to thirty-four. Another major difference is education. Almost 16 percent of nonemigrants, but fewer than 1 percent of the emigrants, have no formal education. Nearly half of the emigrants have junior high school education, whereas close to 50 percent of the nonemigrants have only an elementary school education. Thus, if education is used as a proxy for socioeconomic status, it is clear that emigrants from Fujian are not at the bottom of socioeconomic hierarchy.[6]

Culture of Seafaring

Unlike earlier Fujian emigration to either Nan Yang (Southeast Asia) or the United States, the current illegal immigration is highly risky. For example, the *Golden Venture* traveled 112 days, passing Thailand, going

Table 4. Sociodemographic Characteristics of Emigrants and Nonemigrants, Fujian, 1995

Variables	Emigrant (%)	Nonemigrant (%)
Sex		
Male	74.1	50.79
Age (yr.)		
0–14	0.55	29.59
15–19	8.26	8.2
20–34	68.04	27.43
35+	23.14	34.77
Mean Age	29.21	29.03
Marital Status		
Unmarried	37.95	22.41
Married, spouse present	61.22	68.02
Remarried, spouse present	0.55	1.7
Divorced	0	0.65
Widowed	0.28	6.53
Education		
No formal education	0.28	15.88
Literate	0	3.75
Elementary school	27.42	48.23
Junior high school	47.92	22.42
High school	19.39	7.32
Junior college and above	4.99	1.56
Place of Origin		
City	17.36	14.34
Town	17.08	8.33
Rural	65.56	77.33

Source: Liang and Zhang (1999).

through Africa (Kenya and the Ivory Coast), and finally reaching Queens in New York City (Schemo, 1993b). The Fujianese aboard suffered from the lack of food and poor nutrition, isolation, and extremely poor sanitary conditions (Schemo, 1993b; 1993a). It is hard to imagine that the average Chinese could endure such an ordeal. Do Fujianese have any particular characteristics that make them exceptionally risk taking? We argue that their familiarity with sea life facilitates the voyage to the United States.

The sea is a way of life for many Fujianese. Because Fujian is located on the southeastern coast of China, many Fujianese depend on fishing for a living. They are more familiar with life at sea and are not afraid of its difficult conditions. Mr. Chen, a fisherman in Fujian, said: "There is a risk of not being able to return for every fishing trip. But how can you catch fish without going to the sea? For me, going to America is just like another fishing trip." Another informant expressed it this way: "I am from Changle, we are sons of the sea. Our life depends on the sea for generations. . . . My wife does not worry about me when I go on a fishing trip for days because she knows I am going to be ok" (cited in Xin 1993). This unique way of life and culture helps the Fujianese overcome the fear of a voyage of several months and of enduring the conditions that would perhaps be unbearable for most non-Fujianese.

The deep connection with sea life can be traced throughout in Fujianese history and in Fujian's folklore. A well-known Chinese scholar of the Ming dynasty wrote: "Hai zhe min ren zhi tian ye" [sea is the field for Fujianese] (Wang, 1994: 4). Because of the lack of arable land, the Fujianese have for many years earned their living by fishing. There is also a saying that Fujian has a silk road on the sea. During the Ming dynasty, Fujianese took advantage of several port cities and the ready availability of good-quality lumber for shipbuilding to transport silk and cotton from Jiangsu and Zhejiang Provinces for export to other countries (Wang, 1994).

The most famous folktale is of Mazu, the sea goddess. Legend has it that Mazu always helps people through hardships and, in particular, rescues fishermen when they face crises at sea. Even today, before fishermen in Fujian go fishing, they pray to Mazu to protect them. This tradition has been carried over to the Fujianese immigrant community in New York. In February 1999, during the annual parade of the Lunar Chinese New Year in Flushing and Manhattan's Chinatown, we observed floats carrying statues of Mazu.

History and folklore are suggestive of the Fujianese's close attachment to the sea, but they are not a substitute for a rigorous and systematic analysis. Therefore we measured the importance of the fishing industry in the current Fujianese economy. Compared with other provinces in China, the fishing industry accounts for 17 percent of the total agricultural output in 1992—the highest proportion among all the provinces of mainland China (SSB, 1993). The fishing industry is clearly more important in Fu-

jian than in other provinces. Moreover, the total value of the fishing industry output places Fujian in fourth place behind Guangdong, Shandong, and Zhejiang (all coastal provinces) (SSB, 1993).

The importance of fishing is even more evident if one looks at the five
immigrant-sending regions—Fuzhou, Fuqing, Changle, Lianjiang, and
Pingtan. On average, more than half (54%) the agricultural output value
is related to fishing industries of these regions (SSB, 1994). This is particularly the case for Lianjiang and Pingtan Counties, whose fishing outputs
account for 69 percent and 75 percent of the total agricultural outputs,
respectively (SSB, 1994).

Despite the unique economic structure in the immigrant-sending communities, which is dominated largely by fishing-related industries, the rich
historical evidence, and folklore linking Fujianese culture with sea life, we
are by no means suggesting that most emigrants are fishermen before their
departure.[7] Instead, we argue that life at sea is familiar to many Fujianese
who live in these regions and that this familiarity prepares them well for
the sometimes dangerous journey to the United States or other destination countries.

Snake People and Snakeheads

Given the significant income and wage differentials in Fujian, the Fujianese are clearly motivated to migrate to the United States. However,
many Fujianese cannot make the journey on their own. Many players assist in this process: snakeheads, or *she tou* (smugglers), who organize the
entire smuggling process; corrupt Chinese officials, who make sure that
the Chinese Coast Guard conveniently disappears when ships carrying illegal immigrants leave for international waters (Kwong, 1997); contacts
in many transit countries who arrange for charter flights to the United
States or are subcontracted to help the immigrants across the U.S. border;
enforcers in New York whose task is to threaten and torture illegal immigrants until they pay their debts; and, finally the snake people, or *ren
she*[8] (the illegal migrants), who usually endure long journeys to and harsh
working conditions in the United States. The smuggling of undocumented
Fujianese is a complex and difficult operation that does not succeed without an extremely careful plan and collaboration around the globe.

The snakeheads are much more sophisticated than the "coyotes" who help Mexicans cross the U.S.-Mexican border. Their organizations are transnational and have access to the most advanced technology for communication. Their passport and visa factories have the capacity to make fake passports of any country, fake visas to the United States, and any other documents that are needed. They are also able to obtain the most up-to-date information and plan the best possible routes for smuggling people.

The smuggling process typically begins in the communities in Fujian, where smugglers go to recruit potential migrants. Most experts in the study of human smuggling believe that the mastermind of today's smuggling organization is located in Taiwan (Kwong, 1997; Myers, 1997). Such earlier smuggling was pretty much a mom-and-pop operation with limited contacts around the globe and involved smuggling only a few individuals at a time. These operations were run mostly by Cantonese, people from Guangdong Province, another coastal province not far from Fujian (Myers, 1997). However, it was not until the "Taiwan connection" was established that smugglers had access to sophisticated technology and were able to transport large numbers of people with high rate of success.

The ability to establish a global smuggling network seems to be an unintended consequence of the Cold War. After the defeat of the Kuomintang (KMT) by Mao Zedong's People's Liberation Army in 1949, KMT head Chiang Kai-shek was preparing to regain mainland China when the opportunity arose. As an integral part of this strategy, the Intelligence Bureau of the Military National Defense (IBMND) was cultivating all its connections among those who fled China (many of whom had connections with criminal organizations [Kwong, 1997]). According to Myers (1997) and Kwong (1997), with funding and training from the CIA, the IBMND turned the KMT Third Army in Myanmar and Thailand into "Chinese Irregular Forces," who were alleged to be involved in heroin production and export. In the late 1950s, again with further support from the CIA, Taiwan expanded its technical and economic assistance to countries in Africa, Central and South America, and the Caribbean islands. "Thousands of Taiwanese were transferred to work in aid programs . . . and many thousand more Taiwanese emigrated to these obscure countries" (Myers, 1997: 106). Although there is no direct evidence of the Taiwan government's involvement in human smuggling, there is no doubt that Taiwanese crime organizations have taken advantage of the foundations laid by the Taiwan government, and the U.S. law enforcement officials strongly suspect that Taiwan's military and intelligence communities are involved in and profit from the human smuggling trade (Kwong, 1997: 87). In any event, it is clear that smugglers have a dense network that reaches every part of the world: Fujian, Taiwan, Hong Kong, the Golden Triangle (northern mountain region of Myanmar, Thailand, and Laos), Latin America, Africa, and New York's Chinatown.

The Taiwanese have another advantage in smuggling Fujianese to the United States other than geographical proximity: the cultural linkage between Fujian and Taiwan. Many people in Taiwan (80% by some estimates; see "Experimental Region of Collaboration," 1999) are the descendants of Fujianese who migrated to Taiwan many years ago. Though the local dialects are not entirely identical, the Taiwanese and Fujianese have many similar cultural traditions, such as praying to the sea goddess Mazu for safety. This cultural homogeneity facilitates communication and builds a sense of trust, which is essential for smuggling people thousands of miles away from their homes.

There are several strategies for smuggling snake people into the United States. One strategy is to use fake documents that allow them to land directly at airports in the United States. In this case, the snake people first buy fake Taiwanese, Singaporean, Malaysian, or South Korean passports to apply for U.S. visas as citizens of these countries. Often through travel agencies in the United States and China, snake people also mingle with different delegations from China. The only difference is that snake people will simply disappear upon arrival at the destination. Often they are picked up by the smugglers and assigned to work in restaurants or garment factories in the New York metropolitan area. This strategy continues to be used. On December 27, 1997, eight Fujianese were about to board Air China Flight 981 from Shanghai to New York's JFK airport. Chinese immigration inspector Chen Haiyin noted that all eight Fujianese held Chinese passports and U.S. immigration visas but looked suspicious, so she detained them for further inspection of the documents. It turned out that all eight visas were forged ("$120,000 Bought 8 Pages," 1997).

The second strategy requires snake people to pass through transit countries in other parts of the world before they reach the United States. Some snake people travel on foot and by bus from China's Yunnan Province (southwestern China) to Thailand and other Southeast Asian countries

206 .... Case Studies: Mexico, Russia, and China

and then take flights to the United States (Liu, 1996; Myers, 1997). "Between eastern and western processing and holding centers, more than 43 countries played a transit role in airborne and seaborne smuggling" (Myers, 1997: 117). Mexico is a major transit country for snake people. Once they arrive in Mexico, local subcontractors take them across the U.S.-Mexican border.

Another variation of this channel is for snake people to arrive in Canada using Hong Kong passports, since holders of Hong Kong passports do not need visas to enter Canada. Once in Canada, the snake people will be transported to the United States. On December 10, 1998, Doris Meissner, the commissioner of the Immigration and Naturalization Service, announced the crackdown of a smuggling ring that had brought more than thirty-six hundred illegal Chinese immigrants into the United States over the previous two years (Chen, 1998; Holmes, 1998). The ring, consisting mainly of Chinese and members of a Native American tribe, transported immigrants through an upstate New York Indian reservation that was guarded minimally by the U.S. Border Patrol.

Another strategy is to smuggle snake people by sea. Snakeheads often use crumbling freighters or fishing vessels owned by Taiwanese. Between 1991 and 1993, thirty-two ships with a total of fifty-three hundred Chinese were found in the waters of Japan, Taiwan, Indonesia, Australia, Singapore, Hawaii, Guatemala, El Salvador, Honduras, and the United States (Chin, 1996: 157). In sum, whatever strategies snake people use to enter the United States, it is clear that they cannot make it to the United States without the involvement of snakeheads.

New York's Chinatown plays a pivotal role in this process as well. For a good part of this century, crime and gang activity have been part of life in New York's Chinatown (Chin, 1996; Kwong, 1996), but it was not until recent years that members of Chinatown's organized crime organizations became involved in smuggling immigrants from China, among other things (Cooper, 1996).[9] In New York, the smugglers (often in the name of "welcoming and receiving organizations") are responsible for picking up the snake people and escorting them to Chinatown for employment and sometimes sending them to work outside New York if opportunities are available. They also make sure that all snake people are taken care of by enforcers to collect the smuggling fees. In some cases, enforcers use severe physical torture and sometimes sexual abuse to collect the smuggling debt (Chin, 1997; Kwong, 1997).

Summary and Discussion

This chapter has striven comprehensively and systematically to examine undocumented immigration from China's Fujian Province. It first provided a historical overview of emigration from Fujian Province, showing that emigration from Fujian is not a new phenomenon. This historical legacy has stimulated contemporary out-migration because of the lifestyle overseas Fujianese display when they visit Fujian. What is new, however, is the extremely dangerous form this new migration has taken. One important fact that has often been overlooked is that since they live on the east coast of China, many Fujianese are used to life at sea and risk taking as a way of life. This trait makes them particularly good candidates for being snake people.

We suggest that the sense of relative deprivation driven by China's transition to a market economy and the large amount of remittance sent to Fujian are other critical factors in the decisions of Fujianese to immigrate to other countries. Even though the standard of living in Fujian has risen, people at the bottom of the income hierarchy feel poorer than they actually are when they see others getting rich so quickly. In addition, our data clearly show that people who live in these immigrant-sending communities are not poor compared with those in the rest of China or in the rest of Fujian. We suggest, as Massey (1995) pointed out, that in one way or another China's transition to a market-oriented economy has planted some seeds for migration.

What distinguishes Fujianese immigration from other cases (such as the Mexican) is the heavy involvement of the transnational smuggling network. Although the involvement of this network increases the success rate of smuggling, it also increases the cost, which makes this type of migration not accessible to everyone. However, this pattern began to change recently. During our fieldwork in the summer of 1994, we found that snakeheads have started using some new tactics in recruiting potential snake people. For example, they send women with children to chat with potential snake people, which makes the recruitment less threatening, and recruiters often tell potential snake people stories of success of former townspeople to show how easy it is to go to the United States and become rich.

There have also been some changes in the way smugglers collect money. Although the smuggling fee in most cases is still $30,000–$35,000 or even higher, the way snakeheads collect money is different. Some snakeheads do not collect any money until the snake people arrive in the United States (most likely New York City). Other snakeheads lend snake people some money before the departure, which makes the emigration option very attractive. Over time, snakeheads seem to make offers that are difficult to refuse, and because of the high success rate, more and more Fujianese are drawn into the process of illegal migration to the United States.

The entry of large numbers of Fujianese into New York and especially their concentration in Manhattan's Chinatown have implications for the ethnic economy and politics of the city. Increasingly, the Fujianese, as new blood in Chinatown, are playing a greater role in the Chinese community and in many ways are rivaling the old-timers from Guangdong and Taiwan. Lii (1996a, 1996b, 1997) noted that Fujianese have taken control of almost all the takeout places in the New York area that used to be owned by ethnic Chinese from Guangdong and Southeast Asia. The entry of a large number of Fujianese immigrants is also providing a new source of labor for the garment industry, which often pays less than the minimum wage (Kwong, 1996). Furthermore, there has been a heavy concentration of Fujianese immigrants in some sections of Manhattan's Chinatown; for example, some have called East Broadway "Fuzhou Street" (Cooper, 1996; Kinkead, 1992). At the same time, there is also evidence that Fujianese are expanding their businesses to Texas and Indiana (Einhorn, 1994).[10]

The emergence of the Fujianese community introduces new dynamics of "transnational politics" in Chinatown. Most Fujianese are pro–mainland China. In contrast, the Chinatown old-timers are more likely to be pro-Taiwan. So, for the first time in 1995, a Fujianese-led organization (the United Chinese Associations of New York) celebrated China's National Day on October 1 (Kwong, 1996), but the Chinatown old-timers (led by the Chinese Consolidated Benevolent Association) continued to celebrate October 10 ("double 10" as some call it), the day of the birth of the Republic of China. So far both celebrations have been peaceful.

However, Tommy Chan (the deputy inspector of the Fifth Precinct, where Chinatown is located) is caught in the middle of these "transnational politics" and tries to keep a balance between the pro-Taiwan Cantonese oldtimers and pro–mainland Fujianese newcomers (Lii, 1996b). As more and more immigrants from Fujian arrive each day, the extent of "transnational politics" is likely to be further intensified.

NOTES

An earlier version of this chapter was presented at the 1996 annual meetings of the American Sociological Association, New York City, August 21, 1996, and a conference at the New School for Social Research in 1997. We thank Hector Cordero-Gozman, Josh DeWind, Greta Gilbertson, Sean-Shong Hwang, Peter Kwong, Pyong Gap Min, and Philip Yang for their helpful comments and constructive suggestions on earlier versions of this chapter. This project is supported, in part, by grants from the National Institute of Child Health and Human Development (1R55HD/OD3487801A1 and 1R29 HD34878–01A2) and Queens College Presidential Research Award, whose support is gratefully acknowledged.

1. Among the 286 people aboard the *Golden Venture,* 10 died trying to swim to shore (Faison, 1995): 246 were from Fujian and 40 were from Wenzhou in Zhejiang Province (also on the east coast) (Kwong, 1994).

2. During the late 1950s and 1960s, however, many Fujianese escaped to Hong Kong in search of political and economic freedom.

3. Statistics used in this paragraph have been adjusted for inflation.

4. Some even go further in arguing that it is precisely because of Fujian's recent economic growth that some peasants are able to pay snakeheads (smugglers) large sums of money to emigrate (Xin, 1993; Ye, 1995).

5. Obviously only Fujianese immigrants who have already obtained green cards are able to return.

6. We also compared the socioeconomic and demographic characteristics of emigrants in the 1995 sample survey conducted in Fujian with Chin's (1997) sample selected from illegal migrants in Manhattan's Chinatown and found that the results are amazingly similar.

7. Our field trips in Fujian suggest that many people switched from fishing to other types of businesses because the fishing industry has been declining in recent years owing to overfishing.

8. According to Xin (1993: 131), these terms were first used by people from Guangdong, who initiated the process of undocumented migration to the United

States. Legend has it that if one transports a single snake, it is easy for the snake to die on the road. But if one transports many snakes together, they will rely on one another and are likely to survive to their destination. Historical records also suggest that the indigenous Fujianese used snakes as totems for worship (Wang, 1994: 15).

9. Chin's (1998) recent research implies that human smuggling is not so much organized crime as crime that is organized. Chin argued that although certain members of organized crime groups are involved in human smuggling, it is not clear that their participation is sanctioned by their organizations.

10. During the course of our research, we also came across Fujianese who are working in Connecticut and Rhode Island.

REFERENCES

Alexander, Garth. 1973. *The Invisible China: The Overseas Chinese and the Politics of Southeast Asia.* New York, Macmillan.

Butterfield, Fox. 1996. "Three Are Indicted in Plot to Smuggle Chinese Aliens into New York." *New York Times,* October 10.

Cao, Guilin. 1995. *To Du Ke* (Human smuggling). Beijing: Modern Publishing House.

Chan, Sucheng. 1990. "European and Asian Immigration into the United States in Comparative Perspective, 1820s to 1920s." In *Immigration Reconsidered: History, Sociology, and Politics,* edited by Virginia Yans-McLaughlin, 37–75. New York: Oxford University Press.

Chen, David. 1998. "China to Chinatown, Via Canada." *New York Times,* December 20, Metro Section.

Chin, Ko-lin. 1996. *Chinatown Gangs: Extortion, Enterprise, and Ethnicity.* New York: Oxford University Press.

———. 1997. "Safe House or Hell House?: Experiences of Newly Arrived Undocumented Chinese." In *Human Smuggling: Chinese Migrant Trafficking and the Challenge to America's Immigration Tradition,* edited by Paul J. Smith, 169–95. Washington, D.C.: Center for Strategic and International Studies.

———. 1998. "The Social Organization of Chinese Human Smuggling." Paper presented at conference titled "International Migration and Transnational Crime," Rutgers University at Newark, May 15.

"China Arrested 256 Snake Heads in 1995." 1996. *People's Daily,* overseas ed., January 29.

China Map Editorial Committee (CMEC). 1993. *Handbook of Updated Chinese Maps*. Beijing: China Map Press.

China News Digest (CND). 1996. "Survey of 40 Cities in China." August 23.

China Population Census Office (CPCO). 1993. *Tabulations from 1990 China Population Census*. Beijing: China Statistics Publishing House.

China Population Sample Survey Office (CPSSO). 1997. *Tabulations from 1995 China 1% Population Sample Survey*. Beijing: China Statistics Publishing House.

Cooper, Michael. 1996. "New Mission for Lin Ze Xu, Hero of Old." *New York Times*, June 2.

Crane, George T. 1990. *The Political Economy of China's Special Economic Zones*. New York: M. E. Sharpe.

Einhorn, Bruce. 1994. "Send Your Huddled Masses, and a Hot and Sour Soup." *Business Week*, November 14.

Espenshade, Thomas. 1995. "Unauthorized Immigration to the United States." *Annual Review of Sociology* 21:195–216.

"An Experimental Region of Collaboration between Fujian and Taiwan Was Established." 1999. *People's Daily*, overseas ed., March 15.

Faison, Seth. 1995. "Asian Gang Members Arrested in Kidnapping." *New York Times*, March 22.

Fritsch, Jane. 1993. "One Failed Voyage Illustrates Flow of Chinese Immigration." *New York Times*, June 7.

Gurr, Ted Robert. 1969. *Why Men Rebel?* Princeton: Princeton University Press.

He, Qinglian. 1996. "Analysis of Social Stratification in China." *China News Digest*, July 26.

Heer, David. 1992. *Undocumented Mexicans in the United States*. ASA Rose Monograph Series. New York: Cambridge University Press.

Herbert, Bob. 1996. "Freedom Birds." *New York Times*, April 5.

Ho, Pingti. 1959. *Studies on Population in China: 1368–1953*. Cambridge: Harvard University Press.

Holmes, Steven A. 1998. "Ring Is Cracked in Smuggling of Illegal Chinese Immigrants: Route Ran through Indian Land in New York." *New York Times*. December 11. Metro Section.

Hood, Marlowe. 1997. "Sourcing the Problem: Why Fuzhou?" In *Human Smuggling: Chinese Migrant Trafficking and the Challenge to America's Immigration Tradition*, edited by Paul J. Smith, 76–92. Washington, D.C.: Center for Strategic and International Studies.

Institute of Modern Chinese History of Chinese Academy of Social Sciences (IMCHCASS). 1983. *Modern Chinese History* (in Chinese). Beijing: China Youth Press.

Khan, Azizur Rahman, and Carl Riskin. 1998. "Income and Inequality in China: Composition, Growth, and Distribution of Household Income, 1988–1995." *China Quarterly* 154:222–32.

Kinkead, Gwen. 1992. *Chinatown.* New York: HarperCollins.

Kristof, Nicholas. 1993. "We Think of the U.S. as a Kind of Heaven." *New York Times,* July 21.

Kwong, Peter. 1994. "China's Human Traffickers." *Nation,* October 17, 422–25.

———. 1996. *The New Chinatown.* Rev. ed. New York: Hill and Wang.

———. 1997. *Forbidden Workers: Illegal Chinese Immigrants and American Labor.* New York: New Press.

Li, Fangfang. 1995. *Two Beijing Playboys in New York* (in Chinese). Beijing: Qunzhong Press.

Liang, Zai. Forthcoming. "Demography of Illicit Emigration from China: A Sending Country's Perspective." *Sociological Forum.*

Liang, Zai, and Toni Zhang. 1999. "Emigration and Housing Conditions in Fujian, China." Paper presented at the annual meeting of the Population Association of America, New York City, March 26.

Lii, Jane H. 1996a. "The Chinese Menu Guys." *New York Times,* sec. 13, pp. 1–2 and 11–12, "The City." July 28.

———. 1996b. "The Tightrope of Tommy Chan." *New York Times,* sec. 13, pp. 1–2 and 8–9, "The City." October 20.

———. 1997. "The New Blood in Chinatown: on the Eve of Hong Kong Takeover, a Revolution Takes Hold in Lower Manhattan." *New York Times,* "The City." June 22.

Lin, Jan. 1998. *Reconstructing Chinatown: Ethnic Enclave, Global Change.* Minneapolis: University of Minnesota Press.

Liu, Ningrun. 1996. "The Gangsters on the Black Trail." *China Times,* no. 7.

Liu, Xiaozhu. 1995. "Income Distribution in Chinese Society." Working paper series no. 2. Beijing: China Strategic Institute.

Lyons, Thomas. 1994. "Economic Reform in Fujian: Another View from the Villages." In *The Economic Transformation of South China,* edited by T. P. Lyons and Victor Nee, 141–68. Cornell East Asia Series no. 70. Ithaca, N.Y.: Cornell University East Asia Program.

———. 1998. "Intraprovincial Disparities in China: Fujian Province, 1978–1995." *Economic Geography* 74:405–32.

Massey, Douglas S. 1995. "The New Immigration and Ethnicity in the United States." *Population and Development Review* 21:631–52.

Massey, Douglas S., Rafael Alarcon, Jorge Durand, and Humberto Gonzalez. 1987. *Return to Aztlán: The Social Process of International Migration from Western Mexico.* Berkeley: University of California Press.

Massey, Douglas S., Jaquin Arango, Graeme Hugo, Ali Kouaouci, Adela Pellegrino, and E. Edward Taylor. 1994. "An Evaluation of International Migration Theory: The North American Case." *Population and Development Review* 20:699–751.

———.1998. *Worlds in Motion: Understanding International Migration at the End of the Millennium.* New York: Oxford University Press.

Massey, Douglas S., and Audrey Singer. 1995. "New Estimates of Undocumented Mexican Migration and the Probability of Apprehension." *Demography* 32:203–13.

McFadden, Robert D. 1993. "Chinese Abroad Are Seized for Illegal Entry." *New York Times,* June 7.

———. 1998. "Illegal Immigrants Seized after Jersey Shore Landing." *New York Times,* June 1.

Meyers, Willard H., III. 1997. "Of *Qinqing, Qinshu, Guanxi,* and *Shetou:* The Dynamic Elements of Chinese Irregular Population Movement." In *Human Smuggling: Chinese Migrant Trafficking and the Challenge to America's Immigration Tradition,* edited by Paul J. Smith, 93–133. Washington, D.C.: Center for Strategic and International Studies.

Nee, Victor. 1996. "The Emergence of a Market Society: Changing Mechanisms of Stratification in China." *American Journal of Sociology* 101:908–49.

Nee, Victor, and Brett De Bary Nee. 1972. *Longtime Californ': A Documentary Study of an American Chinatown.* Stanford: Stanford University Press.

Noble, Kenneth B. 1995. "In California, Smuggled Refugees of Golden Venture Protest Long Detention." *New York Times,* December 2.

"$120,000 Bought 8 Pages of Copy Paper." 1997. *Xinmin Evening News.* http://www.hsm.com.cn/html/fztd.htm

Pan, Lynn. 1990. *The Sons of the Yellow Emperor: A History of Chinese Diaspora.* Boston: Little, Brown.

Parish, William, and Ethan Michelson. 1996. "Politics and Markets: The Dual Transformations." *American Journal of Sociology* 101:1042–59.

Portes, Alejandro. 1997. "Immigration Theory for a New Century: Some Problems and Opportunities." *International Migration Review* 31:799–825.

Portes, Alejandro, and Ruben G. Rumbaut. 1996. *Immigrant America: A Portrait.* Berkeley: University of California Press.

Poston, Dudley L., Jr., Michael Xinxiang Mao, and Mei-Yu Yu. 1994. "The Global Distribution of the Overseas Chinese around 1990." *Population and Development Review* 20:631–45.

Schemo, Diana Jean. 1993a. "Chinese Immigrants Tell of Darwinian Voyage." *New York Times,* June 12.

———. 1993b. "Survivors Tell of Voyage of Little Daylight, Little Food, and Only Hope." *New York Times,* June 7.

Skelton, Ronald. 1996. "Migration from China." *Journal of International Affairs* 49 (2): 434–55.

Smith, James P., and Barry Edmonston. 1998. *The Immigration Debate: Studies on the Economic, Demographic, and Fiscal Effects of Immigration.* Washington D.C.: National Academy Press.

Smith, Paul J., ed. 1997. *Human Smuggling: Chinese Migrant Trafficking and the Challenge to America's Immigration Tradition.* Washington, D.C.: Center for Strategic and International Studies.

Spence, Jonathan D. 1991. *The Search for Modern China.* New York: W. W. Norton.

Stark, Oded. 1991. *The Migration of Labor.* Cambridge, Mass.: Basil Blackwell.

Stark, Oded, and J. Edward Taylor. 1989. "Relative Deprivation and International Migration." *Demography* 26:1–14.

State Statistical Bureau (SSB). 1993. *China Statistical Yearbook.* Beijing: China Statistics Press.

———. 1994. *Fujian Statistical Yearbook.* Beijing: China Statistics Press.

Stouffer, Samuel A., E. A. Suchman, L. C. DeVinney, S. A. Star, and R. M. Williams Jr. 1949. *The American Soldier: Adjustment during Army Life.* Princeton: Princeton University Press.

Sung, Betty Lee. 1967. *Mountain of Gold: The Story of the Chinese in America.* New York: Macmillan.

Tilly, Charles. 1978. *From Mobilization to Revolution.* New York: Random House.

Treaster, Joseph B. 1993. "Behind Immigrants' Voyage, Long Reach of Chinese Gang." *New York Times,* June 9.

Tsai, Shih-shan Henry. 1983. *China and the Overseas Chinese in the United States, 1868–1911*. Fayetteville: University of Arkansas Press.

Wang, Yaohua. 1994. *Overview of Fujianese Culture* (in Chinese). Fuzhou, China: Fujian Education Publishing House.

Warren, Robert, and Jeffery S. Passel. 1987. "A Count of the Uncountable: Estimates of Undocumented Aliens in the 1980 Census." *Demography* 24:375–93.

The World Bank. 1996. *World Development Report 1996: From Plan to Market*. New York: Oxford University Press.

Xie, Yu, and Emily Hannum. 1996. "Regional Variation in Earnings Inequality in Reform-Era Urban China." *American Journal of Sociology* 101:950–92.

Xin, Yan. 1993. *Hell in Paradise* (in Chinese). Beijing: Tuanjie Press.

Ye, Wenzhen. 1995. "An Analysis of Illegal Immigration from Coastal Region of Fujian Province." *Historical Study of Overseas Chinese* (in Chinese) 1:28–36.

Zhou, Min. 1992. *Chinatown: The Socioeconomic Potential of an Urban Enclave*. Philadelphia: Temple University Press.

Zhu, Guohong. 1991. "A Historical Demography of Chinese Migration." *Social Sciences in China* 12:57–91.

8 ▪▪▪▪▪▪▪ The Social Organization of Chinese Human Smuggling

Ko-Lin Chin

A year after the United States had established diplomatic relations with the People's Republic, China liberalized its immigration regulations in order to qualify for most-favored-nation status with the United States (Dowty, 1987).[1] Since 1979, tens of thousands of Chinese have legally immigrated to the United States and other countries (Seagrave, 1995). U.S. immigration quotas allow only a limited number of Chinese whose family members are U.S. citizens or who are highly educated to immigrate to or visit America (Zhou, 1992). Beginning in the late 1980s, some of those who did not have legitimate channels to enable them to immigrate, especially the Fujianese, began turning to human smugglers for help (U.S. Senate, 1992).

Smuggled Chinese arrive in the United States by land, sea, or air routes (Smith, 1997). Some travel to Mexico or Canada and then cross U.S. borders illegally (Glaberson, 1989). Others fly into major American cities via any number of transit points and make their way to their final destination (Lorch, 1992; Charasdamrong and Kheunkaew, 1992; U.S. Senate, 1992). Entering the United States by sea was an especially popular method between August 1991 and July 1993 (Zhang and Gaylord, 1996). During that time, thirty-two ships carrying as many as fifty-three hundred Chinese were found in waters near Japan, Taiwan, Indonesia, Australia, Singapore, Haiti, Guatemala, El Salvador, Honduras, and the United States (Kamen, 1991; Schemo, 1993; U.S. Immigration and Naturalization Service, 1993), though in the aftermath of the *Golden Venture* incident, the use of the sea route diminished significantly (Dunn, 1994).[2]

U.S. immigration officials estimated that at any given time in the early 1990s as many as four thousand Chinese were waiting in Bolivia to be shuttled to the United States by smugglers (Kinkead, 1992); several thousand more were believed to be waiting in Peru and Panama. American officials maintained that Chinese smuggling rings have connections in fifty-one countries that were either part of the transportation web or were involved in the manufacturing of fraudulent travel documents (Freedman, 1991; Kamen, 1991; Mydans, 1992). According to a senior immigration official who was interviewed in the early 1990s, "at any given time, thirty thousand Chinese are stashed away in safe houses around the world, waiting for entry" (Kinkead, 1992: 160).

Unlike Mexican illegal immigrants who enter the United States at relatively little financial cost (Cornelius, 1989), illegal Chinese immigrants reportedly must pay smugglers about $30,000 for their services (U.S. Senate, 1992). The thousands of Chinese smuggled out of their country each year make human trafficking a very lucrative business (Mooney and Zyla, 1993; Smith, 1997). One case illustrates the point: a forty-one-year-old Chinese woman convicted for human smuggling was alleged to have earned approximately $30 million during the several years of her smuggling career (Chan and Dao, 1990b). In 1992, a senior immigration official estimated that Chinese organized crime groups were making more than $1 billion a year from human smuggling operations (U.S. Senate, 1992). Others suggest that Chinese smugglers earn more—about $3.2 billion annually—from the human trade (Myers, 1994).

Little is known about the organizations involved in smuggling Chinese to the United States. In this chapter, I focus on the group characteristics of human smugglers, the extent of their affiliation with Chinese organized crime and street gangs, and the role of corruption in the human trade.

Research Methods

This study employs multiple research strategies, including a survey of three hundred smuggled Chinese in New York City, interviews with key informants who are familiar with the lifestyle and social problems of illegal Chinese immigrants, a field study in the Chinese immigrant community of New York City, two research trips to sending communities in China, and a systematic collection of media reports.

Group Characteristics

A smuggler I interviewed in 1994 insisted that nobody really knows how many Chinese smuggling groups exist worldwide, but she guessed that there were approximately fifty. Other estimates vary widely, from only seven or eight ("Chinese Social Worker Discusses His Observations," 1990) to as many as twenty or twenty-five (Chan, Dao, and McCoy, 1990; Burdman, 1993a). According to some observers, Chinese people-trafficking groups are well-organized, transnational criminal enterprises that are active in China, Hong Kong, Taiwan, Thailand, and the United States (Myers, 1992; U.S. Senate, 1992; Burdman, 1993b), but there are few empirical data to support this observation.

A smuggler I once asked to characterize a Chinese smuggling network said: "It's like a dragon. Although it's a lengthy creature, various organic parts are tightly linked." According to my subjects, a smuggling organization includes many roles:

- Big snakeheads, or arrangers/investors, often Chinese living outside China, generally invest money in a smuggling operation and oversee the entire operation but usually are not known by those being smuggled.
- Little snakeheads, or recruiters, usually live in China and work as middlemen between big snakeheads and customers; they are mainly responsible for finding and screening customers and collecting down payments.
- Transporters in China help immigrants traveling by land or sea make their way to the border or smuggling ship. Transporters based in the United States are responsible for taking smuggled immigrants from airports or seaports to safe houses.
- Corrupt Chinese government officials accept bribes in return for Chinese passports. Law enforcement authorities in many transit countries

are also paid to aid the illegal Chinese immigrants entering and exiting their countries.

- Guides move illegal immigrants from one transit point to another and aid immigrants entering the United States by land or air. Crew members are employed by snakeheads to charter or work on smuggling ships.
- Enforcers, themselves mostly illegal immigrants, are hired by big snakeheads to work on the smuggling ships. They are responsible for maintaining order and for distributing food and drinking water.
- Support personnel are local people at the transit points who provide food and lodging to illegal immigrants.
- U.S.-based debt collectors are responsible for locking up illegal immigrants in safe houses until their debt is paid and for collecting smuggling fees. There are also China-based debt collectors.

According to data collected in New York City and the Fuzhou area, a close working relationship links the leaders and others in the smuggling network, especially the snakeheads in the United States and China. More often than not, all those in the smuggling ring belong to a family or an extended family or are good friends. If a smuggling group is involved in air smuggling, the group may also need someone to work as a snakehead in such transit points as Hong Kong or Thailand.

When I visited Fuzhou, I interviewed a number of people who belonged to a ring that smuggled Chinese by air. A woman in charge of a government trade unit in Fuzhou City recruited customers and procured travel documents. She interacted only with government officials who helped her obtain travel documents; her assistant dealt with customers directly, recruiting, collecting down payments, signing contracts, and so forth. She recruited a partner, a childhood friend and member of the Public Security Bureau, who was responsible for securing travel documents for the ring's clients. A female relative in Singapore acted as a transit point snakehead. She traveled to countries such as Thailand, Indonesia, and Malaysia to set up transit points in those countries.

The primary leader and investor in the ring, based in New York, was responsible for subcontracting with members of a Queens-based gang to keep immigrants in safe houses and collect their fees after arrival in the

United States. If the fee was to be paid in China, the female snakehead's assistant in China would collect it. It was not clear to me how profits were distributed among members of the smuggling ring or how money was actually transferred from one place to another.

Most smuggling groups reportedly specialize in either air or sea smuggling. According to Zhang and Gaylord (1996), only groups with ties to organized crime groups in Asia engaged in the complicated, large-scale operations of sea smuggling, but snakeheads involved in air smuggling may venture into sea smuggling. A thirty-two-year-old housewife from Fuzhou who left China by boat alleged that her snakehead was involved in both.

Not all smugglers are affiliated with criminal groups, Zhang and Gaylord notwithstanding. A forty-year-old male store owner from Changle described his female snakehead, who specialized in sea smuggling, as "a Taiwanese with good reputation who came to China to be a snakehead. She was involved in sea smuggling for the first time when I was recruited by her. After that, she transported several boatloads of people to the United States. . . . She visited Fuzhou often. After our ship arrived in Los Angeles, [her] husband and a group of people picked us up."

Some U.S. authorities are convinced that Chinese smugglers of immigrants also bring heroin from Southeast Asia into the United States (U.S. Senate, 1992). Senator William Roth Jr., the Delaware Republican who directed a Senate investigation on Asian organized crime, claimed that some human smugglers are former drug dealers (Burdman, 1993a), and there is evidence to support this view. One of the first groups of Chinese to be charged with human smuggling had previously been indicted for heroin trafficking ("INS Undercover Operation," 1985), and a Chinese American who owned a garment factory in New York City's Chinatown was charged with both heroin and human trafficking ("Chinese Merchant Arrested," 1992). Moreover, during an undercover operation, Chinese smugglers offered heroin to federal agents posing as corrupt immigration officers in exchange for travel documents (DeStefano, 1994). U.S. officials also claim that smuggled Chinese are asked by snakeheads to carry heroin into the United States, presumably to finance their illegal passage (Chan and Dao, 1990c). Mark Riordan, INS assistant officer for Hong Kong, suggested that "smugglers make even more when illegals who can't raise the fee carry heroin in exchange for their trip" (Chan and Dao, 1990a: 14).

I asked my respondents whether their snakeheads asked them to carry drugs or to commit crimes to subsidize their illegal passage. Of the three hundred respondents, only one admitted he was asked by his snakehead to transport two bags of opium from the Golden Triangle (northern mountain region of Myanmar, Thailand, and Laos) to Bangkok, Thailand. None of those who left China by sea saw any illicit drugs aboard the sea vessels. It is not clear whether human smugglers are typically involved in heroin trafficking. Based on my interviews, I conclude that only a small number are.

Organized Crime, Gangs, and the Human Trade

Law enforcement and immigration officials in the United States have asserted that Chinese triads, tongs, and street gangs are involved in human smuggling (U.S. Senate, 1992)[3] and claim that Hong Kong–based triads are responsible for the massive movement of undocumented Chinese to the United States via Hong Kong (Torode, 1993a). As Bolz (1995: 148) put it, "Triads have taken over the smuggling of illegal immigrants from smaller 'mom and pop' organizations as an increasingly attractive alternative to drug trafficking because it promises multibillion dollar profits without the same severe penalties if caught."

There is evidence that certain triad members are involved in the human trade. One human smuggler has testified in court that a triad member in Hong Kong was involved in human smuggling (Torode, 1993b), and authorities in California are convinced that the California-based Wo Hop To triad was responsible for the arrival of eighty-five undocumented Chinese on a smuggling boat discovered near Long Beach, California in 1992 ("Many Illegal Chinese Migrants Arrived," 1992). However, no triad member or organization, either in Hong Kong or the United States, has ever been indicted for human smuggling.

U.S. authorities have also claimed that the U.S.-based tongs or community associations, especially the Fukien American Association, are active in the human trade, citing the testimony of New York City police at the 1992 U.S. Senate hearings on Asian organized crime (U.S. Senate, 1992). Leaders of the Fukien American Association, however, have denied that their organization has ever been involved in the illegal alien trade. The president of the association in 1992, labeled by journalists the "Commander-in-Chief of Illegal Smuggling," announced at a press conference that his organization "does not have control over certain individual members and therefore can not be held responsible for their illegal activities. It is unfair to blacken the name of the Fukien American Association as a whole based on the behavior of some non-member bad elements which are not under the control of the Association" (Lau, 1993: 5).

Since 1991 U.S. authorities have also asserted that Chinese and Vietnamese street gangs are involved in smuggling. After a 1991 article in the *San Francisco Examiner* linked Asian gangs and human trafficking (Freedman, 1991), numerous media accounts depicted Chinese gangs in New York City as collectors of smuggling payments. Gang members allegedly picked up illegal immigrants at airports or docks, kept them in safe houses, and forced them to call their relatives to make payments. For their services, gangs reportedly were paid between $1,500 and $2,000 per smuggled immigrant. None of these news articles implied that gangs were involved in transporting immigrants from China to America (Strom, 1991).

After the *Golden Venture* incident, U.S. immigration officials and law enforcement authorities began to view Chinese gang members not as "service providers" to smugglers but as smugglers themselves who were capable of transporting hundreds of illegal immigrants across the Pacific Ocean (Lay, 1993; Wang, 1996) and charged that the Fuk Ching gang was responsible for the *Golden Venture* tragedy itself (Burdman, 1993b; Faison, 1993; Gladwell and Stassen-Berger, 1993; Treaster, 1993). According to the authorities, the gang not only invested money in the purchase of the *Golden Venture* but also was directly involved in recruiting prospective immigrants in China.

In a crackdown on Chinese gangs, members of the White Tigers, the Green Dragons, and the Fuk Ching were indicted for transporting people from borders and coastal areas to New York City and collecting debts for human smugglers. According to court materials in a murder case involving the Fuk Ching gang, Ah Chu, a snakehead, paid a member of the Fuk Ching $500 a head to pick up five illegal immigrants near the Mexican border. Ah Chu also gave the gang member $150,000 to go to California, where he paid a group of Mexicans $500 for each illegal alien they brought in. According to the gang member, Ah Chu was not a member of the Fuk Ching but a partner or friend of the big boss, Ah Kay. The gang member also made two trips to Boston to pick up illegal aliens, transporting seven people by van from Boston to New York City on each trip. For this and for serving time in another case, Ah Kay allegedly paid him $10,000 (Superior Court of New Jersey, 1995).

At the trial, a street-level leader of the Fuk Ching acknowledged that his gang boss paid him $3,000 for transporting 130 illegal immigrants from Boston to New York in a Ryder truck, adding that his gang had smuggled 300 immigrants from China to the United States. Another Fuk Ching defendant testified that he was paid $200 to $300 a week for watching the "customers." However, no Chinese gang members, not even members of the Fuk Ching gang—who were widely believed to be the most active in human trafficking—were charged with transporting illegals from China to the United States. Nevertheless, U.S. authorities completed an undercover operation called Operation Sea Dragon and concluded that "a highly sophisticated, compartmentalized network of Asian gangs in different parts of the United States" was deeply involved in human smuggling (Branigin, 1996: A12).

When asked what role Chinese gangs play in the human trade, a Chinese American immigration officer told me that in the past Chinese gangs had only collected fees for smugglers but that more recently they have been getting into the smuggling business themselves. They now "plan the trips, invest the needed capital, and collect the debt in America."

Although tongs and gangs are allegedly involved in the human trade, little is known about the nature and extent of their involvement, other than what is suggested by these anecdotal accounts. Nor is it clear whether smuggling operations are sponsored by tongs and gangs jointly or carried out by tong members and gang members on an ad hoc basis. Some observers, including some law enforcement authorities, disagree that smuggling organizations are closely linked with gangs or tongs and regard the connection as, at best, haphazard. One Hong Kong police officer claimed that "some of these people are in triads, but it isn't so organized. It's just a question of a couple of people with the wherewithal to put together a criminal scheme to smuggle illegal immigrants" (DeStefano et al., 1991: 8). Another observer concluded that "contrary to popular belief, people who deal in this business [human smuggling] are normally shop or business owners, not gang or 'Mafia' members" ("Former Smuggler Claims Immigration Graft," 1994: A2).

Asked by a reporter how he was related to members of organized crime, a New York–based smuggler denied any connection between snakeheads and gang members:

> What do you mean by "members of organized crime groups"? These people [debt collectors] are nothing more than a bunch of hooligans who like to bully people in Chinatown. These guys are getting out of control; they are willing to kill people for money. Yet, people like us who are in this business could not conduct our business without them. Most illegal immigrants are decent people; however, there are also some criminals. If I don't hire thugs to collect money, I may not get paid. . . . When the immigrants I smuggle arrive here, my debt collectors will go to the airport to pick them up and lock them up somewhere. They collect the smuggling fees, and I pay them $2,000 per immigrant. (Nyo, 1993: S4)

Willard Myers has also concluded that traditional organized crime groups such as the triads, tongs, and gangs do not dominate the human trade. In criticizing U.S. law enforcement strategies against human smuggling among the Chinese, Myers (1994: 4) suggested that "Chinese transnational criminal activity is carried out as a form of entrepreneurial activity by and among persons who are linked by language (dialect group) and lineage (ancestral birth place), who may or may not be a member or affiliate of an organization recognized by law enforcement."

The testimony of my respondents, although a limited sample, tends to support the conclusion that human smuggling is not closely associated with organized crime, as has commonly been alleged in criminological literature (Maltz, 1994). No doubt members of triads, tongs, and gangs are, to a certain extent, involved in trafficking Chinese, but I believe that their participation is neither sanctioned by nor even known to their respective organizations. *Triads, tongs,* and *gangs* are frightening terms that are often used to generate panic and can result in discrimination against ethnic and racial minorities. The "organized crime and gang" problem is perpetuated by the law enforcement community to justify greater investment in the traditional criminal justice apparatus. The media contribute to this view because organized crime and gang problems are easily sensationalized for public consumption. My data, however, suggest that the Chinese trade in human smuggling is not a form of organized crime but rather a "business" controlled by many otherwise legitimate groups, both small and large, working independently, each with its own organization, connections, methods, and routes. A smuggler once told me, "It's like a Chinese story about eight angels crossing a sea: every angel is extremely capable of achieving the goal due to her heavenly qualities." None of these groups, however, dominates or monopolizes the lucrative trade. When U.S. authorities indicted eighteen Chinese for human trafficking, they found that these defendants belonged to five smuggling groups, with several defendants belonging to more than one group (DeStefano, 1994).

I also found that, contrary to the assertions of Myers (1994), Hood (1993, 1997), and Zhang and Gaylord (1996), that immigrant smuggling is not necessarily dominated by ethnic Chinese from Taiwan but is a global business initiated by Chinese Americans of Fuzhou extraction and supported not only by Taiwanese but also by Chinese and non-Chinese in numerous transit countries. In short, the human trade is in many ways like any other legitimate international trade, except that it is illegal. Like any trade, it needs organization and planning, but it does not appear to be linked with traditional "organized crime" groups.

Government Corruption and Human Trafficking

Reasoning that China is a tightly controlled society, U.S. authorities have suspected Chinese law enforcement authorities, as well, of involvement in the smuggling of immigrants to the United States (Burdman, 1993c; Engelberg, 1994). In such a well-policed state, how could smugglers covertly transport tens of thousands of people and escape the notice of Chinese authorities (U.S. Senate, 1992)? They must either be accepting bribes or be actively involved themselves in transporting people out of China.

An officer of the INS enforcement division told me that "people in the Fujian Public Security Bureau have to be involved in alien smuggling. They take bribes from smugglers and either turn a blind eye on illegal immigration or provide logistical support. The INS has evidence to show that Chinese law enforcement authorities are behind alien smuggling." Some of my subjects made the same point. A female immigrant who was deported back to China by Mexican authorities told me that a group of smugglers transported her and hundreds of others from Fuzhou to a seaport on Chinese military trucks. She believed that the military trucks were used by the snakeheads to avoid inspection by local authorities.

There are many legitimate channels available to Chinese citizens who wish to travel abroad—for instance, advanced study, exported laborers, participating in an official or business delegation, visiting relatives abroad, or joining a Hong Kong or Macao tour. It is reported that Chinese government officials and government-owned travel agencies are actively facilitating the departure of a large number of Chinese immigrants through such means (Burdman, 1993c). To understand how allegedly corrupt officials might be involved in the human trade, one needs to examine the nature and operation of some of the government-sponsored labor and economic affairs organizations in the Fuzhou area.

In China, there is a fine line between illegal immigration and legally exported labor ("Is the Chinese Communist Government Sponsoring 'Labor Export' to Taiwan?" 1989). In the coastal areas, there are numerous government-sponsored labor-export companies that work closely with foreign-based labor-import companies to move tens of thousands of Chinese workers overseas, mainly to Southeast Asian countries where there is a labor shortage (Kwong, 1997). It is not always clear, however, which components of their operations are legal and which are illegal, nor is it always clear whether these companies are involved in the human trade on an organizational level or whether only individual employees are involved unbeknownst to their employers.

Whatever the case, those of my subjects who left China with the aid of a labor-export company professed satisfaction with the company's services. A thirty-five-year-old computer clerk from Fuzhou told this story:

> I sought help from a company, a government agency specializing in exporting labor, to leave China. The company worked along with a company in Singapore to help people leave China as laborers. When I got in touch with the company, it was agreed that I should pay the company $2,000 for a passport and an application fee. After I reached the United States, I would pay an additional $26,000. They told me it would take about seven days to get to the United States and it would be safe. After the meeting with the company, I left China within 24 days. I flew to Singapore from Fuzhou, with a Chinese passport and a Singapore visa. They were all genuine documents. After staying in Singapore for two weeks, the Singapore company

provided three of us with photo-sub Singapore passports [passports on which the original holder's picture is replaced with the respondent's picture] to fly to Los Angeles via Germany.

It is possible that employees of these state-run labor-export companies are bribed by snakeheads behind the backs of company officials. A government employee from Fuzhou City said:

In China, I worked for a government agency [a labor-export company]. The main purpose of the agency was to make money by means of assisting people to go abroad as export labor. I used my position in the company to help a friend obtain tourist passports. My friend told me he was only helping his friends and relatives to immigrate. I wasn't quite sure what was he doing exactly. Later, I learned that those who left China with the passports I provided to him had attempted to go to the United States illegally via a third country. How did that happen? Well, while they were attempting to board a plane in Indonesia with fake travel documents, they were arrested and deported back to China. The Public Security Bureau investigated the case and discovered that I was the one who supplied them with the Chinese passports. They accused me of being a snakehead. My boss ordered me to quit while the investigation was going on. I had nowhere to appeal. In China, the punishment for being a snakehead is severe—equal to the punishment for murderers and drug traffickers. After evaluating all my options, I decided to flee China.

Government employees may play another role in facilitating the illegal movement of Chinese. Since China adopted the open door policy and implemented economic reforms in the late 1970s, the government has sent many official delegations abroad to enhance international ties. Human smugglers seized the opportunity to bribe the people who decide the makeup of these official delegations. A forty-four-year-old male from Changle explained how his big snakehead got him and others included in a business delegation to the United States by writing to officials at the local government department in charge of the visit.

Reports of government employees' involvement in smuggling have also appeared in the Chinese media, as when a newspaper reported that four high-ranking Xian City officials had been convicted of trafficking in people. According to the report, the officials knowingly allowed twenty-three people from Fuzhou to leave China with official passports as members of a business delegation. The report revealed that smugglers paid the chairpersons of the city's Economic Affairs Committee and Foreign Affairs Committee about $90,000 for making the arrangement ("Xian Officials Fired," 1993). Another Chinese media account revealed that the director of the Public Security Bureau angrily denounced "some labor export companies for helping Chinese to go abroad illegally, [who] were in reality 'slave traders' who were only interested in collecting a certain amount of money from the immigrants and allowed the people they helped export to run wild in the world community" (Zi, 1993: S5). In a 1997 media account, 150 officers and soldiers of the Shenzhen Border Patrol Army who were bribed by human smugglers were arrested for allowing more than 8,000 Chinese citizens to leave China illegally ("150 Members of the Shenzhen Border Patrol Army Were Arrested," 1997).

According to a number of my respondents, their snakeheads were either former or active Chinese government employees. One described his snakehead as "a government employee working as a middleman for a big snakehead who was his relative." The snakehead of another respondent "was a government official responsible for recruiting customers locally [who] referred them to his younger brother who lived abroad."

Some government officials in many transit countries are allegedly bribed by human smugglers as well, either to look the other way or to provide help to immigrants (DeStefano, 1997). When asked whether smugglers make kickbacks to immigration police in Thailand, one smuggler replied, "That's the essential part of the business" ("Former Smuggler Claims Immigration Graft," 1994: A2). One of my respondents said that public officials assisted him in Thailand. "Because we had no documents, we were arrested by the Thai police and detained for seven days. Later, our snakehead bribed the Thai officers to release us." Another respondent recalled how he passed through Thailand: "I got past Thai immigration by means of *maiguan* (buying checkpoint). That is, my snakehead slipped a $100 bill in my passport. A Thai immigration officer took the money, stamped my passport, and I went through."

Immigration officers in other countries were also reported to have accepted bribes from smugglers. In 1993, immigration officers in Hong Kong were involved in a bribery case concerning people trafficking

(Gomez and Gilbert, 1993), and in 1995 an immigration officer stationed at the Buenos Aires airport was arrested for aiding Chinese smugglers ("Argentina Government Smashes an Alien Smuggling Ring," 1995).

Some of my respondents reported that Mexican authorities played an important role in facilitating the movement of Chinese to the United States via Mexico. A corroborating newspaper account reported an incident in which Mexican authorities, presumably after being bribed, allowed Chinese immigrants in their custody to "escape." "There were about 300 Chinese confined in a detention center in Mexicali. They were not worried at all because they had been told by their snakeheads that their Mexican guards would all 'fall asleep,' after which they would be transported to the airport for deportation. One night, as predicted by the snakehead, all the guards suddenly 'disappeared,' and the Chinese escaped. They all eventually crossed the border and entered the United States" ("Smuggled Chinese Escaped," 1993: A1). The Washington, D.C.–based Interagency Working Group (1995) also concluded that the trade in illegal immigrants is supported by rampant corruption among officials in various transit countries such as Belize, Panama, Guatemala, and the Dominican Republic.

There is no shortage of evidence that government officials, both within China and at various transit points, help to facilitate the clandestine movement of people abroad.

NOTES

Support for this research was provided by Grant SBR 93-11114 from the National Science Foundation. The opinions are those of the author and do not necessarily reflect the policies or views of the National Science Foundation.

1. I use *China* to refer to the People's Republic of China, and *Chinese,* unless otherwise indicated, to denote legal or illegal immigrants from, or citizens of, the People's Republic. *Taiwan* refers to the Republic of China on Taiwan, and *Taiwanese* refers to immigrants from, or citizens of, Taiwan.

2. Most Americans became keen observers of the plight of illegal Chinese immigrants in June 1993, when the *Golden Venture,* a human cargo ship with more than 260 passengers aboard, ran aground in shallow waters off a New York City beach. Eager to complete their dream journey to the United States, ten Chinese citizens drowned while attempting to swim ashore.

3. Chinese triads began as secret societies three centuries ago, formed by pa-

triotic Chinese to fight the Qing dynasty, which they considered oppressive and corrupt. When the Qing government collapsed and the Republic of China was established in 1912, triads degenerated into criminal groups (Morgan, 1960). Most triad societies now have their headquarters in Hong Kong, but their criminal operations have no national boundaries (Booth, 1991; Black, 1992; Chin, 1995). Tongs were established in America as self-help groups by the first wave of Chinese immigrants in the mid-nineteenth century (Dillon, 1962). Historically, tongs have been active in gambling, prostitution, extortion, and violence (Chin, 1990, 1996).

REFERENCES

"Argentina Government Smashes an Alien Smuggling Ring" (in Chinese). 1995. *World Journal*, October 14, A3.

Black, David. 1992. *Triad Takeover: A Terrifying Account of the Spread of Triad Crime in the West*. London: Sidgwick & Jackson.

Bolz, Jennifer. 1995. "Chinese Organized Crime and Illegal Alien Trafficking: Humans as a Commodity." *Asian Affairs* 22:147–58.

Booth, Martin. 1991. *The Triads*. New York: St. Martin's Press.

Branigin, William. 1996. "U.S. Seeks Fugitive Falls Church Man after 3-Year Alien-Smuggling Probe." *Washington Post*, April 21, A12.

Burdman, Pamela. 1993a. "Huge Boom in Human Smuggling—Inside Story of Flight from China." *San Francisco Chronicle*, April 27, A1.

———. 1993b. "How Gangsters Cash In on Human Smuggling." *San Francisco Chronicle*, April 28, A1.

———. 1993c. "Web of Corruption Ensnares Officials around the World." *San Francisco Chronicle*, April 28, A8.

Chan, Ying, and James Dao. 1990a. "Crime Rings Snaking." *New York Daily News*, September 23, 14.

———. 1990b. "Merchants of Misery." *New York Daily News*, September 24, 7.

———. 1990c. "A Tale of 2 Immigrants." *New York Daily News*, September 24, 21.

Chan, Ying, James Dao and Kevin McCoy. 1990. "Journey of Despair: Out of China, into Desperate Debt." *New York Daily News*, September 23, 4.

Charasdamrong, Prasong, and Subin Kheunkaew. 1992. "Smuggling Human Beings: A Lucrative Racket That Poses a Threat to National Security." *Bangkok Post*, July 19, 10.

Chin, Ko-lin. 1990. *Chinese Subculture and Criminality: Non-traditional Crime Groups in America*. Westport, Conn.: Greenwood Press.

———. 1995. "Triad Societies in Hong Kong." *Transnational Organized Crime* 1 (Spring): 47–64.

———. 1996. *Chinatown Gangs: Extortion, Enterprise, and Ethnicity*. New York: Oxford University Press.

"A Chinese Merchant Arrested for Trafficking Heroin and Humans" (in Chinese). 1992. *Sing Tao Daily*, October 10, 32.

"A Chinese Social Worker Discusses His Observations of Alien Smuggling Activity in Fujian" (in Chinese). 1990. *Sing Tao Daily*, July 14, 24.

Cornelius, Wayne. 1989. "Impact of the 1986 US Immigration Law on Emigration from Rural Mexican Sending Communities." *Population and Development Review* 15 (4): 689–705.

DeStefano, Anthony. 1994. "Feds Crack 'Snakehead' Alien Smuggling Ring." *New York Newsday*, November 10, A79.

———. 1997. "Immigrant Smuggling through Central America and the Carribean." In *Human Smuggling: Chinese Migrant Trafficking and the Challenge to America's Immigration Tradition*, edited by Paul J. Smith, 134–55. Washington, D.C.: Center for Strategic and International Studies.

DeStefano, Anthony, David Kocieniewski, Kevin McCoy, and Jim Muvaney. 1991. "Smuggling Rings Victimize Clients." *New York Newsday*, January 6, 8.

Dillon, Richard. 1962. *The Hatchet Men: The Story of the Tong Wars in San Francisco's Chinatown*. New York: Coward-McCann.

Dowty, Alan. 1987. *Closed Borders: The Contemporary Assault on Freedom of Movement*. New Haven: Yale University Press.

Dunn, Ashley. 1994. "After Crackdown, Smugglers of Chinese Find New Routes." *New York Times*, November 1, A1.

Engelberg, Stephen. 1994. "In Immigration Labyrinth, Corruption Comes Easily." *New York Times*, September 12, A1.

Faison, Seth. 1993. "Alien-Smuggling Suspect Eluded Immigration Net." *New York Times*, June 10, A1.

"Former Smuggler Claims Immigration Graft." 1994. *Nation* (Bangkok), November 9, A2.

Freedman, Dan. 1991. "Asian Gangs Turn to Smuggling People." *San Francisco Examiner*, December 30, A7.

Glaberson, William. 1989. "6 Seized in Smuggling Asians into New York." *New York Times*, May 5, B3.

Gladwell, Malcolm, and Rachel Stassen-Berger. 1993. "Human Cargo Is Hugely Profitable to New York's Chinese Underworld." *Washington Post*, June 7, A10.

Gomez, Rita, and Andy Gilbert. 1993. "Immigration Officer Charged over Passport Forgery." *South China Morning Post*, October 20, 1.

Hood, Marlowe. 1993. "The Taiwan Connection." *South China Morning Post*, December 27, 11.

———. 1997. "Sourcing the Problem: Why Fuzhou?" In *Human Smuggling: Chinese Migrant Trafficking and the Challenge to America's Immigration Tradition*, edited by Paul J. Smith, 76–92. Washington, D.C.: Center for Strategic and International Studies.

"INS Undercover Operation Crushes a Taiwanese Alien Smuggling Ring." 1985. *Centre Daily News* (in Chinese), May 9, 3.

Interagency Working Group. 1995. "Presidential Initiative to Deter Alien Smuggling: Report of the Interagency Working Group. Summary." Unpublished.

"Is the Chinese Communist Government Sponsoring 'Labor Export' to Taiwan?" (in Chinese). 1989. *United Daily News*, May 12, 1.

Kamen, Al. 1991. "U.S. Seizes Illegal Aliens from China." *Washington Post*, September 5, A5.

Kinkead, Gwen. 1992. *Chinatown: A Portrait of a Closed Society.* New York: HarperCollins.

Kwong, Peter. 1997. *Forbidden Workers: Illegal Chinese Immigrants and American Labor.* New York: New Press.

Lau, Alan Man S. 1993. Statement by Alan Man S. Lau, chairman of Fukien American Association, at a press conference held at 125 East Broadway, New York, September 28.

Lay, Richard. 1993. "The Gangland Fiefdom of Terror." *South China Morning Post*, June 27, 4.

Lorch, Donatella. 1992. "A Flood of Illegal Aliens Enters U.S. via Kennedy: Requesting Political Asylum Is Usual Ploy." *New York Times*, March 18, B2.

Maltz, Michael. 1994. "Defining Organized Crime." In *Handbook of Organized Crime in the United States*, edited by Robert Kelly, Ko-lin Chin, and Rufus Schatzberg, 21–38. Westport, Conn.: Greenwood Press.

"Many Illegal Chinese Migrants Arrived in the US in Taiwanese Fishing Boats, Triads Are Alleged to Be Behind the Illegal Operations" (In Chinese). 1992. *Sing Tao Daily*, March 6, 23.

Mooney, Paul, and Melana Zyla. 1993. "Bracing the Seas and More: Smuggling Chinese into the US Means Big Money." *Far Eastern Economic Review*, April 8, 17–19.

Morgan, W. P. 1960. *Triad Societies in Hong Kong.* Hong Kong: Government Press.

Mydans, Seth. 1992. "Chinese Smugglers' Lucrative Cargo: Humans." *New York Times,* March 21, A1.

Myers, Willard. 1992. "The United States under Siege: Assault on the Borders: Chinese Smuggling 1983–1992." Manuscript in author's possession.

———. 1994. "Transnational Ethnic Chinese Organized Crime: A Global Challenge to the Security of the United States, Analysis and Recommendations." Testimony of Willard Myers, Senate Committee on Foreign Affairs, Subcommittee on Terrorism, Narcotics and International Operations, April 21.

Nyo, Ming-sen. 1993. "Why So Many Chinese Illegals Coming to the US?" (in Chinese). *World Journal Magazine,* August 29, S4.

"150 Members of the Shenzhen Border Patrol Army Were Arrested for Working for Snakeheads" (in Chinese). 1997. *World Journal,* October 17, A13.

Schemo, Diana Jean. 1993. "Survivors Tell of Voyage of Little Daylight, Little Food, and Only Hope." *New York Times,* June 7, B5.

Seagrave, Sterling. 1995. *Lords of the Rim: The Invisible Empire of the Overseas Chinese.* New York: G. P. Putnam's Sons.

Smith, Paul J. 1997. "Chinese Migrant Trafficking: A Global Challenge." In *Human Smuggling: Chinese Migrant Trafficking and the Challenge to America's Immigration Tradition,* edited by Paul J. Smith, 1–22. Washington, D.C.: Center for Strategic and International Studies.

"Smuggled Chinese Escaped from Mexican Authorities" (in Chinese). 1993. *World Journal,* August 25, A1.

Strom, Stephanie. 1991. "13 Held in Kidnapping of Illegal Alien." *New York Times,* January 2, B3.

Superior Court of New Jersey. 1995. *State of New Jersey vs. Dan Xin Lin et al.* Bergen County, Law Division, Indictment No. S-644–94.

Torode, Greg. 1993a. "Immigration HQ Criticized over Illegals." *South China Morning Post,* February 10, 3.

———. 1993b. "Triads Use HK Agency for Illegals." *South China Morning Post,* March 15, 1.

Treaster, Joseph. 1993. "Behind Immigrants' Voyage, Long Reach of Chinese Gang." *New York Times,* June 9, A1.

U.S. Immigration and Naturalization Service. 1993. "Vessels That Are Known to Have Attempted to Smuggle PRC Nationals into the United States." Report in author's possession, August 17.

U.S. Senate. 1992. *Asian Organized Crime.* Hearing before the Permanent Sub-committee on Investigations of the Committee on Governmental Affairs, October 3, November 5–6, 1991. Washington, D.C.: U.S. Government Printing Office.

Wang, Zheng. 1996. "Ocean-going Smuggling of Illegal Chinese Immigrants: Operation, Causation, and Policy Implications." *Transnational Organized Crime* 2 (1): 49–65.

"Xian Officials Fired for Receiving Bribes from Human Smugglers" (in Chinese). 1993. *Wen Wei Pao,* November 6, 1.

Zhang, Sheldon, and Mark Gaylord. 1996. "Bound for the Golden Mountain: The Social Organization of Chinese Alien Smuggling." *Crime, Law, and Social Change* 25: 1–16.

Zhou, Min. 1992. *Chinatown: The Socioeconomic Potential of an Urban Enclave.* Philadelphia: Temple University Press.

Zi, Ye. 1993. "The Doom of the *Golden Venture*" (in Chinese). *World Journal Weekly,* August 15, S-5.

9 ▪▪▪▪▪▪▪ Impact of Chinese Human Smuggling on the American Labor Market

Peter Kwong

Chinese organized crime has developed human smuggling into a truly global business, shepherding some one hundred thousand people per year to a range of destinations including Japan, Canada, Australia, the United States, France, Holland, and other parts of Europe. Profits from the Chinese smuggling network are reported to be in the range of $3.1 billion U.S. per year (Kaihla, 1996). However, this human smuggling system can only be sustained on the premise that illegals, once they have arrived in a host country, can secure employment to pay off their debts. Employers will hire them only if their services are cheaper and if they demand fewer benefits and less labor protection than the legal workers. The most important impact of illegals on the host society is, therefore, on its labor supply and labor conditions.

More than two hundred thousand Chinese illegal aliens have arrived in this country during the past two decades (Nin-lung, 1996: 63). Most of them work in a substandard underground economy. They are recruited to serve the needs of the decentralized, restructured American economy. Not only are they cheap, but hiring them serves the important objective of bringing readjustment to the balance of power between labor and capital in this country, established since the 1930s. The destruction of the powerful labor movement that was able to make significant gains in collective bargaining, higher wages, health and retirement benefits, unemployment compensation, and other social welfare safety nets is the chief objective of this new business order in the United States.

The best way to achieve this objective is by hiring the least organized and most vulnerable labor available—the new immigrants or, better yet, the undocumented aliens who have no protection at all. Therefore the issue of Chinese illegal migration is more of a labor than an immigration problem. As long as there is demand for cheap and pliable labor, there will be jobs for the illegals and a market for human smugglers in which they can go on making huge profits.

Background

The majority of the Chinese illegals have come from the area around the city of Fuzhou in Fujian Province and a smaller portion from the area around the city of Wenzhou in the neighboring Zhejiang Province up north. As the human smuggling network expands in search of new recruits, illegal aliens from other parts of China are slowly entering this flow as well.

Fuzhounese illegals began to arrive in the early 1970s, when Fuzhounese seamen who worked on foreign vessels started jumping ship in New York Harbor (Nin-lung, 1996: 51). Most of them were single men without legal status. Few could become legalized residents. A handful arranged phony marriages with ABC (American-born Chinese) girls, paying them three thousand dollars to go through the ritual of a bogus marriage.

With or without legal status, however, as soon as the seamen became established economically, they started bringing in members of their families from China. This was the beginning of the Fuzhounese human smuggling network: a few primitive, simple schemes concocted by enterprising travel agencies to exploit this eager market of naturalized merchant mariners. The main challenge was transporting the relatives from Hong Kong to New York.

In the late 1960s, at the height of the Cultural Revolution, the Chinese Communist government opened the border between China and Hong Kong, thinking it might destroy the British colony by flooding it with penniless refugees. Many Fuzhounese with family connections in New York seized the opportunity of this chaotic period to go to Hong Kong, some by swimming across the Shenzhen River. Once in Hong Kong they gained refugee status and were thus entitled to exit visas.

The travel agencies' task was to obtain, usually through bribery, entry visas for the refugees from countries such as Bolivia, Guatemala, or Mexico. When they arrived in those countries, the refugees were then easily escorted across the Mexican border into the United States. During the days when the border controls were at a minimum, the smuggling fee was a mere eighteen hundred dollars.

This route via South America was already well traveled by Taiwanese criminals—often tax cheats but occasionally including more serious offenders, including embezzlers and violent criminals—in the 1970s. In fact, the very first illegal Fuzhou emigrants used phony Taiwanese passports. This Central American option became even more popular after 1978, when Deng Xiaoping initiated the liberal "open door policy." After the border controls relaxed, thousands of Fuzhounese illegals arrived in New York.

The modern era of human smuggling began with the passage of the Immigration Reform and Control Act of 1986 (IRCA). The act contained an amnesty provision granting legal status to all those who could prove that they had resided in the United States as undocumented aliens before January 1, 1982. IRCA was a bonanza for the Fuzhounese illegals already in the U.S. With a stroke of the pen they became legal. Even the would-be illegal immigrants who were still in China could become legal if they arrived in time to hand in their application by November 1988. There were plenty of crooks in Chinatown willing to provide them with the back-dated employment records and tax receipts needed for the application—if they could come up with five hundred to six hundred dollars.

The result was a mad rush. The Taiwanese crime syndicate, which had made most of its money in the past through heroin trafficking (Hood, 1994), suddenly realized the profit potential in cash-rich, recently legalized Fuzhounese Americans, who were willing to pay almost any amount to get their relatives out of China before the deadline. The syndicate immediately dispatched agents to Fuzhou to build up smuggling networks by hiring locals as recruiters.

Soon the syndicate had muscled in on the operations of the existing small-scale travel agencies in Chinatown, adding its own facilities and a sophisticated, worldwide smuggling network to transform illegal immigration into an international corporate enterprise. It was a low-risk and high-profit operation for the syndicate, which quickly raised smuggling fees tenfold to eighteen thousand dollars per person—the origin of the New York City street nickname for a Fuzhounese illegal: "the Eighteen-Thousand-Dollar Man."

Suddenly, going to the United States became the only topic of conversation in Fuzhou. Stories of this or that lucky neighbor whose relatives in the United States cared enough to pay the smuggling fee spread like wildfire. People knew that if their relatives acted fast enough, they too could obtain legal resident status.

In the aftermath of the Tianenman Massacre in 1989, President George Bush compromised with China's critics by issuing an executive order permitting all Chinese students in the United States to adjust their immigration status so that they could not be forced to return if they faced political repression. In a later order, Executive Order 12711, the president instructed the State and Justice Departments to give "enhanced consideration" to individuals who expressed fear of persecution related to forced abortion or coerced sterilization (Russell, 1995: 39–87). The new order extended the promise of legal status to almost all Fuzhou immigrants, who could now be classified as refugees, fleeing past or threatened persecution by forced abortion and sterilization.

The 1986 IRCA, together with the 1989 and 1990 Bush executive orders, not only gave a huge number of Fuzhounese illegals the opportunity for lawful existence in this country but also assured their relatives of the option of legal immigration. The Fuzhounese evidently had enough seed population to grow through this legal process. But some relatives who could enter the United States legally did not want to wait the usual period—which, for, say, the wife of a permanent resident, could be three to four years. For a sibling it could be as long as eight years.

Those who did not have relatives to sponsor their legal immigration were given the hope that once they arrived on American soil they could apply for political asylum based on the Executive Order 12711's provision construing China's one-child policy as "persecution." The information provided by the smuggling network was that the asylum application process would take a long time; once in the country, even those denied asylum could still appeal and easily evade deportation indefinitely. While waiting for their hearings and appeals, the asylum seekers could get legal work permits and a job. Thanks to such convenient legal decisions, the smuggling operation kept expanding. The largest number of Chinese illegals ever entered the United States between 1988 and 1993. The cost of smuggling keeps growing: it had reached $22,000 per person in 1988 and $35,000 in the early 1990s.

During this period, the overall U.S. border surveillance was so lax that the Chinese smugglers used ships to transport aliens across the Pacific and unloaded them directly off American shores, first on the West Coast and then directly off the East Coast, until the *Golden Venture* incident in the summer of 1993, which shocked the American authorities into action. By 1994, a dozen new routes opened a variety of new staging areas in Central America, Eastern Europe, and the Caribbean (Smith, 1996). Most Chinese illegals no longer traveled by ships but via air and more often than not with "valid" visas—F-1 student visas, H-1 temporary work permits, diplomatic passports, or visas issued for official trade delegations—provided by the smugglers. So even with the tightened immigration controls intended in the harsh 1996 Illegal Immigration Reform and Immigrant Responsibility Act, the flow of Chinese illegal migration has continued. There are reports of new arrivals every week. Human smugglers are developing new sources of supplies from the central and coastal provinces of Zhejiang, Sichuan, Shandong, and Anhui—and from wherever there are villages with significant past overseas emigration and wherever there are large enough "seed populations" that have accumulated sufficient capital to support migrant trafficking. In the meantime, the smuggling fee for Fuzhounese has edged up to forty-two thousand dollars.

Most human smuggling systems simply provide assistance in border crossing, like the "coyotes" who charge at most a few hundred dollars for sneaking a client across the U.S.-Mexican border. Chinese smuggling services are much more comprehensive. Their package includes passage out of China, a transit location or locations as the case requires, and transport to a final destination. Their charges are also the highest.

The high fee the smugglers charge has nothing to do with the actual cost of transportation, but that is how much the smugglers can command. To maintain such high profits, Chinese smuggling operators have to enter into complex financial arrangements with their clients that continue even years after the illegals' arrival, because they are being paid by them from income yet to be realized.

In the early stages of the human smuggling industry, some snakeheads extended credit, allowing their clients to pay the debt off in monthly installments. However, as the smuggling business grew, keeping track of credit allowances became a nuisance. In addition, a lengthy involvement with a freely roaming client made brushes with law enforcement more likely. These days, smugglers expect potential illegal immigrants first to raise fifteen hundred dollars in China. On arrival, they will be held in safe houses until all their debts are paid (Chin, 1996).

That amount is usually borrowed from relatives in the United States at 3 percent interest. To pay off, for example, $30,000 in three years means approximately $10,000 a year, or $800 a month. The smugglers prefer to shift the responsibility of keeping track of the debt payments to other parties, be they relatives, local gangs, local loan sharks, or village associations. Still, the perpetuation of this whole smuggling system calls for an overall stable debt-paying environment. The smuggling operators are constantly taking measures to make sure that debts are honored for all parties concerned, even if they are not to them.

Structured Violence

Regular use of violence is one way to instill fear in the minds of the illegals in order to gain their compliance. Smugglers usually pay enforcers to terrorize the illegals during the voyage to the United States. However, the worst abuses of illegal immigrants occur in New York safe houses while they wait for their relatives to come up with the final payment. To encourage the relatives to raise the funds by borrowing from various sources more quickly, the smuggling networks contract with violent youth gangs. The enforcers begin to abuse the illegals as soon as they arrive at the safe houses, at times forcing them to talk to their relatives on the phone while undergoing torture.

The police claim that there are some three hundred safe houses holding newcomers in New York City (Chan, 1993). They are usually located in basement cellars, and all illegals have to spend some time in one before being released. The immigrants are obliged to eat, sleep, and urinate in the same place as more than a dozen inmates, all of whom are confined to one room. They are starved, deprived of fresh air and sunlight, and beaten regularly. At times they are ordered to inflict pain on one another. Many are shackled and handcuffed to metal bed frames. Males are told that they could be killed; the females are threatened with work in a whorehouse. One thing the smugglers always make sure of is that their victims do not dare to inform the authorities or testify against them in court—not even to talk about their experience with other illegals. They are never allowed to forget that the smugglers control the whole community.

For victims who were unable to pay off their smuggling fees, the snakeheads simply have the unfortunate debtor incarcerated. In 1992, the Brooklyn Police Robbery Squad stumbled upon a human-smuggling scheme while investigating a youth-gang extortion case. When they broke into an apartment building in the Hispanic section of Sunset Park, they found thirteen undocumented Fuzhounese, some of whom had been incarcerated in the cellar for as long as fourteen months. They were virtual slaves to the enforcers, who were members of the Fuching (Fujian Youth) Gang. During the day, the victims worked at restaurants and laundries affiliated with organized crime.

Fear of physical violence, however, is not the only way to extract compliance from indebted illegals. Bringing pressures from members of their families in China is another way.

Illegal Migration as a Family Enterprise

Illegal migration from a poor country like China is a costly proposition. No one individual is capable of initiating exodus without being part of a "family migration project." The project runs like a relay team. The family first pools all its resources and social connections to send one young, capable, and dependable male abroad. In the beginning, he has to work for others in the United States to pay off his debts. The ideal narrative from here on goes like this: once his debts are paid, he begins to save to bring other family members over. He familiarizes himself with his new environment and selects a business that is likely to succeed as a "family enterprise"—a takeout restaurant, for instance, as is commonly the case with the Fuzhounese. The migration relay begins. The next in line to be sent overseas may be his wife, but most likely it will be a male sibling who will maximize the family's capital accumulation—a hardworking, "productive" male is preferable. A wife is considered as a prime candidate for migration if the family wants to have a child born in the United States to secure its future legal footing.

Once this early core group, the "seed population," begins to get established—when it accumulates enough savings for a down payment on a takeout restaurant in the Bronx, for instance—other family members are brought over one by one: wives and sisters to help out as cashiers, grandparents to look after the children, and so on. The children will be put to work as soon as they are old enough to act as translators and delivery boys or girls—forming the second generation of the family's "corporate venture."

The migration engine does not stop there. The wives do not abandon their original families—they and their in-laws' family will assist their siblings and parents by linking them into the migration chain. The siblings can then start a new cycle of family migration, thus extending the network to people with different surnames and eventually encompassing an entire community of neighbors and fellow villagers. The chain can eventually include not just the population of a whole village but an entire dialect group.

The strong sense of family and kinship loyalty that underlies group migration should not be seen purely in cultural and moral terms, because it is ultimately informed by an explicit economic rationale. Bringing family members into the migration chain is seen by the Fuzhounese as a chance to extend their economic power, by bringing in a relative either as a business partner or as cheap labor. To the Chinese in America who came early, Fuzhounese immigrants represent the rock bottom of the economic ladder in the community. They can move upward only if they accumulate some capital, and for that Fuzhounese need cheap and dependable labor. Their kin back home are the ideal candidates.

A Deadly Embrace

What the Fuzhounese are caught up in, however, is not a normal rural and kinship-based migration chain. Their migration has been helped by an organized human smuggling network, whose only concern is making a profit—not maintaining family ties and kinship unity. The network is interested in the Fuzhounese as potential clients only if two critical conditions exist: one, the client can pay; two, the client can be trusted to keep the operation secret from law enforcement.

Established by seamen who had jumped ship in the early 1970s, a "seed population" in New York has helped the Fuzhounese to fulfill the first condition. This seed population was expanded with the 1986 amnesty program and President Bush's 1989 executive order, which provided legal status for Chinese already in this country. The resulting relatively large legal resident community of Fuzhounese had accumulated enough savings to pay smugglers for shipping their relatives over. The Fuzhounese fulfill the second condition of the smuggling networks by the virtue of their proven dedication to their family migration projects, for which they are willing to keep quiet and even tolerate abuse by snakeheads.

In China, family members of Fuzhounese immigrants have a very different understanding of the smugglers and the conditions in America than might be expected of an exploited population. Those who are waiting to emigrate look to the smugglers as the providers of an essential service. If there is a debt-payment dispute, the family in China as a rule sides with the smugglers, typically convinced that its own members in the United States are at fault. The snakeheads have devised their own propaganda and misinformation campaign in order to attract as many innocent people as possible onto the smuggling journey. When I confronted the relatives of illegals in China with accounts of torture, kidnapping, rape, and other abuses perpetrated by the snakeheads, they usually responded that the snakeheads have every right to punish those who are lazy and unwilling to pay off their debts. In a way, the snakeheads have already immunized the Fuzhounese from being critical of the human smuggling process.

After years of this type of indoctrination, the Fuzhounese in China have come to believe that America is a land of opportunity, where anyone can work for two years to pay off their smuggling debts and then, in a couple more years, buy a business. Those unable to do so are considered *mei-zu-shi,* useless and lacking in ambition. Even those family members not expecting to immigrate to the United States want to make sure the migration project succeeds so that their future in China will be assured by overseas remittances.

Of course, the Fuzhounese in America know that the snakeheads are far from perfect, but they are too intimidated to challenge them. They cannot fight back lest they jeopardize the chances of other family members to make the trip. Besides, their relatives in China are vulnerable. The snakeheads could threaten family members there with violence or extortion. This kind of situation is taken seriously because local authorities are not likely to intervene. More than anything, however, they keep quiet in order to maintain their "face" and family honor. The smugglers are therefore using the strong kinship ties of the Fuzhounese to keep their clients in line.

Reaching the Limit

There are limits, however, to how far the Fuzhounese's resources could be exploited. The smuggling operations are increasingly limited by the U.S. Fuzhounese immigrant community's finances. As more Fuzhounese come, the debts are accumulating and will eventually reach a point where the indigenous community will no longer be able to service their debt. Paul Smith of Pacific Forum estimates that between 1991 and 1994, there were 25,000 Fuzhounese illegals entering the United States yearly (Smith, 1994: 60–77). That means that at least 100,000 illegal Fuzhounese, not counting the thousands who came before and after that period, paid $30,000 each—a grand total of $3 billion. No new immigrant community can withstand this amount of debt.

By 1992 the influx of Fuzhounese illegals had reached a saturation point. Members in the community were having increasing difficulty raising the smuggling funds. To counter this trend, the snakeheads tried to squeeze more out of the illegals and their relatives by force. Kidnapping and torturing of illegals were the inevitable consequences. In the meantime, knowing the importance of family structure to the Fuzhounese, the snakeheads used every means possible to exploit that weakness. They kidnapped and tortured those illegals with relatives to ensure speedy payment. They enlisted the support of debtors' families in China to exact maximum pressure on them (*World Journal*, March 1995: B2). Most of all, they forced the illegals themselves to collect funds from their relatives.

These wayward indebted illegals are also recruited to be the enforcers. At times they simply go off on their own to prey on others as a way of paying off their own debts. They have been known to seize clients who have already paid and torture them in safe houses to force their relatives to pay again. As the hardship of debt burden increases, more Fuzhounese are being forced into crime. The civic order of the Chinatown community is sliding into chaos. The atmosphere of fear and insecurity intensifies.

Finally, the snakeheads, in order to maintain the volume of their business, developed a modified form of "kinship sponsoring system." Rich Fuzhounese restaurant and garment factory owners and gambling and prostitution kingpins, who are legal and came to this country earlier, stepped in to sponsor new groups of "distant relatives." The snakeheads, knowing the reputation and reliability of the sponsors, smuggled the new recruits at a discount, some even entirely on credit. These new recruits have to work for the sponsors as unpaid labor for several years while the enforcers ensure their complacency through control over their relatives in China. They are, therefore, trapped in a state of virtual indentured servitude.

Modern-Day Coolies

Employers, of course, prefer Fuzhounese because they are cheaper and because they must accept almost any conditions in order to pay off their debts to the snakeheads. In fact, many employment agencies specialize in illegals. For instance, it is a well-known fact among short-term labor employers' circles that agencies around East Broadway in New York's Chinatown specialize in undocumented Fuzhounese workers. The posted employer requests come from all over the East Coast, including New Jersey, Connecticut, and Maine, even from Ohio and North Carolina.

In the past ten years, undocumented Fuzhounese have penetrated deeply into the garment, construction, and restaurant trades in New York. Many of their employers are not Chinese. Non-Chinese-owned small electronics factories in New Jersey, construction companies specializing in loft renovation in Soho, and Long Island farms alike use Chinese employment agencies to find Chinese labor contractors who will take care of selection, transportation, payment, and management of their workers. In fact, if one looks into the kitchens of most mid-priced continental or American restaurants in Manhattan, one is likely to find a number of Fuzhounese working there. When a construction company can hire a skilled carpenter for fifty dollars a day and an unskilled one for even less, without ever even having to know the workers' pay scale, why should it matter what kind of conditions the workers are laboring under?

With the flood of desperate, undocumented aliens willing to work, Chinese employers are in a position to depress the labor conditions to the limits for all other workers as well. Wages in the Chinatown garment industry, already low by American standards before the arrival of the Fuzhounese, have declined even further. Home work, thought to have disappeared in America fifty years ago, is a common phenomenon in Chinatown, as is child labor, which has pushed down the already low wage scale in the garment industry.

Testifying in 1995 at a Senate hearing for antisweatshop legislation, Mrs. Tang, a schoolteacher in Guangdong Province who had immigrated ten years ago to Brooklyn, recalled that in the early eighties she worked eight hours a day and earned forty to fifty dollars a day. Today, with competition from the Fuzhounese, she slaves twelve hours a day to make a paltry thirty dollars (*World Journal,* September 26, 1996: B4). For her, it is almost as if she has to work twice as long to make the same amount of money.

Those who have worked in the industry for some time and are physically no longer able to keep up the pace are assigned to lesser jobs, such as cutting threads, and make even less. Immigrants from Fuzhou, who are usually younger, choose to work at nonunion shops in order to get more take-home pay, still averaging about forty dollars a day.

Competition from the illegals is forcing documented Chinese workers to settle for less if they want to maintain steady employment. Employers lay off workers as soon as their work orders are completed. In the slower months, from November to the end of the year, seamstresses make less than two hundred dollars a month. For immigrants paying off enormous debts, this sum is absurdly, desperately low. They line up outside the factory long before the doors open to be the first ones to begin work. At night, they refuse to quit even after ten, just to be able to get a few more pieces done for a few more dollars. Some of the seamstresses on sewing machines are known not to drink anything during the day lest they interrupt their work, calculated on piece rate, by going to the bathroom. One Cantonese garment lady has testified to a congressional committee that Fuzhounese illegals work until two in the morning, sleep in the factory, and start again right after sunrise. Sometimes, if they are not able to complete a given order, they ask their children to come in to help (Baoqing, 1996: B1) Now even Fuzhounese men work on the sewing machines, competing with the traditionally all-woman labor force.

Not surprisingly, the illegals have the best chance of getting and keeping a job. The employers like them because they are young, committed, and willing to work long hours and also for their docility and uncomplaining nature. Some employers are interested only in undocumented workers. Longtime residents must either follow their example or lose their jobs. Thus employers have effectively erased the distinctions between legal and illegal immigrant workers. It is not surprising that the Chinese legal immigrants resent the undocumented interlopers, who they say have marginalized everybody's labor and worsened everybody's conditions. In every Chinatown discussion about workplace conditions, the Fuzhounese, the *wu-sun-fun* (people with no status), are the target of scorn.

The most egregious practice at both unionized and nonunion Chinese garment factories in New York is withholding workers' legitimate wages. This problem has reached epidemic proportions. Previously, the normal withholding period was three weeks; now anything under five weeks is considered good. The length of wage withholding has become the single criterion used by garment women in choosing a factory. Of course, there is never a guarantee; after the employment starts, the employer can claim cash flow problems or manufacturers' nonpayment to postpone his own wage payments. After a few weeks of unpaid wages, the workers are faced with the difficult decision of whether to hope against hope and work for another week or quit and cut their losses (Kwong, 1997: 104).

Employers are violating the most basic right of a worker—to be paid after the work is done. If the workers ask for their back pay, they are given excuses. If they push further, they are blacklisted (never to be hired by any other contractor in the Chinese community), threatened with informing their illegal status to the INS, or even threatened with gang violence. In the meantime, the employers let their accountants figure out how much back pay and taxes they owe, to help them decide when to close the shop down, change to a new corporate entity, and reopen at a new location.

Taking legal action against employers almost never succeeds. In the first place, the employers do not believe that illegals would dare to file complaints against them, because of their illegal status. Even then there are hundreds of complaints against Chinese employers for back wages filed with the New York State Labor Department, but so far there have been only two convictions. The first was brought in 1993, but the workers have yet to collect any back payment. More recently, in September 1996, workers won back wages totaling fifty-nine thousand dollars—for work done between August 1992 and November 1993. More typically, employers simply take advantage of legal loopholes and opt for bankruptcy proceedings whenever they face pressure for back wages. Workers arrive one morning to find the factory gates closed without a forwarding address or any other information. The same owners soon reopen nearby under a new corporate title with an altered partnership, refusing legal responsibility for the defunct factory.

The illegal Chinese workers were also used for union busting. In 1994, the owners of the Silver Palace Restaurant—one of Chinatown's largest restaurants, which was unionized in 1980—locked out all their union workers, claiming that their wages were too high. The locked-out union workers picketed the restaurant for more than seven months. "If the owners win this one," the leader of the picketing workers stressed, "employers all over Chinatown could impose any kind of conditions they want on the working people, no matter whether they are legal or undocumented. We are then nothing but slaves" (interview with Kwong Hui, leader of the picketing workers). The issue is no longer just the treatment of illegals. In Chinatown, where employers use illegals to depress wages for all legal workers, they have transformed the problem into a class struggle between labor and management.

Ineffective Enforcement of Labor Law

To blame all the problems that Chinatown workers face on Chinese employers, however, is too easy. This is not just a Chinese internal problem, as some people would like one to believe. Chinese contractors are behaving this way because they know they can get away with it, because they know that no American institution will intervene to impose standard rules and regulations to protect the weak and the vulnerable in the Chinese community.

The performance of the Labor Department can be described at best as ineffective, passive, and slow. According to its own reports, 90 percent of the factories in Chinatown are sweatshops. Yet it rarely initiates action.

If it is criticized, its typical first response is to claim that it is understaffed; it then blames the workers for not coming forward. When they do come forward, the Labor Department takes months to investigate the case, while the workers are exposed to retribution by the bosses: to come forward means risking being fired or even physically harmed. And in the end, after a long wait, nothing usually comes of it: the Labor Department claims that the owner's corporate entity has changed and that the defendant cannot be found. Even when an errant owner is convicted, the punishment is minimal—at the worst, the labor violations are judged a misdemeanor. The workers are usually forced to settle, and they generally get only a small portion of the wages owed. But so few cases have been prosecuted so far that no employer in Chinatown needs to worry.

The labor union—most of the Chinese workers in Lower Manhattan are members of the Union of Needletrades, Industrial and Textile Employees (UNITE)—is not performing much better. It can also be best described as ineffective, passive, and slow. What's worse, the union's representatives tend to have a better relationship with the owners than the workers, and they regularly side with them (Kwong and Lum, 1988: 899).

The workers, thus, have nowhere to turn. They are silenced and trapped in their own ethnic environment, which is completely controlled by the employers. Employers are using every means available to squeeze extra profits, including laying off workers to collect unemployment compensation while still asking them to work for less.

The long hours and low wages have taken a toll on the physical condition of many Chinatown workers. After several years of working like machines chasing after the piece rate, for twelve hours a day and seven days a week, workers begin to develop physical ailments. Seamstresses generally complain of sore arms, back and shoulder pains, and swollen feet. Bronchial asthma is also common; it is caused by prolonged exposure to the chemicals used in treating fabrics. Working more than eighty hours a week has also led to all sorts of relatively uncommon problems—pinched nerves, headaches, dizzy spells, heart palpitations, missed menstrual cycles, and insomnia—overwork symptoms not well known in this country since the turn of the century. Once sick, the workers are slowed down and are not able to earn enough to be eligible for medical insurance. This is the time when they find out that their employers have not been paying dues for their Workmen's Compensation and Social Security benefits.

For illegals, their priority is to pay off debts, and they simply cannot get sick. Mr. Lan, who left his wife and children behind in Fuzhou, came here illegally five years ago and worked hard to pay off his huge smuggling debt. Under heavy pressure and emotional stress, his health declined. His wife, realizing his predicament, came illegally to help him out. But this doubled his debt, and his health deteriorated to the point that he could no longer work. Thus the whole family started to depend solely on his wife's income as a seamstress—just to survive. The debts remained. One day, when his wife was out working, he hung himself (*World Journal*, March 1, 1996: B1).

American Business Climate

The U.S. government's ineffectiveness should be seen in the context of America's demand for cheap labor. For some time now the American economy has been emphasizing growth through deregulation and increased labor productivity. The most effective way to achieve this is by employing nonunionized labor. Immigrant labor is even better, not only because it is not organized but also because it is less protected. Following this logic, undocumented labor is the best: entirely unregulated and thus the most productive. If we push this logic one more step, then the most productive labor would be the "unfree" undocumented immigrant labor, such as the indebted Fuzhounese workers. Therefore, their unchecked entry into this country in such large numbers is in the spirit of the current American economic philosophy.

American corporations have responded to global competition through a strategy of restructuring that calls for production decentralization. Decentralization under a subcontracting system, the corporations can still control prices and product quality through competition among the many small suppliers. The competition among the small suppliers is so intense that they have to accept a low rate of profitability, which forces them to abandon the capital investment needed to maintain modernized production as well as the desire to train and upgrade their workforce (Luria, 1996: 11–16). While they bear the brunt of the ups and downs of the market fluctuation, the small suppliers have the additional responsibility of managing the workforce, trying to minimize labor costs by adopting tactics of union busting, and freezing or cutting wages. Typically they will hire less educated and less skilled workers—often immigrant labor. Illegal immigrants are best of all, since they are not organized or legally protected.

In short, to win competitively, small firms employ what is called a "low road" strategy. The losers are the employers who do precisely what common sense says they should do: invest, train, innovate, and hire well-educated legal workers. The recent efflorescence of sweatshops in the apparel industry in New York and Los Angeles, for instance, should not be a surprise.

On the other end, the ineffectiveness of labor law enforcement has political support. Some of the most important elected officials in New York, for instance, are susceptible to political influence from employers. They lack concern for labor issues and have no qualms about taking contributions from sweatshop operators.

Governor George Pataki attended a banquet at Jing Fong Restaurant in New York's Chinatown in November 1995 to award the "Outstanding Asian American Award" to Cheng Chung-ko, the owner/manager of the restaurant. Yet in 1997, the New York State Attorney General's Office filed suit against Cheng's restaurant, charging it with cheating fifty-eight workers of more than $1.5 million in tips and wages. Attorney General Dennis Vacco asserted that fifty-eight Jing Fong employees who worked sixty or more hours weekly were paid just $65 to $100 a week. They should have earned more than $300 with overtime (Greenhouse, 1997: A5).

Universal Enforcement of Labor Standards

As long as there is no effective labor enforcement, employers will have the incentives to hire illegals, and the flood of illegal immigration will continue. Harsh immigration restrictions will not stop this flow because they do not address the heart of the problem: the ever healthy demand of American business for vulnerable, unprotected labor. Even with all the public attention generated by the *Golden Venture* fiasco, Chinese illegal migration has continued. It will continue because the sensational headlines, punitive legislation, and political demagoguery all work together to reinforce the essential appeal of illegal Chinese laborers to the American businesses that employ them: illegal aliens continue to be cheaper, more pliable, and more dependent on their employers than legitimate labor. More than any other single fact, this explains how human smuggling has grown in the last half of the last decade of the twentieth century into an industry boasting $4 billion in annual profits.

If our objective is to prevent employers from hiring and exploiting illegal workers so American working conditions will not deteriorate, we need a different logic and a different approach. This is essentially a labor and not an immigration issue.

The only way to immunize American workers from the damage caused by the presence of illegal alien laborers is by across-the-board enforcement of all U.S. labor laws, affecting all employers in the United States—whether foreign or U.S. citizens, employing foreign documented, undocumented, or domestic labor. Strict enforcement means adherence to American labor standards, particularly in regards to the minimum wage, the forty-hour workweek, and OSHA health and safety regulations.

Strict enforcement also means uncompromising prosecution of reported violations without regard to whether the information was provided by an American-born worker, a legal, or an illegal immigrant. Only then will all the victims speak out and the labor abuses stop. At the same time, the extension of American labor standards to all workers will eliminate employers' incentive to recruit and exploit illegals and also put a brake on the barbaric human smuggling trade.

REFERENCES

Baoqing, Lin. 1996. *World Journal*, August 26, B1.

Chan, Ying. 1993. *Daily News*, September 10.

Chin, Ko-lin. 1996. "Safe House or Hell House?: The Experiences of Newly Arrived Undocumented Chinese." Paper presented at the Conference on Asia Migrant Trafficking: The New Threat to America's Immigration Tradition, Honolulu, July 25–27, sponsored by the Pacific Forum CSIS.

Greenhouse, Steve. 1997. "Big Chinatown Restaurant Sued on Wages and Tips." *New York Times*, January 24, A5.

Hood, Marlowe. 1994. "The Taiwan Connection." *Los Angeles Times*, October 9, 1.

Kaihla, P. 1996. "The People's Smugglers." *Maclean's*, April 29.

Kwong, Peter. 1997. *Forbidden Workers: Illegal Chinese Immigrants and American Labor.* New York: New Press.

Kwong, Peter, and Jo Ann Lum. 1988. "How the Other Half Lives Now." *Nation,* June 18, 899.

Luria, Daniel. 1996. "Why Markets Tolerate Mediocre Manufacturing." *Challenge* 11–16 (July/August): 11–16.

Nin-lung, Liu. 1996. *Chinese Snakepeople [Choong Kuo Ren Tsai Tsao].* Hong Kong: Nineties Monthly/Going Fine.

Russell, Sharon Stanton. 1995. "Migration Patterns of U.S. Foreign Policy Interest." In *Threatened People, Threatened Borders: World Migration and U.S. Policy,* edited by M. Teitelbaum and M. Weiner, 39–87. New York: Norton.

Smith, Paul. 1994. "The Strategic Implications of Chinese Emigration." *Survival* 36 (2): 60–77.

———. 1996. "Illegal Chinese Immigrants Everywhere, and No Letup in Sight." *International Herald Tribune,* June 28, 1.

"The Worsening Fuzhouese Gang Violence." 1995. *World Journal,* B2.

PART III

The Politics of Human

Smuggling

10 ▪▪▪▪▪▪ The Law at a Crossroads: The Construction of Migrant Women Trafficked into Prostitution

Nora V. Demleitner

In the late 1970s and throughout the 1980s, news reports proliferated about women and girls forced into prostitution in some Asian countries, which were heralded as tourist paradises for men from highly industrialized nations. While the accounts of abuse and torture that followed the abduction, seduction, or outright sale of young women into prostitution were shocking, for those who did not visit those countries, they were merely tales of faraway atrocities.

Globalization and increasing migration have dramatically expanded the location of women and (female) children who are being forced to prostitute themselves. The one-way street has been opened to two-way traffic: Men from wealthy countries go abroad for sexual "adventures"; women from poorer states migrate to the men's home states. Today these women and girls can be found in Tel Aviv, Berlin, Amsterdam, Milan, New York City, and rural Florida.[1] As human trafficking and forced prostitution have moved into our midst, they have also moved onto the political agenda of the Western, industrialized world.[2]

Human trafficking has been characterized as extremely violent, of "industrial scale" (U.N. Commission on Human Rights, 1995: 1), and involving huge profit margins. Since organized criminal groups are alleged to dominate trafficking, it has been portrayed as a security threat to Western countries, akin to drugs and weapons smuggling (Anderson et al., 1995: 156–67).[3]

Human trafficking and forced prostitution could be approached in multiple ways: as a moral issue, a public order problem, a labor question, a human rights problem, a migration issue, or a matter of (organized) crime (Wijers and Lap-Chew, 1997: 157–78). Because of the ways in which trafficking has been depicted in Western Europe, North America, and Australia, most of the focus has been on the migration and organized crime components of trafficking.

The emphasis on trafficking as a migration problem has also led to the criminalization of trafficking victims who generally violate prostitution and immigration laws. Despite their traumatic victimization, these persons tend to receive only very limited, if any, assistance from the governmental authorities in the countries in which they were forced to work as prostitutes and in their home countries. Neither regular admonitions by United Nations agencies (U.N. Commission on Human Rights, 1995: 2, 4) nor accusations by women's organizations have changed this approach. However, with the increasing entry of women from central and Eastern Europe into Western Europe and the United States, the dual abuse that these women suffer at the hands of traffickers and governments has been more highly publicized.[4] Moreover, it has become clear that the immediate deportation of trafficking victims because they are undocumented migrants generally thwarts the successful prosecution of the traffickers.

Much of the reluctance to help trafficked women effectively can be ascribed to the social ambivalence that surrounds their construction as prostitutes and as undocumented migrants. Often unreflected and stereotyped images of the women have driven the application of laws and the implementation of policies that have characterized them as offenders rather than victims.[5] Only powerful images, such as the forced prostitution of very young girls or brutal forms of physical abuse amounting to torture, have succeeded in overcoming the negative attitude toward prostitutes and "illegal" migrants, which is reflected in the reluctant passage and enforcement of antitrafficking laws. Although compelling depictions of victimhood may be able to counteract the negative constructions of the women, they also carry with them dangers as they construe women generally as helpless and in need of rescuing.[6] Since many migrant women do not fit this image, they are unlikely to benefit from a framework that aids only the "typical" victim. Therefore, the depiction of trafficking victims as victims may not provide substantial assistance to most of the women. Rather than attempting to replace the current construction of trafficked women with that of "victims," we must question the image of the prostitute and the "illegal alien" that drives the implementation of current law and the further use and abuse of trafficked women by the state.[7]

The Legal Construction of "Illegal" Migrants

Trafficking "Illegal" Migrants

In recent years, highly industrialized countries in Europe, North America, and Asia have increasingly restricted legal, long-term immigration. Although certain highly skilled immigrants and close family members, primarily spouses and minor children, of citizens will still be admitted, almost all others are excluded from legal migration.

For many foreigners even short-term visas, which include entry permits for tourists, seasonal workers, fiancé(e)s, and, in some countries, models and dancers, are difficult to obtain. The demand for these visas far exceeds the supply; and many of these visas are, explicitly or implicitly, reserved for the educated and affluent. Because of sexual inequality around the world, which results in men as a group being better educated and wealthier than women as a group, men are the more likely beneficiaries of long- and short-term entry permits that allow them to work legally or at least put them in the position to earn higher wages than in their home countries, even in illegal employment.

However, many women in the less industrialized and less developed world also frequently desire to migrate to improve their own and their family's economic situation, especially in light of high unemployment or the availability of only low-paying jobs at home. The media portrayal of Western economies and the accounts of other migrants promise higher-paying employment and a better life abroad. Often the women's home governments support migration to decrease unemployment and population pressures and to increase foreign remittances and the wealth of their people. Some countries have not even shrunk from promoting sex work for women.[8]

Not surprisingly, the contraction of legal immigration in the Western world combined with global economic inequality has caused an upsurge in illegal or undocumented migration. Potential migrants may be willing to attempt illegal border crossings; procure visas illegitimately, such as through marriage fraud; or stay on even after the expiration of a short-term visa. Such a combination of legal and illegal methods is typical for entry into Western countries (International Organization for Migration [IOM] and International Centre for Migration Policy Development, 1999: 72).

While in decades past illegal migration tended to be an individual matter, with the increasing fortification of borders by Western countries, organized groups have begun to assist migrants in crossing international borders, gaining short-term entry visas, and even finding (fraudulent) spouses (Wijers, 1998: 72). However, these services do not come cheap, and the migrants and their families often become deeply indebted to traffickers. Traffickers then use that debt to pressure these migrants. For female migrants that has meant forced labor in sweatshops or forced prostitution.

Even though much has been written about undocumented migration, the number of migrants, whether trafficked or entering on their own or with the help of smugglers, is subject to conjecture. The media, governments, and nongovernmental organizations publicize increasingly higher figures (Campani, 1998: 231–32). The U.S. Department of State has spoken of fifty thousand women trafficked into the United States every year (U.S. House of Representatives, 1999). Precise data, however, are difficult to collect because of the clandestine nature of all undocumented migration and the impossibility of determining how many of these migrants will move on to third states or return to their home countries. Moreover, definitional questions and uncertainties pose a substantial difficulty in accurately assessing the number of individuals trafficked. Frequently, all undocumented migrants, whether smuggled or trafficked, are considered together.[9]

Data on trafficked migrants no longer focus exclusively on their number but have shifted to the amount of money organized criminal groups make from human trafficking. This reconfiguration further commodifies human beings and equates them with other trafficked goods, such as drugs, rather than treating them as individuals. Moreover, such a change in focus does not solve the definitional problems inherent in the term *trafficking*.

Despite its frequent use in popular and academic discourse, the meaning of the term *trafficking* is ambiguous. Three primary meanings are distinguishable. To many the term is synonymous with *illegal entry*. The European Union's definition of trafficking, on the other hand, ties entry into a member state to sexual exploitation or abuse, with sexual exploitation connoting forced prostitution (Council of the European Union, 1997). The link between trafficking and forced prostitution severs the connection between women who are forced to work in the sex industry, women who are trafficked into forced labor generally (Bindman, 1998: 65), and men who are trafficked. The issue of whether trafficking for sexual exploitation and other slaverylike employment should be treated separately has been fiercely contested and has caused a rift in the antitrafficking community. The United Nations General Assembly depicts trafficking more broadly as connecting the "illicit and clandestine movement of persons across national or international borders" to sexual or economic oppression and exploitation, which can take the form of "forced domestic labour, false marriages, clandestine employment and false adoption" (Chuang, 1998: 87).[10] One of the most comprehensive definitions suggested construes trafficking as "consist[ing] of all acts involved in: within or across borders; whether for financial or other gain or not; and in which material deception, coercion, force, direct or indirect threats, abuse of authority, fraud, or fraudulent non-disclosure is used; for the purpose of placing a person forcibly, against her/his will or without her/his consent; in exploitative, abusive or servile situations, such as forced prostitution, sweatshop labor, domestic servitude or other abusive forms of labor or family relationships, whether for pay or not" (Stewart, 1998: 16).

All these definitions attempt to focus attention on the illegality of the traffickers' actions rather than the migrants'. They also highlight particularly the subjugation and abuse of the person trafficked and may lead states to protect the victims of this practice (Chuang, 1998: 88).

However, so far Western countries have deemed illegal migration, with or without the help of traffickers, a menace to their economic and social well-being and their territorial integrity. Ultimately, they have considered illegal migrants and traffickers threats to their national security (Vernez, n.d.: 1, 8).

The Portrayal of Undocumented Migrants as Criminals

Although many migrants, and especially those who are undocumented, become the victims of crime, including forced labor and forced prostitution, in the countries of destination, generally undocumented migrants are portrayed as *lawbreakers* (Demleitner, 1997: 43; Pickup, 1998: 47). That label, however, deprives them of the compassion and empathy that generally extends to crime victims.

Many of the offenses ascribed to undocumented migrants pertain to violations of the immigration laws, such as staying in the country without legal permission, evading an official border crossing, and obtaining fraudulent documents; other offenses grow out of the experience of illegal migration, such as the use of fraudulent work permits and the violation of tax laws.[11] Additional violations arise out of the often desperate situation in which undocumented migrants find themselves on their travels or upon arrival at their destination. However, the public portrayal of migrants as criminals is much less differentiated. Frequently, all noncitizens are aggregated and treated as potential offenders without regard to their personal situation or the type of law violated (Demleitner, 1997: 43–44). This perception is often reinforced by law enforcement activities against traffickers that lead to the indiscriminate arrest of traffickers and trafficked persons alike. Like the citizenry, however, migrants encompass law violators, victims, victims/lawbreakers, and those who do not fall into any of the above categories.

The situation is most complex, morally and legally, when the lawbreaker becomes a victim. Smugglers—as well as immigration officials and police in transit countries or countries of destination—exploit and abuse many of the migrants who enter without documents. In addition to all the risks that their male compatriots shoulder, female migrants face threats to their bodily integrity because of the ever present, added risk of sexual abuse by the smugglers, male migrants, and even police and immigration officials. Others find themselves either outrightly forced into prostitution or horribly abused and degraded as sex workers, or both.

Even if they are victimized, however, these undocumented migrants continue to be classified as criminals because of their immigration status and attendant offenses they may have committed.

Female Migrants and Sexual Abuse

Historically most migrants were men who were later joined by their spouses, but increasingly women migrate on their own rather than in response to familial or spousal migration. Many view emigration as the sole avenue to find any or more lucrative employment or a more attractive marriage partner. Often it is the economic and familial structure in their home countries that prompts women to leave to provide a better life for themselves and their families. High female unemployment, a negative economic outlook, and the economic and social oppression of women cause many of them to depart their home countries in search of a better future.

While some of these women succeed in finding lucrative and fulfilling employment or an attractive marriage partner abroad, many are less lucky. Most of them end up crossing international borders either without documentation or with fraudulent papers. For an appropriate fee, traffickers facilitate both the illegal border crossing and the provision of fraudulent entry documents. However, since women are generally less able than men to procure the amount of money demanded by the smugglers, they are frequently forced to tie their destiny to the smugglers in a form of debt bondage that requires them to work for the smuggling organization until they have paid off their debt. The labor demanded may take the form of sweatshop employment or of forced sex work.

Although there is no generally recognized legal definition of *forced prostitution,* for the purpose of this chapter it will refer to women or girls who are compelled to engage in sexual acts with strangers in exchange for commodities with the compulsion emanating from either physical violence and abuse, threats to their lives or bodily integrity or those of their families, emotional and physical coercion based on their indebtedness to the smugglers and procurers, and/or their presence in a foreign country without legal status and any support network. This definition ties forced prostitution to trafficking into a geographical area, including a foreign country, in which the women have no connections, do not speak the language, have no legal status, or are not permitted to work.

Like the number of undocumented migrants as a whole, the number of women forced into prostitution is undetermined and possibly indeterminate. Not only is it difficult to classify women as being "forced" or "voluntarily" working in prostitution, but, as prostitution is largely concealed, it is also difficult to obtain any reliable data on the practice.[12]

Despite the recent discovery of trafficking groups that forced young Mexican, Thai, and Korean women into prostitution, not much attention has been paid to forced prostitution in the United States. Israel, on the other hand, appears to deny the existence of forced prostitution even though a number of Russian women have charged that they were forced into prostitution upon arrival in Israel. In Germany the forced prostitution of women from central and Eastern Europe and the former Soviet republics has triggered almost hysterical commentary, especially since trafficking has been tied to the Russian Mafia.

Many media reports focus on the very small number of women who were forcibly abducted from their home country, transported to Western Europe, and there forced into prostitution. Although these cases do occur, they constitute the least likely scenario of sexual slavery (Schroeder, 1995: 236–37). Nevertheless, they are frequently used as paradigmatic cases of forced prostitution because these women represent the innocent, the "true" victim, a victim who did not choose to migrate illegally, let alone prostitute herself. While technically these women were illegally in the country in which they were abused, neither the police nor the public view them as illegal migrants but rather—and correctly so—as the victims of kidnappers. The stories that surround this group of women are reminiscent of the newspaper accounts published at the turn of the century in the United States about the abduction of innocent women—either recent immigrants or women from small towns and rural areas—who were taken to American cities for prostitution (James, 1977b: 11). At that time it was assumed that both groups of women would want to be repatriated—to their city or country of origin.

The more likely scenario of how migrant women are forced into prostitution involves those women who want to migrate to an economically more prosperous country and leave their home country voluntarily. However, these women do not form a cohesive group. Some of them will neither know nor suspect that they will be forced into prostitution. Often traffickers promise them legal immigration status and legitimate employment as domestic workers or in the service industry; sometimes they promise marriage. Some women may suspect or assume that the traffickers expect them to engage in prostitution to pay off their debt; others may have planned to migrate to work as prostitutes. While some women may have already worked as prostitutes in their home countries, others may envision that they could engage in that activity long enough to pay off the smugglers. Whatever their situation, none of these women agreed to the inhumane, forced, and oppressive circumstances in which they would find themselves once abroad. Nevertheless, legally all of them are undocumented migrants who entered or stayed in a country without legal permission. And, "in most countries . . . state policy on trafficking in women derives from policy on aliens" (Rayanakorn, 1995: 15).

The women may be tried for immigration violations and ultimately be deported to their countries of origin, often at their own expense. Traffickers, pimps, and brothel owners use the legal situation to their advantage. To immobilize their victims psychologically and prevent their escape, frequently they threaten the women with deportation. Since deportation implies risks to the women's families because of the still existing smuggling debt, public humiliation, and ostracization owing to disclosure of the woman's activity, and possibly further victimization, this threat is highly effective.

Even though policymakers and legislators know of the legal vulnerability of trafficking victims, almost no country has made serious attempts to change its immigration laws to protect women in forced prostitution. Their reluctance to act may be due to three reasons. First, they fear that granting any special benefit to forced prostitutes may either increase the number of women who seek to be categorized as such or may allow smuggling networks to exploit such a legal change to their advantage. While both effects may seem unlikely, the despair of some migrants may know no boundaries, and the ingenuity of the traffickers knows none either.

Second, in their struggle against illegal migration, most Western countries seem to be more concerned about closing potential loopholes and stopping illegal migrants than disturbed by the victimization and sacrifices their policies cause.[13] Therefore, any exception to the anti-immigration policy may be viewed as weakness or as an invitation to further undocumented migration.

Third, because of the legal construction of prostitutes, trafficking victims, even though forced into prostitution, may not be sympathetic enough as victims to bring about legal change. Ultimately, the law would have to protect persons who fall into two groups that are not generally held in high regard—undocumented migrants and prostitutes. Therefore, the women's dual status as (illegal) migrants and prostitutes may exacerbate the lack of interest in their fate.

The Legal Construction of "Prostitutes"

Gender stereotypes have long supported the existence of (female) prostitution. Since men's need for sex is deemed biologically based and therefore uncontrollable, many men around the world have been socialized to expect sexual access to women (James, 1977a: 39).[14]

Prostitution has been characterized as "the oldest profession," but in Western countries it has been tied to immorality, and especially the immorality of women. Courts in the United States have characterized prostitutes as "fallen women," whereas they have described their customers as respectable members of the community (Haft, 1977: 24). The early research on prostitution focused exclusively on the women involved in the exchange and attempted to discover their motivations. In addition, studies of forced prostitution in Western countries so far have provided little to no insight into the customers of women who are forced into prostitution. However, the customers could be potentially important in alerting authorities to the existence of forced prostitution (Altink, 1995: 51–52).

Legally prostitution is being approached in one of three ways: legalization, decriminalization, or criminalization.[15] In the United States prostitution and attendant activities, such as solicitation, are outlawed in all states, with the exception of Nevada. Not surprisingly, such a prohibitionist legal regime is reflected in the immigration laws, which allow for the exclusion of suspected prostitutes at the border and the deportation of noncitizens for engaging in prostitution.

The official criminalization of prostitution does not necessarily reflect on whom the burden of enforcement proceedings will fall. While prostitutes, their customers, and their procurers are subject to criminal penalties, recently localized drives against (male) customers notwithstanding, enforcement efforts have traditionally focused on the (female) prostitutes. The women, particularly those working on the streets, are easily identified, powerless, and therefore most likely to become police targets (James and Withers, 1977: xiv). Frequently, women will be charged with prostitution offenses even if it is suspected that they were forced into prostitution (Rosenberg, 1998).

In other countries, such as Germany, prostitution is governmentally regulated, even though procuring and pimping are criminalized. Decriminalization allows the police to stay in close contact with registered prostitutes and use them as informal informants. Even in countries that regulate prostitution, in general only citizens or long-time permanent residents are permitted to work as prostitutes.[16] Moral opprobrium continues to attach to the work of prostitutes, who are considered a "necessary evil." The moral requirements for migrants tend to be higher than those for the "native" women, a small group of whom are permitted to "service" men. Any female migrant who is perceived as intending to engage in prostitution will be excluded at the border; those convicted of a prostitution-related offense will be removed.

The Netherlands has recently taken an additional step and fully legalized prostitution. Prostitution is considered a form of work (Sterk-Elifson and Campbell, 1993: 196; Gillan, 1999).[17] The Dutch government views the right to self-determination as so broad that it permits every individual to choose freely how to use her body, even if she decides to prostitute herself. With this legal change, the government also hopes to combat forced prostitution more effectively. However, it is unlikely that the Dutch government will provide work visas to non-EU citizens who would like to work as prostitutes in the Netherlands.

Because of the Dutch legalization policy, since 1994, European Union documents explicitly distinguish between *prostitution* and *forced prostitution*. The latter term refers to the situation of women who are compelled to prostitute themselves either because of physical violence or duress, or who were lured into prostitution through misrepresentations. Generally, these women are non-EU nationals who hail from the former USSR, Eastern Europe, and Asia.

The distinction between *voluntary* and *forced* prostitution has angered women's organizations that argue for the abolition of all prostitution because its practice denigrates and humiliates all women. On the international scene the most vocal and best known of these organizations is the Coalition against Trafficking in Women (CATW), spearheaded by Kathleen Barry. Together with the International Abolitionist Federation and a few other groups, the CATW charges that the distinction between forced and voluntary prostitution fails to recognize that all prostitution is forced in some way (Edwards, 1997: 72–74; Murray, 1998: 52–53). It also claims that the increasing legitimation of prostitution in Europe in the 1980s was responsible for the rise in trafficking (Raymond and CATW, 1995).

The debate surrounding the treatment of prostitution has caused rifts between antitrafficking organizations and between feminists in the north and the south (Seabrook, 1996: 144). Despite what appeared to be successes of the CATW's position in the 1980s, the distinction between forced and voluntary prostitution remains dominant because it falls within the liberal legal tradition that has traditionally distinguished between actions that are forced because of social circumstances, on the one hand, and duress, on the other. While it is not the function of this chapter to map a position on the question whether all prostitution is forced, the existing legal framework and the prevailing public attitude toward prostitution will color a country's legal and political approach to forced prostitution. As much as the advocates in the struggle against forced prostitution have attempted to leave the question of prostitution generally unresolved, this avoidance strategy has caused conceptual confusion and prevented the development of a consistent antitrafficking program (Reanda, 1991: 226).

Independent of the legal framework, women who work as prostitutes are identified with their work: they *are* prostitutes, a fact that remains unchanged even after they leave prostitution. When women are forced into prostitution through the threats, coercion, or abuse of others, they can also expect to be defined by their past (or present) status. Not surprisingly, enforcement of antitrafficking laws is often absent or low because of the attitude of law enforcement and the judiciary with respect to sex workers (Skrobanek, Boonpakdee, and Jantateero, 1997: 97–98; Heine-Wiedenmann, 1992: 123–27). When the laws are enforced, their impact often falls on the women rather than the traffickers, replicating enforcement patterns against prostitution generally.

The Impact of Legal Constructions: "Solutions" That Are None

Since the turn of the century, the international community has labeled the trafficking of women and forced prostitution as abuses of the most grievous type (Demleitner, 1994: 167–79). Means to combat these practices encompassed punitive measures—severe penalties for procurers and pimps—and prevention, rescue, and rehabilitation of the victims of the white slave traffic (Berkovitch, 1999: 41).

Today trafficking and forced prostitution are labeled human rights violations. They are outlawed explicitly in a number of international treaties and conventions (Demleitner, 1994: 172–78), including the Convention on the Elimination of All Forms of Discrimination against Women (Toepfer and Wells, 1994).[18] Signatory states obligate themselves to take all measures to combat trafficking and the exploitation of prostitution. This includes devising effective penalties for traffickers and procurers, rehabilitating and training former prostitutes, but also attacking what are perceived as the root causes of prostitution, including "underdevelopment, poverty, drug abuse, illiteracy, and lack of training, education and employment opportunities" (U.N. Centre for Human Rights, 1994: 13–14). Over time different emphases have been set in the international arena in combating trafficking (Reanda, 1991: 211, 219), and with them have changed the strategies, the commitment of resources, and the view of the participants (Fitzpatrick, 1994: 537).

Startling, however, is the apparent overall lack of political will in the receiving and sending countries to protect the victimized women. Although international cooperation with respect to most criminal activity is still sorely inadequate, the women's status as undocumented migrants and as prostitutes may exacerbate the lack of interest and collaboration in the detection of networks that traffic women and force them to prostitute themselves. The depiction of the women forced into prostitution and their ambiguous legal position as offenders and victims have made it difficult for countries to develop a coherent policy of enforcement against the traffickers and of protection and support for the women. Tied inexorably to trafficking, forced prostitution has become primarily an immigration problem. Governments seem to assume that to deter undocumented migration, no migrant, however abused, should be able to benefit from her illegal entry or stay but rather must be deported. This holds particularly true for migrants who appear of dubious morality. The ambivalence displayed toward the victimized women often makes it difficult, if not impossible, to convict the traffickers and procurers.

One of the crucial problems in the enforcement of antitrafficking laws

is the lack of a coherent definition for *forced* prostitution. This definitional problem is partly due to the ambivalence about prostitution in
many societies and even the feminist community (Murray, 1998: 52–53).
While advocates of the position that only forced prostitution, defined as
prostitution under conditions of physical and emotional abuse, is a human rights violation shape the current antitrafficking agenda, countries
have found it difficult to define *force* in domestic antitrafficking legislation comprehensively and accurately.[19] It is striking, however, that although frequently traffickers and brothel owners could be indicted for a
whole host of criminal activities, including debt bondage, kidnapping, or
extortion, such prosecutions appear rare (Wijers and Lap-Chew, 1997:
152).

Many of the potential receiving countries have worked on preventing
the arrival of trafficked women in their territory. These proposals are designed to shelter the women from exploitation and abuse, but they also
serve to dissuade women from migrating.[20] Most of these preventive measures center around publicity campaigns warning the women of the dangers of sexual and other abuse should they cross the border (Pickup, 1998:
48).

More distressingly, although often hailed as a panacea, these campaigns are problematic (Wijers and Lap-Chew, 1997: 169). They are designed to create a fear of leaving one's country and help immobilize
women in their current position. They also create a dutylike obligation on
women to abstain from certain behavior that is characterized as high-
risk.[21] Ironically, some of the educational materials used have had an effect contrary to that envisioned as they portray the possibility of riches to
be found in prostitution in the West. Additionally, women from Eastern
European countries tend to be little concerned about the morality of being engaged in illegal activities because of their experiences under Communism, when everyone seemed to do something illegal (Altink, 1995:
159–60).

Some of the legal changes the potential host countries have made have
proven counterproductive, especially since "often, 'trafficking' is used by
states to initiate and justify restrictive policies" (Doezema, 1998: 45).
Canada, for example, grants visas to dancers and models, which tends to
mean strippers who are at high risk of being forced into prostitution (Godfrey, 1998b). Since antitrafficking and feminist groups have strongly crit-

icized these visa categories, to prevent exploitation, Canada has begun to require that women coming as exotic dancers be professional strippers (Godfrey, 1998a) and has dramatically limited the number of women admitted into the country under this visa category (Heinzl, 1999). However, in response, trafficking organizations have apparently encouraged women to enter Canada claiming refugee status and then forced them to work as strippers and prostitutes (Godfrey, 1999). Therefore, de jure or de facto bans on immigration that appear attractive for protective purposes may lead to increased rather than decreased exploitation.[22] It may be more effective to schedule follow-up visits for those visa recipients who are likely to be victimized.[23] However, when Belgium required a number of protective measures for women who entered under "artist" visas, the issuance of such visas in Belgium stopped. This measure probably caused traffickers to bring women into Belgium illegally or obtain "artist" visas for other countries that did not have such a protective framework (IOM, 1995: 20).

Protective measures are problematic not only because of the reaction of traffickers but also because of the measures' paternalistic nature, which causes women to be further disadvantaged. For example, abolishing the visa categories for dancers would further limit women's opportunities for legal migration and drive yet more of them into the arms of traffickers. In addition, it reinforces already existing value judgments about the work women do as strippers and models. Finally, governments may feel that entry restrictions absolve them of responsibility for persons trafficked into their states (Caldwell, Galster, and Steinzor, 1997).

Another example is visa requirements for citizens of countries from which women seem disproportionately involved in forced prostitution. For example, Germany introduced a visa requirement for citizens of the Philippines and Thailand, as entrants from those countries were disproportionately women (Lipka, 1989: 132–33). The result of such requirements is not the end of forced prostitution. Traffickers will either bring women into the country illegally or with fraudulent documents, or shift to trafficking women from countries without a visa requirement. Both occurred in Germany. The former dramatically increased the cost for Filipinas and Thai women, which increased their debt and dependence on the traffickers. At the same time, the number of women from central and Eastern Europe who are forced into prostitution in Germany has risen dramatically (Streiber, 1998: 5). Another consequence of such a governmental response is the stigmatization of all women hailing from certain countries as potential prostitutes or undocumented migrants ("Russian Envoy," 1999; Braun, 1989: 294).[24] Therefore, any measures further hindering women's entry must be carefully weighed against their disadvantages, as they pertain to potential migrants and women as a whole.

Practically, situations of forced prostitution are difficult to uncover. Forced prostitution generally comes to the attention of either immigration officials or those investigating sexual offenses. Sometimes, trafficking networks are discovered through proactive policing in the form of undercover work. However, police often find trafficking groups difficult to infiltrate because they are run either by extended families or by ethnically homogeneous gangs. Occasionally one or more of the trafficked women are able to flee the subhuman conditions under which they are forced to labor. Such escapes are less likely to occur or to be successful if the women are psychologically coerced and under the impression that their abusers will retaliate against them or their families. The women will also not attempt to flee if threatened with deportation or if they are afraid of the police, often because of experiences with corrupt and abusive police in their home countries. Alternatively, in countries in which prostitution is regulated or legalized, registered prostitutes may tip off the police, often because they resent competition. Such tips are less likely if the trafficked women's "customers" are drawn exclusively from a group of men that does not patronize registered prostitutes.[25] Finally, customers may inform the police once the prostitutes confide in them.

Discovery guarantees the women no protection. As in rape cases, the burden of proof for women forced to work as prostitutes seems often reversed. Unless they can demonstrate their lack of consent to prostitute themselves, law enforcement officials appear to assume that they worked as prostitutes in their home countries or knew what was expected of them in the receiving country. The only woman who will be able to escape moral doubt is the one who was snatched off the streets by criminals, drugged, taken across an international border, raped, and then chained to a bed or at least severely beaten to engage in sex for money, paid to her captors.

Often the media focus on the fate of teen girls, frequently emphasizing their virginity, who were kidnapped and sold into prostitution (Murray,

1998: 55; Doezema, 1998: 43). Alternatively, they report on conditions amounting to torture and possibly culminating in the death of one of the women.[26] Presumably such stark portrayals of abuse will allay any doubt as to the forced nature of the women's involvement in prostitution. They could never have chosen such abuse.

This picture of captive and underaged migrants not only dominates media reports but is also prevalent in depictions of forced prostitution by human rights organizations. This focus resembles the emphasis of the turn-of-the-century crusaders who fought the white slave traffic. They created the image of "helpless innocent young women being 'ruined,' transported, and sold by traffickers to brothels in other countries" (Berkovitch, 1999: 38). This depiction created national and international backing for the anti–white slave trafficking movement and galvanized women and men alike (ibid.).[27] The goal of such portrayals is to engender public sympathy for the victims and remove any potential stigma from the victimized women. The result of such a strategy, however, may be less benign. Once it becomes obvious that only a small number of women have been victimized in such egregious manner (Campani, 1998: 256), interest in and sympathy for all other women forced to work as prostitutes might evaporate, leaving them with less protection. Another problematic aspect of this discourse is the depiction of women as powerless, helpless, and pure.[28] The legal process may tend to declare any woman not fitting this childlike image—and most victims of unscrupulous traffickers will not conform to this model—as unworthy of support and protection.[29]

Much more common than the tortured and abducted victim is the woman willing to be smuggled across an international border, either knowing or suspecting that her stay and employment may be illegal but not expecting to work as a prostitute. Most of the women trafficked and forced into prostitution have shown courage and initiative in attempting to change their situation through migration (Wijers, 1998: 70). Many are assertive, well-educated, independent, self-possessed, and strong women. When forced into prostitution, many of the women suffer some physical abuse, but more prevalent is serious emotional coercion based on their illegal status and debt to the traffickers. This situation creates a dilemma for law enforcement because the women intentionally broke the laws of their country.[30] Once classified as "illegal" migrants rather than as victims, the women will be deported and possibly even penalized. The prosecution of the traffickers will most likely depend on the amount of harm the woman has suffered, especially in terms of physical abuse.

Another group of women found in forced prostitution consists of those who were either willing to engage in prostitution abroad or at least knew that this was likely. The authorities of the receiving countries view this subset of women not only as "illegal" migrants but also as of dubious morality and therefore undesirable. Even though a number of countries, including Germany, have passed legislation that treats all women forced into prostitution alike independent of whether they had worked as prostitutes in their home countries, in reality police, prosecutors, and courts continue to discriminate against these women throughout the criminal justice process. Moreover, for women who plan on continuing to work as prostitutes after having been liberated from a forced situation, "compassion turns into indifference or outright hostility" (Wijers, 1998: 77).

Often the last group of women dictates the approach law enforcement officials take to all migrant women who are sexually abused and forced into prostitution abroad. Akin to the attitude frequently displayed toward (date) rape victims, police and prosecution often doubt that the women were forced into prostitution. Rather, they view the migrants as complicit in the trafficking and prostitution, especially when the women do not show any signs of physical abuse. As is the case with other sex offenses, often the victim is blamed because she "should" have known what was going to happen or because she "should" have acted differently. This attitude fails to appreciate that these women reacted to the economic and social situation in their home countries in the only way possible.

Even though the women's fate may evoke empathy, especially if the abuse they endured was severe, their primary portrayal as illegal immigrants and "loose" women rather than victims of violent crime supports demands for their removal (Wijers, 1998: 72). Therefore, the legal "solution" currently offered to these trafficked women is deportation to their home countries. Some of the women choose deportation so that the traffickers do not assume that they cooperated with law enforcement officials. Others want to return home as quickly as possible and not relive the abuse they endured. However, even women who do not want to return to their home countries because they fear for their lives are being deported.

In some cases women willing to testify against the ringleaders of the trafficking and forced prostitution ring were deported prior to trial. Some of these prosecutions were dismissed because the main witnesses could not be re-called to testify in court.[31] While ostensibly the lack of cooperation between law enforcement and immigration authorities causes such prosecutorial failure, the inability to convict the traffickers might be indicative of the primary construction of forced prostitutes as illegal migrants and the hierarchy of goals in Western countries. The removal of undocumented migrants is of primary importance, independent of their situation. The receiving country is not seen as sharing any blame in their victimization, even though it was unable to prevent their victimization in its territory.

Deportation implies not only return to the conditions the women attempted to leave in the first place but often also intimidation and threats by the smuggling operation either because the women owe the traffickers money for the failed trip or because they testified or are perceived to have provided information against the procurers. Upon their return home, many of the women can also be expected to be shunned by their families and friends for being deported or, if their prior experience becomes known, being prostitutes.

To prevent the women from continuing to work as prostitutes in their home countries and presumably from attempting to return to the country to which they had wanted to migrate, some Western European countries have now begun to offer "rehabilitation" programs to victimized women, ranging from vocational training to psychological counseling. The choice of the term *rehabilitation* is telling.[32] How many *victims* generally need to be rehabilitated?

Legal and logistical hurdles to the successful prosecution of traffickers may be overcome more successfully if the will existed to protect the victims. However, the current legal treatment of migrant women who are forced to prostitute themselves serves to stigmatize them as double outcasts. Largely the legal and social construction of the female victims drives the lax enforcement of existing laws against forced prostitution. In many respects the way in which trafficked women are being treated is comparable to the treatment of victims of gang-related attacks in the United States. Police and courts tend to view them either as having contributed to the crime or as criminals when they belong to another gang (U.S. Department of Justice, 1996: 14–15).

Forced prostitution is caused in part by current migration laws, reinforced by gender inequalities, and supported by the precarious legal position of the victims. Because of the current restrictive immigration climate and the continued oppression of women around the globe, we can expect to witness the growth of trafficking networks and an increase in the exploitative situations in which migrants, and especially women, find themselves. Therefore, it is crucial to reevaluate the portrayal of the victims and to grant them more effective protection.

Recommendations

Respect and Protection

Currently, discussions about female migration and prostitution are often grounded in unsupported and even dubious claims. Fragmented and anecdotal stories drive the discourse. Quantitative empirical analysis and data are missing (Streiber, 1998: 22). The absence of hard data can be ascribed to the secretiveness of the activity, the lack of reporting by the victims of forced prostitution, and the still low priority trafficking seems to have for many law enforcement agencies, despite statements to the contrary (IOM, 1995: 7). Divergent claims with respect to the magnitude of trafficking and forced prostitution may also be due to the differing definitions of the phenomenon.

Resolution of numerical claims may help chart a more effective course in the protection of victims. Should the number of women forced into prostitution be smaller than expected, the receiving countries may be more willing to grant them protection within their territory. Should the number be larger than projected, the focus is likely to shift further to preventive strategies and repatriation. Whatever the ultimate goals, the debates surrounding victim protection must be grounded in better empirical knowledge about the scope of the problem.

Anthropological and sociological studies exist that document dramatic differences between trafficked women, but often a "one size fits all" model drives prescriptions to assist the victims. However, "even today the practice of prostitution pertains more specifically to certain groups of immigrant women and certain countries" (Campani, 1998: 231). Is this a function of divergent social settings in the sending countries, their economic development, or rather different male-female relationships? How may women differ overall by nationality in terms of the pressure exerted upon them to work as prostitutes?[33] What conditions await the women in their home countries upon repatriation? Answers to these questions must be ascertained to allow for precisely targeted legal solutions.

Some policy and legal responses should, however, apply to all women forced to work in prostitution. First, the women should not be incarcerated based on their violation of criminal laws or their status as undocumented migrants (Heine-Wiedenmann and Ackermann, 1992: 340). Both situations, however, occur frequently and indicate the preeminence of concerns about illegal migration over compassion. Second, victims of forced prostitution should not be subject to penal sanctions or be deported.[34] To prevent deportations, closer cooperation is required between immigration services on the one hand and the police and prosecutors who develop the case against the traffickers on the other.

The prevention of negative consequences, however, is insufficient. The victimized women should also be granted protection and assistance, and that not only in exchange for their assistance in law enforcement efforts against their abusers.[35] To create effectively targeted programs and help empower the women forced into prostitution, such support programs should be developed in conjunction with trafficking victims rather than designed solely by government officials and feminist organizations (Skrobanek, Boonpakdee, and Jantateero, 1997: 18). Currently, two bills are pending in the United States Congress that would allow specifically for the temporary (and permanent) protection of victims of human trafficking.[36] Ultimately, we must empower these women by presenting them with realistic options for their future, including permission to stay and repatriation, which they may choose depending on their personal goals and situation. Should humanitarian and gender-based considerations not suffice in structuring a comprehensive strategic package, practical law enforcement reasons also counsel to pursue such a path. Otherwise the state will not act much differently than the traffickers and "us[e] women as witnesses for combatting organized crime in [its] interest . . . without allowing them the corresponding protection" (Wijers, 1998: 77).

The Netherlands and Belgium were the first countries to grant trafficked women who would testify against their abusers a temporary right to stay while the case went to trial. Although the two countries have been praised for their progressive program, this presents a very limited approach (Rayanakorn, 1995: 21–22) in which the state uses the victims for its own purposes. The United States also has a visa category that allows trafficking victims to stay while assisting in the investigation and prosecution of the traffickers.[37]

The moral and legal ambiguities created by the women's status as former prostitutes, albeit forced, and as illegal migrants often make the women reluctant to cooperate in criminal proceedings against their abusers, even though they would like to see them punished. If they do not participate in the prosecution out of fear for their lives and those of family members or because they were treated as accomplices rather than victims, chances are that the accused will go free.

Police and prosecutors mistrust the women's testimony. If the women succeed in convincing law enforcement authorities of their credibility, defense attorneys will attack their testimony as untrustworthy because of their prior work as prostitutes. To escape criminal actions against themselves, the women must often enter into "deals" with the prosecution that the traffickers' lawyers may use in court to allege bias.

Most distressingly, the host countries generally do not grant the women long-term financial and physical protection. Therefore, the women should be provided with the legal tools to demand compensation from the traffickers. The United States allows for civil causes of actions against violent offenders whose actions were motivated by gender. Therefore, trafficking victims and women forced into prostitution may be able to recover compensatory and punitive damages from their victimizers.[38] Other countries provide similar opportunities for compensation.

Some women may require permanent protection from their victimizers, but others will only need to be sheltered prior to and during the trial. Temporary isolation from the prostitution milieu will prevent the victimizers from influencing the women's testimony (Reinhardt, n.d.: 6). As temporary relocation is more cost-effective and decreases the administrative burden on law enforcement, it should be made available whenever necessary. In the United States similar programs have been put in place to protect the victims and witnesses in gang prosecutions (U.S. Department of Justice, 1996).

Women whose lives would be threatened even after the trial should be able to benefit from permanent witness protection programs. Most of the European countries at this point do not have a witness protection program comparable to the U.S. federal witness protection program,[39] but they have developed relocation programs that entail the changing of the identity of witnesses. In light of their high cost and logistical burden, permanent witness protection efforts can be expected only infrequently (Reinhardt, n.d.: 6). So far, trafficking victims have often been unlikely to benefit from full-fledged protection programs because their knowledge of the trafficking and procuring operation, while helpful, will generally not justify the expense of their protection. However, there is limited judicial precedent in the United States for forcing the offenders who necessitated the relocation to pay for the witness protection program.[40] To increase protection and distribute the cost of witness protection, a regional rather than national approach might be desirable in certain parts of the world.[41]

Those women assisting the prosecution whose lives would be endangered by the traffickers in their home country must be provided with long-term guarantees of security. However, most schemes currently under consideration or in place are administratively burdensome, dependent on the goodwill of prosecutors, and do not guarantee permanent residence. The United States holds out the promise of permanent legal residence as a reward for witnesses assisting their new home country in its crime-fighting function.[42] The European Parliament has called for the grant of permanent residency status to victims of trafficking (Chuang, 1998: 102). Short-term visa status often proves of little avail to the women. Many prefer to be deported so as to avoid giving the traffickers the impression that they assisted law enforcement agencies (IOM and International Centre for Migration Policy Development, 1999: 77).

The Netherlands permits the grant of permanent residency to trafficking victims on humanitarian grounds. Despite its legal availability, this benefit is rarely granted (IOM, 1995: 25). An alternative approach may be to encourage trafficking victims to petition for asylum based on their fear of persecution upon their return home. Their persecution would be based on membership in the group of former forced prostitutes. If their home government is unable to protect them from potential violent attacks by the traffickers, the women should be granted asylum. Moreover, women who would be ostracized and socially stigmatized because of their previous status should also be able to benefit from such a regime. While the potential for abusing such benefits exists, it is unlikely, in part because of the biases of police and prosecutors, in part because the requirements for such status remain high (Altink, 1995: 47).

Mere protection of the women's physical lives is insufficient. The victims of forced prostitution should be provided with "support services," not "rehabilitative" measures.[43] The Netherlands provides a partial model for this approach. Among the support services offered there is counseling, akin to the type generally provided for victims of sexual violence. Whether skills training is appropriate and advisable should depend on the individual victim and her plans for the future.[44] Should she contemplate returning to her home country, potential skills training should primarily include the victim's interests and abilities but also take into account the economic situation in her home country. Such support measures can be funded in different ways, including out of restitution payments ordered against convicted traffickers or out of a general victims' fund.

Not all women will want to stay in the receiving states. Those who choose to return to their home country should be given free transportation (Murray, 1998: 64). Support programs should also be continued there. Counseling and shelters may be of particular importance (Pickup, 1998: 48). For any of these measures, it is important that the trafficked woman be allowed to make an informed decision whether to participate. The focus on the victim's needs and desires will lead to her empowerment and explicitly recognizes her as an independent individual rather than stigmatizing her as a victim for whom others will make decisions (agisra, 1990: 11).

Although the protection of individual victims is important, more comprehensive approaches are necessary to control trafficking and provide its victims with realistic survival chances.

Creating Opportunities

In the concern about individual trafficking victims, Western countries should remember that their victimization does not occur in a social and political vacuum. Rather, national and global structures of power and privilege cause and aggravate this type of abuse. Among those structures are not only gender-based domination in the sending and receiving states but also economic power relationships between north and south and between East and West. Therefore, the concern about human trafficking and forced prostitution may be largely symptomatic of global and domestic economic disparity and gender inequality.[45] Frequently, Western economic policies, in the guise of free trade and market liberalism, have exacerbated poverty and unemployment in the developing world (Seabrook, 1996: 134). Even developmental aid has contributed to a further deterioration in the position of women (Braun, 1989: 296). A growing consumer culture, combined with traditional assumptions about gender relationships, has led to the breakup of families, which in turn appears to fuel much of the trafficking (Campani, 1998: 259n. 15). As governments in the developing world have grown dependent on the remittances of migrants, they have done little to protect intending migrants from abuse. Therefore, the international economic framework, also in light of gender considerations,[46] must be reconsidered to prevent women and men from being forced to migrate to better their lives. While some of the underlying problems have been recognized and acknowledged and international organizations have suggested remedies, in Western countries these considerations seem to have taken a backseat compared with the emphases on criminalization and prosecution of traffickers and the repatriation of their victims.

As long as a global imbalance exists between wealthy and poor states and the media glamorize life in highly industrialized countries, legal and undocumented migration will continue. However, in recent years wealthy nations have increasingly closed their borders to migrants even though their governments' economic policies have frequently fostered migration pressures (Martin, 1999: 834). Because of the global distribution of power and education, women who have traditionally received fewer market skills have been disproportionately deprived of the legal opportunity to move. However, the developed world also appears to demand an increasing number of low-paid workers in the domestic sector and in the services industry, including sex work. Traditionally, these positions have been available to women (Chant, 1992: 198). In light of their limited options and the demand for their services in Western countries, women may act rationally in crossing international borders with the help of traffickers, even though they realize that they may have to or could be coerced to work in prostitution, at least for a limited period of time. Therefore, long-term strategies that attack these types of inequalities must be actively pursued rather than paid mere lip service.

Forced prostitution could not exist without customers. We must learn more about the clients of trafficked women who work in prostitution. While much of the discussion seems to be on targeting them to decrease the demand for prostitution—an approach grounded in abolitionist ideals—practically it might be more useful to co-opt potential customers so that they will report potential trafficking situations to law enforcement authorities. Therefore, the criminalization of clients would prove counterproductive if the goal is to protect trafficked women.

The current portrayal of victims, however, may prevent us from acknowledging a disconcerting truth. Although applied to the English debate about prostitution and white slavery in the last century, the critique of the portrayal of victims as sexually innocent and passive who were violated by evil individuals may hold equally true today. "Had they allowed themselves to see that many young girls engaged in prostitution not as passive, sexually innocent victims but because their choices were so limited, the reformers would have been forced to recognize that the causes of juvenile prostitution were to be found in an exploitative economic structure" (Gorham, 1978: 355). In the long run only a fundamental change in global economic inequities and an opening of Western countries to migration will undermine the power of traffickers and prevent the victimization of women.

Conclusion

The construction of women forced into prostitution as illegal migrants and as immoral has informed and prevented effective policy making and law enforcement against the traffickers. The portrayal of trafficking victims has also hampered the provision of legal protection and assistance to them. The receiving countries must break the negative imagery and tackle the stereotyped framework underlying their legal approaches to trafficking and forced prostitution. Should this not occur, it will become blatantly obvious that Western concerns about forced prostitution are instrumental, tied to illegal migration rather than the exploitation of human beings. Humanitarian considerations and the empowerment of women, however, should drive the prevention of trafficking and forced prostitution and the protection of its victims.

NOTES

A special note of gratitude extends to Rey Koslowski and David Kyle, the two editors of this volume, to Hans-Jörg Albrecht, Deborah Anker, Christopher

McCrudden, Michael D. Smith, and Michael Tonry. Sincere thanks go the *Polizeipräsident* for Middle Franconia, Dr. Max von der Grün, and his staff in the sex crimes unit. My lengthy discussions with them have shed light on forced prostitution, human trafficking, and the treatment of prostitution in Germany.

1. In recent years a few traffickers have been prosecuted in the United States, among them the members of a family who forced twenty Mexican women and underage girls to work as prostitutes in rural Florida (Wilson, 1998).

2. Examples are the creation of the Working Group on Trafficking in Women and Children within the U.S. Department of Justice in 1998 and the various European Union antitrafficking initiatives.

3. European Union action plans to combat trafficking have highlighted the connection between organized crime and human trafficking. Nevertheless, some commentators have argued that Western countries' perceptions of threats to their national security emanating from organized criminal groups in central Europe and the Newly Independent States (NIS) that focus on "drugs, illegal immigration, prostitution and forms of protection, car ringing" are exaggerated (Hebenton and Spencer, 1998: 30).

4. Whether this is a result of the increasing number of women trafficked into prostitution in Western Europe and the United States or because of latent racism in favor of white women is debatable.

5. This is not only true for the host countries but also for the sending states. In the Philippines the portrayal of "Filipina migrant entertainers [as] the Other[,] the prostitute[,] the willing victim . . . and the heroine" has driven policies regulating their condition (Tyner, 1996: 77).

6. The race and ethnicity of the women may also affect these constructs and engender yet more discrimination against them (Murray, 1998: 58–60). This holds particularly true for Asian women.

7. This chapter addresses the trafficking of *women* and does not deal with the issue of underaged *girls* who are forced into prostitution. International conventions and national laws treat children substantially differently than adults.

8. The suggestions of Russian politicians to export Russian women for sex work and to turn Russia into a sex tourist paradise, made possible by the "service" of Russian women, are only shocking because of their frankness. More traditional has been the practice of politicians in some Asian states to market their countries as tourist paradises, with the special attraction of prostitution (agisra, 1990: 15), and to use prostitution as a tool for economic development in this way.

9. The Human Rights Caucus has put together a fact sheet discussing succinctly the differences between trafficking and smuggling (Human Rights Caucus, n.d.).

10. Wijers and Lap-Chew describe various definitions of *trafficking* in national laws (1997: 149–51). The divergent legal definitions demonstrate the difficulty in assessing accurately the scope of trafficking and forced prostitution.

11. The proposed draft for a supplemental instrument to the as of yet uncompleted United Nations Convention against Transnational Organized Crime would exempt the persons trafficked from criminal liability and punishment "on account of such trafficking and transport" (U.N. General Assembly, 1999).

12. An example of the uncertain scope of forced prostitution is drawn from a newsmagazine article: "A conservative estimate by Jonas Widgren, of the International Centre for Migration Policy Development in Vienna, reckons that 400,000 people are smuggled into the European Union each year; others suggest that is simply the number of girls brought into the EU and forced into prostitution" ("A Single Market in Crime," 1999).

13. Another example of this phenomenon is the increasing number of deaths from heatstroke, hypothermia, and drowning along the U.S.-Mexican border.

14. Although male prostitutes have been the topic of media reports and movies, they constitute only a small percentage of all prostitutes, and even they tend to serve primarily men.

15. Frequently, other terms are used to describe the same tripartite division. Among them are *abolitionist, regulationist,* and *prohibitionist* (Reanda, 1991: 203). An overview of prostitution legislation in select countries is provided in *Prostitution: An International Handbook on Trends, Problems, and Policies* (Davis, 1993).

16. In the member states of the European Union (EU) that condone prostitution, at least unofficially citizens of other EU countries may also work as prostitutes.

17. Were prostitution universally classified as a form of legal employment, the International Labor Organization's (ILO) International Convention on the Protection of the Rights of All Migrant Workers and Members of Their Families would cover all prostitutes, whether working legally or without documentation. This convention, which includes a reporting requirement and an optional complaint mechanism, would provide women trafficked into prostitution with an international forum to publicize their exploitation and a legal basis for compensation claims. The ILO already considers child prostitution to fall under the forced labor conventions that cover children.

18. Even within the human rights framework, international and regional doc-

uments have set different priorities in their antitrafficking strategies, depending on whether they view forced prostitution primarily as discrimination, as a violation of the principles of equality, or as a deprivation of human dignity (Fitzpatrick, 1994: 556).

19. An example is the German antitrafficking provisions that have been frequently criticized by legal scholars because of their ambiguity and the difficulties in application that result (Kelker, 1993; Heine-Wiedenmann, 1992: 126–30).

20. In that respect these campaigns pursue the same purpose as the attempts at urging country girls to stay in their hometowns around the turn of the century when it was feared that they would be forced into prostitution in the cities (Connelly, 1980: 122).

21. In the domestic context, David Garland has classified such publicity campaigns as part of a responsibilization strategy designed to achieve private action to prevent the occurrence of crime (Garland, 1996: 452–53).

22. The U.S. Commission on Immigration Reform has proposed a ban on immigration to Saipan for "foreign contract workers engaged in exploitative occupations" (U.S. Commission on Immigration Reform, 1997: 21), which includes employment that may lead to sexual abuse.

23. This is not a novel idea. The League of Nations proposed in the 1920s that "governments should exercise supervision over the employment of girls in theaters and music halls, in order to secure that no attempt should be made to induce them to lead immoral lives" (Berkovitch, 1999: 78). However, my proposal is not motivated by a belief in the frailty of women but rather by an understanding of the greater likelihood of victimization of men and women who live in a country with whose language, customs, and legal framework they are unfamiliar.

24. A similar fate may befall men. When men from certain countries are disproportionately identified as traffickers, all men from these states are subject to stigmatization as criminals and traffickers ("Russian Envoy," 1999).

25. Not much information exists about the customers of women forced into prostitution, but there is some indication that in Germany young, male asylum applicants, who could not otherwise afford a prostitute, may frequent these women, especially when the traffickers bring them to the men's living quarters. In the United States migrant farmworkers were the primary customers of the Mexican women forced into prostitution in rural Florida.

26. Concerns about the trafficking victims do not motivate such reporting. Rather, the combination of sex, prostitution, and crime increases the audience (Dreixler, 1998: 203).

27. As Eileen Scully indicates in her work (this volume, Chapter 3), that description of white slaves at the turn of the century was incorrect.

28. The characterization of trafficked women as "products" akin to illegal narcotics or arms also fortifies the impression of women as goods rather than as free-willed human beings.

29. Women who do not fit the victim image become easily categorized as offenders (Henderson, 1998: 586).

30. If the migrant was forced to work in prostitution, a duress defense is available to charges of violating antiprostitution laws.

31. Currently, most countries expect the women who returned home, either voluntarily or involuntarily, to cover transportation costs to the trial subject to later reimbursement. This makes it virtually impossible even for willing witnesses to testify against their abusers.

32. In the late 1800s, the Progressive Party offered "'Christian rehabilitation'" to women who had fallen into "white slavery" (James, 1977b: 11).

33. Studies in Italy have shown that women's nationality is related to differences in age and levels of education. The latter affect the living and working conditions of the women (Campani, 1998: 249–50). A recent IOM study also found some illuminating differences between trafficked women by nationality. Distinctions that may allow for the creation of a targeted legal response pertained, for example, to the way in which the women were recruited and how they entered the country in which they were forced to work in prostitution (IOM, 1995: 14–18).

34. A group of human rights organizations has developed *Human Rights Standards for the Treatment of Trafficked Persons* (Human Rights Caucus, 1999). They include a list of strategies designed to protect trafficked persons, including a temporary stay of deportation and no criminal prosecution for activities connected to them having been trafficked.

35. International working groups in this area and the European Parliament (EP) have made similar recommendations (European Parliament, 1996).

36. The bills are S. 600 (106th Cong., 1st sess.), entitled "International Trafficking of Women and Children Victim Protection Act of 1999," introduced by Senator Paul Wellstone, and H.R. 3244 (106th Cong., 1st sess.), entitled "Trafficking Victims Protection Act of 1999," introduced by Representative Christopher Smith.

37. The recently introduced "International Trafficking of Women and Children Victim Protection Act of 1999," S. 600, proposes to grant every trafficking victim a stay of up to three months in the United States unless the individual has an asy-

lum petition pending or is involved in civil or criminal litigation, in which cases he or she would be permitted to stay until the proceedings are completed. The bill would also require that trafficking victims not be incarcerated and that they be granted any protection needed.

38. 42 U.S.C. § 13981 (1999). The women forced to prostitute themselves in southern Florida won restitution orders against the members of the family who trafficked them (Smith, 1999).

39. 18 U.S.C. § 3521 (1999). The program has not been designed to protect "innocent" witnesses but rather those who can provide inside information on criminal organizations.

Italy and Sweden have protection programs similar to but less comprehensive than the U.S. program. Germany also makes the protection of endangered witnesses possible through changing their identity but does not provide an explicit legal basis for such a procedure (Soiné and Soukup, 1994).

40. In *United States v. Malpeso,* 126 F.3d 92 (2nd Cir. 1997), the appellate court affirmed a district court's decision ordering the defendant to pay restitution to the FBI for relocating the victim and his family. Similar arguments have also been made in Germany (Reinhardt, n.d.: 7).

41. Cooperation of this type might be especially likely within the European Union, which has already approved plans to protect witnesses in the fight against organized crime. The government of Trinidad and Tobago has suggested a regional plan for the Caribbean (Zagaris, 1996).

42. The antitrafficking bills pending in the U.S. Congress also promise permanent residency.

43. This language is taken from recommendation No. 19 issued by the Committee on the Elimination of Discrimination against Women, which suggests that states provide support services to victims of violence (U N. Centre for Human Rights, 1994: 31).

44. Trafficking victims from Eastern Europe and the former Soviet Union are generally more highly educated than women from Southeast Asia (Shelley, 1999: 1). Therefore, their education and support needs will be different from those of women who did not complete secondary schooling.

45. A similar concern had been voiced during the white slave era (Daly, 1988: 173).

46. In many countries, the unemployment rate for women is a multiple of that for men (IOM and International Centre for Migration Policy Development, 1999: 68).

REFERENCES

agisra. 1990. *Frauenhandel und Prostitutionstourismus.* München: Trickster Verlag.

Altink, Sietske. 1995. *Stolen Lives: Trading Women into Sex and Slavery.* London: Scarlet Press.

Anderson, Malcolm, Monica den Boer, Peter Cullen, William Gilmore, Charles Raab, and Neil Walker. 1995. *Policing the European Union.* Oxford: Clarendon Press.

Berkovitch, Nitza. 1999. *From Motherhood to Citizenship: Women's Rights and International Organizations.* Baltimore: Johns Hopkins University Press.

Bindman, Jo. 1998. "An International Perspective on Slavery in the Sex Industry." In *Global Sex Workers: Rights, Resistance, and Redefinition,* edited by K. Kempadoo and J. Doezema, 65–68. New York: Routledge.

Braun, Eva. 1989. "Zur politischen Dimension von Frauenhandel." In *Frauenhandel in Deutschland,* edited by Tübinger Projektgruppe Frauenhandel, 286–97. Bonn: Verlag J. H. W. Dietz Nachf.

Caldwell, Gillian, Steven Galster, and Nadia Steinzor. 1997. *Crime and Servitude: An Exposé of the Traffic in Women for Prostitution from the Newly Independent States.* Washington, D.C.: Global Survival Network.

Campani, Giovanna. 1998. "Trafficking for Sexual Exploitation and the Sex Business in the New Context of International Migration: The Case of Italy." *South European Society and Politics* 3:230–61.

Chant, Sylvia. 1992. "Conclusion: Towards a Framework for the Analysis of Gender-Selective Migration." In *Gender and Migration in Developing Countries,* edited by S. Chant, 197–206. London: Belhaven Press.

Chuang, Janie. 1998. "Redirecting the Debate over Trafficking in Women: Definitions, Paradigms, and Contexts." *Harvard Human Rights Journal* 11:65–107.

Connelly, Mark Thomas. 1980. *The Response to Prostitution in the Progressive Era.* Chapel Hill: University of North Carolina Press.

Council of the European Union. 1997. *Joint Action to Combat Trafficking in Human Beings and Sexual Exploitation of Children.* Joint Action 97/154/JHA, February 24.

Daly, Kathleen. 1988. "The Social Control of Sexuality: A Case Study of the Criminalization of Prostitution in the Progressive Era." In *Research in Law, Deviance, and Social Control,* edited by S. Spitzer and A. Scull, 9:171–206. Greenwich, Conn.: JAI Press.

Davis, Nanette J., ed. 1993. *Prostitution: An International Handbook on Trends, Problems, and Policies.* Westport, Conn.: Greenwood Press.

Demleitner, Nora V. 1994. "Forced Prostitution: Naming an International Offense." *Fordham International Law Journal* 18:163–97.

———.1997. "The Fallacy of Social 'Citizenship,' or the Threat of Exclusion." *Georgetown Immigration Law Journal* 12:35–74.

Doezema, Jo. 1998. "Forced to Choose: Beyond the Voluntary v. Forced Prostitution Dichotomy." In *Global Sex Workers: Rights, Resistance, and Redefinition,* edited by K. Kempadoo and J. Doezema, 34–50. New York: Routledge.

Dreixler, Markus. 1998. *Der Mensch als Ware.* Frankfurt am Main: Peter Lang.

Edwards, Susan. 1997. "The Legal Regulation of Prostitution—a Human Rights Issue." In *Rethinking Prostitution,* edited by G. Scambler and A. Scambler, 57–82. London: Routledge.

European Parliament. 1996. "Resolution on Trafficking in Human Beings." A4–0326/95. In *Official Journal of the European Communities* No. C 32/88–93 February 5.

Fitzpatrick, Joan. 1994. "The Use of International Human Rights Norms to Combat Violence against Women." In *Human Rights of Women: National and International Perspectives,* edited by R. Cook, 532–71. Philadelphia: University of Pennsylvania Press.

Garland, David. 1996. "The Limits of the Sovereign State." *British Journal of Criminology* 36:445–71.

Gillan, Audrey. 1999. "Dutch Make Oldest Profession Just a Job." *Guardian,* October 30.

Godfrey, Tom. 1998a. "Blitz on Foreign Strippers: Feds Require Interview before Arrival." *Toronto Sun,* June 24.

———. 1998b. "Woman Was Sex Slave." *Toronto Sun,* July 16.

———. 1999. "Strip Their Rights: Peelers Claim Refugee Status." *Toronto Sun,* July 22.

Gorham, Deborah. 1978. "The 'Maiden Tribute of Modern Babylon' Re-examined: Child Prostitution and the Idea of Childhood in Late-Victorian England." *Victorian Studies* 21:353–69.

Haft, Marilyn G. 1977. "Legal Arguments: Prostitution Laws and the Constitution." In *The Politics of Prostitution,* 2d ed., edited by J. James, J. Withers, M. Haft, S. Theiss, and M. Owen, 20–36. Seattle: Social Research Associates.

Hebenton, Bill, and Jon Spencer. 1998. "Law Enforcement in Societies in Transition." *European Journal of Crime, Criminal Law, and Criminal Justice* 6:29–40.

Heine-Wiedenmann, Dagmar. 1992. "Konstruktion und Management von Menschenhandels-Fällen." *Monatszeitschrift für Kriminologie und Strafrechtsreform* 75 (2/3): 121–30.

Heine-Wiedenmann, Dagmar, and Lea Ackermann. 1992. *Umfeld und Ausmass des Menschenhandels mit ausländischen Mädchen und Frauen.* Stuttgart: Kohlhammer.

Heinzl, Mark. 1999. "Canada's Government Gets Skimpy with Work Visas for Exotic Dancers." *Wall Street Journal,* April 5.

Henderson, Lynne. 1998. "Co-Opting Compassion: The Federal Victim's Rights Amendment." *St. Thomas Law Review* 10:579–606.

Human Rights Caucus. N.d. *Clarification: Trafficking and Smuggling.* www.hrlawgroup.org/site/programs/traffic/No3.htm

———. 1999. *Recommendations and Commentary on the Draft Protocol to Prevent, Suppress, and Punish Trafficking in Persons, Especially Women and Children, Supplementing the United Nations Convention Against Transnational Organized Crime.* www.hrlawgroup.org/site/programs/traffic/No3.htm

International Labor Organization. 1990. *International Convention on the Protection of the Rights of All Migrant Workers and Members of Their Families,* adopted by General Assembly Resolution 45/158, December 18.

International Organization for Migration. 1995. *Trafficking and Prostitution: The Growing Exploitation of Migrant Women from Central and Eastern Europe.* Geneva: International Organization for Migration.

International Organization for Migration and International Centre for Migration Policy Development. 1999. *Migration in Central and Eastern Europe—1999 Review.* Geneva: International Organization for Migration.

James, Jennifer. 1977a. "Answers to the 20 Questions Most Frequently Asked about Prostitution." In *The Politics of Prostitution,* 2d ed., edited by J. James, J. Withers, M. Haft, S. Theiss, and M. Owen, 37–63. Seattle: Social Research Associates.

———. 1977b. "The History of Prostitution Laws." In *The Politics of Prostitution,* 2d ed., edited by J. James, J. Withers, M. Haft, S. Theiss, and M. Owen, 9–19. Seattle: Social Research Associates.

James, Jennifer, and Jean Withers. 1977. "Introduction." In *The Politics of Prostitution,* 2d ed., edited by J. James, J. Withers, M. Haft, S. Theiss, and M. Owen, xiii–xviii. Seattle: Social Research Associates.

Kelker, Brigitte. 1993. "Die Situation von Prostituierten im Strafrecht und ein freiheitliches Rechtsverständnis-Betrachtung der Situation nach dem 26. Strafrechtsänderungsgesetz." *Kritische Vierteljahresschrift für Gesetzgebung und Rechtswissenschaft 76* (3): 289–312.

Lipka, Susanne. 1989. *Das käufliche Glück in Südostasien: Heiratshandel und Sextourismus,* 3d ed. Münster: Verlag Westfälisches Dampfboot.

Martin, Michael T. 1999. "'Fortress Europe' and Third World Immigration in the Post–Cold War Global Context." *Third World Quarterly* 20:821–37.

Murray, Alison. 1998. "Debt-Bondage and Trafficking: Don't Believe the Hype." In *Global Sex Workers: Rights, Resistance, and Redefinition,* edited by K. Kempadoo and J. Doezema, 51–64. New York: Routledge.

Pickup, Francine. 1998. "More Words but No Action?: Forced Migration and Trafficking of Women." In *Gender and Migration,* edited by C. Sweetman, 44–51. Oxford: Oxfam.

Rayanakorn, Kobkul. 1995. *Special Study on Laws Relating to Prostitution and Traffic in Women.* Bangkok: Research and Action Project on Traffic in Women.

Raymond, Janice G., and Coalition Against Trafficking in Women. 1995. *Report to the Special Rapporteur on Violence against Women.* www.uri.edu/artsci/wms/hughes/catw

Reanda, Laura. 1991. "Prostitution as a Human Rights Question: Problems and Prospects of United Nations Actions." *Human Rights Quarterly* 13:202–28.

Reinhardt, Andreas J. n.d. "Frauenhandel-eine moderne Form des Slavenhandels (Teil 2)." *MFDP* 265:4–8.

Rosenberg, Amy S. 1998. "13 Women Arraigned in Prostitution Case." *Philadelphia Inquirer,* October 9.

"Russian Envoy on Immigrants, Peace Process, Iranian Arms." 1999. *Yedi'ot Aharonot* (Tel Aviv), March 1.

Schroeder, Friedrich-Christian. 1995. "Irrwege aktionistischer Gesetzgebung-das 26. StÄG (Menschenhandel)." *Juristenzeitung* 5:231–38.

Seabrook, Jeremy. 1996. *Travels in the Skin Trade: Tourism and the Sex Industry.* London: Pluto Press.

Shelley, Louise. 1999. "Human Trafficking: Defining the Problem." *Organized Crime Watch—Russia* 1 (2): 1–2.

"A Single Market in Crime." 1999. *Economist.* http://www.economist.com/editorial/freeforall/current/sa3284.html (visited October 16, 1999).

Skrobanek, Siriporn, Nataya Boonpakdee, and Chutima Jantateero. 1997. *The Traffic in Women: Human Realities of the International Sex Trade.* London: Zed Books.

Smith, Stephanie. 1999. "Women Smuggled into U.S., Forced into Prostitution Try to Recoup $1M." In *Palm Beach Daily Business Review,* April 8.

Soiné, Michael, and Otmar Soukup. 1994. "'Identitätsänderung,' Anfertigung und Verwendung von 'Tarnpapieren.'" *Zeitschrift für Rechtspolitik* 12:466–70.

Sterk-Elifson, Claire, and Carole A. Campbell. 1993. "The Netherlands." In *Prostitution: An International Handbook on Trends, Problems, and Policies,* edited by N. Davis, 191–206. Westport, Conn.: Greenwood Press.

Stewart, Alison N. 1998. "Report from the Roundtable on the Meaning of 'Trafficking in Persons': A Human Rights Perspective." *Women's Rights Law Reporter* 20:11–19.

Streiber, Petra. 1998. *Internationaler Frauenhandel.* Berlin: Freie Universität Berlin.

Toepfer, Susan Jeanne, and Bryan Stuart Wells. 1994. "The Worldwide Market for Sex: A Review of International and Regional Legal Prohibitions Regarding Trafficking in Women." *Michigan Journal of Gender and Law* 2:83–128.

Tyner, James A. 1996. "Constructions of Filipina Migrant Entertainers." *Gender, Place, and Culture* 3:77–93.

U.N. Centre for Human Rights. 1994. *Fact Sheet No. 22—Discrimination against Women: The Convention and the Committee.* Geneva: U.N. Centre for Human Rights.

U.N. Commission on Human Rights, Subcommission on Prevention of Discrimination and Protection of Minorities. 1995. *Report of the Working Group on Contemporary Forms of Slavery on its twentieth session. Draft programme of action on the traffic in persons and the exploitation of the prostitution of others.* E/CN.4/Sub.2/1995/28/Add.1, June 13.

U.N. General Assembly, Ad Hoc Committee on the Elaboration of a Convention against Transnational Organized Crime (First Session—Vienna, January 19–29, 1999). 1999. *Draft Elements for an International Legal Instrument against Illegal Trafficking and Transport of Migrants (Proposal Submitted by Austria and Italy).* A/AC.254/4/Add.1, December 15.

U.S. Commission on Immigration Reform. 1997. *Immigration and the CNMI.* Washington, D.C.: GPO.

U.S. Department of Justice, Office of Justice Programs, Office for Victims of Crime. 1996. *Victims of Gang Violence: A New Frontier in Victim Services.* Washington, D.C.: U.S. Department of Justice.

U.S. House of Representatives, Subcommittee on International Operations and

Human Rights. 1999. *Hearing on "Trafficking of Women and Children in the International Sex Trade."* Testimony of Theresa Loar, Director, President's Interagency Council on Women and Senior Coordinator for International Women's Issues, U.S. Department of State, September 14.

Vernez, Georges. n.d. "National Security and Migration: How Strong the Link?" Manuscript in author's possession.

Wijers, Marjan. 1998. "Women, Labor, and Migration: The Position of Trafficked Women and Strategies for Support." In *Global Sex Workers: Rights, Resistance, and Redefinition,* edited by K. Kempadoo and J. Doezema, 60–78. New York: Routledge.

Wijers, Marjan, and Lin Lap-Chew. 1997. *Trafficking in Women: Forced Labour and Slavery-Like Practices in Marriage, Domestic Labour, and Prostitution.* Anraad: Foundation Against Trafficking in Women and Global Alliance Against Traffic in Women.

Wilson, Catherine. 1998. "20 Women Forced into Prostitution." Associated Press, April 24.

Zagaris, Bruce. 1996. "Trinidad Government Leads Witness Protection Initiative." *International Enforcement Law Reporter* 12:266–68.

11◾◾◾◾◾◾◾◾Immigrants, Smuggling, and Threats to Social Order in Japan

H. Richard Friman

During the mid-1990s, Japanese debates over immigration turned to the threat posed by illegal Chinese migrants—primarily male unskilled workers—and the smuggling networks facilitating their entry. Government and media reports attributed the rise in migrant smuggling to the shifting interests of foreign organized crime groups, especially the "Snakehead" (in Japanese, *jato*) syndicate rumored to be directed by Hong Kong's 14K triad. Police and immigration officials argued that Snakehead's targeting of Japan reflected two displacement effects, the first stemming from the U.S. crackdown on illegal Chinese immigration in the aftermath of the *Golden Venture* incident and the second from the reversion of Hong Kong to the People's Republic of China. As smuggling incidents surged in early 1997, the Maritime Safety Agency (MSA) noted further that the diversion of its resources to deal with a major oil spill had opened a unique window of opportunity for smugglers to expand their operations into Japan (NPA, 1997; "14K Gang," 1997; "Inside Story of 'Chinese Mafia,'" 1997; "Oil Spill," 1997; "Snake Head Gangs," 1997).

Reports of the Snakehead threat, however, were not limited to migrant smuggling. Police officials noted that the new wave of immigration was responsible for a crime spree threatening public safety and social order.

Annual *White Papers on Police* illustrated the Chinese propensity toward criminal behavior with statistics and graphical presentations positing that Chinese in Japan were responsible for more than 40 percent of crime by foreigners but constituted less than 13–16 percent of the foreign visitor (*rainichi gaikokujin*) population. To explain this behavior, police officials stressed the expansion of the membership of 14K affiliates in Japan but stopped short of arguing that this criminal propensity of the new illegals was necessarily inherent to all Chinese. A more common claim was that the combination of Japan's slowing economy and especially the debt burdens incurred by the new immigrants had forced many into a life of crime. Japanese officials argued that to prevent a disruption to migrant trafficking operations, the Snakehead syndicate had facilitated the trafficking shift to Japan by offering its services at a discount. The migrant would rely on borrowed funds or pay a partial fee with the remainder to be paid by relatives in China or by the migrant after securing employment in Japan. The funds in the case of the latter mode of repayment would be routed back to China through what police identified as an extensive underground money-laundering network ("In Japan, a Thriving Business," 1997; "Money Pipeline Helped Illegals," 1997; "Illegal Chinese Hide in Shadows," 1997; "Police Target Illegal Foreign Workers," 1998).

The Japanese concerns over migrant smuggling do reflect a kernel of truth. Smuggling incidents have increased since the late 1980s, as have criminal offenses by Chinese immigrants. However, several pieces are missing from the prominent explanations of the extent and nature of the problem. One set of missing pieces lies in the inconsistent, official conceptualization of migrant smuggling networks and the misleading public presentation of criminal statistics. The second set of pieces missing from the prominent explanations includes a discussion of Japan's history of labor brokering with China and the ramifications of the ongoing transition taking place in Japanese organized crime.

To explain why these pieces are missing, this chapter argues that discussions of the Snakehead threat to Japan partially reflect a broader pattern of state agents constructing foreigners as threats to social order. Though often referred to as a newcomer to immigration, Japan has a long history of arguments linking immigrants and crime. In the past, these arguments surfaced during periods of severe dislocation such as the anti-Korean riots in the aftermath of the 1923 Tokyo earthquake and the incidents of gang warfare between Japanese and *sankokujin* (literally, "three country people," referring to Korean, Taiwanese, Chinese) over black markets during the early years of the American occupation (Aldous, 1997; Morris-Suzuki, 1998: 105). Crime-by-foreigner arguments have resurfaced in Japan since the late 1980s in the context of increased immigration and especially with the collapse of the bubble economy.

This chapter offers a preliminary exploration of crime-by-foreigner arguments in Japan in the context of concerns over the Snakehead threat of the mid-1990s. To do so, the chapter's first section addresses the question of the extent of migrant smuggling and the crimes committed by illegal Chinese migrants. The second section turns to the issues of labor demand and organized crime missing from the prominent discussions of migrant smuggling. The third section explores the construction of the Snakehead as a threat to social order in Japan.

Snakeheads and Chinese Crime

Even a brief overview of agency reports, official statements, and media analyses of the Snakehead threat reveals inconsistencies in the conceptualization of the smuggling networks linking China and Japan. For example, the networks are often discussed as being directed by either a single organization or multiple organizations, while Japanese are members, allies, or victims of Snakehead operations. In contrast, the most prominent statistics on the criminal propensity of illegal Chinese migrants suffer from the selective presentation of Japanese crime data.[1]

Snakeheads

According to the International Organization for Migration, human smuggling occurs when "money (or some other form of payment) exchanges hands; and a facilitator (or 'trafficker') arranges passage across an international border; and such passage is illegal; and the movement is voluntary" (Smith, 1997: 9). During the 1990s, and in the aftermath of high-profile incidents such as the *Golden Venture,* Chinese traffickers began to attract extensive international attention. Taiwanese snakeheads, or "alien smugglers," played an integral role in facilitating the movement of migrants from China's Fujian Province abroad (Myers, 1997: 97–104;

Zhang and Gaylord, 1996: 5–8). The term *snakehead* stems from the "image of slithering from point to point along clandestine routes" (Chin, 1997: 190). The expansion of the Taiwanese smuggling industry of the 1990s drew upon established drug transit routes and existing migrant smuggling networks that had facilitated the earlier, smaller-scale movement of Fujian Chinese to the United Sates and elsewhere (Myers, 1997: 105–6). Rather than a single smuggling network, snakehead groups exist at multiple levels of the illegal migration process—local, national, international, and host country. Moreover, snakehead groups vary extensively in size and formal organizational structure (Zhang and Gaylord. 1996: 6–11).

In contrast, the Japanese discussion of the Snakehead threat lacks this sense of nuanced complexity. All too often, migrant smugglers are referred to by enforcement agencies, and in turn the media, as members of a single, foreign organization. For example, according to Shirakawa Katsuhiko, the chairman of the National Public Safety Commission, Snakehead is "a Hong Kong based criminal syndicate which deals in illegal immigrants" ("Japan-China Talks on Illegals Set," 1997). Similarly, National Police Agency (NPA) officials in reports and testimony before the Diet tend to refer to the "Hong Kong criminal syndicate Snakehead" in the singular, though occasionally acknowledging that the term refers more broadly to Chinese brokers that facilitate the smuggling process (e.g., "More Gangs Aiding Illegals," 1997; "Snake Head Gangs Step up Smuggling," 1997; "Profits Keep People-Smuggling Boom Alive," 1997). Immigration officials, operating under the Ministry of Justice, and MSA officials reveal a similar pattern.

References to the participation of Japanese in migrant smuggling operations also have been inconsistent. As discussed below, by the mid-1990s enforcement authorities began to acknowledge the role of Japanese organized crime (the *yakuza*) in migrant smuggling cases. But authorities continued to posit that the guiding force in such operations remained Chinese. Perhaps the best example of this pattern was the August 1997 revelation of an international smuggling network linking China, Hong Kong, Cambodia, Europe (France, Italy), the United States, and Japan. The number of Japanese arrested in the case led to reports noting the Cambodian-based operation of the "Snakehead crime group, which is predominantly Chinese," and "directed by a Chinese leader" in which Japa-

nese nationals were used to smuggle Chinese into the United States and
Europe by passing them off as relatives. The following month, the police
turned to investigating the syndicate for its role in the rash of illegal entries of Chinese into Japan (e.g., "3 More Snakeheads," 1997; "Police Go
International," 1997).

Illegal entries of groups of Chinese by boat have been the focal point
of the Japanese debate over the migrant smuggling. As seen in table 5, official figures on the number of these incidents increased in 1993 and remained relatively stable until a surge in 1997.[2] As is the case for drug trafficking and money laundering, interdiction rates in the illicit global
economy offer only a limited sense of the extent of actual movements of
people (Friman and Andreas, 1999). Moreover, as an illicit stream becomes prioritized, the resources devoted (or redirected) toward interdicting it often increase, leading to a subsequent jump in official statistics
concerning the trade. Implicitly drawing from the practice of drug enforcement agencies, immigration officials and scholars have also posited
that Japan is only interdicting roughly 10 percent of the illegal migrant
traffic into the country (e.g., "Japan Cracks Down," 1997; "Japan Worries about a Trend," 1997; "Snake Head Gangs Step up Smuggling,"
1997). References to this calculation became a recurrent theme during discussions over further immigration controls in the spring of 1997.

In March, enforcement agencies and the press revealed data noting the
surge in group smuggling incidents and apprehensions of illegals. The figures emphasized that twenty-eight incidents had taken place by the end
of February alone involving 692 illegals, more than the entire previous
year. These figures and the Japanese concerns were picked up by the U.S.
press, and in turn the U.S. press reports were reprinted verbatim in the Japanese press as proof of international recognition of the magnitude of the
Snakehead problem (e.g., "Smugglers Flood Japan," 1997). Though incidents and apprehensions increased during the remainder of the year, the
10 percent claim of interdictions remains suspect. During the mid-1990s,
concerned Japanese citizens noticed even small groups of Chinese wan-
dering lost in the countryside and around train stations and immediately
contacted the police. In light of this pattern, the likelihood that an additional 7,000 Chinese could be offloaded by boat illegally into Japan during the first two months of 1997, or roughly 12,000 Chinese during the
course of the year, without detection is an overstatement at best. Even

Table 5. Illegal Entry by Groups of Migrants (*Shudan Mikko*), Interdiction Incidents, and Apprehensions, 1990–1999

Year	Total Incidents	Total Apprehended	Chinese Apprehended
1990	1	18	18
1991	4	89	89
1992	14	396	383
1993	7	335	329
1994	13	467	360
1995	13	324	151
1996	29	679	542
1997	73	1,360	1,209
1998	64	1,023	815
1999	44	770	682

Source: Personal correspondence from National Police Agency; Mo (1997: 55); Keisatsucho (1998b: 229); and Smugglers Flood (1997).
Note: Group smuggling attempts were primarily by boat.

with the heightened attention by Japanese authorities on smuggling by boat, the figures for 1998 and 1999 also suggest that the pace of migrant smuggling along this path may be slowing.

Crime by Chinese

During early 1997, in the midst of the surge in migrant smuggling incidents of Chinese and fears of a Chinese crime wave, the chief of the Investigation Bureau of the NPA, Higuchi Tateshi, observed that "Japanese society is completely unprepared for these people" ("Japan Worries about a Trend," 1997). However, part of the difficulty in preparation lies in the tendency of enforcement agencies and, in turn, the Japanese media to overstate the criminal propensity of foreigners. In the mid-1990s, reports of crime by Chinese began to replace the high-profile stories of unemployed Iranians waylaying young, diet-obsessed Japanese schoolgirls to sell them methamphetamine (e.g., "Foreigners Help Teens," 1996; Friman, 1996: 974–75; "Stimulant Drug Dealers Expand Operations" 1996; Schreiber, 1997: 83–84). As Sugita Kazuhiro, head of the NPA's Security Bureau, noted in early 1997, "crimes by Chinese syndicates have had a serious impact on Japan's security. It is imperative to arrest would-be illegal immigrants" ("National Police Agency and Maritime Safety Agency Hold Discussion," 1997). The director general of the MSA, Muto Kabun, argued further that "it is true that [illegal Chinese immigrants] have brought narcotics into the nation or forged pachinko pre-paid cards, jeopardizing peace and order in Japan" ("National Police Agency to Dispatch Officials," 1997).

The most common statement by government officials, pundits, and the media was that Chinese committed more than 40 percent of crimes by foreigners but constituted only 16 percent of foreigners in Japan. The statement often glossed over the distinction between legal foreign visitors, illegal foreign visitors, and total numbers of foreigners, including permanent foreign residents—*zainichi gaikokujin*—such as the roughly 700,000 Koreans and 150,000 Chinese living in Japan (Mori, 1997: 136; Sassen, 1998: 65; for a larger estimate of the Chinese population, see Mo, 1998: 44–47). The still rarer observation was to place these figures in the broader context of total crime statistics, in which "only about one percent of all crimes in Japan are committed by non-Japanese" ("Inside Story of 'Chinese Mafia,'" 1997; "Japan, China Must Fight Illegal Entry," 1997; "Japan Worries about a Trend," 1997).

Statistics on crime by foreigners can be shaped by a number of factors beyond the scope of this chapter, including potential bias in enforcement patterns, the nature of crime reporting by victims, and discretionary steps by street-level enforcement agents (Herbert, 1996; Friman, 1996). Other practices that can overstate crime patterns are the tendency of the police to arrest and rearrest a single individual for multiple crimes and to compare the foreign visitor population (overwhelming male and in prime working age) to the full Japanese population (male, female, and elderly) (e.g., NPA, 1997: 113–14). These caveats aside, the presentation of criminal statistics plays an essential role in shaping public and governmental concerns over migrant smuggling. More important, this presentation has overstated the Snakehead threat.

Japanese criminal statistics are divided into two broad categories: penal code violations and special law violations. Penal code offenses include felonies, violent offenses, and larceny; special law offenses include issues such as drug crimes, prostitution, and immigration regulations. Penal law data have played the central role in the broader debate over crime by for-

Table 6. Penal Code Violations by Visiting Foreigners (*Rainichi Gaikokujin*), Total and by Top Three Nationalities/Areas of Origin, 1987–1997

Year	Total	First	F/T%	Second	Third
1987	1,871	778 C	42	312 K	169 F
1988	3,020	1,643 C	54	398 K	148 F
1989	2,989	1,709 C	57	392 K	112 U
1990	2,978	1,288 C	43	517 K	151 F
1991	4,813	1,732 C	36	728 K	561 I
1992	5,961	1,933 C	32	876 K	771 I
1993	7,276	2,668 C	37	987 K	544 I
1994	7,183	2,942 C	42	775 K	470 P
1995	6,527	2,919 C	45	752 K	386 P
1996	6,026	2,661 C	44	732 K	326 F
1997	5,435	2,320 C	43	522 K	329 V

Source: Keisatsucho (1997: 400–01; 1998a: 128–29; 1999: 261).

Note: C refers to Chinese, including those from the People's Republic, Taiwan, and Hong Kong; K refers to North and South Korean. The third largest groups include Filipino (F), American (U), Iranian (I), Peruvian (P), and Vietnamese (V).

eigners, though references to specific categories of special law violations such as drug crimes also garner attention. The 40 percent figure of crimes by Chinese reflects penal code violations, though a number of media reports have glossed over this distinction (e.g., "Japan Cracks Down on Snakeheads," 1997). The NPA also publishes statistics—both those for public consumption and those for use by in-house researchers—in a compartmentalized manner. Separate sections on crimes by foreigners do not compare their offenses with the total number of penal and special law violations. More important, the statistics on specific types of penal or special law offenses make no distinction according to immigration status (e.g., between legal visiting foreigners, illegal migrants, illegal overstayers, or permanent foreign residents).

The statistics presented in table 6 illustrate total arrests for penal code violations by visiting foreigners and a breakdown by the top three nationalities/areas of origin. From 1987 through 1997, these statistics suggest that Chinese have been the leading foreign violators of Japan's penal code followed by Koreans (North and South), and a shifting mix of Iranians, Filipinos, Americans, Peruvians, and Vietnamese. For Japanese enforcement officials, the upturn in the raw numbers and percentage of Chinese violations beginning in 1993 (table 6) and the increase in migrant smuggling incidents (table 5) support the linkage between illegal migrants and crime. However, the figures used to support this linkage are problematic. The category of Chinese migrants in table 5, for example, refers to persons from the People's Republic. The category of Chinese offenders in table 6, by contrast, includes persons from the People's Republic, Taiwan, and Hong Kong. Moreover, the figures in table 6 reveal nothing as to whether these Chinese violators, regardless of specific area of origin, were legal foreign visitors, visa overstayers, or members of groups of illegals smuggled into Japan. In effect, all Chinese crime has become Snakehead-related.

Table 6 also reveals nothing as to the types of penal code violations committed by the visiting Chinese. To make more specific claims, enforcement agencies and the media have selectively turned to data such as those presented in table 7. The table reveals penal code violations for all foreigners (visiting and permanent) in 1996, broken down by specific categories of penal code violations. Enforcement officials have turned to the finding that the primary crimes committed by Chinese were larceny offenses to support the view that illegal Chinese migrants have turned to crime to meet financial obligations to their Snakehead smugglers. However, the figures are not disaggregated enough by area of origin or immigration status to support such arguments fully. Moreover, the table reveals other patterns that suggest a less threatening picture of crime by Chinese in Japan. For example, Chinese accounted for roughly 1 percent of total penal code violations and less than one-half a percent of violent crimes (assaults, battery, and the like). Relative to other foreigners, Chinese also fall well short of the 40 percent figure for penal code violations.

The second piece of the argument on the criminal propensity of Chinese—pointing to criminal offenses relative to Chinese as 16 percent of the foreigner visitor population—is also suspect. In addition to the practice of conflating all Chinese into one nationality category, estimates of the *rainichi gaikokujin* population tend to be calculated from official figures on those legally in Japan as collected under Japan's alien registration law. These figures would not include illegal entrants such as those Chinese brought in by boat through migrant smuggling operations. As a result, the foreign visitor population and the Chinese percentage of this pop-

Table 7. Penal Code Violations in 1996, by Total Arrests (Japanese and Non-Japanese), Arrests of Foreigners (Visiting and Permanent), and Arrests of Chinese (Visiting and Permanent)

	Total	Foreigners	Chinese	Chinese Total (%)	Chinese Foreigners (%)
Penal Code	295,584	10,741	3,140	1	29
Felony	5,459	329	72	1	22
Violent	37,110	1,225	114	0.3	9
Larceny	162,675	5,486	1,869	1	34

Source: Keisatsucho (1997: 1, 389).
Note: Additional penal code offenses include intellectual crimes (e.g., counterfeiting), moral (e.g., gambling), and a broad category of others. The category of Chinese includes those from the People's Republic, Taiwan, and Hong Kong.

ulation would be understated in official figures. In contrast, relative Chinese criminality would be overstated by including those illegals not captured in official immigration statistics but arrested for penal code violations. In effect, by positing a massive surge in illegal immigration enforcement authorities face contradictions in their own arguments on the subsequent criminal threat. In the absence of more accurate statistics than those currently in use in public discussions of the Snakehead threat, the more extensive the migrant smuggling, the greater the potential flaw in the argument that Chinese are disproportionally prone to crime.

Sources of the Snakehead Threat

Efforts to explain migration dynamics commonly explore an array of possible push and pull effects. The discussion of migrant smuggling in Japan has emphasized the push effects of economic and political uncertainty in China and the presence of organized smuggling networks controlled by Chinese organized crime. To a lesser extent these discussions also have addressed the pull effects of relative Japanese economic prosperity, lax security, and domestic Chinese affiliates of the Snakehead network. However, other pull effects such as Japan's demand for low-skilled labor and the growing interest of Japanese organized crime in the financial gains from migrant smuggling have attracted still less attention.

Labor Demand and Paths of Access

Although Japan's demand for unskilled labor has been a major theme in the broader discussions of immigration, the ramifications of this demand for the rise of migrant smuggling remain underexplored. Scholarship on Japanese demand patterns commonly points to needs generated by the construction, manufacturing, and service booms of the 1980s bubble economy. These dynamics combined with declining Japanese birth rates, a limiting socioeconomic structure regarding women and elderly in the workplace, labor market inefficiencies shaping employment practices in the service sector, and a general aversion of younger Japanese to unskilled, labor-intensive jobs (e.g., Cornelius, Martin, and Hollifield, 1994; Shimada, 1994). Though faced with rising demand, employers lacked the legal framework for recruiting unskilled labor through the front door of Japanese immigration regulations. In brief, the import of unskilled workers was prohibited. As a result, employers turned to a number of side and back doors or indirectly explored these options by working through layers of subcontractor cutouts.

Access patterns for unskilled foreign workers (*gaikokujin rodosha*) into Japan have varied by country of origin. Through the early 1990s, migrants from countries such as Bangladesh, Pakistan, and Iran could draw on labor brokers at home and in Japan to take advantage of visa-exemption accords negotiated during the 1970s. These migrants would gain access into Japan as tourists but would engage in illegal work and overstay their visas (Mori, 1997). Lacking the option of exploiting similar visa-exemption accords, mainland Chinese migrants sought access to Japan through paths such as admission to Japanese language and vocational schools (on a *shugakusei* visa) (e.g., Friman, 1996: 969; Herbert, 1996: 107–16; Mori, 1997: 22). Japanese regulations on such schools—and the outside work prohibitions on students attending them—had eased during the mid-1980s as part of the Nakasone administration's pledge to educate 100,000 students by the year 2000. New mainland Chinese entrants surged through this side door into the Japanese labor market. The mainland students were typically from Fujian Province, mid- to late twenties in age, and 50–60 percent male. Their numbers increased from 113 new Chinese students in 1982 to 7,178 in 1987, and 28,256 by 1988, the last figure constituting roughly 74 percent of all entrants through this category into Japan (Herbert, 1996).

In response to growing evidence of language schools serving primarily as side doors into the unskilled labor market, however, Japanese authorities slowly began to impose new regulations. These steps included new visa provisions in 1989 requiring proof of a financial guarantor and new restrictions in 1990 reducing the maximum allowable outside work by students to twenty hours per week. Seeking to offset these changes, brokerage agencies emerged in China and Japan offering potential students "forged fictitious documents" of financial support and proof of acceptance from a Japanese language school. However, even tighter regulations through the mid-1990s and the ebb and flow of post-Tiananmen emigration provisions decreased the accessibility of the student path into Japan. By 1989, new Chinese students entering Japan had dropped to 9,142, roughly half of the total number of entrants. In 1992, new Chinese students increased to 16,265 out of a total of 27,000 students. By 1996, however, these numbers had fallen dramatically as only 2,567 new Chinese students, roughly 30 percent of the total foreign students, entered Japan on the *shugakusei* visa (Herbert, 1996: 107–16; "BRIGHT Idea," 1997).

The concurrent decline in student visa access by Chinese into Japan and the rise of migration through smuggling incidents suggest that the latter emerged, in part, as a replacement path into the Japanese labor market.[3] Given economic conditions in Japan, this argument of a pull effect initially appears unconvincing. The collapse of the bubble economy and Japan's economic recession of the mid-1990s adversely affected employment opportunities, especially for illegal labor (Mori, 1997: 74, 76–77). In addition, illegal workers were displaced by the 1990 Immigration Act's provisions for side-door access by *nikkeijin*, unskilled, primarily Latin American labor of Japanese descent (e.g., Shimada, 1994; Mori, 1997: 10; Sassen, 1998: 60–62). However, though well short of full employment conditions, demand for unskilled Chinese workers still exists in Japan.

As larger firms turned to meeting labor needs through the *nikkeijin*, medium and especially smaller firms essentially were priced out of the legal unskilled labor market. Illegal migrants from Asia offered such firms both a cheaper alternative to the *nikkeijin* and a labor force better able— than Iranians, for example—to pass cursory inspections by immigration authorities (Mori, 1997: 63–65, 112). Opportunities for Chinese workers also arose in the context of the post–Kobe earthquake reconstruction projects and the extensive work required for the Nagano Winter Olympics. Contractors interviewed in Nagano in early 1998, for example, noted that they did not want to use (Chinese) illegals but had "no choice" given the labor needs. The source of the Chinese illegals, media reports argued further, appeared to be linked with Snakehead smuggling networks. The Nagano incident also revealed, however, that although opportunities for Chinese illegals exist in Japan they can be fleeting. Following the completion of the Olympic construction projects in 1997 and through 1998, police and immigration officials waged a large-scale crackdown on illegals in the Nagano area designated "Operation White Snow" ("Illegal Aliens Who Helped Build Game Sites," 1998; "Nagano's Foreign Workers Sent Home," 1998).

The *Yakuza* and Migrant Smuggling

Japanese authorities increasingly have acknowledged the growing role of the *yakuza* in alien smuggling as part of a larger trend toward linkages between foreign and domestic organized crime groups. Police arrest reports and subsequent media stories have noted instances of the *yakuza* affiliation of Japanese arrested in conjunction with migrant smuggling incidents. These reports reveal the participation of members of minor organized crime groups as well as affiliates of the major syndicates such as the Yamaguchi-gumi (e.g., "Failed Snakehead Operation," 1997; NPA, 1997; "Smuggling Chinese into Japan," 1997). The most common explanation for why the *yakuza* might be participating in the migrant trade has been economic. The collapse of the bubble has adversely affected illicit operations as well as organized crime's incursion into the stock market and real estate markets during the boom of the 1980s (often termed the expansion of the economic, or *keizai yakuza*). Less attention in the public debate has been focused on the longer history of organized crime's participation in labor brokering and its increased reliance on brokering of illegals as an unintended impact of antiorganized crime legislation.

For all the images of corporate networks, intensive education, and lifetime employment that dominate the public perception of Japan, unskilled labor has remained an essential part of the Japanese economy. Major

Japanese cities all contain day laborer settlements (*yoseba*) with long histories, such as Kotobuki in Yokohama, Kamagasaki in Osaka, and San'ya in Tokyo. Labor brokers, tied into state agencies (e.g., employment offices through the Ministry of Labor) or illegal, private networks, link unskilled day laborers with construction and other jobs (Fowler, 1996: 35–40; Komai, 1995: 142–43; Stevens, 1997: 22, 26, 28). The *yakuza* have played an integral role in the construction industry as well as the *yoseba* areas, brokering labor supplies, running protection, drug, and gambling operations, and serving as a check on freelance crime. In some areas, the *yakuza* also have served as a check, implicitly state-supported, on union organizing among day laborers. In others, the *yakuza* have been less successful, with union conflicts erupting into full-scale violence (Fowler, 1996: 20–25).

By the mid-1980s, *yakuza* brokering of labor was still focused primarily on Japanese workers. Even as illegal foreign workers began to settle in and around the *yoseba* areas, Ministry of Justice figures estimated that only 14 percent of foreigners were being brokered by the *yakuza* (Herbert, 1996: 64, 79–84; Komai, 1995: 28). The reason for the limited involvement was primarily based on cost considerations relative to other sources of income. For example, Wolfgang Herbert (1996: 65) notes a 1989 interview with a Yamaguchi-gumi lawyer who observed that "recruiting male migrant workers and acting as agent for them is not seen as being lucrative enough to warrant large-scale *yakuza* involvement." The one exception to this pattern of involvement with foreigners was with female migrants and a shift earlier in the decade in the entertainment/sex industry. During the 1970s, the *yakuza* played an integral role in facilitating the sex tourism business from Japan into East and Southeast Asia. By the early 1980s, faced with growing protest in the host countries, the *yakuza* shifted focus toward recruiting, smuggling, and job placement for women from the Philippines, Thailand, and other countries into the lucrative Japanese sex industry (e.g., Herbert, 1996: 28–29; Sellek, 1996: 159–75; Komai, 1995: 77–78).

By the mid-1990s, however, the *yakuza* interest in male migrant labor had changed. According to Raisuke Miyawaki (1997), a former NPA official in charge of organized crime operations, the *yakuza* began to shift activities into a number of new areas with the collapse of the bubble economy, including "smuggling illegal aliens into the country." One sign of the competitive shift into migrant smuggling, according to police analysts, was that contending *yakuza* groups were even accepting smaller profit percentages from their Chinese counterparts. They were settling for 20 percent rather than a 50 percent share, which had distinguished earlier efforts at *yakuza* participation (e.g., "More Gangs Aiding Illegals," 1997; "Smuggling Chinese into Japan," 1997). Yet the reasons for the shift were not solely tied to changing economic circumstances.

The Anti–Organized Crime Law of 1992 increased the means by which Japanese authorities were able to interfere in the activities of organized crime groups, including protection rackets and gang-owned or -operated establishments (Kaplan, 1996; Friman, 1999). Subject to increased monitoring and declining revenues, membership in the *yakuza* began to fall. Organized crime groups turned to consolidation efforts to stem their losses, and violent conflicts erupted between and within syndicates over possible dissolution of affiliates, protecting established revenue sources, and capturing new areas of expansion.

By August 1997, these tensions had erupted into the gangland-style slaying of the number two official of the Yamaguchi-gumi (Takumi Masaru) in a Kobe hotel lobby and a subsequent onset of gang warfare in cities including Kobe, Osaka, and Tokyo (e.g., "Gang Boss Gunned Down," 1997; "Mobster Slaying Tied to Power Struggle," 1997; "Succession through a Gun Barrel," 1997). The wave of retaliatory shootings and firebombings prompted extensive police crackdowns and the accelerated introduction of new antigang legislation with measures to increase police powers under the Japanese criminal code, further adding to pressure on the *yakuza* (e.g., "Cabinet Approves 3 Bills," 1998; "Govt to Beef Up Fights," 1996; New Antigang Law," 1997; "Recent Violence Destabilizing Tokyo Underworld," 1997). In this context, Japanese organized crime groups have gone further underground. Some groups have increased their willingness to subcontract higher-profile operations—such as street-level drug trafficking—to foreigners. More important, syndicates and lower-level affiliates have turned their efforts to expanding less traditional sources of revenue, including cooperation with migrant smuggling networks (e.g., "Smuggling Chinese into Japan," 1997).

The Construction of the Snakehead Threat

The selective presentation of smuggling and crime data and the relative absence of discussions of the impact of Japanese labor demand and government anticrime campaigns lead to the question of why these pieces have been missing from the discussion of the Snakehead threat. The remainder of the chapter turns to the enforcement agencies that have played a central role in defining this issue, offering the primary information as to the extent of migrant smuggling, its ramifications, and its sources. One possible explanation for the absence of a more nuanced exploration of migrant smuggling lies in the simple, narrow self-interest of state enforcement agencies in the postbubble economy. A second, broader explanation lies in constructed norms concerning the sources of social order in Japan and the place of enforcement agencies in defending that order.[4]

Self-Interest

As argued by Masao Miyamoto (1994: 79–80), conflict over scarce economic resources and influence is extensive between and within the Japanese ministries. To obtain leverage, bureaucrats provide information to the media, knowing full well the media's reliance on the ministries for access to information and the media's tendency to oversell issues/threats (*mondai,* or problems) to the public to enhance readership. The information can be leaked or provided through official reports written for public distribution. As the information from official sources generates "public concern" (demonstrated in the media headlines and reports and subsequent public reaction), the ministry, bureau, or section can point to this concern as justification for greater financial and staff resources (see also Van Wolferen, 1993: 130, 305).

With the collapse of the bubble economy, Japanese ministries soon faced extensive economic pressures. In addition to falling revenue allocations from the Ministry of Finance, ministries were confronted with external as well as internal demands for reorganization as a means to decrease financial and staff requirements. That Japanese enforcement agencies in this context turned to stressing the criminal threats posed by the late 1980s wave of immigration has not gone unnoticed. Herbert (1996: 175) argues that "for the agencies of control themselves and for the framers of criminal policy, the postulation of rising crime rates [by foreigners] serves to legitimize demands for more financial resources and staff in the sector 'internal security.'" Such arguments, raised in the context of "public concern" with the threat of crime by foreigners (*gaijin-*

hanzai), have been successful in generating support from the Ministry of Finance. This support has facilitated the expansion of the enforcement bureaucracy with staff allocations, new departments, new task forces, and crime-fighting equipment and training (author interviews with police, immigration, and MSA officials, 1995; Friman, 1996).

The narrow self-interest of enforcement agencies helps to explain the construction of the issue of migrant smuggling. The picture of a single Snakehead organization, directed by Chinese affiliated with the infamous 14K crime group, smuggling crime-prone Chinese migrants into Japan is threatening. The picture is clearly more threatening than if enforcement agencies posed the existence of multiple smuggling networks, illegal migrants who are not prone to engage in additional criminal behavior, the culpability of Japanese employers, and the unintended results of anti–organized crime legislation on the *yakuza*. Moreover, the enforcement bureaucracy has benefited from the Snakehead threat. For example, the public image of the MSA as defender of Japan's coastal waters has improved since the early 1990s, when the agency was consistently and publicly chastised by the police for failing to do its part in curtailing the illicit drug trade (e.g., "MSA Thwarts Smuggling," 1996; "Possible Smuggling Vessel Chased," 1998). MSA, immigration, and national and prefectural police officials also have obtained support for new task forces and operations, foreign travel, and penalties to respond to the threat of alien smuggling and related crime (e.g., "Task Force Set Up," 1997; "Task Force Formed," 1998). For example, immigration provisions introduced during 1997 added new offenses and penalties for migrant smuggling. These included increasing the penalties for assisting illegal entry from an earlier maximum of eighteen months in prison to up to ten years or a Y10 million fine ("Cabinet OKs Tougher Law," 1997; "Immigration Bill Passes," 1997).

Homogeneity Myths and Social Order

However, to attribute the absence of the more nuanced conceptualization of Chinese migrant smuggling and its sources to the narrow self-interest of enforcement agencies for increased resources would be misleading. Scholarship on Japan as well as interviews of national and prefectural level police officials over the past four years on questions of foreigners and crime suggest a more complex process at work. In his analysis of Japanese security issues, Peter Katzenstein (1996: 19, 22) argues for a focus on the "politically contested," constitutive norms that "express actor identities" and help to "define . . . and thus shape behavior." Perhaps the most pervasive constitutive norm in Japan is that of collective identity, conceptualized as Japan as a homogeneous country with the primary sources of its domestic social order deriving from this homogeneity (Yoshino, 1992).

Clearly, though less diverse than other advanced industrial democracies, Japan is not homogeneous, nor has it ever really been. The homogeneity myth, stridently promoted in the late 1800s and early 1900s, has recast, discounted, or simply ignored portions of Japan's history. These portions include the migrations that shaped the country's origins and the forced migration of Koreans and Chinese earlier in the century. They also include the postwar compromises that shaped the rise of a permanent foreign resident population and, in turn, the impact of the most recent waves of immigration of the 1980s and 1990s (e.g., Smith, 1995: 181–207; Hingwan, 1996: 52–53; Morris-Suzuki, 1998: 79–109). However, despite growing local efforts at greater integration of immigrants into Japanese society, the constitutive norm of Japan as a homogeneous country—and especially the belief that this collective identity facilitates social order—is institutionalized and still carries weight.[5]

This is particularly the case within the more conservative state agencies that constitute Japan's enforcement bureaucracy. For enforcement officials, immigration, especially the uncontrolled nature of migrant smuggling, poses a threat to the country's homogeneity and, in turn, the heart of Japan's social order. As observed by one immigration official, Yamanaka Masanori, illegal migrants "come to Japan through the black market, ignoring the system of immigration control, so this problem shakes the very foundation of the Japanese government" ("Japan Worries about a Trend," 1997; also see Herbert, 1996). The Japanese police have always had difficulty in dealing with the country's minority populations. By the mid-1990s these difficulties had increased with new languages and the wider cultural diversity of the immigrant population. Where the police would often seek to hold immigration officials accountable for the access of illegal workers through violations of the country's visa system (e.g., overstayers), the rise in migrant smuggling incidents bypassed the immigration control process entirely and posed additional challenges and responsibilities for the police. The prominence in these incidents of mainland Chinese, who by 1993 were already a source of concern for the police and the *yakuza* alike in major cities such as Tokyo, added to the problem (e.g., Friman, 1999).

In short, operating under the linkage between homogeneity and social order, Japanese enforcement officials have perceived illegal Chinese migrants as disproportionate criminal threats. They view the very dynamic of migrant smuggling as driven more by external than internal dynamics, and more by organized Chinese gangs than by a varied array of smuggling networks. In addition, enforcement officials have used this interpretation to seek acknowledgment of the migrant smuggling threat from the broader public and to obtain support for a more active response.

Conclusion

During the bubble economy of the 1980s, Japan implicitly tolerated and relied on illegal immigration by male, unskilled workers. Immigration reforms in 1990 reaffirmed the country's formal opposition to such immigration but introduced a series of partially regulated side doors into the labor market that allowed access by unskilled workers. By the mid-1990s, however, migrant smuggling, especially from China, had added a new dynamic to the Japanese immigration debate. Japanese enforcement authorities posited the rise of the Snakehead threat, suggesting a single organization of smugglers directed by the 14K crime group. Moreover, the illegal migrants were responsible for a growing wave of crime by foreigners throughout Japan.

This chapter has argued that though incidents of migrant smuggling have increased since the early 1990s, the Snakehead threat has been oversold by Japanese enforcement authorities and, in turn, by the media. Through the selective use of statistical data, authorities have overstated the extent and nature of migrant smuggling as well as the relative criminal propensity of Chinese immigrants. Authorities also have downplayed the pull effects of Japanese labor demand for illegal Chinese workers and the diversification of *yakuza* operations in the face of antigang legislation. Their reasons for doing so reflect a combination of narrow self-interest in the context of postbubble economy pressures on the Japanese bureaucracy and the broader perception of illegal (Chinese) migrants as posing a threat to Japan's collective identity and the all-important, and related, linkage between homogeneity and social order.

NOTES

1. This chapter does not explore the potential for bias in arrest patterns. For a partial discussion, see Friman (1996).

2. During the summer of 1989, Japan faced thirty-seven incidents of smuggling by boat. The roughly thirty-five hundred people posing as Vietnamese refugees were soon revealed to be from Fujian Province. Though playing a role in the immigration debate, the incidents preceded the deliberations over the Snakehead threat (Komai, 1995: 177–86; Herbert, 1996: 126–27).

3. An additional path would be to enter as company trainees under visa programs modified under the 1990 and subsequent regulations. Mori (1997: 117) posits that of the approximately fifty thousand corporate trainees in Japan during the mid-1990s, 40 percent were from China.

4. The social construction of threats to public order is explored in an array of sociological literatures including work on moral panics (e.g., Goode and Ben-Yehuda, 1994; Sampson and Lauritsen, 1997; Thompson, 1998).

5. Interpretations of Japanese social order by foreign scholars also point to the impact of homogeneity. Classics in this vein include the work of L. Craig Parker (1987) and David H. Bayley (1991).

REFERENCES

Aldous, Christopher. 1997. *The Police in Occupation Japan: Control, Corruption, and Resistance to Reform.* London: Routledge.

Bayley, David H. 1991. *Forces of Order: Policing Modern Japan.* Berkeley: University of California Press.

"BRIGHT Idea to Halt Illegal Entry." 1997. *Asahi Evening News,* August 5.

"Cabinet Approves 3 Bills to Fight Organized Crime." 1998. *Daily Yomiuri,* March 14.

"Cabinet OKs Tougher Law on Immigration." 1997. *Daily Yomiuri.* March 5.

Chin, Ko-lin. 1997. "Safe House or Hell House?: Experiences of Newly Arrived Undocumented Chinese." In *Human Smuggling: Chinese Migrant Trafficking and the Challenge to America's Immigration Tradition,* edited by Paul J. Smith, 169–95. Washington, D.C.: Center for Strategic and International Studies.

"Chinese Mafia Taking Root in Japan's Cities." 1998. *Mainichi Daily News,* March 14.

Cornelius, Wayne, Philip L. Martin, and James F. Hollifield. 1994. *Controlling Immigration: A Global Perspective.* Stanford: Stanford University Press.

"Failed Snakehead Operation." 1997. *Daily Yomiuri,* June 15.

"Foreigners Help Teens See Worms in Their Rice Bowls." 1996. *Mainichi Daily News,* November 3.

"14K Gang Invades Japan." 1997. *Asahi Evening News,* February 13.

Fowler, Edward. 1996. *San'ya Blues: Laboring Life in Contemporary Tokyo* Ithaca, N.Y.: Cornell University Press.

Friman, H. Richard. 1996. "Gaijinhanzai: Immigrants and Drugs in Contemporary Japan." *Asian Survey* 36 (10): 964–77.

———. 1999. "Obstructing Markets: Organized Crime and Drug Control in Japan." In *The Illicit Global Economy and State Power,* edited by H. Richard Friman and Peter Andreas, 173–97. Boulder, Colo.: Rowman & Littlefield.

Friman, H. Richard, and Peter Andreas, eds. 1999. *The Illicit Global Economy and State Power.* Boulder, Colo.: Rowman & Littlefield.

"Gang Boss Gunned Down in Kobe Hotel." 1997. *Daily Yomiuri,* August 29.

Goode, Erich, and Nachman Ben-Yehuda. 1994. "Moral Panics: Culture, Politics, and Social Construction." *Annual Review of Sociology* 20:149–71.

"Govt to Beef up Fights against Organized Crime." 1996. *Daily Yomiuri,* June 17.

Herbert, Wolfgang. 1996. *Foreign Workers and Law Enforcement in Japan.* London: Kegan Paul International.

Hingwan, Kathiane. 1996. "Identity, Otherness, and Migrant Labor in Japan." In *Case Studies on Human Rights in Japan,* edited by Roger Goodman and Ian Neary, 51–75. Surrey, England: Japan Library.

"Illegal Aliens Who Helped Build Games Sites Seen Facing Sweep." 1998. *Japan Times,* February 4.

"Illegal Chinese Hide in Shadows." 1997. *Asahi Evening News,* March 30.

"Immigration Bill Passes Upper House." 1997. *Daily Yomiuri,* April 26.

"In Japan, a Thriving Business in Illegal Immigrants." 1997. *International Herald Tribune,* March 4.

"Inside Story of 'Chinese Mafia' Operating in Japan—Frightening Infiltration." 1997. *Sentaku,* U.S. Embassy, Office of Translation Services.

"Japan, China Must Fight Illegal Entry." 1997. Editorial printed in *Daily Yomiuri,* February 27.

"Japan-China Talks on Illegals Set." 1997. *Daily Yomiuri,* March 5.

"Japan Cracks Down on Snakeheads." 1997. *Japan Times,* October 18.

"Japan Worries About a Trend: Crime by Chinese." 1997. *New York Times*, March 12.

Kaplan, David. 1996. "Yakuza Laughing All the Way from the Bank." *Asahi Evening News*, February 14.

Katzenstein, Peter J. 1996. *Cultural Norms and National Security: Police and Military in Postwar Japan*. Ithaca, N.Y: Cornell University Press.

Keisatsucho. 1997. *Hanzai Tokeisho, Heisei 8nen no Hanzai* (Criminal statistics in 1996). Tokyo: Keisatsucho.

————. 1998a. *Hanzai Tokei Binran, Heisei 9* (Concise crime statistics handbook, 1997). Tokyo: Keisatsucho.

————. 1998b. *Keisatsu Hakusho 1997* (White paper on police). Tokyo: Keisatsucho.

————. 1999. *Keisatsu Hakusho 1998* (White paper on police). Tokyo: Keisatsucho.

Komai, Hiroshi. 1995. *Migrant Workers in Japan*. London: Kegan Paul International.

Miyamoto, Masao. 1994. *Straitjacket Society: An Insider's Irreverent View of Bureaucratic Japan*. Tokyo: Kodansha International.

Miyawaki, Raisuke. 1997. "Underworld Protected by Discriminatory Administrative Practices: Wage All-Out War against Organized Crime!" *Ronza* (August), U.S. Embassy, Office of Translation Services, October.

Mo, Bangfu. 1997. "Jato to Kyuzyosuru Mitsukosha" (Snakehead and rapid increase in smuggled persons). *Chuo Koron* 5:52–59.

————. 1998. "The Rise of the Chinese Mafia in Japan." *Japan Echo* 25 (1): 44–47.

"Mobster Slaying Tied to Power Struggle." 1997. *Mainichi Daily News*, August 30.

"Money Pipeline Helped Illegals." 1997. *Daily Yomiuri*, March 1.

"More Gangs Aiding Illegals, Police Say." 1997. *Daily Yomiuri*, January 21.

Mori, Hiromi. 1997. *Immigration Policy and Foreign Workers in Japan*. New York: St. Martin's.

Morris-Suzuki, Tessa. 1998. *Re-inventing Japan: Time, Space, Nation*. Armonk, N.Y.: M. E. Sharpe.

"MSA Thwarts Smuggling of Illegal Aliens." 1996. *Daily Yomiuri*, January 26.

Myers, Willard H., III. 1997. "Of Qinshu, Guanxi, and Shetou: The Dynamic Elements of Chinese Irregular Population Movement." In *Human Smuggling: Chinese Migrant Trafficking and the Challenge to America's Immigration Tra-*

dition, edited by Paul J. Smith, 93–133. Washington, D.C.: Center for Strategic and International Studies.

"Nagano's Foreign Workers Sent Home without a Medal." 1998. *Mainichi Daily News*, January 25.

"National Policy Agency and Maritime Safety Agency Hold Discussion to Fortify Smuggling Controls." 1997. Excerpted from *Nihon Keizai Shimbun*, March 5, U.S. Embassy, Office of Translation Services.

"National Police Agency to Dispatch Officials in Effort to Cope with Increasing Mass Smuggling." 1997. Excerpted from *Mainichi Shimbun*, March 5, U.S. Embassy, Office of Translation Services.

"New Antigang Law to Target Gangsters' Offices from Today." 1997. *Japan Times*, October 1.

National Police Agency [NPA]. 1997. *White Paper on Police 1996* (excerpt). Tokyo: Japan Times.

"Oil Spill Crisis Opens Shore to Wave of Chinese." 1997. *Mainichi Daily News*, February 7.

Parker, L. Craig. 1987. *The Japanese Police System Today: An American Perspective*. Tokyo: Kodansha International.

"Police Go International in Crackdown on Snakehead." 1997. *Mainichi Daily News*, September 10.

"Police Target Illegal Foreign Workers." 1998. *Japan Times*, March 13.

"Possible Smuggling Vessel Chased over 3,000 Km." 1998. *Daily Yomiuri*, January 8.

"Profits Keep People-Smuggling Boom Alive." 1997. *Mainichi Daily News*, February 3.

"Recent Violence Destabilizing Tokyo Underworld." 1997. *Mainichi Daily News*, September 9.

Sampson, Robert J., and Janet L. Lauritsen. 1997. "Racial and Ethnic Disparities in Crime and Criminal Justice in the United States." In *Ethnicity, Crime, and Immigration: Comparative and Cross-National Perspectives*, edited by Michael Tonry, 311–74. Chicago: University of Chicago Press.

Sassen, Saskia. 1998 *Globalization and Its Discontents*. New York: New Press.

Schreiber, Mark. 1997. "Juvenile Crime in the 1990s." *Japan Quarterly* 44 (April–June): 78–88.

Sellek, Yoko. 1996. "Female Migrant Workers in Japan: Working for the Yen." *Japan Forum* 8 (2): 159–75.

Shimada, Haruo. 1994. *Japan's Guest Workers: Issues and Public Policies.* Tokyo: University of Tokyo Press.

Smith, Herman W. 1995. *The Myth of Japanese Homogeneity: Social-Ecological Diversity in Education and Socialization.* Commack, N.Y.: Nova Science Publishers.

Smith, Paul J. 1997. "Chinese Migrant Trafficking: A Global Challenge." In *Human Smuggling: Chinese Migrant Trafficking and the Challenge to America's Immigration Tradition,* edited by Paul J. Smith, 1–22. Washington, D.C.: Center for Strategic and International Studies.

"Smugglers Flood Japan with Illegal Boat People." 1997. *Daily Yomiuri,* March 24.

"Smuggling Chinese into Japan Proves a Lucrative Business." 1997. *Japan Times,* February 7.

"Snake Head Gangs Step Up Smuggling of Immigrants." 1997. *Asahi Evening News,* October 5.

"Snakehead Pay Process Uncovered." 1997. *Asahi Evening News,* August 22.

Stevens, Carolyn S. 1997. *On the Margins of Japanese Society: Volunteers and the Welfare of the Urban Underclass.* London: Routledge.

"Stimulant Drug Dealers Expand Operations to Towns near Tokyo." 1996. *Daily Yomiuri,* May 21.

"Succession through a Gun Barrel." 1997. *Asahi Evening News,* September 3.

"Task Force Formed to Nab Foreigners Staying Illegally." 1998. *Daily Yomiuri,* January 27.

"Task Force Set Up to Tackle Wave of Chinese Illegals." 1997. *Daily Yomiuri,* February 26.

Thompson, Kenneth. 1998. *Moral Panics.* London: Routledge.

"3 More Snakeheads Nabbed Overseas." 1997. *Mainichi Daily News,* August 5.

Van Wolferen, Karel. 1993. *The Enigma of Japanese Power.* Tokyo: Charles E. Tuttle.

Yoshino, Kosaku. 1992. *Cultural Nationalism in Contemporary Japan: A Sociological Inquiry.* London: Routledge.

Zhang, Sheldon X., and Mark S. Gaylord. 1996. "Bound for the Golden Mountain: The Social Organization of Chinese Alien Smuggling." *Crime, Law, and Social Change* 25:1–16.

12 ▪▪▪▪▪▪ The Sanctioning
of Unauthorized Migration
and Alien Employment

Mark J. Miller

The apparent proliferation of human trafficking in the post–Cold War period has renewed longstanding concerns over prevention of exploitation of international migrants. This was evidenced by the convening of conferences on human trafficking by the United Nations in January 2000 and by the International Organization for Migration in 1994. The draft program for the Migration Branch of the International Labor Organization circulated in 1999 also reflected the growing concern and suggested that member states were prepared to cooperate to deter human trafficking better.

The post–Cold War flurry of bilateral and multilateral antitrafficking diplomacy in many respects echoed the alarm sounded a century earlier over victimization of international migrants, especially women and children. What was then commonly termed the white slave trade weighed heavily upon Italy-U.S. fin-de-siècle relations, for instance, and constituted a major concern for the Roman Catholic Church, then as now a significant transnational actor affecting domestic and international politics. By 1904, owing to the efforts of activists such as Bishop Scalabrini, the founder of the Scalabrinian order, twelve European states proposed an International Convention for the Suppression of the White Slave Traffic. In

1921, under the auspices of the League of Nations, thirty-three states met to affirm their intent to "secure more completely the suppression of the traffic in women and children" (Kang, 1999). The 1921 convention was revisited in 1949 by the United Nations, which proposed the Convention for the Suppression of the Traffic in Persons and the Exploitation of the Prostitution of Others. Hence, post–Cold War concerns over human trafficking were scarcely unprecedented. Calls for more intensive regulation of international migration have arisen from many quarters and for diverse reasons. State action has long been viewed as a possible antidote to victimization of international migrants.

Post–Cold War concerns over human trafficking arose, however, in a global context very different from those that prevailed in 1904, 1921, or 1949. Precisely how fundamentally different the global or international systems were at the various junctures is problematic. There is no consensus among students of international relations that enables incontrovertible characterization of given periods in global history, as various schools of analysis perceive greater and lesser degrees of continuity and discontinuity. Nevertheless, much scholarship would suggest that post–Cold War concerns over human trafficking arose at a time when the potential for effective countermeasures by states seemed bleak.

Many scholars of international relations and history have written about the decline or retreat of the national state, its hollowing out, demise, and waning (Hobsbawm, 1990; Ruggie, 1993). Others have written about the growing disjuncture between territorially bounded states and transnational socioeconomic and political processes (Sassen, 1988). Still others view the erosion of national states and their capacity to govern and regulate as part and parcel of globalization (Mittelman, 1997). Many analysts of neoliberal cast celebrate the putative decline of the national state as positive and beneficial. If market forces are such that they reduce governments to tinkering around the edges (Cerney, 1995), perhaps it is too much to expect states to take effective steps to prevent exploitation of international migrants. A number of scholars have suggested that governmental regulation of international migration is anomalous in view of the ascendency of neoliberalism in the post–Cold War period. The apparent proliferation of international criminal organizations with the capacity and the financial incentive to smuggle aliens has been interpreted as additional evidence of a broader systemic transformation.

On the subject of human trafficking, however, one does not see smug satisfaction arising from the putative withering away of the state. Even the most resolute intellectual foes of the sovereign state appear alarmed by the depravity and harm caused by human trafficking. For some, the root problem is governmental regulation of international migration. Do away with it and thereby eliminate the need for human smuggling. Visions of a border-free world, however, are at best premature, if not utopian. The most compelling scholarship on the question of the state and international migration has suggested that what states do through their international migration policies still matters a great deal (Weil, 1997). Many have seriously underestimated the importance of states and their policies. In other words, those who look to governments for an antidote to the scourge of human trafficking in post–Cold War global affairs do not necessarily look in vain. States in the transatlantic area most notably have track records on dealing with human trafficking and illegal migration. Interpreting or assessing them, however, is more akin to an art than a science. A major reason for this state of affairs is the difficulty of measuring illegal migration.

When contemplating the possibility of effective governmental countermeasures to human trafficking, a key, and as yet inadequately answered, question arises over the differentiation of human trafficking from illegal migration. Specific national laws and a longstanding international convention specifically proscribe human trafficking. Illegal migration is also by definition proscribed. However, illegal or unauthorized migration often is viewed as benign and has been unofficially tolerated by some governments in the transatlantic area. Human trafficking, on the other hand, is universally condemned because it endangers aliens, harms or degrades them in unacceptable ways. Is unauthorized migration and alien employment distinct from human trafficking, or is there a continuum between them? Is the difference between routine unauthorized employment of aliens and enslavement of alien workers a difference of degree or of kind? Is it possible to condone illegal migration on the one hand and to condemn human trafficking on the other? Is it possible to dismiss state capacity to regulate international migration with one breath and to call for more effective countermeasures against the crime of human trafficking in the next?

States of the transatlantic area have responded to illegal migration and human trafficking. Indeed, as a general rule, they were better equipped to punish wrongdoing by and against aliens at the twilight of the twentieth century than at its dawn. But there have been persistent obstacles to deterrence of unauthorized alien employment by punishing employers, which is central to modern immigration control strategy. By tracing the evolution of employers' sanctions and their implementation through transatlantic comparisons, one can elucidate important dimensions of the politics of international migration and crime. There is a terrible paradox. On the one hand, many transatlantic democracies, most notably the United States, have in fact countenanced illegal employment of aliens. On the other hand, when they better enforce laws against illegal migration, they create conditions conducive to more extreme forms of criminality, including human trafficking. However, exploitation of international migrants preceded regulation of international migration, which arose for many purposes and reasons, some of which were scarcely noble. It is worth recalling, however, that many states were called upon to curb abusive or exploitative employment of immigrants more than a century ago. Bilateral and multilateral efforts to that end commenced back then.

The Development of Employer Sanctions

Imperial Germany began to organize recruitment of foreigners for employment in agriculture. Eventually, bilateral accords were signed to regulate seasonal agricultural employment. Some foreign workers, however, violated the terms of their entry. Deportation was the punishment. Yet employers who hired the unauthorized foreign workers were also culpable. By the interwar period, when international migration in Europe generally ebbed, German labor law included sanctions for unauthorized employment of aliens (Miller, 1986).

During World War II, the United States resumed recruitment of Mexicans for temporary employment, mainly in southwestern agriculture. A U.S.-Mexican accord was to regulate the recruitment and employment of the Mexican workers. Justified by a wartime manpower emergency, what came to be known as the Bracero Program brought some 5 million Mexicans to the United States between 1942 and 1964. Mexico became concerned with alleged abuse and mistreatment of its citizens in Texas. It discouraged Mexicans from working there and called upon the United States to adopt laws that would punish employers who employed unauthorized Mexican workers. By 1952, both houses of the U.S. Congress had adopted immigration bills that included an employer sanctions provision. However, Lyndon Baines Johnson became the chairman of the House-Senate conference committee appointed to reconcile the two bills. He appears to have single-handedly written what came to be known as the Texas Proviso to the Immigration and Naturalization Act of 1952. The proviso was interpreted as exempting employers from punishment for unauthorized employment of aliens. Hence it was that unauthorized employment of aliens was not unlawful in the United States until November 1986, when the Immigration Reform and Control Act (IRCA) took effect (Miller, 1989).

In Western Europe, many states adopted laws punishing unlawful employment of aliens in the 1970s. In several instances, the adoption of employer sanctions was preceded by laws punishing trafficking or smuggling of aliens. In France, for instance, several decades of postwar toleration, even tacit approval, of illegal immigration gave way to mounting concern. Outrage over migrant housing and employment conditions grew. Indifference to exploitation of foreigners and the annual toll of deaths and work accidents gave way to a *prise de conscience*. The French government embarked upon a long effort to implement its immigration laws and to curb illegal migration.

By 1976, it established an interministry agency to monitor the enforcement of laws to prevent illegal migration, illegal employment of aliens, and worker trafficking (Miller, 1994). At roughly the same juncture, Germany and the Netherlands adopted similar measures. German measures differed from French steps in that they were directed against illegal employment in general, which subsumed illegal employment and trafficking of aliens. By 1990, France's enforcement strategy would change and mirror the German approach. Illegal employment was a key dimension of underground economies. Most transgressors were citizens, but unauthorized employment of aliens was considered a crime and, when aggravated by exploitation of alien employees, a serious offense punishable by heavy fines and the possibility of imprisonment.

Not all Western European states adopted employer sanctions in the 1970s. The United Kingdom considered but did not adopt employer sanctions in the 1970s in part because illegal migration was not viewed as particularly alarming or prevalent. This would change in the 1990s. Western European experiences with adoption and enforcement of laws punishing unauthorized employment of aliens informed the U.S. debate over adoption of similar deterrent measures in the 1980s. The heated debate over the wisdom of laws punishing illegal employment of aliens in the United States contrasted sharply with a broad political consensus in support of such measures in Western Europe.

A number of problems in the enforcement of employer sanctions in Western Europe were apparent prior to adoption of IRCA in 1986. To summarize, too few enforcement personnel and budget resources were committed. Courts often did not regard illegal employment of aliens as constituting a serious offense and judged employers accordingly. Employers adapted to countermeasures by going further underground. Overall assessments of the deterrent effect of employer sanctions were mixed. Most Europeans seemed to favor more aggressive enforcement of such laws. A pattern of incremental adjustment of laws and enforcement strategies emerged. Slowly, many European states built capacities to punish employers, but progress was painstaking and expensive.

Meanwhile, across the Atlantic, the United States debated the wisdom of employer sanctions. The Select Commission on Immigration and Refugee Policy appointed by President Carter and headed by Father Theodore Hesburgh recommended the adoption of employer sanctions and of a counterfeit-resistant employment eligibility document (Select Commission on Immigration and Refugee Policy, 1981). It was widely assumed by advocates of employer sanctions that they could only be effective if there was a reliable way to verify authorization for employment. However, Congress did not mandate implementation of a counterfeit-resistant employment eligibility document in IRCA. It did make knowing employment of unauthorized aliens a punishable offense. Employers were henceforth required to fill out an I-9 form to certify employment eligibility for all new hires. But many documents could be used to prove eligibility, including some that were easily forged. The U.S. president was empowered, however, to implement a secure employment eligibility document if false documentation led to widespread circumvention of the intent of the 1986 law.

Active enforcement of the employer sanctions provision of IRCA began after a legalization period and a period of education about the new law. Evaluation of the effectiveness of the 1986 law is difficult, but most would concur that it has had a less-than-hoped-for impact. It is commonplace to hear U.S. employer sanctions enforcement dismissed as a failure. Yet there is enforcement, and fines are levied. Indeed, many employers have complained about enforcement actions. They often attempt to bring political pressure to bear on the Immigration and Naturalization Service (INS) agents who do the bulk of enforcement to get them to desist. Controversies sparked by INS enforcement raids led to a temporary discontinuation of enforcement activities in 1998.

A number of factors have weakened enforcement of employer sanctions in the United States. Primary responsibility for enforcement lies with the Immigration and Naturalization Service. Historically, the INS was a weak and poorly administered agency, underfunded and mismanaged. This pattern was not accidental: a number of scholars have suggested that members of the U.S. Congress beholden to special interests, particularly those of labor-intensive agriculture, consistently strove to weaken and emasculate the INS (Calavita, 1992). It was only in the 1990s under the Clinton administration that the INS began to receive long-needed appropriations enabling it to hire additional personnel and to modernize its operations. The Clinton administration also brought in by far the most professionally competent senior administrative team in history. The infusion of money, personnel, and superior management transformed a long-lackluster agency, but the legacy of decades of neglect and underfunding could not be quickly erased, and monumental problems and issues of managing U.S. immigration continued. This hampered employer sanctions enforcement.

The INS has many missions. This multiplicity has led to calls for reorganization such as a proposal by the Commission on Immigration Reform. Despite major increases in personnel and budgets, enforcement of employer sanctions has been only one of several priorities. In the 1990s, the INS focused on improving border enforcement and the removal of criminal aliens, more so than enforcement of employer sanctions. The number of enforcement agent hours dedicated to enforcement of the law against illegal employment of aliens was insufficient. Moreover, INS agents were not well prepared by background for workplace inspections. U.S. Department of Labor inspectors were better prepared by background to carry out workplace inspections, but it took several years for a Memorandum of Understanding to be worked out between the INS and USDOL to cooperate in enforcement of employer sanctions.

As in Western Europe, enforcement was targeted to strike at the worst forms of illegal alien employment and to maximize the educational effect of the limited capability of the U.S. government to enforce the 1986 law. This strategy made sense. One result was a strategy to target certain industries known to rely heavily on illegally employed aliens. In 1997 and 1998, an INS enforcement team focused on I-9 violations in meatpacking industries, especially poultry-processing plants. These enforcement actions resulted in hefty fines being levied and the detention and repatriation of hundreds of unauthorized alien workers. However, many of the fines were negotiated down or forgiven, and affected employers sought to bring political pressure to bear to stop INS enforcement actions that disrupted production; an extremely costly matter in meatpacking industries.

Employer sanctions enforcement in the United States proceeded despite enormous handicaps. Authorities were required to notify agricultural employers several days prior to inspection visits. A variety of documents were permitted to be used to establish employment authorization through completion of the I-9 form. This resulted in widespread counterfeiting of documents and subsequent circumvention of the law (General Accounting Office, 1999).

In the mid-1990s, the INS began to experiment with a system to verify employment eligibility prior to hiring. Employers voluntarily communicated I-9 form information for prospective or new hires to an office in Washington, D.C., which then verified that the documents supplied, such as alien employment authorization numbers, were authentic. However, only non-U.S. citizen employment eligibility was verified. The documents of individuals claiming to be U.S. citizens were not verified. All an unauthorized alien had to do was to borrow bona fide documents or purchase forged ones and claim that he or she was a U.S. citizen. Firms would duly record the corresponding information on I-9 forms, which could be inspected. But alien workers falsely claiming U.S. citizenship could circumvent the verification system in this way.

In a number of cases, the INS and firms agreed to cooperate in order to preclude "disruptive" INS site visits or "raids." Firms promised to participate voluntarily in the employment eligibility verification system described above and to permit inspections of their I-9 forms in return for a cessation of raids. Although constituting a sign of progress in employer sanctions enforcement, which requires the active cooperation of firms, such arrangements ran the risk of providing an illusion of compliance with immigration law while circumvention continued. Only the implementation of a counterfeit-resistant employment eligibility document such as envisaged by Father Hesburgh and the Select Commission on Immigration and Refugee Policy appeared capable of rendering U.S. employer sanctions enforcement more credible. But the implementation of an employment eligibility document would be expensive, perhaps costing 5 billion dollars, and there was much political resistance to it led by the American Civil Liberties Union and several employer groups. Even several unions affiliated with the AFL-CIO, perhaps the staunchest supporter of adoption of employer sanctions in the 1970s and 1980s, called for rescinding employer sanctions in 2000. This ambivalence reflected the growing weight of illegal immigrants in U.S. unions, especially in industries experiencing gains in union membership.

A reenactment of U.S. debates over employer sanctions took place during the heated run-up to the adoption of the 1996 immigration law, widely perceived as anti-immigrant and restrictionist in character. The 1996 law stripped many legal resident aliens of U.S. government benefits, some of which were later restored, and increased the capacity of the U.S. government to detain and remove criminal aliens and asylum seekers denied recognition as refugees. Most significant, however, the 1996 law did not authorize the counterfeit-resistant employment eligibility document or additional hiring of enforcement personnel for employer sanctions enforcement. Indeed, the U.S. Congress legislated additional barriers to effective enforcement of the 1986 law.

Employer sanctions enforcement in Western Europe in the 1990s was more credible than in the United States but still appeared insufficient. In France, periodic recourse to legalization policy attested to the continuation of a certain but unknown level of illegal immigration. Legal changes in the 1990s adversely affected legally resident aliens in France, making it more difficult for them to marry or to reunite with their families. These "reforms" also made it easier for French authorities to deport criminal aliens. Critics suggested that the policy and legal changes "manufactured" illegality of status. When the Socialist Party returned to power in 1997, it largely embraced this critique and authorized legalization for certain classes of aliens adversely affected by the laws and policies implemented by Conservatives. About eighty thousand aliens were legalized.

By the 1990s, French government statistics on enforcement of laws against illegal employment revealed that most infractions concerned French citizens, not aliens (Délégation interministérielle, 1998). Noncitizen employers, however, were disproportionally sanctioned for illegal employment of aliens and were also disproportionally punished. Enforcement was evident in the fines and prison terms meted out. However, some alien employers simply disappeared and thereby eluded fines and prison terms. Enforcement of employer sanctions, among other measures, made it quite difficult for many who aspired to go to France, if need be illegally, to realize their project. Compared with the 1950s and 1960s, France had a much more credible arsenal of laws and policies to deter illegal alien employment. Nevertheless, much unauthorized employment persisted, as did cases of extreme exploitation and trafficking. Kurds arriving in Italy paid substantial fees to be smuggled across French territory into Germany. France was by no means hermetically sealed, but it did mount serious efforts to detect and discourage such flows, as attested to by the stopping of four thousand Iraqi citizens in the first ten months of 1997 alone (Abdulkarim, 1998).

As in the United States, the availability of sophisticated fraudulent documents hampered West European efforts to enforce laws against illegal employment of aliens and worker trafficking. Dutch authorities interviewed in 1998 reported a growing problem of aliens using forged European Union passports to circumvent immigration and employment restrictions. Despite reinforcement of German enforcement personnel, illegal alien employment remained widespread in certain German industries, such as construction.

Barriers to effective deterrence of illegal alien employment in Western Europe appeared more surmountable than in the United States, because of a broad political consensus in support of policies to reduce illegal immigration. Western European political parties and political elites appeared more responsive to public opinion than their American counterparts despite the general perception that West European enforcement efforts were insufficient. In Germany, the legacy of the Nazi period weighed on enforcement efforts. Authorities cringed at anything remotely resembling a police state. Nevertheless, personal identification was required of all citizens and aliens, which in no way seemed to diminish civil liberties. In the 1990s, the Netherlands implemented a new universal identification requirement for Dutch citizens and resident aliens alike. This was not done for immigration control purposes, but it suggested that a more reliable way of verifying identities and therefore eligibility for employment or receipt of social services could be implemented without damage to civil liberties.

The Need for Balanced Assessments of Governmental Policies

Viewed against the checkered history of efforts to curb illegal alien employment in the transatlantic area, growing concern over human trafficking in the post–Cold War period can be put in perspective. First, human trafficking is a longstanding concern. States were called upon to curb it at least a century before the post–Cold War period. The laws and regulations pertaining to immigration that evolved over the past century were intended in part to prevent mistreatment of immigrants. Organized labor in particular had a major stake in the prevention of immigration, which resulted in immigrants being vulnerable to exploitation by unscrupulous employers or criminals. Fears over immigrants undercutting wages and working conditions or being used by employers to break strikes or weaken union organization efforts frequently led to restrictive stances, at times manifestly tinged with racist overtones. Concurrently, homeland governments and various social actors such as religious organizations also sought to reduce abuse of immigrants.

It was clear long ago that not all international migration was beneficial to all concerned. Sometimes, it resulted in manifest injustice, when immigrants were horribly exploited or subjected to unacceptable transportation, living, or employment conditions. Yes, these immigrants often voluntarily agreed to subject themselves to such treatment in a bid to better their lives or those of loved ones. But there is a limit beyond which such volition becomes socially and politically unacceptable. In other instances, immigrants were duped or coerced into such conditions. States were right back then to attempt to curb abuse of immigrants just as states should attempt to curb human trafficking in the post–Cold War period.

Immigration policies, in other words, are not necessarily evil or oppressive, contrary to the impression created by some public and scholarly discourse in the post–Cold War period. Antistatist bias has marred much public and scholarly discourse. While it is outside the scope of the present chapter to elaborate, there has been a troubling tendency to ignore beneficial effects and potentials of immigration policies in the rush to castigate them as draconian and restrictive. This overview of employer sanctions enforcement suggests that such characterizations are woefully misplaced. A strong case could be made that transatlantic democracies should do much more than they have to curb illegal migration and illegal employment of immigrants.

But then there's the paradox. Although understanding of illegal immigration dynamics is fragmentary, there are ample reasons to suspect that efforts to curb and punish illegal entry and illegal alien employment have created greater incentives for criminals to organize illegal entry and employment, which results in greater victimization of aliens. This appears to be the inevitable by-product of efforts to regulate migration. Much, indeed too much, has been made of untoward or perverse effects of efforts to prevent unlawful migration. In general, these effects have been anticipated, but states strive nevertheless to make their public policies credible and authoritative. The result sometimes is that the medicine makes the illness worse. When such dynamics become manifest, a change of public policy appears advisable.

However, it is scarcely self-evident, for instance, at what level measures to curb illegal migration foster human trafficking. In practice, there is a gradation between smuggling and illegal employment of aliens that is considered less harmful than trafficking or enslavement of immigrants. Other proposed remedies are problematic in their own right. For instance, temporary foreign worker admissions policies are often advocated as a pragmatic and humane alternative to clamping down on illegal immigration and thereby generating incentives for worker trafficking. Transatlantic immigration history, however, is replete with well-known patterns of temporary foreign worker exploitation and abuse. The contingent legal rights of temporary foreign workers render these workers vulnerable, and temporary foreign worker policy often appears to foster illegal migration, not diminish it (Miller and Martin, 1982).

Optimally, transatlantic democracies will authorize generous levels of legal immigration that accord legally admitted resident aliens equality of rights, save perhaps in the realm of voting and standing for public office.

Legal immigration systems best protect immigrants because they confer democratic legitimacy to immigrant settlement and immigration transpires within the rule of law. All illegal immigration tends to weaken or erode legal immigration frameworks, which makes patterns of tacit approval of illegal migration deplorable. Moreover, past periods of benign neglect of illegal migration and of large-scale seasonal foreign worker or guest worker policies created enduring legacies.

Employers in heavily affected industries, typically labor-intensive agriculture, construction, hotels and restaurants, domestic services, and garments, became dependent on low-wage, often servile labor. Such dependency did not arise from dual labor markets but from historical processes in which state policies actively or passively contributed to perceived employer dependency on foreign labor. An erosion of labor standards and wages often resulted, making employment in the sector steadily less attractive to citizen workers or resident aliens. When legal recruitment opportunities were curbed, as in 1964 in the United States or 1973 and 1974 in Germany and France, respectively, the economic sectors that had become heavily dependent on legally admitted foreign workers would continue to have recourse to illegally hired foreign workers. Efforts to curb illegal employment practices therefore often attempted to alter enrooted behavior. Moreover, in labor-intensive agriculture, decisions to plant certain crops and land values reflected presumptions concerning the availability of abundant low-wage labor. These legacies became major obstacles to late-twentieth-century efforts to curb illegal migration and unauthorized employment of aliens.

Legacies of past policies, however, do not suffice to explain illegal immigration or its more problematic and reprehensible subset—human trafficking. Global developments examined elsewhere in this volume have rendered states in the transatlantic area more vulnerable and permeable to human trafficking. Transatlantic states that have made the least progress toward development of credible policies to deter illegal migration in general are probably the most vulnerable to human trafficking in the post–Cold War era. Italy would appear to be much more at risk than the Netherlands.

The post–Cold War specter of human trafficking has already led to renewed calls for more effective immigration control policies and harsher penalties for the perpetrators of such crimes. Perhaps public revulsion over enslavement and trafficking will result in more effective governmental counteraction. However, it is crystal clear that effective countermeasures to human trafficking will require the elaboration of a comprehensive approach to regulation of international migration that so far has proven elusive.

One can justifiably fear that transatlantic democracies will become inured to human trafficking and become as complacent about it as some have been toward illegal immigration. Many pundits and scholars have suggested, after all, that states have become a residual variable and that they can do little to alter the march of history dictated by deep structural forces and globalization. Mercifully, the obituaries for sovereign states are premature, and post–Cold War visions of democratization and growing respect for human rights will demand a coordinated effort to curb human trafficking. Could concern over human trafficking combined with growing concerns over migration and security provide the heretofore deficient political will to make immigration laws more credible?

Toward More Credible Governmental Responses to Human Trafficking

Laws matter: there is a difference between societies that do and do not sanction employers for the unauthorized employment of aliens. Societies without employer sanctions laws, such as the United States before 1986, tolerate and encourage illegal immigration. The vast majority of states attempt to regulate international migration, and they view unauthorized migration with varying degrees of concern.

The starting point, then, is incrimination of unauthorized employment of aliens, using two distinct but related strategies:

1. Employer sanctions should be part of a broader campaign against illegal work that usually principally involves citizens rather than noncitizens.
2. Employer sanctions should be a component of a broad strategy to deter and punish illegal migration.

By focusing on illegal alien employment as a particularly socially harmful aspect of illegal employment in general, governments can keep distinct legal immigrants and immigration, and illegal immigration. Moreover, enforcement of employer sanctions becomes labor law enforcement in addition to immigration law enforcement.

The wisdom of such an approach became apparent in the French case between 1972 and 1984. Part of the French enforcement problem arose from confusion over terms such as *illegal employment* and *clandestines,* thus mixing legal immigration and illegality. It was only in the 1990s with substitution of *dissimulated* for *clandestine* and *illegal employment* that a full and precise clarification and distinction was achieved. Hence, the legal text incriminating unauthorized alien employment should make clear that such employment is a particularly harmful instance of a broader class of infractions involving illegal employment.

There is a tendency for lawmakers to underscore the priority they attach to deterring illegal immigration by increasing fines, jail terms, and other punishments for illegal employment of aliens. However, if those punishments are viewed as too severe by labor inspectors and court systems, increasing penalties can be counterproductive. Ideally, an employer sanctions law would provide prosecutors with the flexibility to mete out heavy punishments against employers who profit enormously from illegal employment of aliens, including jail time for recurrent and worse offenders. However, the law should be flexible enough to enable prosecutors to prevent employers from viewing the fines simply as the cost of doing business. The law punishing illegal employment in Germany was amended to give courts the discretion to increase fines enormously in such cases.

Progressive fines and possible jail terms for illegal alien employment should be complemented by further penalties that enable authorities to confiscate goods, machines, vehicles, and properties used for recurrent or more severe forms of illegal alien employment, specifically worker trafficking and human smuggling. Moreover, wayward employers should be barred from bidding for public contracts. Employer sanctions should also apply to beneficiaries of illegal employment practices by subcontractors. Finally, governments should be empowered to disclose and publicize actions taken to punish wayward employers.

Illegal alien employment often involves several infractions against labor laws, immigration laws, and social security regulations. In such instances, multiple punishments may be appropriate. However, prevalent legal doctrine holds that one can only be punished once for an offense, so sanctions laws must make clear that governments are empowered to pursue way-ward employers for numerous infractions arising from illegal employment.

Employer sanctions laws should require all employers to record or transmit verifiable information concerning the eligibility of a prospective employee for employment before the onset of employment, with specific and appropriate punishments for failure to do so. Moreover, there should be stiff penalties for usage of fraudulent documents or fraudulent use of bona fide documents and for the manufacture and sale of fraudulent doc-uments. Authorities charged with verification of prospective employee el-igibility for employment should be empowered to cross-check their data for compliance with related laws and regulations such as social security requirements. These legal innovations presuppose a reasonably secure system for identification of persons and for verifying their identities.

Legal innovation alone will not suffice. Best practices also require ef-fective enforcement of employer sanctions. The simultaneous, multiple violations that often characterize illegal alien employment necessitate interagency coordination and cooperation. Minimally, ministries (or de-partments) of Labor, Justice, and Immigration and social security agen-cies need to establish interagency structures to coordinate and facilitate enforcement of laws that punish illegal alien employment extending from the national level to administrative subunits to the local level.

The interagency structures should be charged with reporting on en-forcement of laws against illegal employment, especially illegal employ-ment of aliens, as well as with training and public information functions. Enforcement personnel from various services charged with enforcement of immigration, labor, and social security laws often require training to alert them to the law's enforcement by other agencies and the social harm arising from illegal employment practices. The mandate of the interagency structures should also include awareness building of the harm done by il-legal employment in critical audiences, such as judges and prosecutors, and the general public.

No amount of interagency coordination will suffice if inadequate re-sources are devoted to the enforcement of laws against illegal alien em-ployment. It may be necessary, as in France, to develop a body of en-forcement agents specializing in the enforcement of laws against illegal employment of aliens. One of the major functions of the interagency structures should be to monitor and ensure that sufficient enforcement agents are devoted to the enforcement of laws against illegal alien employment. Credible and effective administrative systems must be put in place for recovery of fines, and administrative or court discretion to reduce or forgive fines should be limited and closely monitored by the interagency structures.

The employment of illegal aliens is primarily a labor market offense, and thus labor and related agencies should take the lead in enforcement. The roles of various police services and immigration agencies should be secondary but complementary. For example, police involvement may be required to arrest and possibly incarcerate certain employers, and immigration service agents may be required to verify documents. The growing role of organized crime in human trafficking increasingly necessitates deeper involvement of police agencies, security and intelligence agencies, and, in extreme instances, militaries in coordinated enforcement actions.

Concepts of security have evolved significantly in the post–Cold War period. Broader strategies against illegal immigration involve much more than enforcement of laws against illegal employment of aliens. However, credible enforcement of employer sanctions remains an irreplaceable component of any coherent strategy to deter illegal immigration.

Best practices also require the involvement of civil society in the enforcement of laws against illegal employment of aliens. All laws have a symbolic function; their goal is voluntary compliance. Involvement of social actors, especially trade unions and employer groups, in securing voluntary compliance and aiding in the detection and punishment of noncompliance is critical. History and institutional frameworks endow governments with quite different capacities to mobilize civil society to help implement laws against illegal employment of aliens.

Germany's pattern of social partner involvement in industrial relations appears advantageous. France's industrial relations are less institutionalized, but France has made progress toward mobilizing social forces to better ensure compliance with laws against illegal work, such as the recent agreements signed between the French Ministry of Labor and various professional groups that allow businesses injured by competitors who employ illegal workers to seek legal redress.

Prevention of illegal alien employment, like any form of illegal employment, is preferable to its repression. The shift to a strategy to reduce incentives for illegal hiring of aliens makes a great deal of sense but must be cognizant of mounting evidence of coercive worker trafficking and virtual enslavement of human beings.

Perceptions of government capacities to control international migration and prevent illegal immigration affect perceptions of legitimacy, identity, and security. Support for parties and governments, especially in Europe, can crumble or mushroom over immigration issues. The politicization of immigration questions makes mobilization of civil society in support of effective enforcement of employer sanctions a democratic imperative. This appears better and more widely understood in Western Europe than in the United States. However, understanding of the high stakes involved in constructing credible strategies of immigration control in democratic settings is generally lacking even among political elites, including foreign policy and security communities.

REFERENCES

Abdulkarim, Amir. 1998. "Les Kurdes irakiens en Europe, nouveaux 'Boat People.'" *Revue Européenne des Migrations Internationales* 14 (1): 263–75.

Calavita, Kitty. 1992. *Inside the State*. New York: Routledge.

Cerney, Philip G. 1995. "Globalization and the Changing Logic of Collective Action." *International Organization* 49 (4): 595–625.

Délégation interministérielle à la lutte contre le travail illégal. 1998. *La lutte contre le travail illégal*. Paris: La documentation francaise.

General Accounting Office. 1999. "Illegal Aliens: Fraudulent Documents Undermining the Effectiveness of the Employment Verification System." July T-GGD/HEH-99-175.

Hobsbawm, Eric J. 1990. *Nations and Nationalism since 1780*. Cambridge: Cambridge University Press.

Kang, Jool Nie. 1999. "Trafficking in Women: The Challenge in Global Governance." Honors thesis, University of Delaware.

Miller, Mark J. 1986. *Employer Sanctions in Western Europe*. New York: Center for Migration Studies.

———. 1989. "Continuities and Discontinuities in Immigration Reform in Industrial Democracies: The Case of the Immigration Reform and Control Act of 1986." In *Immigration in Western Democracies—The United States and Western Europe*, edited by Han Entzinger and Jack Carter. Greenwich, Conn.: JAI Press.

———. 1994. "Towards Understanding State Capacity to Prevent Unwanted Migration: Employer Sanctions Enforcement in France, 1975–1990." *West European Politics* 17 (2): 140–67.

Miller, Mark J., and Philip Martin. 1982. *Administering Foreign-Worker Programs.* Lexington, Mass.: D. C. Heath and Co.

Mittelman, James H., ed. 1997. *Globalization: Critical Reflections.* Boulder, Colo.: Lynne Rienner.

Ruggie, John G. 1993. "Territoriality and Beyond: Problematizing Modernity in International Relations." *International Organization* 47 (1): 139–74.

Sassen, Saskia. 1988. *The Mobility of Labor and Capital.* Cambridge: Cambridge University Press.

Select Commission on Immigration and Refugee Policy. 1981. *U.S. Immigration Policy and the National Interest.* Washington, D.C.: U.S. Government Printing Office.

Weil, Patrick. 1997. *The State Matters: Immigration Control in Developed Countries.* New York: United Nations.

13........Economic Globalization,

Human Smuggling,

and Global Governance

Rey Koslowski

The rapidly advancing information, communication, and transportation technologies that are driving economic globalization are also propelling international migration and fostering transnational crime. These two aspects of globalization have become intertwined. The international migration of criminals has become a means of expanding local and national criminal organizations into transnational operations, and human smuggling is a form of transnationally organized crime that increases illegal migration.

Although migration scholars might have reservations about analyzing human smuggling because of potentially inflammatory linkages of immigrants to crime, a sober assessment of these linkages is necessary, for despite the lack of attention to human smuggling in the migration literature, policymakers are already drawing their own conclusions about such linkages and are beginning to act upon them. The Group of Eight (G-8) noted after its May 1998 summit, "Globalisation has been accompanied by a dramatic increase in transnational crime . . . [that] takes many forms, including . . . smuggling of human beings (G-8, 1998b)."

American and European foreign policymakers are increasingly placing international migration together with transnational crime in new institutional frameworks set up to deal with the emerging challenges of the post–

Cold War world. As a former U.S. State Department official in the recently established Global Affairs division put it, "President Clinton directed the administration several years ago to develop a strategy to combat a threat which is a criminal threat, an immigration threat, a human rights threat, and a national security threat, the threat posed by transnational migrant smuggling, alien smuggling, trafficking in persons" (Winer, 1997). These new policy-making organs are being focused on the problem of human smuggling as states cooperate within fora such as the European Union (EU) and the G-8 as well as within the United Nations and the International Organization for Migration (IOM).

Ironically, as states tighten border controls and asylum policies, they have indirectly prompted more people to get into the smuggling business—increased restriction drives up the costs of illegal migration and increases the profits of human smuggling. Now states are stepping up cooperation to combat transnational criminal organizations and human smuggling in particular. Human smuggling, however, is often "crime that is organized" (Finckenauer and Waring, 1996) rather than a new line of business of easily identifiable traditional criminal organizations. International cooperation to combat human smuggling may provide another demonstration of the challenges posed to states, and international organizations composed of states, when they confront the side effects of globalization.

The argument proceeds in three steps. The first section examines human smuggling in the larger context of the processes of economic globalization that have facilitated both increasing international migration and transnational crime. The second section examines state and multilateral responses to human smuggling as well as the linking of migration and crime in the policy-making process. The third section considers some of the policy dilemmas involved in combating human smuggling, including the difficulties of targeting migrant traffickers and the unintended consequences of tougher border controls.

Economic Globalization, International Migration, and Transnational Crime

Economic globalization has largely been driven by the collapse of Communism and the spread of capitalist economic systems throughout the so-called Second and Third Worlds, combined with the fundamental technological changes that have drastically reduced the cost of communication and transportation (Korbin, 1997). For example, since 1945, average ocean freight costs have dropped 50 percent, air transport by 80 percent, and transatlantic telephone calls by 99 percent (Auguste, 1998: 16). This globalization of economic activities facilitates both increasing international migration and the expansion of transnational crime. Increasing international migration and expanding transnational crime do not simply share a common accelerator in economic globalization and technological change; the very processes of globalization have intensified the very real intersection of these two phenomena.

According to neoclassical economic theory, the liberalization of international capital markets, which has become the hallmark of globalization, should decrease migration (see, e.g., Weintraub and Stolp, 1987; Layard et al., 1992: chap. 1). Recent trends, however, have not always followed neoclassical logic. For example, large-scale direct investment by U.S. companies in South Korea, Taiwan, and China was accompanied by an increase in migration from these East Asian countries to the United States rather than a decrease (Sassen, 1988). Indeed, increased investment in developing countries and increased trade often have the reverse effect than that expected, at least for the immediate term, as has been the case with illegal migration to the United States from Mexico (Massey, 1998). While increased investment may increase the number of available jobs and decrease the wage differentials among developed and developing countries, surplus disposable income often becomes "migration capital" used to pay for international travel and to pay for smugglers who increase the chance of a successful border crossing (Kyle, 1996; Spener, this volume, Chap. 5; Singer and Massey, 1998). Similarly, a large proportion of the Chinese who are smuggled into the United States are from Fujian Province, a coastal province with one of China's fastest-growing regional economies (Liang and Ye, this volume, Chap. 7). Moreover, smuggled Chinese are usually from the middle-class families that can afford stiff cash down payments (approximately fifteen hundred dollars) required by smugglers before embarkation (Hessler, 2000).

The rapidly advancing information, communication, and transportation technologies that are driving economic globalization and propelling international migration are also fostering transnational crime. There is a long tradition of understanding organized crime in terms of models derived from generalized depictions of the Sicilian Mafia in which criminal hierarchies are dominated by "godfathers" who order foot soldiers to do their bidding. When such criminal activity takes place in two or more countries, it is then considered transnational in nature. In contrast, some criminologists have argued that criminals are more like highly competitive entrepreneurs whose organizations, to the extent that they exist at all, are more like informal trade associations and old boys' networks (Reuter, 1983). Between these two positions lies the depiction of criminal organizations as underground governments, rather than armies, and as illicit corporations competing in various markets, rather than individual entrepreneurs with informal ties (Naylor, 1995).

In a sense, transnational organized crime groups are not all that different from transnational corporations (TNCs) in that they both run border-transcending economic enterprises—the major differences are that TNCs' business is legal whereas organized crime groups deal in illegal trade (drugs, stolen goods, prostitution) and use illegal means (extortion, theft, money laundering, murder) to realize their profits (Williams, 1995). Just as technological change has globalized production and markets of legal goods and services, it has a similar impact on illegal production and markets. As Susan Strange points out, local and national crime organizations have expanded to global operations; the expansion is often a response to expanding markets for illegal commodities; increasing revenue has facilitated favorable treatment by states (i.e., corruption); and the globalization of financial markets and services facilitates the financing of illegal trade and the laundering of ill-gotten gains into "legitimate" businesses and investment instruments (Strange, 1996: 110–21).

Despite the historical legacy of human smuggling and the recent surge in cases, migration scholars have been slow to analyze the phenomenon. Part of the problem is that migrants are all too often implicitly or explicitly identified with criminality in political rhetoric when in fact migrants are more likely to be the victims than the perpetrators of crime (see Miller, 1998). For example, some conservative members of the U.S. Congress are quick to point out that undocumented aliens are criminals by virtue of their illegal crossing or visa overstay, and certain European politicians are quick to attribute the spread of organized criminal activity in Western Europe to increasing migration from the former Soviet Union. Indeed, Helmut Kohl and Gerhard Schroeder may have disagreed on citizenship and migration policy during Germany's 1998 federal election campaign; however, they both agreed on fighting crime by deporting foreigners who are convicted of crimes. In the face of the exaggeration of immigrant criminality and the propensity of politicians to allow immigrants to become scapegoats in the heat of election campaigns, it is tempting for migration scholars to overcompensate for such knee-jerk reactions by avoiding any discussion of crime among migrants.

Just as it is preposterous to assert that all Sicilian immigrants in the United States are members of the Mafia, it is also foolish to contend that none are. The fact of the matter is that local criminal organizations may expand their operations abroad through emigration and recruitment within migrant communities abroad and the transportation and communications revolutions are facilitating this process. For example, the numbers of foreign-born Russians in New York City and Berlin who are involved in criminal organizations with origins in Moscow may be rather small; however, their activity has expanded the scope of Russian organized crime beyond Russia's borders. Some members of these organizations may be native-born Americans and Germans, but many are indeed migrants from Russia (Finckenauer and Waring, 1996; Finckenauer, this volume, Chap. 6).

It is important to note that the expansion of local gangs to become border-spanning transnational criminal organizations through the migration of members is not always a matter of migration to the advanced industrialized countries of the West from former Communist countries in the East and developing countries of the south. For example, stepped-up enforcement of the U.S. policy of deporting noncitizens who have completed their prison sentences has inadvertently led to the expansion of Los Angeles gangs to El Salvador. Having fled the Salvadoran civil war as children in the 1980s, these gang members often speak very little Spanish. They have been deported to "home" countries (often without notification) in which they no longer have close family members or job prospects in an economy recovering from years of conflict. Without jobs, but with considerable survival skills learned on the streets of Los Angeles and in U.S. prisons, many deportees turn to crime in an environment characterized by relatively weak civilian law enforcement (Rohter, 1997). Los Angeles gangsters recruit local Salvadoran youth into the American gang culture and maintain ties with their associates from back in the United States, often returning to the United States illegally. For example, a gang started by Salvadoran immigrants in Los Angeles, Mara Salvatrucha, has become pan-Hispanic in membership and has established branches in Seattle, San Francisco, Washington, and El Salvador (Sontag, 1997).

Finally, it is necessary to point out that members of human smuggling organizations in the receiving countries and the employers who illegally hire the smuggled labor are often themselves migrants. For example, most "enforcers" who collect debts from illegal Chinese workers in New York or the owners of the sweatshops or restaurants who employ them are from the Chinese immigrant community (Chin, this volume, Chap. 8; Kwong, this volume. Chap. 9). Similarly, immigrants owned and operated the Houston-based "transportation companies" that moved smuggled Mexicans and Central Americans to Washington, D.C. (Moreno, 1998). It is believed that the trafficking of central and Eastern European women to Western Europe is primarily controlled by Russian and Ukrainian organizations; the women are then forced into prostitution by various local gangsters, many of whom are not nationals of the countries in which they operate. For example, Viennese police arrested Turkish and Yugoslav gangsters holding Hungarian and Slovak women, and, in a major sweep of twenty locations in North Rhine Westphalia, twenty-four women from Eastern Europe were freed from German, Albanian, Turkish, and Italian gangsters (IOM, 1998a).

Human smuggling is a form of transnationally organized crime that increases illegal migration, and the international migration of criminals has become a means of expanding local and national criminal organizations into transnational operations. In confronting globalization, policymakers have implicitly, if not explicitly, linked migration and crime, particularly with their focus on human smuggling. Although such linkage has at times been overdrawn for political reasons, the reality of human smuggling by criminal organizations and transnational criminal activity among migrants, not the least being the smuggling and employment of illegal migrants, helps one understand the resonance of such linkages among the publics to which politicians appeal.

Policymaking and Multilateral Cooperation

Policymakers have linked migration and crime not only in their rhetoric but also in their actions. Policy making on this issue has evolved in three steps. First, post–Cold War foreign policy making has been re-structured in a way that has elevated international migration and transna-tional crime to the "high politics" of international security while at the same time associating the two by placing them together in new institu-tional frameworks. Second, policy initiatives emanating from this re-structuring have increasingly focused on the problem of human smuggling in a way that solidifies and justifies the earlier institutional linkages. Third, in combating human smuggling, policymakers have increasingly turned to multilateral cooperation on the regional and global level.

In attempting to deal with post–Cold War policy issues associated with globalization, policymakers in the United States and Europe have often restructured policy-making institutions in ways that associated interna-tional migration with transnational crime. For example, Title VI of the 1991 Maastricht Treaty institutionalized intergovernmental cooperation on Justice and Home Affairs (JHA), the so-called Third Pillar, in which European foreign policymakers put cooperation on migration policy, asy-lum, and external borders together with cooperation on drugs, fraud, and other issues of law enforcement. Moreover, cooperation in Justice and Home Affairs is being increasingly focused on the growing problem of hu-man smuggling. Similarly, in 1993 the incoming Clinton administration reorganized the State Department to include an Office of the Under Sec-retary for Global Affairs, which "coordinates U.S. foreign relations on a variety of global issues, including: democracy, human rights and labor; environment, oceans and science; narcotics control and law enforcement; population, refugees and migration; women's issues."[1]

Human smuggling prompted European Union action as early as 1993, when the JHA Council agreed to a set of recommendations for member states to combat trafficking in women and children (JHA, 1993). More recently, JHA ministers refocused their attention on human smuggling, particularly on the trafficking in women and children by Russian Mafias (JHA, 1996) and the transportation of Turkish and Iraqi Kurds to Italian shores by Turkish and Italian criminal organizations. The EU and other ministers involved in the so-called Budapest Process dealing with illegal migration as well as representatives from relevant international organi-zations, such as the IOM, adopted recommendations in areas including "harmonization of legislation to combat trafficking in aliens" and "link-age in trafficking in aliens and other forms of organized crime" ("Conference of Ministers," 1997: 3–6). In January 1998, EU foreign ministers adopted a forty-six-point plan directed at reducing the numbers of Kurds arriving illegally in the EU ("Influx of Kurds," 1998: 4–6). Germany pressed for implementation of the plan as it expressed fears that Kurds arriving in Italy would easily move on to Germany ("Justice and Home Affairs," 1998). The January Action Plan aims to reduce the entrance of Kurds from Turkey and Iraq as it describes them as "illegal refugees" as well as "illegal immigrants." The council stated that these migrants "almost always make use of traffickers, of whom the majority appear to be part of organized crime networks, with contacts in the EU" (quoted in "Influx of Kurds," 1998: 4). Only three of the forty-six points were devoted to "ensuring that humanitarian aid makes an effective difference," while most points were focused on more restrictive measures—six on "effective application of asylum procedures," six on "preventing abuse of asylum procedures," and twenty on "combating illegal immigration," most of which were devoted to enhanced border control and effective removal (4–6).

The United States has been a bit slower than EU member states with multilateral responses to human smuggling; however, the Immigration and Naturalization Service and the State Department's Global Affairs division have recently begun to act. In 1997 the INS initiated the $8.2 million program Operation Global Reach by opening thirteen offices in sending and transit countries in order to gather information, assist countries in identifying smugglers, provide support for prosecutions, and train law enforcement personnel particularly in order to recognize fraudulent documents.[2] The State Department's Global Affairs division coordinates offshore interdiction of ships used by migrant smugglers and funds INS training for immigration officials from central and Eastern European countries (CEECs), the Newly Independent States (NIS) of the former Soviet Union, and Central American countries.[3]

The fight against human smuggling has become a major focus of the Regional Consultation Group on Migration, composed of Belize, Canada, Costa Rica, El Salvador, Guatemala, Honduras, Mexico, Nicaragua, Panama, and the United States, which met in Puebla, Mexico, in 1996 and in Panama City in 1997.[4] At the third meeting of the group, which took place in Ottawa on March 2, 1998, Colombia, the Dominican Republic, Ecuador, Jamaica, and Peru were invited as observers, as were representatives of the United Nations High Commissioner for Refugees (UNHCR), the Economic Commission for Latin America and the Caribbean (ECLAC), and the IOM. The Regional Consultation Group has encouraged participating states to pass legislation outlawing migrant smuggling and set out to establish a regional network of liaison officers responsible for exchanging information about migrant smuggling. Governments are to provide annual reports on migrant smuggling legislation and provide the IOM with information that will enable it to establish a comparative "matrix." The IOM also organized a January 1998 workshop on migrant smuggling for the Regional Group.[5] In the announcement of Operation Global Reach, Doris Meissner said that this INS initiative was building on the international cooperation achieved through the Regional Consultation Group (Meissner, 1997).

The United States also cooperated with the EU to combat trafficking in women and children from central and East European countries and the Newly Independent States of the former Soviet Union by funding a contract with the IOM to provide education and public information to dissuade Polish and Ukrainian women from getting involved with traffickers (United States and European Union, 1997). In July 1999, the Organization for Security and Cooperation in Europe (OSCE) Parliamentary Assembly adopted a U.S.-initiated "Resolution on the Trafficking of Women and Children" (OSCE, 1999). Moreover, international crime was one of the three major themes of the 1998 G-8 Summit in Birmingham, with an explicit focus on the "organized smuggling of people" (U.S. State Department, 1998). Japan joined European countries and the United States in supporting increased efforts to combat human smuggling, having experienced an increase in the smuggling of Chinese into Japan (Kohli and Macklin, 1998).

The League of Nations and then United Nations have long served as fora for international cooperation against the trafficking of women and children—going back to international cooperation to combat white slavery (see Scully, this volume, Chap. 3). Under the impetus generated by the Bejing UN conference on women and the leadership of certain member states, attention is being refocused on migrant smuggling. Austria took the lead in encouraging fellow UN member states to pass laws that specifically criminalize human smuggling and draft an international convention on the smuggling of illegal aliens (Schuessel, 1997). Such efforts within the UN received support at the May 1998 G-8 summit, where leaders called for negotiation of a UN crime convention to be completed within two years (G8, 1998b). In December 1998, the UN General Assembly initiated an ad hoc committee that was charged with drawing up a comprehensive international convention against transnational organized crime and three additional protocols, one of which is to deal with human smuggling and another with trafficking in women and children.[6] The committee met eleven times and then held a conference in Palermo for signing the new treaty.

The objectives of the human smuggling protocol are twofold: establishing the smuggling of migrants as a criminal offense and facilitating cooperation in the prevention, investigation, and prosecution of the crime of smuggling migrants. To this effect, the draft protocol provides rules for interdicting and boarding ships suspected of carrying illegal migrants, approves of state use of carrier sanctions, and encourages information programs directed at the customers of smugglers as well as information exchanges between states that enable more effective law enforcement. The protocol also calls for strengthening border controls and intensifying cooperation among border control agencies by establishing and maintaining direct lines of communication (UN, 1999).

Human smuggling and the trafficking in women received high-level attention during the October 1999 opening meetings of the General Assembly. At a meeting hosted by U.S. secretary of state Madeleine Albright, fourteen women foreign ministers drafted a letter, which they sent to Secretary General Kofi Annan, that called for stepped-up action to combat trafficking and pledged support of the UN Convention against Transnational Crime. The foreign ministers state, "We recognize the importance of close international cooperation to defeat the traffickers at every stage of their criminal activities" (cited in IOM, 2000).

Although the International Organization for Migration has a smaller membership (seventy-six states) than the UN and is much more specialized and limited as a forum for migration policy making than regional organizations such as the EU, the IOM is becoming a major player when it comes to international cooperation in the area of human smuggling (which quickly becomes evident from the many references above). Created in 1951, the IOM (and its predecessors) have a long history of work in moving refugees to second countries of asylum, voluntary repatriation of refugees, and the return migration of the highly skilled in order to further development in sending countries. At a 1994 IOM-sponsored meeting in Geneva that brought together representatives from sending, transit, and receiving countries, participants asked the IOM to advance the policy discussions of migrant smuggling, organize regional meetings, collect and disseminate information, analyze the problem of trafficking in women for prostitution, and contribute to policy harmonization (IOM, 1994). Since then the IOM has been involved in regional processes dealing with irregular migration and migrant smuggling not only in Europe and the Americas, noted above, but also in East and Southeast Asia, including sponsoring meetings of government representatives (IOM, 1998c) as well as a project returning and reintegrating trafficked women and children from Thailand to Cambodia, Vietnam, China, Burma, and Laos (IOM, 1998b). While the IOM has emerged as the leading international organization in the area of research and policy dialogues devoted to human smuggling in general,[7] operational programs have primarily focused on trafficking in women and children for forced prostitution, whether in terms of publicity campaigns to discourage women from turning to traffickers or return programs with which the IOM is very experienced.

The Dilemmas of Controlling Human Smuggling as a Challenge to Global Governance

Jonathan Winer, the former deputy assistant secretary for law enforcement and crime in the U.S. State Department, put the problem posed by migrant traffickers to foreign policy makers in terms of increased international cooperation. "We are working with the European Union, the International Organization for Migration, the UN and other organizations to develop international cooperation against traffickers, whose organizations transcend all of our national borders, because in a transnational world, no country can defend its own borders or its people, however big or small, without the cooperation of the entire world" (Winer, 1998: 8). International cooperation to strengthen border controls, criminalize human smuggling where laws against it do not already exist, identify and prosecute human smugglers where they do, and provide to women information about the dangers involved in offers of employment abroad are first steps in dealing with the challenges posed by human smuggling. Certain aspects of such cooperation, however, particularly those directed at border control, may potentially exacerbate the problem they were designed to combat. This dilemma arises from a certain misunderstanding of the nature of human smuggling and an underestimation of complex interrelationships between the effects of various migration and refugee policies.

Human smuggling is often depicted in terms of traditional organized crime groups that have added a new line of business to drug smuggling, car theft, and money laundering (IOM, 1996). It may, however, be that human smuggling is more often "crime that is organized" (Finckenauer and Waring, 1996) and committed by people who may have previously not been involved in transnational criminal organizations. Hence, targeting migrant traffickers for prosecution may be harder to execute in practice than it sounds as a policy prescription.

For example, travel agents who sell tickets to migrants without the proper documentation to make the proposed journey legally profit from the illegal transportation of migrants organized by smugglers. Are these travel agents themselves "smugglers" who can be targeted for prosecution? As Ko-lin Chin (this volume, Chap. 8) points out, Chinese migrant smuggling rings are more often than not loose networks of relatives and friends who organize transportation and border crossings for acquaintances as a lucrative business that may even have developed as a supplement to legitimate business. These smuggling networks often use more traditional gangsters involved in other criminal activities such as drug dealing and extortion to enforce debt repayment in the receiving country if necessary; however, enforcers may just be hired hands—thereby outsourcing the dirty work. Law enforcement efforts directed at more easily identified enforcers may not necessarily be very effective in putting out of business the smuggling operations of which they may be a necessary, but replaceable, part.

Of course, whether or not migrant smugglers are gangsters moving into another line of business or businesspeople moving into an illegal activity to help migrants cross borders illegally varies by regions and particular migration flows involved. Winer suggests that in Western Europe and Southeastern Asia "the same criminal organizations may traffic in migrants and narcotics. In other areas, alien smugglers avoid other criminal activities, such as drug trafficking, for which they would risk prosecution and stiff penalties" (1998: 3). For instance, a study of "coyotes" who assist crossings of the U.S.-Mexican border found little evidence of collaboration between coyotes and drug traffickers. Border Patrol agents told of some cases of migrants paying their fees by taking along a "small package." This was not a common practice and was not a mode of transporting drugs from producing areas to the border, in large measure because of the high risks associated with drug smuggling (López Castro, 1998: 972).

The communication and transportation revolutions that have facilitated transnational crime provide only a partial reason for the recent increase in cases of human smuggling. Increasing human smuggling may also be an unintended consequence of the stricter visa and border control policies adopted by individual states and, in the case of Europe, more effective EU cooperation on border control and more restrictive policies adopted by central and Eastern European countries that have applied for EU membership. Very simply: as more restrictive policies increase the obstacles to crossing borders, migrants turn to smugglers rather than pay the increased costs of unaided attempts that prove unsuccessful.

It is important to point out that illegal migrant workers are not the only clientele of human smugglers. While stricter visa policies and more effective border controls lead illegal migrant workers to pay for smugglers' services, restrictive border controls and asylum policies have led those who have fled pogroms, secret police, and civil wars to do the same. For example, Kurds fleeing civil war in Iraq find themselves unable to get official passports from Baghdad; they give up going through regular asylum application channels; they purchase false documents that are readily available in Northern Iraq; and they pay thousands of dollars to the growing numbers of Turkish smugglers for the short but dangerous trip to Greece or Italy (Hemming, 1997). The same substitution effect occurred with Kosovo Albanians. As the conflict between the Kosovo Liberation Army and the Yugoslav police intensified during 1998, increasing numbers of Kosovo Albanians were apprehended while trying to enter the EU illegally. Having accepted the bulk of those fleeing the Bosnian civil war, Germany, as well as Austria, refused to provide temporary protection to the Kosovo Albanians right up until the March 1999 NATO bombing of Yugoslavia and the accompanying refugee crisis ("Germany Cannot Receive Kosovo Albanians," 1998; "No Temporary Protection," 1998). Faced with a low probability of finding a safe haven within the EU by seeking temporary protection or asylum, increasing numbers of Kosovo Albanians turned to smugglers to get them into the EU, particularly to Germany ("More Human Smuggling," 1998; "Large Smuggling Ring," 1998), which, together with Switzerland, already hosted most of the EU's population of Kosovo Albanians. Of the 12,000 persons apprehended while being smuggled into Germany in 1998, the largest group (between 4,000 and 5,000) were Kosovo Albanians (Dalka, 1999). Of the 4,918 persons apprehended while attempting to enter Switzerland in the first half of 1998 (including asylum seekers), 1,594 were Kosovars ("Increasing Number of Persons Arrested," 1999).[8]

Moreover, as Salt and Stein (1997) point out, as the human smuggling business expands, the smugglers, rather than the migrants and asylum seekers, make more decisions regarding where their customers actually go. Part of the smugglers' success in getting migrants across borders is the smugglers' ability to change routes and destinations in order to overcome obstacles placed in their way by states. In a sense, the smugglers gather and process information about the weak links in terms of transportation systems, border controls, and liberal visa and asylum policies and then provide it to their customers. Moreover, smugglers often tutor migrants to say certain things to officials that may enable them to claim asylum, for instance, instructing Chinese migrants to claim they participated in the Tiananmen Square protests or that they have been unable to have a family because of China's "one child policy" (Kerry, 1997: 141). This ratchets up the pressure on receiving states to cooperate with one another and to adopt even more restrictivist border control and asylum policies lest their land borders, airports, and harbors be targeted by traffickers as weak links.

Whether or not stepped-up border controls and stricter visa polices will reduce human smuggling, however, is very unclear owing to the inherent dilemma of control. For example, in response to tougher enforcement of controls on the U.S.-Mexican border, fees charged by "coyotes" have recently doubled or tripled, depending on the area of the border, with fees at San Diego reaching seven hundred dollars (De La Vina, 1998). If tougher border controls increase smugglers' fees beyond that which their customers are willing to pay, controls may decrease smuggling. However, if potential migrants are willing to pay the additional costs while at the same time stiffer border controls prompt more migrants to enter into the market, border controls will most likely increase the profits of human smuggling and entice new entrants into the business.

The willingness of migrants to pay more for smugglers' services is perhaps best demonstrated by Chinese migrants who have been smuggled into Western Europe, North America, Japan, and Australia. For example, as Peter Kwong points out, the average fee to be smuggled into the United States rose from a few thousand in the early 1980s to $22,000 in 1988, to some $30,000–35,000 in 1993; yet at the same time the number of those who purchased the smuggler's services grew (Kwong, 1997). In this case, such high demand for smuggler's services can largely be explained by the willingness of migrants to incur debts against anticipated future earnings and a border-transcending financial system based on the willingness of family members to ensure repayment and the violent enforcement of debt repayment by criminal organizations in the host country or in China if necessary. "Illegal refugees" who are in fact fleeing for their lives may be even more willing to pay higher prices and incur debts than "illegal migrants." If demand for smugglers' services does not respond to increased prices, stepped-up border controls could lead to increased human smuggling at higher profits, which in turn draw more people into the business.

The demand among "illegal migrants" for smugglers' services often depends on anticipated earnings from businesses that are willing to employ smuggled migrants. Hence, increased human smuggling may in large measure be a function of employer demand (Kwong, 1997). The profit potential of exploiting vulnerable indentured labor was highlighted by a recent case in which Italian labor inspectors found 242 immigrants, mostly Chinese, working twelve-hour days in Tuscan leather workshops and earning about eleven dollars per day ("Chinese Exploited," 1998). It is estimated that tens of thousands of women from Russia and Eastern Europe have been trafficked into the EU and forced into prostitution to work off their smuggler's fee and many ultimately end up in debt bondage situations that are highly profitable to pimps and brothel owners (IOM, 1995; Global Survival Network, 1997).

Despite increased employment of smuggled migrants and trafficked forced laborers, enforcement of sanctions against employers for hiring illegal migrant labor in major receiving states has been spotty to say the least (see Miller, this volume, Chap. 12), and it has been particularly weak in the United States (Rojas, 1996). From 1994 to 1996, only 3,765 of the 15,039 U.S. employers charged with knowingly employing illegal migrants received fines; these totaled $34 million, but only $14 million were collected ("INS Enforcement," 1998). That is an average of $3,718 per fine, which is relatively small compared with other costs of doing business. Indeed, antimigrant smuggling initiatives by the U.S. government have so far focused on interdiction on the high seas, targeting smugglers in sending and transit countries, and public information campaigns in sending countries, but little attention has been devoted to reducing demand for smuggled labor, as Kwong points out (1997). According to a veteran U.S. Border Patrol official, such antismuggling initiatives will not be very effective if they are not paired with demand-reducing actions such as mandatory employer verification of employee eligibility using computerized checks of a social security number database, as recommended by the U.S. Commission on Immigration Reform in 1994 but as yet only in place on a pilot project basis.[9] Recent events, however, indicate that strengthening employer sanctions to combat human smuggling appears increasingly unlikely. Labor unions have been a bedrock constituency for sanctions, but the AFL-CIO called for repeal of the employer sanctions law at its February 2000 convention.[10]

Similarly in the EU, the European Council's January 1998 Action Plan is directed at "tackling the involvement of organized crime," but the council remains mute on the demand for illegal labor by employers. European Commission policy recommendations to combat trafficking in women adopted by the JHA Council focus primarily on judicial and police cooperation directed at smugglers, migrants' labor conditions, and the need for victim support (European Commission, 1996; JHA, 1996), rather than the consumer demand for sex with "exotic" foreign women, which fuels a growing industry that capitalizes on vulnerable illegal migrants.

Conclusion

Economic globalization fosters both increasing international migration and transnational organized crime. These two aspects of globalization intersect in the phenomenon of human smuggling, which has in turn drawn the attention of immigration, law enforcement, and foreign ministry officials. North American and European states that have been the primary targets of smugglers and their customers have initiated campaigns to combat human smuggling, and these states have engaged in growing international cooperation aimed against smuggling. Antismuggling initiatives, however, have not come close to matching the recent expansion in the numbers of those smuggled. So far, most states and international organizations have tried to address the problem by increasing migration controls, passing laws against human smuggling, and stepping up enforcement of these laws. Since tighter border controls often yield the unintended consequences of more customers for smugglers and more people entering the smuggling business, the prospects that recent antismuggling initiatives will be very effective remain quite dim. Moreover, since these antismuggling initiatives fail to address the demand for smuggled labor, it is unlikely that target states will be able to accomplish much more than the diversion of flows along their borders and among themselves.

Given that sufficient international cooperation in law enforcement and immigration policies to make a significant impact on smuggling may involve major infringements of participating states' sovereignty, one may anticipate a fair amount of resistance to such cooperation in certain political parties of the states involved. Given that truly effective measures to stop human smuggling involve major restrictions on employers' access to cheap and compliant illegal migrant labor, one may anticipate significant resistance from powerful interest groups. Given that effective work-site enforcement in several countries may involve increased state use of citizens' personal data, which is often perceived as an affront to civil liberties, one may anticipate widespread public outrage.

Nevertheless, the fear of crime, and organized crime in particular, has proven quite effective in moving democratic publics to sacrifice liberties for the sake of their own perceived personal security. Perhaps politicians will prove effective in marshaling popular fears of criminals and the unwanted migrants they bring to galvanize serious international cooperation to curb human smuggling despite the consequences that cooperation may have for state sovereignty, employer profits, and civil liberties.

NOTES

1. See http://www.state.gov/www/global/index.html
2. See http://www.ins.usdoj.gov

3. See http://www.state.gov/global

4. For documents see http://www.iom.ch/migrationweb/Focus_Areas/entrym.htm

5. See Citizenship and Immigration Canada, http://www.ci.gc.ca/english/press/98/9813-pre-html

6. Draft documents can be found at http://www.uncjin.org/Documents/Conventions/conventions.html

7. In addition to the quarterly bulletin *Trafficking in Migrants,* see the book by IOM staff member Bimal Ghosh (1998).

8. For an elaboration on the Kosovo Albanian case, see Koslowski (2000).

9. Author's interview with Eugene R. Davis, deputy chief Border Patrol agent, U.S. Border Patrol in Blaine, Washington, on November 27, 1999; U.S. Commission on Immigration Reform, *U.S. Immigration Policy: Restoring Credibility* (Washington, D.C.: U.S. Government Printing Office, 1994).

10. Statement issued by the AFL-CIO after 2000 convention at: http://www.aflcio.org/publ/estatements/feb2000/immigr.htm. See the *New York Times* opinion-editorial by the secretary-treasurer of the Union of Needletrades, Industrial and Textile Employees (UNITE), Bruce Raynor (1999).

REFERENCES

Auguste, Byron G. 1998. "What's So New about Globalization?" *New Perspectives Quarterly* 15 (1): 16–20.

"Chinese Exploited in Italian Leather Workshops." 1998. Reuters, May 28.

"Conference of Ministers on the Prevention of Illegal Migration." 1997. *Migration News Sheet,* no. 177/97–12 (December), 3–6.

Dalka, Karin. 1999. "Smuggling of Human Beings Experiencing Upswing." *Frankfurter Rundschau,* March 12.

De La Vina, Gustavo. 1998. "Interview with the New Assistant Commissioner for the Border Patrol, Gustavo 'Gus' De La Vina." U.S. Border Control.

"EU Enlargement Must Include Waiting Period of 12 to 15 Years for Free Movement." 1998. *Migration News Sheet,* no.186/98–09 (September), 2.

European Commission. 1996. *Communication from the European Commission to the Council and the European Parliament on Trafficking in Women for the Purposes of Sexual Exploitation.* Brussels, Com(96) 567 final.

Finckenauer, James O., and Elin Waring. 1996. "Russian Émigré Crime in the United States: Organized Crime or Crime That Is Organized?" *Transnational Organized Crime* 2 (2/3): 139–55.

G8. 1998a. The Birmingham Summit, May 15–17, Communiqué.

————. 1998b. The Birmingham Summit, Drugs and International Crime, press release, May 16.

"Germany Cannot Receive Kosovo Albanians." 1998. *Migration News Sheet,* no.186/98–09 (September), 12.

Ghosh, Bimal. 1998. *Huddled Masses and Uncertain Shores: Insights into Irregular Migration.* Doredrecht: Kluwer Law International.

Global Survival Network. 1997. *Crime and Servitude: An Exposé of the Traffic in Women for Prostitution from the Newly Independent States.* Washington, D.C.: Global Survival Network.

Hemming, Jon. 1997. "Alien Smuggling in Turkey." Reuters, November 21.

Hessler, Peter. 2000. "It's the 'Rich' Chinese Who Flee to U.S." *Seattle Post-Intelligencer,* February 10.

"Increasing Number of Persons Arrested for Clandestine Entry." 1999. *Migration News Sheet,* no. 197/99–08 (August), 6.

"Influx of Kurds Prompts Adoption of a 46-Point Action Plan." 1998. *Migration News Sheet,* no. 179/98–02 (February), 4–6.

"INS Enforcement." 1998. *Migration News* 5 (10).

IOM, 1994. "International Responses to Trafficking in Migrants and the Safeguarding of Migrant Rights," Seminar, Geneva, October 26–28.

————. 1995. *Trafficking and Prostitution: The Growing Exploitation of Migrant Women from Central and Eastern Europe.* Geneva: International Organization for Migration.

————. 1996. "Organized Crime Moves into Migrant Trafficking." *Trafficking in Migrants, Quarterly Bulletin,* no. 11 (June): 1–2.

————. 1998a. *Trafficking in Migrants, Quarterly Bulletin,* no. 17 (January).

————. 1998b. *Trafficking in Migrants, Quarterly Bulletin,* no. 18 (June).

————. 1998c. "Third IOM Regional Seminar on Irregular Migration and Trafficking in East and Southeast Asia." *IOM News,* no 3/98.

————. 2000. *Trafficking in Migrants, Quarterly Bulletin,* no. 20 (January).

JHA. 1993. Council of the European Union, "Recommendation on Trafficking in Human Beings." Council Press Release 10550/93 of November 29 and 30.

————. 1996. Justice and Home Affairs, Joint Action 96/700/JHA. *http://europa. eu.int/comm/sg/scadplus/leg/*

"Justice and Home Affairs: EU Struggles to Define CEEC Strategy." 1998. *European Report,* no. 2288, February 4.

Kerry, John. 1997. *The New War: The Web of Crime That Threatens America's Security.* New York: Simon and Schuster.

Kohli, Sheel, and Simon Macklin. 1998. "G8 to Fight 'Slave' Trade into Japan." *South China Morning Post,* May 18.

Korbin, Stephen J. 1997. "The Architecture of Globalization: State Sovereignty in a Networked Global Economy." In *Governments, Globalization, and International Business,* edited by John H. Dunning, 146–71. Oxford: Oxford University Press.

Koslowski, Rey. 2000. "The Mobility Money Can Buy: Human Smuggling and Border Control in the European Union." In *The Wall around the West: State Borders and Immigration Controls in North America and Europe,* edited by Peter Andreas and Timothy Snyder. Lanham, Md.: Rowman & Littlefield.

Kwong, Peter. 1997. *Forbidden Workers: Illegal Chinese Immigrants and American Labor.* New York: New Press.

Kyle, David. 1996. "The Transnational Peasant: The Social Construction of Transnational Migration from the Ecuadorian Andes." Ph.D. diss., Johns Hopkins University.

"Large Smuggling Ring Broken Up." 1998. *Migration News Sheet,* no.186/98–09 (September), 6.

Layard, Richard, Oliver Blanchard, Rudiger Dornbusch, and Paul Krugman. 1992. *East-West Migration: The Alternatives.* Cambridge: MIT Press.

López Castro, Gustavo, 1998. "Coyotes and Alien Smuggling." In *Migration between Mexico and the United States: Binational Study,* vol. 3. Mexico City and Washington, D.C.: Mexican Ministry of Foreign Affairs and the U.S. Commission on Immigration Reform.

Massey, Douglas. 1998. "March of Folly." *American Prospect* (March–April): 22–33.

Meissner, Doris. 1997. "Operation Global Reach News Conference." Federal News Service, June 19.

Miller, Mark. 1998. "The Politics of International Migration and Crime: Reflections on French and U.S. Trends." Presented at the workshop "International Migration and Transnational Crime," Rutgers University, Newark, N.J., May.

"More Human Smuggling across the Eastern Border." 1998. *Migration News Sheet,* no.186/98–09 (September), 5.

Moreno, Sylvia. 1998. "Legal Attack Targets Vans Carrying Immigrants." *Washington Post,* April 22.

Naylor, R. T. 1995. "From Cold War to Crime War: The Search for a New 'National Security' Threat." *Transnational Organized Crime* 1 (4): 37–56.

"No Temporary Protection for Kosovo Albanians." 1998. *Migration News Sheet*, no.186/98–09 (September), 10.

OSCE. 1999. "St. Petersburg Declaration of the OSCE Parliamentary Assembly: Resolution on the Trafficking of Women and Children." Washington, D.C.: Commission on Security and Cooperation in Europe.

Raynor, Bruce. 1999. "Serfs of the Service Economy." *New York Times*, November 16.

Reuter, Peter. 1983. *Disorganized Crime*. Cambridge: MIT Press.

Rohter, Larry. 1997. "Deportees from the U.S. Unwelcome in El Salvador." *New York Times*, August 10.

Rojas, Aurelio. 1996. "Border Guarded, Workplace Ignored." *San Francisco Chronicle*, March 18.

Salt, John, and Jeremy Stein. 1997. "Migration as a Business: The Case of Trafficking." *International Migration* 35 (4): 467–94.

Sassen, Saskia. 1988. *The Mobility of Labor and Capital*. Cambridge: Cambridge University Press.

Schuessel, Wolfgang. 1997. "Statement by Austrian Vice-Chancellor and Federal Minister for Foreign Affairs, Wolfgang Schuessel, to the Fifty-second Session of the United Nations General Assembly, New York, 25 September 1997," Austrian Information Service, Washington, D.C.

Singer, Audrey, and Douglas S. Massey. 1998. "The Social Process of Undocumented Border Crossing among Mexican Migrants." *International Migration Review* 32 (3): 561–92.

Sontag, Deborah. 1997. "Many Deported Felons Return to U.S. Unnoticed." *New York Times*, August 11.

Smith, Paul J., ed. 1997. *Human Smuggling: Chinese Migrant Trafficking and the Challenge to America's Immigration Tradition*. Washington, D.C.: Center for Strategic and International Studies.

"Special Meeting to Combat Illegal Migration." 1998. *Migration News Sheet*, no. 185/98–08 (August), 5–6.

Strange, Susan. 1996. *Retreat of the State: The Diffusion of Power in the World Economy*. Cambridge: Cambridge University Press.

United States and European Union. 1997. Justice and Home Affairs Cooperation EU-US Summit, 5th December 1997, Facts brief 8.

U.S. State Department. 1998. "G-8 Birmingham Summit Overview." Fact sheet released by the Bureau of European and Canadian Affairs, April 30.

United Nations. 1999. "Revised Draft Protocol against Smuggling of Migrants by

Land, Air and Sea, Supplementing the United Nations Convention against Transnational Organized Crime." United Nations General Assembly, December 27, A/AC.254/4/Add.1/Rev.4.

Weintraub, Sidney, and Chandler Stolp. 1987. "The Implications of Growing Economic Interdependence." In Organization for Economic Cooperation and Development (OECD), *The Future of Migration*. Paris: OECD.

Williams, Phil. 1995. "Transnational Criminal Organizations: Strategic Alliances." *Washington Quarterly* 18 (Winter): 57–72.

Winer, Jonathan M. 1997. "Operation Global Reach News Conference." Federal News Service, June 19.

———. 1998. "Organized Crime: Smuggling of Illegal Aliens and Trafficking in Women and Children." Speech given at Amerika Haus, Vienna, April 27.

⬛⬛⬛⬛⬛⬛⬛⬛⬛ Contributors

Peter Andreas is an assistant professor of political science at Reed College in Portland, Oregon. He is the author of *Border Games: Policing the U.S.-Mexico Divide* (2000) and coeditor of *The Wall around the West: State Borders and Immigration Controls in North America and Europe* (2000).

Ko-Lin Chin is an associate professor in the School of Criminal Justice, Rutgers University–Newark. Dr. Chin is the author of *Chinese Subculture and Criminality* (1990) and *Chinatown Gangs* (1996) and coeditor of *Handbook of Organized Crime in the United States* (1994). His most recent book is *Smuggled Chinese: Clandestine Immigration to the United States* (1999).

John Dale, a Ph.D. candidate in the department of sociology at the University of California, Davis, is a lecturer at San Francisco State University. His dissertation is entitled "Transnational Strategies for Democratic Engagement: The Free Burma Movement, '8.8.88' to 9.9.99.'"

Nora V. Demleitner is a professor of law at St. Mary's University School of Law in San Antonio, Texas, and has been a visiting professor at the University of Michigan Law School, the University of Freiburg, Germany, and the Scuola Superiore in Pisa, Italy. Currently, she is an editor of the *Federal Sentencing Reporter* and a director of the American Society of Comparative Law. The recipient of two Max Planck fellowships, she has written numerous articles and chapters on comparative law, international gender issues, and sentencing.

James O. Finckenauer is a professor of criminal justice at the School of Criminal Justice, Rutgers University and the director of the International Center, National Institute of Justice. His books include *Scared Straight! and the Panacea Phenomenon* (1982), *Russian Youth* (1995), and *Organized Crime in America* (1995). Professor Finckenauer is the editor of the *Journal of Research in Crime and Delinquency* and president of the International Association for the Study of Organized Crime.

H. Richard Friman is an associate professor and assistant chair of political science at Marquette University. During 1994–95 he was a visiting Fulbright scholar with the National Research Institute of Police Science at the Japanese National Police Agency in Tokyo. His recent publications include *Narco-Diplomacy: Exporting the U.S. War on Drugs* (1996), *Patchwork Protectionism* (1990), and "Gaijinhanzai: Immigrants and Drugs in Contemporary Japan" (*Asian Survey* 36, no. 10 [October 1996]).

Khalid Koser is a lecturer in human geography at University College London and a member of the Migration Research Unit. His most recent books are *The New Migration in Europe: Social Constructions and Social Realities* (1998, coedited with Helma Lutz) and *The End of the Refugee Cycle? Refugee Repatriation and Reconstruction* (1999, coedited with Richard Black).

Rey Koslowski is an assistant professor of political science at Rutgers University–Newark and, recently, a visiting fellow of the Center of International Studies at Princeton University. During the 1996–97 academic year he was also a research associate of the Center for German and European Studies at Georgetown University's School of Foreign Service. He is the author of *Migrants and Citizens: Demographic Change in the European States System* (2000).

Peter Kwong is a professor of urban affairs and planning and the director of the Asian American Studies Program at Hunter College, City University of New York. He is the author of *The New Chinatown* (1996) and *Forbidden Workers: Illegal Chinese Immigrants and American Labor* (1997). Kwong writes regularly for the *Nation* and the *Village Voice,* and is also an award-winning TV documentary producer.

David Kyle is an assistant professor of sociology at the University of California, Davis. Author of *Transnational Peasants: Migrations, Networks, and Ethnicity in Andean Ecuador* (2000), he is an expert adviser on human trafficking for the United Nations High Commissioner for Human Rights' World Conference on Racism (2001).

Zai Liang is an associate professor of sociology at Queens College, City University of New York. His current research (funded by the National Institute for Child Health and Human Development) focuses on the demographic consequences of market transition in China, including internal migration and emigration from China. He also continues working on assimilation of immigrants in the United States, especially the second generation.

Mark J. Miller is a professor of political science at the University of Delaware. His most recent publications include *The Age of Migration*, coauthored with Stephen Castles (1993), and *International Migration and World Politics: A Critical Case for Theory and Policy*, coauthored with R. Denemark (1993). He is currently associate editor of *International Migration Review*.

Eileen Scully is an assistant professor in the history department of Princeton University. She is the author of *Bargaining with the State from Afar: American Citizenship in Treaty Port China* (2000) and *Imperial Campfollowers: Migratory Prostitution in an Age of Empire* (forthcoming).

David Spener is an assistant professor of sociology at Trinity University in San Antonio, Texas. He has written several articles and chapters on U.S.-Mexican border issues and is coeditor, with Kathleen Staudt, of *The U.S.-Mexico Border: Transcending Divisions, Contesting Identities* (1998).

Wenzhen Ye received a Ph.D. in sociology from the University of Utah and conducted postdoctoral work at Princeton University. He is a professor of economics at Xiamen University, China. His main research areas are demography of China and the Asian American population.

Index

abuse: by governments, 258; by smugglers, 153–55, 160n. 14, 240–41; volition issue, 328; of women, 263–66
agricultural industry, 330
Albright, Madeleine, 346
American Bureau of Social Hygiene, 89
Anti–Organized Crime Law (1992) (Japan), 308
Argentina, 78–79
Arizona, 115, 143
Association of Southeast Asian Nations (ASEAN), 43–44
asylum seekers: from China, 238–39; policy issues and, 14, 60–62, 70–72; political issues and, 67–68; smuggling fees, 351; smuggling of, 58–59, 71, 349–50; tutoring of, 350; in Western Europe, 60–62
Australia, 8, 9
Austria, 345, 349
Azuay Province, Ecuador, 34–40, 48–49

Bales, Kevin, 1–2
Barry, Kathleen, 267–68
Belgium, 271, 277–78

Bracero Program (U.S.), 109–10, 321–22
Bristow, Edward, 79
Brownsville, Texas, 143, 150
Budapest, 2
Burma (Myanmar), 13, 40–47, 48, 50–51
Butler, Josephine, 85

California, Los Angeles, 341–42. *See also* San Diego
Canada, 8–9, 206, 270–71
Cañar Province, Ecuador, 35, 36–37
capital, acquiring: for migration, 339; for smuggling operation, 151
Caplan, Elinor, 8–9
Carter administration, 323
Chan, Tommy, 209
Changle, Fujian Province, 195, 196, 198, 199, 203
Checkpoint Charlie, 157
Cheng Chung-ko, 251
Chen Jiageng, 193
children: in garment industry, 246; in Russia, 175; sex tourism and, 94; slave importing scheme and, 40–41; trafficking in, 9, 174; U.S.-Mexico border and, 120–21, 152

364.135
K993

LINCOLN CHRISTIAN COLLEGE AND SEMINARY

117929

3 4711 00180 3248